T0319401

A SHOPPERS' PARADISE

A SHOPPERS' PARADISE

*How the Ladies of Chicago
Claimed Power and Pleasure
in the New Downtown*

EMILY REMUS

Harvard University Press

Cambridge, Massachusetts
London, England
2019

For my parents
and
for Randy

Publication of this book has been supported through the generous
provisions of the Maurice and Lula Bradley Smith Memorial Fund

Library of Congress Cataloging-in-Publication Data

Names: Remus, Emily, 1984– author.
Title: A shoppers' paradise : how the ladies of Chicago claimed power
and pleasure in the new downtown / Emily Remus.
Description: Cambridge, Massachusetts : Harvard University Press,
2019. | Includes bibliographical references and index.
Identifiers: LCCN 2018040566 | ISBN 9780674987272 (alk. paper)
Subjects: LCSH: Women consumers—Illinois—Chicago—History. |
Shopping—Illinois—Chicago—History. | Purchasing power—
Illinois—Chicago—History. | Retail trade—Illinois—Chicago—History. |
Loop (Chicago, Ill.)—History. | Chicago (Ill.)—Economic conditions.
Classification: LCC HC107.I33 C66 2019 | DDC 381.1082/0977311—dc23
LC record available at https://lccn.loc.gov/2018040566

Contents

Introduction

ON HER FIRST EXCURSION into Chicago's central business district, small-town transplant Carrie Meeber, the protagonist in Theodore Dreiser's classic novel *Sister Carrie* (1900), entered one of the great department stores on the city's burgeoning retail corridor, State Street. As she passed along the busy aisles, Carrie was "much affected by the remarkable displays of trinkets, dress goods, stationery, and jewelry." Each counter seemed to offer a dazzling new attraction. "The dainty slippers and stockings, the delicately frilled skirts and petticoats, the laces, ribbons, hair-combs, purses, all touched her with individual desire," wrote Dreiser. Yet such consumer delights lay beyond the reach of the young woman. She was there only to seek employment. In making her way to the management office, Carrie was stirred by the aura of "wealth, fashion, and ease," which set in relief her own shabby clothing and dreary prospects. She "noticed too, with a touch at the heart, the fine ladies who elbowed and ignored her, brushing past in utter disregard of her presence, themselves eagerly enlisted in the materials which the store contained." The pleasures and possibilities of Chicago's consumer institutions seemed to belong not to Carrie but to "her more fortunate sisters of the city," the women of the moneyed classes.[1]

Dreiser's story, which opens with Carrie's arrival in 1889, illuminates Chicago's dynamic commercial landscape at century's end, as the expansion of the consumer economy reshaped urban culture and the built environment. At the center of these transformations were women with disposable income and leisure time. These "fine ladies" came to State Street to savor a profusion of new goods and services. Their consumption aroused the envy of the penniless Carrie.[2] It also sustained the growth of new department stores, restaurants, theaters, grand hotels, soda fountains, and other consumer spaces that catered to female shoppers. The result was an increasingly conspicuous flow of moneyed women into Chicago's central business district, the Loop.

The daily stream of female consumers marked State Street, in the words of the city's boosters, as a "shoppers' paradise," where women and their money could circulate freely.[3] But this paradise had to be created. Until the end of the nineteenth century, Chicago's central business district was hardly welcoming to unchaperoned ladies. Indeed, they were once as out of place in the city center as Carrie found herself to be in the department store. The Loop had chiefly been a male preserve, oriented toward finance, manufacturing, processing, and wholesale. Its buildings and infrastructure, no less than its cultural practices, supported the captains of industry who dominated the urban economy. Women could certainly be found downtown, running errands, attending public events, and working for wages. Yet for most of the nineteenth century, Chicago's Loop was primarily a space that women were expected to move through, not linger in or enjoy. Without a male escort, they were refused service in most hotels, restaurants, cafés, and theaters, while saloons and private clubs simply closed their doors to women. Even dry goods merchants, preoccupied with their wholesale businesses, offered scant amenities to female customers. To eat, drink, rest, or even use a bathroom, Chicago ladies were often forced to return home. In short, they experienced the Loop as mere visitors, not rightful occupants.

The masculine downtown was not to last, however. In the final decades of the nineteenth century, Chicago merchants and entrepreneurs established a range of consumer institutions that invited moneyed women into the central business district. In patronizing these spaces, Chicago ladies helped fuel the city's remarkable commercial growth. Yet they also aroused conflict. Their very presence in the downtown, as well as their conspicuous new habits of consuming, provoked opposition from many industrialists, religious leaders, city officials, and ordinary citizens. As these tensions reveal, incorporating women into a downtown dominated by men—and creating an atmosphere favorable to women's consumption—was not automatic. It required transforming the material and moral landscape of the central business district. While establishing the terms of ladies' public presence, Chicagoans clashed over the appropriate use of urban space, the rights and duties of women, and the moral legitimacy of emerging forms of consumption. This conflict, over gender and space, shaped the creation of a built environment and cultural norms that sustained the growth of American consumer capitalism. It produced the modern consumer city—a place where respectable women could publicly indulge their desires.

Ladies had, of course, purchased goods and services in decades past.[4] They had even done so in dedicated shopping districts.[5] But at the end of the nineteenth century, the scale and pace of American consumption increased exponentially, laying the foundation for a mass consumer society that would consolidate after the Second World War.[6] This growth was driven by innovations in production and distribution that gave rise to new consumer institutions, notably department stores.[7] Dwarfing the size and profits of traditional dry goods houses, these massive retailers pioneered new strategies of enticement to sell a multitude of goods to their primarily female clientele.[8] "They were handsome, bustling, successful affairs, with a host of clerks and a swarm of patrons," Dreiser wrote of Chicago's first examples.[9] Through service and spectacle, department stores kindled consumer desires and encouraged women to linger in the city center.[10] They also stimulated the growth of other retail and service businesses that catered to moneyed women. Tearooms, cafés, confectioneries, and restaurants arose to revive weary shoppers. Opulent new theaters enticed female customers with matinee performances, while recently erected hotels opened their premises to women's club meetings and social events.

As Chicago's downtown came to be nearly saturated with businesses that relied on female consumption, new questions arose over the increasingly conspicuous presence of ladies in public. Some concerns were material and touched on the space women's bodies and apparel occupied at sites also frequented by men. On crowded Loop sidewalks, for example, did women have a right to wear voluminous hoopskirts? When seated in downtown theaters, should they be required to remove their elaborate millinery? Other issues involved public culture and standards of respectability. In new dining spaces, such as tearooms, soda fountains, and confectioneries, could reputable women imbibe alcohol? On downtown streets, was it appropriate for shopping ladies to loiter near store windows or interact with strangers? And what obligation, if any, did civic and business leaders have to protect unescorted ladies from harassment or violence on the streets? Chicagoans battled fiercely over the answers to these questions at the turn of the century and, in doing so, redefined the terms on which women could access the downtown.

Chicago was by no means the only city to confront these matters. Yet no place figured more prominently in the national imagination at the turn of the century. And, indeed, no city played a more decisive role in establishing a national culture of consumption. As historian Asa Briggs observed in his classic study of Victorian cities, the midwestern metropolis was the "shock city" of the era, "a new phenomenon, a portent, a place which the 'clear-minded' had to visit if they wished to understand the world."[11] After the great fire of 1871 demolished the downtown, Chicagoans energetically set about the task of rebuilding. With breathtaking speed, they erected an even grander city on top of the ashes. The growth of this new metropolis astounded contemporaries. Between 1870 and 1910, Chicago nearly doubled its population each decade, expanding from less than 300,000 inhabitants to nearly 2.2 million.[12] Economic development kept pace with demographic expansion.[13] Chicago's commercial success stemmed largely from its location at the center of the nation's vast railroad network. Fully one-third of all railway mileage in the United States connected there, making the prairie city the greatest railroad hub on the planet and giving a ring of truth to the local saying "All roads lead to Chicago."[14]

Hailed as the "Great Central Market," Chicago stood at the center of a national transportation and communication network that circulated new commodities and cultural standards across the United States, helping to define the contours of consumer society.[15] The city's department stores, such as Marshall Field & Co., Carson Pirie Scott & Co., and Siegel-Cooper & Co., were among the largest and most profitable in existence. Their retail divisions attracted visitors from across the country, while their wholesale operations supplied dry goods houses in myriad far-flung cities and small towns.[16] Chicago companies—led by Sears, Roebuck & Co. and Montgomery Ward & Co.—dominated the nation's emergent mail-order trade. Together, these firms generated more than $150 million in sales each year, effectively expanding State Street's reach to Iowa, Nebraska, and beyond. As one industry expert noted, "Millions of people throughout the country who have never been in the city of Chicago do a large part of their shopping there."[17] Chicagoans also spread their cultural influence via national trade journals and lifestyle magazines, such as the *Dry Goods Reporter,* the *Show Window,* and *Red-*

book. "It's Chicago they're looking to," wrote novelist Henry Blake Fuller in 1893 of small-town Americans: "This town looms up before them and shuts out Boston and New York. . . . They read our papers, they come here to buy and to enjoy themselves."[18]

The number of people who came to Chicago "to buy and to enjoy" surged in the final decade of the nineteenth century. In 1893, the city hosted the most celebrated fair in the nation's history, the World's Columbian Exposition. It was, as Fuller claimed, the "year of grace" for Chicago—a moment when the upstart metropolis finally achieved the cultural recognition its boosters had long sought.[19] Led by renowned architect Daniel H. Burnham, the fair's organizers constructed a dazzling neoclassical fairyland, known as the White City, which attracted millions of visitors and inspired international urban planning interest.[20] The exposition's success made Chicago a locus of the City Beautiful movement, whose advocates maintained that attention to urban aesthetics as well as efficiency could better serve the needs of industrial capital.[21] In 1909, this movement culminated with the publication of Burnham's *Plan of Chicago,* a sweeping blueprint for Chicago's growth that solidified the city's reputation as a model of urban progress and innovation.[22] In mere decades, Chicago had gone from a smoldering ruin to the "laboratory of the continent," a place where new metropolitan ideals were forged and tested.[23]

And moneyed women flocked to this dynamic metropolis. They were the wives and daughters of industrialists, merchants, and financiers, as well as of managers and professionals. Their incomes ranged from millionaire to middling. The sums in their purses varied, but these women mixed together in commercial public spaces, belonged to the same clubs and civic associations, and shared notions of respectability. That they did so reflected the particularities of Chicago's class structure, which was, in the words of author Charles Dudley Warner, "as unformed, unselected, as the city itself—that is, more fluid and undetermined than in Eastern large cities."[24] In this midwestern capital of parvenus, where nearly three-quarters of the wealthiest citizens were self-made and where upward mobility seemed within everyone's reach, divisions between old and new money, between middle class and elite, were far less salient than they were in established urban centers.[25] As Chicago novelist Robert Herrick wrote in *The Gospel of Freedom* (1898), "There was a certain social openness, and a willingness to take people for their personal value."[26] In luxurious restaurants and department stores, as well as in modest tearooms and retail shops, moneyed women produced the cultural standards that Chicago businessmen distributed to the rest of the country.

Access to financial resources enabled Chicago ladies to patronize the city's new consumer institutions. But money alone was not enough to ensure entrée. Even before the Great Migration hardened northern racial divides, at a time when African Americans accounted for less than 2 percent of Chicago's population, black women faced discrimination in downtown restaurants, department stores, theaters, hotels, and other enterprises.[27] Although the Illinois Civil Rights Act of 1885 had established that all persons were entitled to enjoy public accommodations, black customers were routinely denied service and otherwise made to feel unwelcome in commercial public space. In 1899, for example, African American journalist and activist Ida B. Wells was prohibited from riding an elevator at the Palmer House hotel, where she was attending a meeting of the Cook County League of Women's Clubs. The hotel's management alleged Wells had been denied entry by mistake. Yet such mistakes were all too common for black consumers at the turn of the century.[28] By contrast, moneyed white women were eagerly courted by downtown businesses. Most of these women were native born; however, a significant number came from Chicago's thriving old immigrant communities—particularly the German, Irish, and Swedish enclaves.[29]

The activities of Chicago's moneyed white women attracted the notice of economist Thorstein Veblen in the 1890s, when he was teaching at the recently founded University of Chicago. In the works he penned while living in the city, most notably *The Theory of the Leisure Class* (1899), Veblen proposed that women's primary function was to bring status to their husbands or fathers through the "conspicuous consumption" of goods and leisure.[30] And certainly Chicago ladies did pass much of their time in this manner. But in focusing solely on their spending habits, Veblen overlooked a crucial component of their daily lives—their engagement in civic affairs. Few cities afforded women greater prospects for participation in public life than Chicago. The World's Columbian Exposition, in particular, opened new public roles to women with the creation of the Board of Lady Managers, headed by Bertha Palmer, wife of millionaire hotelier Potter Palmer.[31] This same period saw Chicago-based reformers such as Jane Addams, Florence Kelley, and Frances Willard rise to national prominence.[32] Joining these celebrated figures in their work were countless other moneyed women whose names were less well-known but who nonetheless devoted time to social reform, philanthropy, education, and city politics.

Crucially, Chicago ladies' public pursuits did not prevent them from savoring the fruits of the city's new consumer institutions. They seemed to glide easily between the settlement house and the opera house, between committee meetings and display windows. Herrick highlighted this distinctive aspect of the city's culture in a scene from *The Gospel of Freedom* in which a young woman visiting Chicago from New England attends a meeting of a prominent women's club. "Why, it's great," she exclaims, "to find all these fashionable women in such stunning clothes taking up these serious interests."[33] Whether they identified as reformers, professionals, philanthropists, clubwomen, society leaders, or some combination thereof, the moneyed women of Chicago regularly exercised their "pecuniary strength" in an expanding urban marketplace.[34]

Chicago ladies were thus advancing into public life as both civic actors and consumers at the turn of the century. Many historians, focusing on the former, have expertly documented the tensions aroused by middle-class and elite female reformers, professionals, and suffragists as they breached the traditional boundaries of their sphere.[35] Yet the incorporation of moneyed women into the public realm as consumers has largely been taken for granted, regarded as "what-goes-without-saying." This development, which occurred at different moments in different cities, was neither natural nor inevitable. Rather, it was "determined by history," to quote cultural critic Roland Barthes.[36] The social integration of the shopping lady into urban life—as well as the insertion of her corporeal form into the urban landscape—evoked profound moral, political, and legal opposition. This conflict, and the consuming practices at its root, shaped the cultural and physical contours of a metropolitan environment that upheld women's role as consumers.

The period between the Columbian Exposition and the publication of Burnham's *Plan* constituted a distinctive epoch in the development of Chicago. It was a formative era of consumer capitalism, when, as economist Simon Patten theorized, a pain economy of scarcity began to give way to a pleasure economy of abundance. Sustaining this shift, Patten argued in *The Theory of Social Forces* (1896), required a radical break from the past, the annihilation of old "ideals, impulses, and institutions."[37] In their place would emerge moral, aesthetic, and social values suited to the new economic conditions. Patten's optimistic assumption that these developments would reap nothing but progress and human happiness has hardly been borne out. Still, his work rightly emphasized the disruptive potential of consumer capitalism. Writing more than a century later, historian Joyce Appleby echoed Patten in arguing that "there can be no capitalism . . . without a culture of capitalism, and there is no culture of capitalism until the principal forms of traditional society have been challenged and overcome."[38] In Chicago, the expansion of the consumer economy did profoundly reshape local "customs, habits, and beliefs," as well as the built environment. But what neither Patten nor Appleby recognized—and, indeed, what existing scholarship has not adequately explored—was the crucial role of gender in this "revolutionary process."[39]

Historians have recently turned to questions of capitalism with renewed interest. A shared assumption of this scholarship has been that the development of capitalism "is a problem to be investigated, not simply assumed."[40] Among its many accomplishments, this literature has exposed the ways that culture, space, morality, and the state enabled capitalist growth. But questions of women and gender have not been central to this work.[41] Women's peripheral place is all the more puzzling given that they controlled as much as 80 to 85 percent of consumer spending in the twentieth century.[42] Yet for all that has been written about women's influence on retail, marketing, and advertising, the conditions enabling women's ascent as consumers remain relatively unexplored.[43] Gender has been central to capitalist development—a connection first exposed by pioneering women's historians, such as Nancy Cott, Christine Stansell, Kathy Peiss, and Jeanne Boydston.[44] Only by taking women and gender into account can historians of capitalism fully understand the evolution of our modern consumer economy and the institutions and environment that support it.

Chicago ladies' consuming practices, and the tensions they evoked, provide new insight into the crucial role of moneyed women in the making and meaning of the urban landscape as the city became a focal point of sociological investigation, literary imagination, and progressive reform at century's end. A new American bourgeoisie wielded cultural, political, and financial capital that dominated the creation of the built environment.[45] Existing scholarship has focused mainly on this era's working-class women, on deviance and vice, and on the experience of female reformers.[46] However, the influence of shopping ladies has started to become apparent.[47] By examining the conflict aroused by their new habits of consumption, this account's vantage point highlights the masculine orientation of the nineteenth-century downtown. It reveals how moneyed women helped establish a city center that accommodated, even invited, their presence. It lays bare these women's imprint on Burnham's *Plan*, upending the assumption that women consumers only began to have a decisive role in downtown development in the 1920s.[48]

At issue is the role of moneyed ladies in the seismic reorientation of American culture at the turn of the century, as women claimed new opportunities for autonomy, heterosociability, and public pleasure. Shop girls and factory operatives, as well as reformers and suffragists, spurred the transformation.[49] But so, too, did consuming ladies. As they ate and drank and shopped downtown, moneyed women ushered in new modes of public behavior that eroded the social and spatial boundaries restricting their lives. They challenged men's exclusive right to enjoy all the pleasures of the metropolitan experience—a right embodied in the figure of the flâneur.[50] Access to public space did not, of course, translate directly into access to the ballot.[51] Nor did it provide an immediate means of achieving financial autonomy. Yet social and spatial relations were mutually reinforcing in the creation of gender regimes, and assumptions about the correct place for women often justified their exclusion from public life.[52] In gaining greater access to the city center, even if that access was circumscribed, women achieved a new purchase on the public realm. They attained the ability to traverse the city center unescorted without compromising their respectability—to see, be seen, socialize, and pursue pleasure away from their homes. In the streets and stores of the retail district, they enacted a female subjectivity that affirmed self-gratification and, in turn, underwrote the consolidation of a culture of accumulation and desire.

The new practices of shopping ladies illuminate how gender ideals constrained and shaped an emergent culture of consumption. Existing literature has highlighted contestation over workingwomen's pursuit of commercial pleasure in dance halls, cabarets, nickelodeons, and other cheap resorts.[53] The account offered here brings to light protests aimed at genteel women and the campaigns waged to restrict their new practices of public leisure and consumption. These women provided the financial resources and cultural authority that upheld the consumer economy. They gained access to the public realm as patrons of refined and feminized commercial spaces.[54] But in entering those spaces, moneyed women also provoked opposition. Chicago lawmakers, reformers, and men of industry drew on traditional notions of femininity to restrain the consuming habits that propelled affluent women into public life. These debates challenge dominant narratives of the growth of consumer society, which hold that the creation of a culture of consumption was nonconsensual and uncontested.[55] Instead, they reveal the fraught formation of a moral and civic landscape that enabled the expansion of consumer society.

As historians of American legal culture have shown, the ability to enjoy public accommodations—including theaters, hotels, and restaurants—became entwined with definitions of freedom and equality in the age of Jim Crow.[56] In 1885, the Illinois Civil Rights Act codified this link and established the right of "all citizens" to "full and equal enjoyment" of "places of public accommodation and amusement."[57] But merely a decade after legally assuring African Americans access to such places, lawmakers, reformers, businessmen, and consumers fought over the terms of women's incorporation into these very sites. In debating those terms, Chicagoans negotiated the meaning of civic equality, as well as the privileges and responsibilities that accompanied participation in the public sphere. Much like the legal transformations that opened public accommodations to African Americans, the commercial changes that brought women into the public realm disrupted established codes of civility and appropriate public conduct.[58] The conflict over Chicago ladies' consuming practices marked a remaking of public culture as women asserted new belonging in the modern metropolis.

Traces of the conflict emerged in newspapers, magazines, fiction, guidebooks, trade journals, and other published materials. Indeed, debates over consumption regularly seeped into public discourse at the turn of the century. But their impress was also left on the law, city council minutes, records of civic organizations, municipal reports, urban planning documents, and the shape of the metropolis itself. Together, these materials illuminate surprising points of friction in a city adapting to a new economic order. My account begins with a chapter introducing the moneyed women, as well as the downtown, at the center of these tensions. Each ensuing chapter explores a particular flashpoint, as Chicagoans responded to ladies' new consuming practices. Chapter 2 probes the streets and sidewalks of the Loop in the 1890s, when lawmakers contemplated a ban on large hoopskirts. Chapter 3 focuses on the growing presence of moneyed women in downtown theaters and the near riot that erupted over ladies' tall theater hats. Chapter 4 examines moral crusades against alcohol consumption by female patrons of department store tearooms, cafés, confectioneries, and soda fountains in the early twentieth century. Chapter 5 brings to light the collaborative efforts of retailers, clubwomen, police, and city officials to curtail street harassment and prostitution in the Loop in order to facilitate the circulation of respectable women as consumers. Chapter 6 considers debates between retailers and industrialists over the appropriate use of downtown streets and the failed attempt to introduce a shopping time limit, which would have prohibited moneyed women from accessing the Loop during rush hour. It also reveals how these debates shaped Burnham's 1909 *Plan*.

In contemporary American society, women dominate retail landscapes, and popular culture upholds the figure of a woman "born to shop." The notion, then, that the consuming practices of moneyed women once posed a spatial and cultural problem for the nation's cities is unexpected. Yet just over a century ago, urban inhabitants battled over the incorporation of these practices into public life. On the dusty sidewalks of Chicago, and within the city's elegant theaters, restaurants, department stores, and hotels, this conflict comes into view. In the clash over consumption and public space, Chicagoans transformed the built environment, gender norms, and civic culture. They established a new downtown that women and men could occupy together.

1

Moneyed Women and the Downtown

IN THE SUMMER OF 1891, New York writer Julian Ralph spent several weeks in Chicago to observe preparations for the World's Columbian Exposition. His visit formed the basis of a series of essays for *Harper's New Monthly Magazine* that explored Chicago's civic and economic landscape. Ralph's pen dwelt on the city's singular growth in the two decades since the great fire of 1871 decimated the downtown. He spoke of the monumental achievements of Chicago capitalists, of the "energy, roar, and bustle" of the business district.[1] Yet upon returning to the metropolis two years later to attend the exposition, Ralph concluded that his initial work had overlooked one of Chicago's most distinctive features—its "gentle side," the realm of art, literature, philanthropy, and civic betterment. In this domain, he contended, Chicago ladies took the lead. While their menfolk threw themselves into the hurly-burly of moneymaking, the city's women devoted themselves to bringing order, culture, and beauty to the urban environment—to civilizing the capitalist city. Through their clubs and causes, they exerted a "softening influence" over public affairs, without engaging in the crass commercial life of the metropolis. They were, Ralph maintained, removed from the market, "creatures apart from the confusion—reposeful, stylish, carefully toileted, serene, and unruffled."[2]

As represented in Ralph's essay, Chicago's commercial world rarely intersected with the gentle sphere over which ladies presided. But the city was not as neatly divided as the writer supposed. To be sure, most moneyed women devoted more time to club activities, socializing, and domestic cares than to capital accumulation. But they were nonetheless daily embedded in the relations of the market—as consumers. Invited by the operators of new consumer spaces, such as department stores, restaurants, theaters, and grand hotels, Chicago ladies were spending ever more time in the central business district. Not only errands brought them into this blossoming commercial realm. Increasingly, their entire social and cultural worlds operated there. A lady of 1890s Chicago might find herself going downtown to attend a club meeting at the Palmer House, a committee luncheon at the tearoom of Schlesinger & Mayer, a benefit concert at the Auditorium Theater, or a lecture at Central Music Hall. Indeed, the very civilizing pursuits that Ralph regarded as being isolated from the business realm were drawing ladies into commercial spaces and commercial exchanges.

Chicago's "gentle side" thus converged with the masculine sphere of commerce via the activities of moneyed ladies. A similar fusion could be observed in other American cities during this period. But in Chicago, as Ralph noted, moneyed women had seized an unprecedented degree of involvement in public affairs. "I do not believe," he reflected, "that in any older American city we shall find fashionable women so anxious to be considered patrons of art and of learning, or so forward in works of public improvement and governmental reform as well as of charity." In Ralph's view, Chicago had given birth to "a new character for the woman of fashion," one who asserted herself in the public realm as well as in genteel society. To illustrate his claim, Ralph pointed to Chicago's most prominent social leader, Bertha Honoré Palmer, wife of millionaire merchant and hotelier Potter Palmer. Mrs. Palmer commanded Chicago society in a way "not altogether improperly likened" to Caroline Astor's influence over New York's elite social set, the Four Hundred. Yet unlike Astor, Palmer exerted herself in the civic sphere.[3] Most notably, she served as president of the Columbian Exposition's Board of Lady Managers, in which capacity she oversaw construction of the fair's Woman's Building, represented the board before Congress, lobbied foreign governments, and supervised hundreds of volunteers.[4]

Ralph was far from alone in stressing the civic engagement of Chicago women; it was a theme often repeated in literature and social commentary. As Robert Herrick wrote in *The Gospel of Freedom*, "Chicago is the great home for intelligent woman. Here she moulds the destinies, the civilization of millions of eager human beings . . . She organizes immense reforms, she institutes educational benefits, she advances shoulder to shoulder with men in a common fight against the demons of want and vice."[5] Writer Emily Wheaton struck a similar chord in "The Russells in Chicago," a *Ladies' Home Journal* serial about a Boston couple who moves to the Midwest. Chicago women, Wheaton suggested, were "real thinking machines, on earth for a purpose, and that purpose was not to stay at home to be simply mothers and housekeepers."[6] Instead, they were "up to everything and doing everything."[7]

Chicago's reputation for fostering women's participation in public life owed itself, in part, to the celebrity achieved by women such as Palmer amid the triumph of the Columbian Exposition. Also influential was the fact that the city was home to many of the nation's most prominent female reformers—Jane Addams, founder of Hull House (a settlement house); Frances Willard, president of the Woman's Christian Temperance Union; Florence Kelley, chief factory inspector for the state of Illinois and later head of the National Consumers League; and Ida B. Wells, journalist and anti-lynching activist.[8] Yet many less famous individuals helped extend Chicago women's reach into the public sphere. Associated with a wide range of organizations and causes, these moneyed women infused social activities with public service, mingling cultural privilege with civic consciousness.

Among these public-spirited ladies was Frances Macbeth Glessner, wife of industrialist John Jacob Glessner, a partner in one of the nation's largest farm machinery manufacturers. Frances Glessner (1848–1932) shared with many of her contemporaries a keen interest in Chicago's civic and cultural development. She was best known for helping to establish the city's first permanent professional symphony, an organization she nurtured financially and socially until her death. She was an early member of two of the city's first women's clubs: the Fortnightly and the Chicago Woman's Club. Glessner also served for many years as an officer of the Chicago Society of Decorative Art, later the Antiquarian Society of the Art Institute of Chicago, which provided a market for women's handicrafts. At the behest of the first president of the new University of Chicago, she founded a reading group for faculty wives, which met at her home every Monday morning for more than thirty years.[9]

Glessner's commitment to public life was typical for a woman of Chicago's moneyed classes. She stands out because of a journal she kept between 1879 and 1915, which chronicles her daily activities, social engagements, and domestic concerns. Composed of fifty-two leather-bound volumes now preserved at the Chicago History Museum, Glessner's journal offers a remarkable window into the experiences of moneyed women at a formative moment in Chicago's development. With Glessner as a guide, the ladies who inhabited this bustling metropolis, as well as the built environment their activities transformed, come vividly into focus.

Like most Chicagoans of their generation, Frances Glessner and her husband, John, came from somewhere else. The couple had met in the 1860s in Springfield, Ohio, where John, then a bookkeeper in an agricultural implements firm, boarded in the home of Frances's mother. Frances's father, a failed merchant, had taken a job out of state, leaving his six children to help supplement the earnings he sent home. Frances was teaching school and assisting with her mother's boarders when she "inspired the love" of her future husband. After John was made a partner in his firm in 1870, the Glessners married and moved to Chicago to establish a new headquarters for Warder, Bushnell & Glessner. With John guiding sales from Chicago, the business prospered and became a key competitor to the McCormick Harvesting Machine Company. Meanwhile, Frances oversaw the household's domestic affairs, raised two children, and managed a handful of servants (fig. 1.1).[10]

Chicago was a small city of 300,000 inhabitants and seemingly endless commercial opportunity when the Glessners arrived in 1870. The couple initially rented a small frame house on the West Side, near Union Park. Four years later, with John's success growing, they bought a stately brick home a few blocks away.[11] In 1885, the Glessners affirmed their financial and social status by purchasing the last open lot on Chicago's most exclusive residential street, Prairie Avenue. They commissioned the renowned Boston architect Henry Hobson Richardson to design the property, a fortresslike granite building that contrasted sharply with the ornate Victorian mansions then lining the avenue. Once the Glessners moved into their distinctive new home in late 1887, their nearest neighbors included the households of George Pullman, Philip Armour, Marshall Field, and other leading capitalists.[12]

Like their neighbors and most moneyed Chicagoans, the Glessners had humble upbringings. John Glessner grew up on an Ohio farm, where he helped his father with agricultural tasks and with editing the local newspaper, which his father owned.[13] Frances, raised in a family where

Figure 1.1 Like most moneyed Chicago women of her era, Frances Macbeth Glessner was active in civic, philanthropic, and cultural affairs. She helped bring the first permanent symphony to Chicago and belonged to several prominent women's clubs. Her husband, John J. Glessner, earned his fortune as a manufacturer of agricultural implements.   Courtesy of Glessner House Museum, Chicago, Illinois.

money was always tight, brought few financial assets to the marriage. Such backgrounds were characteristic of their peers. Unlike their counterparts back East, Chicago's most affluent citizens had not inherited their wealth—they had made it. More than 70 percent of Chicago's wealthiest men in 1892 had earned their own fortunes, compared to just 30 percent in New York and Boston.[14] Chicago's reputation for creating self-made men was a source of local pride, as many visitors discovered. "Nearly all of Chicago's prominent citizens are self-made and proud of it," observed etiquette expert Emily Post when passing through on a cross-country tour. "Millionaire after millionaire will tell you of the day when he wore ragged clothes, ran barefooted, sold papers, cleaned sidewalks, drove grocers' wagons, and did any job he could find to get along."[15]

In contrast to eastern cities, where most fortunes dated back two or more generations, Chicago society was less established and, in turn, less exclusive.[16] It was, in the words of novelist Henry Blake Fuller, "wide enough to include the best as well as the worst." As one of a minority of Chicago-born residents, Fuller was a close observer of the city's social life. Society in his hometown, Fuller asserted in an 1897 article for *Atlantic Monthly,* was "unregulated, in the main, by anything like tradition, authority, forms, and precedents."[17] In such a young metropolis, class distinctions were flexible, even imperceptible. The designation "new money" lost much of its meaning in an environment without an established elite. Similarly, the line between middle class and upper class mattered little to people whose family and friends spanned the spectrum—and who may themselves have moved from one end to the other. Instead of pedigree, Chicagoans were said to value upward mobility, talent, and hard work. As Fuller's friend and fellow novelist Hamlin Garland wrote in 1895, "Chicago society isn't the New York Four Hundred. We're all workers here."[18]

Unfinished and rapidly evolving, Chicago society remained accessible to most moneyed women in the decades after the 1871 fire. Residents were building from scratch a city as well as its social categories. Novelist Emily Wheaton emphasized the "great lack of social and caste distinctions" as late as 1902. "They seemed to take everybody on faith out here," declared Wheaton's Boston-born protagonist. "There was no fuss or formality about society at all. They either liked you, or they didn't like you."[19] This flexibility ensured that women married to millionaire merchants and industrialists shared more in common with the wives of doctors, managers, and engineers than did their counterparts back East. Chicago's moneyed women, from the truly rich to those of middling status, spent time together as members of clubs and civic organizations, contributed to the same philanthropic causes, attended the same cultural events, and upheld the same values. Significantly, they also patronized the same commercial spaces, mingling together in theaters, tearooms, cafés, hotels, and department stores. As one travel writer remarked, "Chicago people have a character all their own, among those of large cities, through the constant meeting with one another, in the shopping district and at the clubs."[20]

Women's clubs in particular facilitated social mixing in Chicago. The Chicago Woman's Club, the largest and most prominent in the city, boasted a membership of more than five hundred in the early 1890s.[21] Founded in 1876, the club initially focused on the discussion of literary and philosophical topics. By the late 1880s, however, it had turned to the "practical work" of reform, tackling issues ranging from child labor and compulsory education to prison conditions and age-of-consent laws.[22] The activism of the Chicago Woman's Club impressed Julian Ralph, who described it as "the mother of woman's public work" after his 1893 visit. "I know of no such undertakings or cooperation by women elsewhere in our country," he claimed.[23] Other women's clubs, such as New York's Sorosis or Boston's New England Woman's Club, predated the Chicago organization.[24] But these groups never achieved the same degree of public influence as the Chicago Woman's Club, which, at the height of its authority in the late 1890s, helped establish the first juvenile court in the United States.[25]

The ranks of the Chicago Woman's Club were, in Ralph's words, "made up of almost every kind of woman." Among their number were "ultrafashionable society leaders," such as Bertha Palmer and Ellen Martin Henrotin, wife of the founding president of the Chicago Stock Exchange.[26] Frances Glessner became a member in 1886, while still living on the West Side.[27] These "wealthy and fashionable women" were joined by progressive reformers, such as Jane Addams, Frances Willard, and Julia Lathrop, as well as a number of female professionals, such as physicians Sarah Hackett Stevenson and Julia Holmes Smith, lawyers Myra Bradwell and Catherine Waugh McCulloch, and journalists Mary H.

Krout and Helen Starrett.[28] Fleshing out the membership rolls were in-dividuals that Ralph referred to as "plain wives and daughters"—women of moderate means who were neither society doyennes nor reform ex-perts.[29] These ladies, to quote the club's own *Annals,* were "simply home-women." Each member of the club, no matter her financial situation, was expected to shoulder her "share of the world's work" and contribute $10 in annual dues.[30]

Organizations such as the Chicago Woman's Club encouraged the women of the city to maintain broader social circles than did their counterparts back East, as evidenced by Glessner's own social life. Glessner often interacted with the women of Chicago's wealthiest fami-lies. Peppered throughout her journal are references to such figures as Palmer; Henrotin; Malvina Armour, wife of meatpacker Philip D. Armour; Hattie Pullman, wife of railroad mogul George Pullman; and Nannie Field, first wife of retailer Marshall Field. But Glessner's club activities also encouraged intimacy with budget-conscious professionals and house-wives. Among her close friends, for example, was Dr. Sarah Hackett Stevenson, whom Glessner met through the Fortnightly, which focused chiefly on intellectual pursuits. Born in a small Illinois town, Stevenson worked for several years as a teacher before completing her medical training and becoming the first female member of the American Medical Association.[31] Another of Glessner's close friends from the Fortnightly was Ellen Mitchell, the first female member of the Chicago Board of Education. Married to a grain broker, Mitchell lived on a small income, once confessing to Glessner that "every cent of money that I have used has been such an anxiety to me." Glessner recorded assisting her friend in a variety of ways, such as paying her Fortnightly dues, giving her cash, and treating her to cab rides and other small items she "couldn't afford to buy."[32]

Glessner's club memberships also facilitated regular intercourse with progressive reformers, most of whom belonged to the Chicago Woman's Club. She often noted meals, meetings, and casual conversations with "Miss Addams," "Miss Willard," and the like. In 1903, Glessner furthered her reform connections by joining the Everyday Club, a group of forty civic-minded female Chicagoans who, as Glessner put it, "all stand for something." In addition to Addams and Lathrop, the club's ranks in-cluded Lucy Flower, a child welfare activist; Mary Bartelme, Chicago's first female judge; Ella Flagg Young, the superintendent of Chicago Public Schools; and numerous other women reformers.[33]

While class lines in Chicago were often flexible, other social distinctions proved more rigid—especially race. In the era of the World's Fair, African Americans constituted just 1.3 percent of Chicago's population.[34] Nevertheless, racism profoundly shaped the city's social hierarchy. Practically any white woman of modest means could, in the words of Emily Wheaton, "easily crawl under the fence that hedges society."[35] Yet even the wealthiest black women were denied entry. The operation of this "color line," though never explicitly articulated, was evident in Glessner's journal. Its pages offered no hint of association with black women and, indeed, seldom took notice of black people at all. On rare occasions, Glessner mentioned African Americans who served her at hotels, restaurants, or elsewhere in Chicago and beyond. Not once, however, did she bother to record any of their names. African Americans simply did not figure into Glessner's social world.

The racial divisions operating in Chicago society became a focus of national press attention in 1894, when the Chicago Woman's Club considered admitting its first African American member. Fannie Barrier Williams, a former teacher and wife of a lawyer, had won acclaim during the World's Fair as a speaker at both the World's Congress of Representative Women and the Parliament of Religions. She had also served as "clerk in charge of colored interests" for the Woman's Building—a position created as consolation after black women protested their exclusion from the Board of Lady Managers.[36] In that role, Williams forged strong connections to white female reformers and "well-known society leaders," a handful of whom proposed her name for membership in the Chicago Woman's Club.[37] No formal policies prohibited black women from joining, yet several members strongly objected to Williams's admission. The debate dragged on for fourteen months and drew the interest of newspapers and women's clubs across the country.[38] At last, with public scrutiny mounting, the club agreed to admit Williams and passed a resolution declaring that membership did not hinge on "race, color, creed, or politics."[39] The victory proved hollow, however. For the next thirty years, Williams remained the only African American member of the Chicago Woman's Club.[40]

The "historic contest" over Williams's admission exposed the overt discrimination faced by Chicago black women long before the Great

Migration amplified racial tensions in the urban North.[41] In addition to being excluded from many clubs, African Americans in Chicago were often denied access to commercial spaces enjoyed by white patrons. Such discriminatory treatment inspired a series of lawsuits after 1885, when Illinois passed a Civil Rights Act guaranteeing equal access to public accommodations. The first successful case was brought in 1888 by Josephine Curry, an affluent black woman. Curry sued People's Theater, located at State and Harrison Streets, after she paid for main floor tickets but was shown to segregated seats in the balcony. The verdict against the theater was eventually upheld by the Illinois Supreme Court.[42]

Curry's victory did not stop Loop establishments from discriminating against African American customers, however.[43] In the following decade, black Chicagoans initiated civil rights suits against restaurants, cafés, and theaters.[44] Still, many downtown businesses continued to provide segregated accommodations or deliberately poor service to black patrons. In fact, such behavior was often encouraged by proprietors. Even in establishments that maintained official policies of nondiscrimination, managers and workers sometimes refused to comply. In 1914, the *Chicago Defender* recounted one such instance at Marshall Field & Co. A clerk in the store's bargain basement objected to serving Ida B. Wells, then president of the Negro Fellowship League. After Wells complained to a manager, the clerk screamed, "I don't have to wait on a black 'nigger' like you." In this case, the clerk was promptly fired while Wells received an apology and reassurance that discrimination based on "race, creed or color had no place in their business."[45] Yet had the victim been anyone other than a prominent reformer with extensive press connections, the clerk's behavior likely would have gone unpunished.

Although less salient than race, religion provided another dividing line in Chicago society. Jewish immigration, particularly from eastern Europe, had accelerated in the late 1870s. By the time of the World's Fair, an estimated 75,000 Jews resided in Chicago, constituting nearly 5 percent of the total population.[46] As their numbers increased, so, too, did anti-Semitism. Even members of the longer established, more affluent German-Jewish community, which had developed in the 1840s and 1850s, were often viewed with suspicion.[47] Glessner, like most of her peers, socialized with moneyed Jewish families. Nevertheless, her private journal contained several anti-Semitic remarks. While vacationing at a mountain resort in New Hampshire, for instance, Glessner lamented that the "jews are as thick as flies in summer here" and she "might as well be spending the summer in the 5th Ave. Synagogue."[48] Compared to African Americans, however, Jewish women easily gained entry to Chicago society—a circumstance reflected in the membership of the Chicago Woman's Club. Whereas Fannie Barrier Williams had battled for months in 1895 to join the Chicago Woman's Club, Jewish women were admitted in 1877, a year after the club's founding. Some even held leadership positions, such as Henriette Greenbaum Frank, who served as president from 1884 to 1885.[49]

Other distinctions of birth or background operated more subtly—and rarely did they result in exclusion from commercial venues or women's organizations. To be sure, residents with roots in Germany liked to socialize and attend church together, just as transplants from the East Coast often sought each other's company. But most Chicagoans shared in common this history of migration, from abroad or elsewhere in the United States. As historian Frederic Cople Jaher documented in his classic study of urban elites, only 6 percent of Chicago's most affluent residents had been born there. Nearly 20 percent were of foreign birth, with German, Irish, and Scandinavian immigrants predominating. The remaining 75 percent hailed from other parts of the United States—and most of these native-born residents had at least one foreign-born parent.[50] Chicago's moneyed citizens were not, of course, as diverse as the overall population of the metropolis. Still, they were a heterogeneous lot, particularly when measured against Boston or New York, where most affluent citizens were native to the region, if not the city itself.[51]

Despite their differences, Chicago's moneyed white residents were knitted together by a shared interest in the prosperity of their city. They firmly believed in their own future as the "ultimate metropolis."[52] Facilitating this destiny absorbed the energies of men and women alike. While responsibility for commercial growth fell most heavily on the menfolk, Chicago ladies shouldered much of the work of civic and cultural development. As writer and social leader Hobart Chatfield-Taylor later observed, the desire to uplift Chicago was "most deeply embedded in the hearts of our women, who play, it seems to me, a more active part in public affairs than do their sisters of the East."[53] In the early 1890s, the scope of this "part" was expanding. Chicago women were seizing new opportunities to participate in the public realm—and, crucially, to explore the commercial landscape blossoming around them.

When the Glessners first arrived in late 1870, mere months before the Great Chicago Fire, the city was only the fifth largest in the United States. Yet already its rapid growth since 1837—the date of official incorporation—was said to "scarcely find a parallel in the history of the world." Dubbed the "great city of the West," Chicago was full of young strivers, big dreams, and few cultural trappings.[54] "It seems as if, on all hands, people came here merely to trade, to make money, and not to live," claimed one early visitor, Swedish novelist Fredrika Bremer. The landscape was then dominated by cheap, hasty construction, with few paved roads or sidewalks and buildings made primarily of wood. As Bremer quipped, Chicago was "very little deserving of its name, 'Queen of the Lake'; for, sitting there on the shore of the lake in wretched dishabille, she resembles rather a huckstress than a queen."[55]

In those pre-fire days, Lake Street, which ran east to west just south of the Chicago River, was the principal business street, where a handful of dry goods merchants clustered together with wholesalers, bankers, and shipping companies. At least one Chicagoan envisioned a grander future for the retail district. In the late 1860s, dry goods merchant Potter Palmer—future husband of Bertha Palmer—quietly purchased nearly a mile of frontage on State Street, then a marshy, lightly trafficked, north–south roadway. Palmer dreamed of developing the street into a fashionable retail boulevard to rival Paris's Champs-Élysées. He began by persuading the city council to widen the street, a task made easier after the great fire leveled the city center in 1871. Next, Palmer constructed an opulent six-story emporium into which he enticed his old business partners, the merchants of Field, Leiter & Co. (the antecedent to Marshall Field & Co.). Three blocks south of this "Marble Palace," he built a luxurious hotel, the Palmer House. With these anchors in place, State Street's future as the spine of the retail district was assured (Map 1).[56]

The next two decades were years of steady growth—for Chicago and the Glessners. While John enlarged his company, the city's population climbed to more than one million. Meanwhile, Palmer and other Chicago merchants slowly expanded the retail district. After 1890, when the midwestern metropolis was selected to hold the World's Columbian

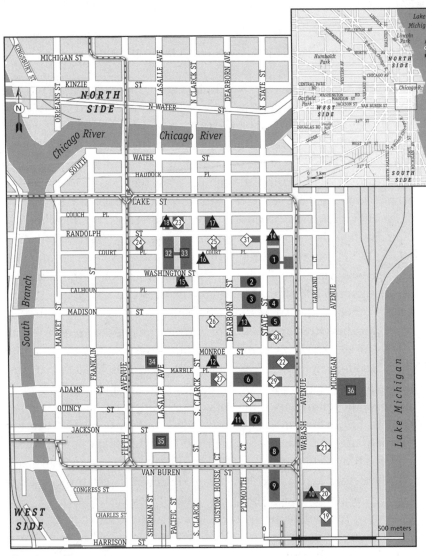

● Department Stores

1. Marshall Field & Co.
2. Carson Pirie Scott & Co.
3. Boston Store
4. Mandel Bros.
5. Schlesinger & Mayer
6. The Fair
7. The Hub
8. Rothschild & Co.
9. Siegel-Cooper & Co.

▲ Theaters

10. Auditorium Theater
11. Great Northern Theater and Hotel
12. Columbia Theater
13. McVickers Theater

14. Central Music Hall
15. Chicago Opera House
16. Grand Opera House
17. Schiller Theater
18. Hooley's Theater

◇ Select Hotels, Restaurants, and Confectioneries

19. Auditorium Annex
20. Auditorium Hotel
21. Richelieu Hotel
22. Palmer House
23. Sherman House
24. Hotel Bismarck
25. Henrici's Restaurant
26. Boston Oyster House

27. H.M. Kinsley's Restaurant
28. Gunther's Candy
29. Berry's Candy
30. Huyler's Candy
31. Kranz's Candy

■ Other Landmarks

32. City Hall
33. Courthouse
34. Woman's Temple
35. Chicago Board of Trade
36. Art Institute

╍╍╍ Elevated Railway Lines

Map 1 Chicago's Loop in the 1890s

Exposition, commercial development along State Street accelerated.[57] A host of department stores, restaurants, grand hotels, cafés, specialty shops, soda fountains, and theaters sprang up, beckoning to moneyed shoppers. The thoroughfare's rapid transformation attracted the attention of visitors, who were urged by residents and guidebooks alike to admire the new consumer abundance. "The great retail houses which we see on either side of the street, as far as the eye can reach, have all grown up during a remarkably brief period," the author of *Picturesque Chicago and Guide to the World's Fair* (1892) reminded readers.[58]

Marveled at by visitors, State Street's developing commercial landscape was the framework of Glessner's ordinary routine at century's end. No matter the season, she visited State Street several times each week—sometimes more than once a day. Shopping most often drew her downtown. According to her journal, "a little shopping," "some shopping," and "more shopping" made up the rhythm of daily life.[59] Glessner also sallied forth to the city center for social and civic activities that made use of the downtown's new consumer spaces. She recorded, for example, attending meetings of the Fortnightly at the elegant Hotel Richelieu, built in 1885, and discussing the Half-Orphan Asylum over lunch at H. M. Kinsley's restaurant, which opened a ladies' lunch room the same year.[60] Glessner often combined these engagements with shopping. "I went down town to a board meeting of the Dec Art Society. Then to the dressmakers, milliners etc.," she wrote in late 1892.[61] Her many public obligations, as well as her consuming practices, guaranteed that rarely would more than a few days pass without the need to make her way to State Street.

In order to reach the retail district, Glessner, like most affluent Chicagoans, could travel by carriage. Her husband noted purchasing the couple's first "small carriage" in 1875, to be followed by numerous others.[62] For more than twenty-five years, the family employed Charles Nelson, a Swedish immigrant, as their coachman.[63] Frances took a carriage for longer trips, such as paying calls on the North Side or exploring the future site of the Columbian Exposition.[64] But she sometimes opted to take a carriage shopping, especially if accompanied by other family members. When her mother was visiting from Ohio, for example, Glessner wrote that Nelson brought "Ma" and Glessner's daughter, Fanny, home while Glessner herself wrapped up her errands at Marshall Field's.[65] Less frequently, she made use of Chicago's growing fleet of hansom cabs, whose rates started at 50 cents a mile or 75 cents an hour.[66]

Glessner recorded taking her first hansom cab ride in 1885 and "enjoyed it very much."[67] She often shared these trips with other ladies. One wet spring day in 1894, for example, Glessner and her neighbor Evaline Kimball, wife of piano manufacturer William Wallace Kimball, were "caught in the rain" downtown and "took a hansom and came home."[68]

In those days, Glessner could easily be caught in the rain, as she often chose to walk to the retail district. When the family resided on the West Side, as they did until 1887, this journey consisted of a one-mile trek down Washington Street, which at the time was lined with tidy single-family homes. Once the Glessners relocated to Prairie Avenue, Frances would walk a mile and a half to the base of State Street and another half mile to its northern end. She made the trip most often when the weather was fine, but she also ventured forth when it was cold and blustery, noting in her journal snow blockades and at least one instance when the "mercury was 10 or more below zero."[69] According to her family, Glessner possessed a "firm step," a trait likely honed by navigating Chicago's unreliable sidewalks.[70] Whereas State Street itself had walkways of cement and limestone, the vast majority of the city's sidewalks were constructed of wood planks.[71] Often poorly maintained and rotting, they varied in height—a peculiar legacy from when the city raised the street grade decades earlier. Recalling this feature, reformer and heiress Louise de Koven Bowen wrote, "When you walked up and down the street you went up and down innumerable steps and swept up the steps neatly with the long trains which were then the fashion in street clothes."[72]

In addition to walking, Chicago ladies took advantage of the public transit system. Glessner often combined the two forms of travel, as in December 1883, when she "walked to Fields dry goods store, bought a few things & came home by cars, feeling better & brighter for the exercise."[73] Throughout her first decade in Chicago, the streetcars ran exclusively on animal power, as they had since commencing service in 1859.[74] Describing this early transit system, Carter H. Harrison Jr., who served as mayor in the early twentieth century, remembered his neighborhood line, "with its seagoing, one-horse rattle-traps, whose drivers had imposed upon them the double duty of serving as money-changer and conductor!"[75] Chicago's first cable car track opened on State Street in 1882 and began whisking passengers from the northern edge of the shopping district to the Near South Side at speeds of nine to twelve miles per hour.[76] The first elevated lines, powered by steam and later electricity, commenced service a decade later, in advance of the World's Fair. By 1897, the iconic Union Elevated Loop had been completed. Circling the business district, the Loop united three distinct elevated railway systems that carried passengers from the North, West, and South Sides. By that point, the midwestern metropolis had more street lines, more track, and longer routes than any other city in the world.[77]

Operated for profit by private transit companies, Chicago's streetcar lines were plagued with overcrowding, especially during peak commuting hours. "A Chicago car at the rush time is a sight which once seen is not easily forgotten," remarked British social reformer William T. Stead after traveling on a North Side streetcar while visiting Chicago for the World's Fair. "Every seat is filled and all the space between the seats is choked with a crowded mass of humanity."[78] The transit line servicing Glessner's South Side neighborhood was less prone to overcrowding than those on the North and West Sides, which were owned by Charles T. Yerkes, the notorious "street-railway magnate" who inspired Theodore Dreiser's *The Titan* (1914).[79] Yet all of Chicago's streetcars drew together in close proximity a diverse collection of riders—men and women, whites and blacks, shoppers and store clerks, executives and secretaries. On one memorable occasion in 1898, Glessner recorded assisting a poor "lame girl" on a crowded State Street car. Glessner was on her way downtown to complete some errands when she noticed the young woman and "helped keep people from stepping on [the girl's] foot."[80]

Traveling to the north side of the retail district, Glessner would have taken the State Street streetcar line to its turnaround at Lake Street, just south of the wholesale corridor that hugged the Chicago River.[81] Stretching more than ten blocks, South Water Market brought together sellers of fruit, vegetables, seafood, meat, dairy products, and other provisions. In the early 1890s, Chicago was home to more than three hundred commission houses, including some of the largest wholesale grocers in the nation. Its merchants received millions of dollars' worth of produce each year via road, rail, and water. Mere blocks from the tip of the State Street shopping district, South Water Market was nonetheless a far cry from the elegant retail landscape enjoyed by Glessner and other ladies. Day or night, the "sidewalks, streets, and stores are alike barricaded with people, teams, and produce," noted one observer in 1895.[82] The entire district, according to another Chicagoan, was a "maze of barrels, and boxes, and gory calves, and chicken-coops redolent with the

unmistakable odor of the badly-kept country barnyard, and huge piles
of sacked potatoes, and egg-cases, squashes, barrels of cider, and hogs
cold and stiff in death, with bits of cob wedged between their gleaming
jaws."[83] It was, simply put, a place that ladies such as Glessner avoided.

Instead of heading north to South Water Street, Glessner would
have disembarked at the State Street turnaround and walked south
toward Randolph Street, the gateway to the retail district. "Here is the
fine trade, the great stores, the concourse of the fashionable world,"
explained travel writer Louis Schick.[84] To the east, at State and Randolph, stood the Central Music Hall, where Glessner attended concerts
and recitals as well as lectures by such speakers as German American
statesman Carl Schurz and Charles Eliot, the president of Harvard University.[85] Lauded as the most acoustically perfect auditorium in the
world, Central Music Hall was one of several elegant theaters that
sprouted up in the city center in the decades following the 1871 fire.[86]
Across the street from Central Music Hall, the glittering plate-glass
windows of jewelers Shourds & Kasper beckoned to passers-by. Elegantly arranged silver spoons and diamond bracelets provided a small
preview of the consumer delights that State Street might yield. On the
opposite corner, Kranz's Candy, one of Chicago's largest confectioneries, served ice cream and bonbons that attracted crowds as easily as "a
weak bank in panicky times."[87]

Glessner would have passed these sites when traveling to her favorite
retail destination—Marshall Field & Co., the first of the large department stores that lined State Street. Then located in an ornate mansard-
roofed building owned by the Singer Sewing Machine Company, the
store occupied only a fraction of the square city block it would later
dominate (fig. 1.2).[88] Yet even in the early 1890s, the retail palace had
an "imposing appearance" that drew throngs of admirers daily. These
crowds pushed the store's retail sales over $8 million the year of the
World's Fair.[89] Glessner had begun frequenting this establishment when
it was still Field, Leiter & Co., noting in her journal when the partnership
dissolved in 1881.[90] She turned to "Field's" for a variety of needs—from
walking dresses and mantels to rugs and table linens.[91] Her preference
may have arisen from a personal relationship with Marshall Field, who,
after 1887, lived nearby on Prairie Avenue. More likely, however, Glessner
was wooed by the store's strategy of courting affluent buyers by carrying
exclusive imports and organizing private showings of new products.[92]

Figure 1.2 This 1894 photograph depicts State Street looking north from Madison Street. Three large department stores are captured by the shot. The six-story white building in the center of the frame is Marshall Field & Co. In the lower left corner, the awning of the Boston Store is visible. To the right, at the edge of the frame, is Mandel Brothers. S. B. Frank, *Great Cities: Chicago* (Chicago: S. B. Frank, 1894), 19. Courtesy of the Newberry Library.

These efforts, as well as the store's elegant atmosphere, made Field's the preferred retailer of many of Chicago's wealthiest shoppers.

Yet Field's was far from State Street's only enticement for women such as Glessner. Along the next six blocks, the thoroughfare was crowded with new retail emporiums offering all manner of consumer goods. "It is not possible to mention all the great shops or stores in detail," observed Chicago guidebook author Harold Richard Vynne in 1892. "There are a few great houses, however, the names of which are in a sense landmarks."[93] At the northern end of State Street, these landmarks included the more established and prestigious department stores— Field's, Carson Pirie Scott & Co., Mandel Brothers, Charles Gossage & Co., and Schlesinger & Mayer. Further south, the newer, more popularly priced stores clustered together—the Fair, Siegel-Cooper & Co., Rothschild & Co., the Hub, and the Boston Store.[94] Unsurprisingly, Glessner concentrated her shopping among the higher-end retailers of north State Street. She favored Field's but also patronized "Gossage's" (later Carson Pirie Scott & Co.) and "Schlesinger's," which she entrusted with the important charge of outfitting her daughter's trousseau.[95]

Although the great department stores dominated State Street's physical landscape—as well as many shoppers' imaginations—Chicago's dry goods merchants had developed their retail operations only recently. Mandel Brothers, which was founded as a wholesaler in 1855, became the first to focus exclusively on retail in 1872.[96] Its competitors were slow to follow suit. Even the Fair, which prioritized retail sales from its inception in 1875, devoted all but the ground floor of its enormous State Street building to the wholesale trade until 1890.[97] State Street's retail commerce grew steadily in the decades after the fire, and each of the major dry goods houses expanded its footprint. By the turn of the century, eight State Street stores were conducting 90 percent of the city's retail business in most lines of merchandise, and the six-block stretch from Randolph to Van Buren had emerged as one of the greatest concentrated shopping districts in the world.[98]

Chicago shoppers also spent time and money beyond the great department stores, in specialty shops and smaller retail houses. Among Glessner's favorites were A. C. McClurg's bookstore, Ernst Weinhober's floral shop, and Madame Caroline Weeks's atelier. But dozens of other retailers also vied for attention. As one observer insisted in 1892, shoppers could obtain "absolutely anything on State Street, from a stick of candy to an elephant."[99] This commercial abundance was evident in city directories from the 1890s. On the east side of a single block of State Street, between Washington and Madison Streets, shoppers could find retail outlets devoted to boots and shoes, corsets, diamonds, dress silks, flowers, furs, men's clothing, photographic prints, precious stones, watches, and wine, not to mention Mandel Brothers department store.[100]

New service institutions, too, beckoned to moneyed customers. On the cross streets that stretched across the retail district, as well as on State Street itself, grand hotels, theaters, restaurants, tearooms, soda fountains, and cafés sought to entice female customers. Many of these spaces had sprung up in the years immediately preceding the World's

Fair. By 1893, Chicago was home to more hotels than any other city in the United States, with at least two or three on every street in the Loop.[101] The most elegant of these hostelries, such as the Auditorium, the Palmer House, and the Great Northern, boasted their own theaters and dining facilities. Outings to these resorts were sprinkled through the pages of Glessner's journal. She recorded, for instance, lunching at the Palmer House and attending social events at the Auditorium.[102]

For moneyed ladies, the experience of "going downtown" was marked by familiar faces. Glessner often wrote of chance encounters with friends and acquaintances. "Mrs. Hall McCormick came in to the Richelieu [hotel] while I was there and we lunched together," Glessner wrote in 1893 of bumping into Harriet Hall McCormick, wife of reaper heir Cyrus Hall McCormick Jr.[103] Similar meetings in other hotels as well as department stores, theaters, and restaurants punctuated Glessner's trips to the Loop. Some of these interactions were impromptu, but most were planned. Indeed, commercial spaces were slowly replacing private parlors and ballrooms as the locus of female social life. When in March 1891, for example, Glessner had to meet with other members of the Fortnightly to discuss a fundraiser for the Visiting Nurse Association, which provided free medical care to needy families, the women conferred over lunch in the tearoom of Marshall Field's—not at home.[104]

Chicago's consumer spaces, which were ever more indispensable to the social lives of moneyed women, relied on the labor of a vast army of service workers—store clerks and cash girls, servers and bellhops, ushers and soda jerks, tram drivers and elevator operators. Many came from the city's largest immigrant communities. In 1890, roughly 30 percent of Chicagoans had been born or had a parent born in Germany, 17 percent in Ireland, and 10 percent in Scandinavia.[105] Immigrant workers found service opportunities in both private homes and downtown commercial establishments. Recalling the predominance of Irish domestics, Arthur Meeker, who grew up on Prairie Avenue, wrote, "There was a perennial confusion of Marys . . . besides the usual complement of Noras and Nellies, Annies and Kates."[106] Immigrant women also worked as hotel maids, waitresses, and store clerks. In most of these spaces, however, male workers continued to outnumber female employees. At Marshall Field's, for example, men held a majority of clerk positions until the early twentieth century.[107] In the restaurant industry, women gained a toehold only after a large waiters' strike in 1903 caused restaurateurs to seek what they believed would be more compliant serving staff.[108]

African Americans also found work in restaurants, hotels, and theaters. Denied access to higher-paying industrial jobs, black Chicagoans were driven into service positions that were "not desirable enough to be contested by whites."[109] In 1900, when approximately 2 percent of the city's population was black, 39 percent of Chicago waiters were African American.[110] Several of the city's finest dining establishments employed all-black waitstaffs, including Arthur Meeker's favorite restaurant. At the Tip Top Inn, according to Meeker, a "corps of beaming African waiters" enhanced a menu of "savoury American food."[111] Black men were also overrepresented as ushers, porters, bellhops, and janitors in consumer spaces.[112] By one estimate, more than 25 percent of employees in Chicago's downtown theaters were black.[113] African Americans did not make inroads as salesclerks, however. State Street department stores notoriously refused to hire black workers. The large stores, reported the *Broad Ax* newspaper, did not "permit colored men or women to work in their stores even as cuspadore cleaners."[114]

White or black, foreign or native, the laboring men and women who sustained Chicago's burgeoning consumer economy attracted little notice from moneyed white women such as Glessner. In more than three decades of journaling, Glessner hardly ever commented on the workers she encountered. On the handful of occasions she did mention service employees, she associated them with charity or gifting. In 1897, for example, she recorded joining several other ladies in providing financial assistance to a widowed "old saleswoman who was at Fields for ten years."[115] The following year, after her daughter's wedding, Glessner sent leftover wedding cake to the seamstresses at Weeks's dressmaking shop, where the bride's gown had been made.[116] For the most part, however, Glessner viewed service workers with little more interest than the dining chairs that filled a restaurant. They were simply fixtures—necessary but unremarkable.

Moneyed men, too, often seemed peripheral to Glessner's view of the city. Women organized the clubs, fundraisers, luncheons, lectures, and dinner parties that occupied her time. In the feminine realm of society, men were often seen as visitors—if they were seen at all. In 1888, Glessner noted with amusement that Mary Elizabeth Sherwood, a New York author and etiquette expert visiting Chicago to give a series of readings, had asked Glessner if the women had "effaced the men here—she had not met them any place."[117] Notably, Sherwood delivered all five of her readings to female audiences in private homes. Had she visited only a few years later, these readings would likely have been held in downtown hotels, restaurants, or theaters. Indeed, as State Street blossomed at century's end, more and more of Glessner's social activities moved into the Loop—a realm long dominated not by women but by men. Increasingly, the lives of moneyed women and men would intersect in Chicago's central business district.

In the early 1890s, despite the growing importance of consumption, the Loop was still firmly oriented toward industrial production. It was a space devoted chiefly to finance, manufacturing, processing, warehousing, and wholesale trade. Of course, most of the city's grain elevators, stockyards, and rail lines lay outside the central business district. Still, the Loop was filled with the institutions and infrastructure that fueled industry—from the Chicago Board of Trade, to insurance companies and commercial banks, to workshops and warehouses. It was also home to the world's largest office towers. The first skyscraper had been built in Chicago in 1885, setting off a wave of steel-frame construction. By 1893, the prairie city held a dozen buildings between sixteen and twenty stories high, while New York lagged behind with just four buildings of comparable height.[118] The occupants of these towering monuments to industrial capital, as Fuller explained in his classic Chicago novel *The Cliff-Dwellers* (1893), were nearly all men—"bankers, capitalists, lawyers, 'promoters'; brokers in bonds, stocks, pork, oil, mortgages; real-estate people and railroad people and insurance people—life, fire, marine, accident; a host of principals, agents, middlemen, clerks, cashiers, stenographers, and errand-boys."[119]

Just as the profiles of Chicago's skyscrapers defined the skyline, the presence of male "cliff-dwellers" determined much of the culture of the downtown. It was their activity and masculine energy that had first interested Julian Ralph when he arrived in Chicago. "I have spoken of the roar and bustle and energy of Chicago," the writer reminded his readers. "This is most noticeable in the business part of the town, where the greater number of the men are crowded together. It seems there as if the men would run over the horses if the drivers were not careful." His perception of Chicago as a "city of young men" was shared by many contemporaries.[120] In the memorable words of Robert Herrick, "The city is made of man."[121]

But as Ralph himself discovered upon returning to Chicago in 1892, moneyed women were asserting new claims to the downtown. They were seizing openings to participate more broadly in public affairs through clubs and civic organizations. They were also moving rapidly into consumer spaces, concentrated on State Street. Accordingly, as the World's Fair approached, moneyed women's presence in the Loop was becoming increasingly conspicuous. Yet as the number of ladies traversing the downtown continued to grow—and to mix with the Loop's male denizens—a vital question arose: In a city that had been "made of man," what was the appropriate place of the moneyed woman?

2

---◆---

The Hoopskirt War of 1893

FOUR CENTURIES after Columbus voyaged to America, Chicago's business and civic leaders proposed to celebrate all of human progress since 1492 in a single magnificent event. The World's Columbian Exposition, as its president, Harlow N. Higinbotham, later explained, was designed to display the "latest discoveries, the newest inventions, the triumphs in art, in science, in education, in the solution of social and even of religious problems."[1] The honor of hosting this event had been won in an open competition with New York, St. Louis, and Washington, and more than three years had been devoted to planning and construction.[2] But as the final touches were placed on the neoclassical fairgrounds, a "pestilence" emerged in Europe that threatened to undermine the exposition's success.[3] This plague came not from cholera-ravaged Hamburg but from the couture houses of Paris, where French fashion designers were said to be reviving steel-banded hoopskirts, or cage crinolines. The rumored return of this voluminous style alarmed many Chicagoans, who feared that millions of behooped, fashion-obsessed visitors would clog the city's streets, public conveyances, and fairgrounds. As a *Chicago Tribune* editorial calling for the creation of an anti-hoopskirt society warned, a crinoline revival would "seriously incommode those who attend the Exposition and make it impossible to see any exhibit where women congregate in any number." Only "manly resistance," critics argued, could contain the scourge and prevent ladies' consumer impulses from undermining civic welfare.[4]

Chicago's city fathers were hardly alone in their opposition to the hoopskirt. The prospect of the style's return provoked outcry across the country and even inspired several states to consider prohibitions on crinoline importation, sale, and use. Yet the stakes of the conflict were especially high for the World's Fair city. As one contemporary travel writer noted, "All eyes are now turned towards this great city of the West."[5] Indeed, in 1893, the entire country—and much of the world—was looking to Chicago for insight into the future of capitalist urbanism. The return of the hoopskirt, with its ungainly dimensions and feminine aesthetic, threatened to disrupt the narrative of progress and innovation the city's leaders were attempting to convey. To safeguard the fair's success, as well as Chicago's glorious future, the fashionable woman needed to be rescued "from her own folly."[6]

American women had succumbed to the "folly" of cage crinoline before. For nearly a decade, from the mid-1850s through the Civil War, women from every region and social background had donned wire-framed petticoats for daily wear.[7] Even at that time, this bouffant style was not without its critics, and many a cartoonist and satirical writer had mocked the hoopskirt's ungainly dimensions.[8] Never before, however, had the hoopskirt figured as an object of public protest and legislative debate. As one anxious style watcher reported in early 1893, "All in all, the threatened invasion of a foreign army could not strike more apparent terror to the hearts and the homes of the multitude."[9]

What accounted for this outcry against crinoline? Why the hoopla over hoops? In part, the conflict turned on new concerns about ladies' conspicuous public presence in a city adapting to an expanding consumer economy. For much of the preceding century, moneyed white women had not been prominent occupants of the downtown. They were advised to move infrequently—and rarely unescorted—through public space and to adhere to traditional ideals of feminine privacy and self-denial. Yet with the rapid growth of the retail and service industries at century's end, profit-minded merchants and entrepreneurs invited women to indulge their desires in a commercial public realm that had once been dominated by men. On the streets of the Loop's flourishing retail district and in recently established restaurants, department stores, theaters, and grand hotels, Chicago ladies not only savored the delights of urban consumption but also ushered in a new ethos of public exposure and conspicuous display. For many observers, these transformations stirred fears that public space and public culture were feminizing—and that male dominion over the public realm was eroding. The outcry against hoopskirts distilled anxieties over the shifting gendered boundaries of the modern consumer city.

But more was at stake in the hoopskirt war than women's public presence. The conflict also marked discomfort with women's growing consumer appetites and the emergent culture of consumption that stimulated their desires. It was a culture preoccupied with fashion, novelty, and accumulation, with self-indulgence instead of the common good.[10] Although produced by American merchants, it was sustained by the everyday practices of moneyed women—women who in early 1893 were said to be placing their consumer longings before the well-being of their city. Ladies had, of course, long been criticized for their interest in fashion and matters of dress. Yet Chicago's crinoline opponents did not dwell on the old specters of vanity and extravagance. Rather, these men, and indeed some women, warned of a disturbing loss of female self-control, as ladies succumbed to the manipulation of merchants and fashion designers. For these critics, the impending hoopskirt invasion laid bare the coercive nature of consumer capitalism, as well as the inability of many women to resist its dictates. In condemning hoops, the style's opponents betrayed a deep ambivalence over the cultural practices promoted by new consumer institutions as well as the potential for consumers to be virtuous citizens.

The hoopskirt war, which ended with the style's resounding defeat, lasted mere months. Yet the consternation aroused in that brief time reveals how seriously Chicago's civic leaders viewed the threat. In opposing crinoline, they sought to control the vision of urban life that would be marketed and sold to millions of fairgoers at the Columbian Exposition. This vision offered limited room, materially or ideologically, for women consumers. It was a vision dominated by the mighty Corliss steam engine and other exemplars of masculine industrial power on display in exhibition halls named for their association with production: Manufactures, Machinery, Agriculture, and Electricity.[11] It was also a vision in which hoopskirts were decidedly out of place. The conflict over crinoline revealed the still uncertain position of women in an industrial economy slowly awakening to the importance of consumer demand.

Even before Congress had officially announced the winning bid to host the Columbian Exposition, Chicago boosters and businessmen were asserting their "place among the cities of the world."[12] The fair, they believed, provided the ideal stage upon which to showcase Chicago's cultural and commercial achievements, its grandeur and power. The men directing the bid and later the fair itself were among Chicago's most influential capitalists, titans who had helped to drive the city's explosive growth. Their ranks included meatpackers and manufacturers, such as Gustavus Swift, Philip Armour, Cyrus McCormick, and George Pullman, as well as bankers, such as Higinbotham, Franklin MacVeagh, and Lyman Gage. They were joined by merchants who had earned their fortunes in wholesale and the burgeoning realm of retail, such as Marshall Field, Potter Palmer, and Levi Leiter. These men—representatives of industry, finance, and trade—sought to project a vision of Chicago that embodied the nation's future, a blueprint for urban development in the age of corporate capital.[13]

Yet in early 1893, it was not the urban future but the sartorial present that absorbed many of the city's residents. As the *Chicago Herald* declared at the time, "To hoop or not to hoop is undoubtedly the question of the moment."[14] For more than three months, since the first hints of fuller skirts had surfaced in the couture houses of Paris, Chicago newspapers and magazines had anxiously anticipated the revival of cage crinoline. Rarely did the vicissitudes of ladies' dress grab headlines beyond the women's page of most periodicals. That winter, however, crinoline sightings and speculation competed with breaking economic and political reports for front-page headlines in mainstream publications.[15] "The press discusses the matter with the space and solemnity that might not be inadequate to a foreign war," noted a correspondent for the *Inter Ocean*. "The annexation of Hawaii; the forthcoming Cabinet of Mr. Cleveland; . . . the relations of Egypt and Great Britain—all these questions, important as they may be, 'pale their ineffectual fires' before the one burning question of the hour."[16] That question—over the hoopskirt's fate—centered on the place of women and consumption in the modern metropolis.

The hoopskirt's initial rise to prominence in the mid-1850s had evoked little overt opposition. On the contrary, many Americans celebrated its arrival for relieving women of the weight and heat of traditional petticoats, which were then worn in heavy layers stiffened with crin, or horsehair. Light and flexible, the cage crinoline was constructed of concentric steel-spring hoops that lifted overskirts up and away from the body (fig. 2.1).[17] Still, the style came with its own peculiar drawbacks. At the height of its popularity, between 1859 and 1864, the hoop-

DRESS AND THE LADY.

Figure 2.1 A cage crinoline, or hoopskirt, was typically constructed of
concentric steel-spring hoops that lifted the wearer's skirt away from the body.
Although the style was better ventilated than a traditional petticoat, its size
made movement more cumbersome. At the peak of the hoopskirt's popularity
in the United States, between the mid-1850s and the mid-1860s, diameters
spanned up to six feet.   "Dress and the Lady," *Harper's Monthly Magazine*, Oct. 1856, 712.

skirt could span up to six feet in diameter, making movement cumbersome and physical closeness nearly impossible.[18] Such unwieldy
dimensions proved a favored target of mid-century humorists.[19] In a
sketch published by *Harper's Weekly*, for example, a lady's maid was
shown suspended on scaffolding in order to reach the waistline of her
fashionable mistress (fig. 2.2).[20] The crinoline was also an object of more

NEW CONTRIVANCE FOR LADY'S MAIDS, Adapted to the Present Style of Fashions.

Figure 2.2 The crinoline's unwieldy dimensions generated humorous critiques in the mid-nineteenth century. In this 1857 image from *Harper's Weekly*, a lady's maid is shown accessing the waistline of her fashionable mistress by climbing onto scaffolding suspended over an enormous hoopskirt.

"New Contrivance for Lady's Maids, Adapted to the Present Style of Fashions," *Harper's Weekly*, July 25, 1857, 480. Art and Picture Collection, The New York Public Library Digital Collections.

sober critique. While moralists denounced the style's tilting frame for exposing ladies' legs to public view, safety advocates claimed that hoops promoted fatal accidents by permitting women to brush unknowingly into hearth fires. Despite such complaints, the hoopskirt dominated American fashion for nearly a decade before deflating into the narrower bustled styles of the late 1860s.[21]

Like most new clothing styles, the mid-century hoopskirt had first reached the United States by way of Paris, the capital of Western fashion. Throughout the nineteenth and well into the twentieth century, French designers maintained a "hegemonic grip" on the sartorial trends of American women.[22] Indeed, women of every social background and region of the United States knew about and at least conservatively adopted French fashions within a year of their introduction in Paris.[23] French directives on shape, color, and trim arrived via numerous channels. Most often, American women encountered French style on the pages of women's magazines, especially *Godey's Lady's Book* and *Peterson's Magazine*. Both of these publications unabashedly cribbed fashion plates from French sources, granting their readers a direct view of Parisian trends. Many women also stayed au courant by consulting dressmakers and store buyers who periodically pilgrimaged to France to view the latest in haute couture.[24] From their ateliers in Paris, French designers shaped the contours of American women's clothes.

Although women of all classes embraced Parisian trends, French fashion was chiefly associated with moneyed women, who possessed the time and resources to closely follow changing modes. In the 1890s, these women obtained their apparel in a marketplace divided between custom dressmakers and ready-to-wear merchants. Mass-production techniques had earlier transformed the market for menswear, ensuring that 90 percent of men's clothing was sold ready-to-wear by century's end. Ladies, by contrast, continued to rely on private dressmakers and seamstresses to create the elaborate silhouettes and intricate details of nineteenth-century fashions.[25] Chicago's most affluent women, such as Bertha Palmer, acquired a significant portion of their wardrobes directly from the couture houses of Paris—either while traveling abroad or via retail importers. At Marshall Field & Co., for example, customers could purchase partially finished French gowns, which were then altered to fit in the store's dressmaking department.[26] More often, however, ladies had their clothes custom-made by local dressmakers who reproduced Parisian styles with the help of French patterns and fashion plates. Many of these dressmakers, or "modistes," adopted French personas to cultivate trade. This trend was reflected in the journal of Frances Glessner, who recorded visiting dressmakers with names such as Madame Anna and Madame Caroline.[27]

Yet even the wealthiest women did not purchase all of their apparel bespoke. Most women also turned to retailers for some ready-to-wear items. These mass-produced fashions consisted chiefly of wardrobe basics, such as gloves, cloaks, and undergarments. Not until the twentieth century, when women's styles became simpler and more streamlined, did the mass production of gowns and shirtwaists begin to reduce reliance on dressmakers.[28] In the 1890s, ready-to-wear purchases for women were still concentrated in two departments—undergarments and accessories. An 1894 advertisement for Marshall Field's recorded the fashion inventory typical of most department stores: handkerchiefs, gloves, capes, hosiery, corsets, and silk umbrellas.[29] By century's end, many such goods had made their way into the homes of Chicago's moneyed families. When ordering lingerie for her daughter's trousseau, for example, Glessner turned not to her favorite dressmaker but to Schlesinger & Mayer department store.[30]

Like most undergarments, the revived crinoline would have been sold in department stores alongside other ready-to-wear manufactured items. In fact, its large-scale production had been successfully implemented three decades earlier. As documented in John Leander Bishop's *History of American Manufactures* (1868), one New York firm—the Eagleton Manufacturing Company—employed hundreds of workers across several mills "converting a rough bar of steel into a finished Hoop Skirt." Each week, the company churned out more than two thousand skirts. Meanwhile, at Douglas & Sherwood's hoopskirt factory, eight hundred women produced an average of three thousand skirts a day, consuming a ton of steel within the same time frame. As the style's popularity waned in the late 1860s, these and other crinoline manufacturers either closed their doors or converted their mills. In early 1893, however, rumors began circulating that foundries were once again preparing machinery for the manufacture of crinoline. "It seems probable," announced a trade report of one large British iron-broking firm, "that some modification of the petticoat may cause a revival of this branch of business for the caging of women of fashion."[31] The crinoline's return seemed imminent.

The first hints of a hoopskirt revival to reach Chicago came not from trade reports but from style watchers in Paris. French designers, warned an *Inter Ocean* correspondent in early November 1892, had introduced flaring skirts supported by a single hoop around the hem. "Alarmists will see in this the certain coming of the hoopskirt," the reporter concluded.[32] Within a week, readers of the *Chicago Tribune* had similarly been advised that fuller, padded skirts were appearing on Parisian streets and would soon hit Chicago. "The Day of Hoops is Not Far Off," the paper predicted.[33] By February, true cage crinolines had yet to grace the models of any French couturiers. Nonetheless, Chicagoans feared an invasion was unavoidable. "The hoop question continues to agitate unduly the public mind," observed a reporter for the *Chicago Daily News*. "Every one is holding his or her breath for the blow to fall—for, do not deceive yourselves, fall it will."[34] Reports from New York, where Parisian trends typically penetrated the United States market first, did little to alleviate the public's fears. "I have no doubt that we are going to see crinolines here again in the spring," affirmed society leader Ward McAllister in an interview printed by several Chicago newspapers. "The decree of fashion appears to have gone forth and there is no gainsaying it. It would be easier to oppose a ukase of the czar of all the Russias."[35]

Yet some women, far from opposing the decree of fashion, welcomed the prospect of a crinoline revival. Although awkwardly sized, hoopskirts offered some appealing features. To begin with, the style enabled a more hygienic pedestrian experience. The sheath dresses then in vogue had trains that dragged through the mud, tobacco spit, and animal waste endemic to downtown sidewalks. Crinoline, by contrast, lifted skirts up and away from the filth of the streets. Highlighting this benefit, actress Lillian Lewis, who had lived in Chicago for several years, declared in 1893, "Let us have crinoline, because it will keep skirts, shoes and stockings clean. Because it will not flop around our ankles like a dishrag. Because it will not sweep up all the dust and drag in all the mud of the street." The stiff wire frames also appealed due to their ability, in Lewis's words, to "keep men at a respectful distance."[36] Although Lewis was invoking the proprieties of Victorian courtship, the advantage of added personal space would have been obvious to any woman who had been pinched, groped, or otherwise harassed on crowded streets or public transit. Not least, the hoopskirt enticed due to its airy, bell-like shape. Anticipating a release from layers of heavy petticoats, one woman exclaimed, "Think how cool they will be in summer! Time and again, I've heard my mother regret [giving up] her hoop-skirts."[37]

Despite such attributes, the hoopskirt's rumored return sparked immediate outrage. Among the style's most outspoken critics were dress reformers. These female activists, who prized comfort, health, and mobility in matters of dress, viewed the adoption of cage crinoline as a backward step in the struggle for "rational" clothing. "It would be like donning the prison bars of the convict," insisted Dr. Mary Walker, a dress reformer known for wearing pants and suitcoats.[38] According to Walker, the hoopskirt interfered "with the everyday duties of women" by hampering freedom of movement. Further, its weight pressed down on internal organs and could cause "mischief with the liver." In her view, the cage crinoline was "barbarous, senseless and dangerous."[39] Walker, then over sixty years old, had rehearsed these critiques decades earlier, in the 1850s, when the hoopskirt was first in fashion. Dress reform then existed solely on the margins of the women's movement, carried on by figures such as Walker and Amelia Bloomer, who made famous the trouser style that still bears her name. Nearly a half century later, however, dress reform was starting to attract interest from mainstream women's organizations.[40]

By the early 1890s, dress reform had emerged as an objective of the National Council of Women. Founded in 1888 at the suggestion of Elizabeth Cady Stanton, the council sought to bring together all organized women's groups in the United States. At the council's first triennial convention in 1891, then president Frances Willard announced the creation of a committee on dress reform.[41] Its charge was to foster styles suitable "for business hours, for shopping, for marketing, housework, walking and other forms of exercise."[42] Over the next two years, the committee worked to define rational new designs to be promoted at the Congress of Representative Women at the World's Fair in Chicago. Its proposals included loosely fitting gowns and pants-like divided skirts—*not* cage crinoline.[43] As dress reformer Helen Gilbert Ecob asserted in an article for *Cosmopolitan*, "We poor reformers denounce the crinoline fashion, on the 'horridly sensible' grounds of health and reason. . . . Surely, the reformer, in her wildest dreams, has never conceived anything more hideous and ugly than the fashions of '93."[44]

Americans had come to expect objections to fashionable dress from female reformers wearing Turkish-style pants and floaty tunics. Less foreseeable was the outcry from those assumed to care little for matters of women's dress: men. "The most impressive thing about the threatened revival of coopered women is the appeals some men are making to women not to do it," proclaimed the *Chicago Herald*.[45] As the paper suggested, male opposition to the hoopskirt was swift and fierce. In January 1893, the *Chicago Tribune* helped initiate the countereffort with an editorial titled "The Anti-Hoopskirt War," which called for collective male action. According to the author, even the most sensible ladies could not resist "that rigorous, despotic, and mysterious creature called Fashion" and, if left to their own devices, would soon adopt the "preposterous and monstrous" hoopskirt. As such, the author argued, "if anything is to be done, it must be done by men and done quickly, for the hoopskirt cages will be here before anyone is aware." He then proposed that male Chicagoans form an Anti-Crinoline League to combat the invasion. "If every man in Chicago," he speculated, "would engage to destroy every crinoline that came into his house it would end the matter then and there."[46]

In contrast to female reformers concerned with health and freedom of movement, male critics dwelt on the spatial problems engendered by crinolines. As the *Chicago Tribune* noted, hoops would cause women to take up "five or ten times the space they do now."[47] Such imposing dimensions may have been tolerated in decades past, when ladies spent more time in the private realm, critics admitted. But hoopskirts would prove an insufferable public nuisance now that moneyed women enjoyed greater access to downtown streets and public spaces. "The monstrosity of hoops is not to be considered nowadays," insisted a correspondent for the *Inter Ocean*. "It was all very well for the days when ladies stayed at home to work crochet tidies, but not for the rush and hurry of these modern times. Moreover, there is no room for them."[48] In an interview published by several Chicago papers, French couturier Gaston Worth expressed similar sentiments. "A crinoline may be made to squeeze into a Sedan chair [an old-fashioned form of conveyance]," he observed, "but there is no room for it in a three-horse omnibus, or in the box or dress circle of a Paris theater." Yet if demand persisted, the designer claimed, he would be forced to incorporate crinolines into his work, despite the likelihood they would be deemed "a dire nuisance by the husbands or fathers who have to pay for them and put up with them."[49]

Concerns about space were not exactly outlandish. Early crinoline reports cited diameters of two feet, but these dimensions were expected to grow.[50] If the revived hoopskirt approached anywhere near its peak mid-century girth of six feet, the style would transform urban spatial dynamics. "Even now," warned one critic, "the sidewalks of our large cities are crowded to an uncomfortable extent during some hours of the day. The adoption of the old bulging, swaying hoopskirt would drive all the men and all the peanut stands into the street."[51] Chicago's downtown sidewalks then ranged from ten to twenty feet in width and, even at their most commodious, were often congested during rush hour.[52] Hoopskirts would certainly exacerbate the problem. Streetcars, too, would be taxed by crinoline-clad riders. Already notorious for insufficient seating, Chicago's largest streetcars were not more than eight and a half feet wide. Their twenty-two-inch benches, arranged in rows up and down both sides of the car, were intended to hold two people each.[53] "What would happen were each woman securely anchored in the middle of a six-foot crinoline[?]" asked a reporter contemplating the hoopskirt in San Francisco. "Crinolines will surely impair the usefulness and destroy what little comfort there is in a streetcar."[54]

The hoopskirt threatened to create genuine spatial problems. But objections to its return were partly rooted in cultural expectations that female bodies occupy as little room as possible, especially in public. Women's spatial claims were typically superseded by those of men, who were assumed to possess a natural right to space.[55] Accordingly, men were often presented as the hoopskirt's chief victims. "With the revival of the hoopskirt," protested one outraged critic, "the capacity of a street car would be reduced about one-half during the shopping hours of the day, and the comfort of the men would be reduced about two-thirds."[56] Male suffering was expected to be especially acute wherever women congregated. "It means less room for the masculine unfortunate in the street cars and all other public conveyances. It means estrangement from his feminine friends at receptions or other functions. It means being crowded everywhere, at home and on the street," lamented another opponent.[57] Even many female commentators highlighted the potential inconvenience to men. "How in the world is unprotected man to get even the smallest corner in an elevator?" wondered Chicago clubwoman and fashion columnist Helen Gale.[58]

Much of the criticism directed at hoopskirts was expressed through satire and comic illustration. Throughout early 1893, newspapers and magazines regularly featured parodies, cartoons, and poems involving crinoline-clad ladies squeezing into crowded public spaces. In one characteristic sketch from *Puck*, illustrator Dick Law proposed a modified hoopskirt that contracted with the pull of a cord. In the accompanying text, Law contended that his device would "materially diminish . . . the area covered by the plague" and preserve "economy of space in our congested thoroughfares."[59] In late January, the *Chicago Tribune* published one of several short poems indicting hoopskirts for promoting congestion on streets and public conveyances:

> And must it come—the skirt of other days
> Amplitudinous and vast, the terror,
> Of pedestrians, the sport of scoffers,

> Shelter of small dogs fleeing from the wrath
> Of bigger ones, space monopolizer
> In the omnibus and gilded chariot
> Of the horse railway! . . .
> The earth is getting crowded.
> There is no room for the hoop-skirt.
> It belongs to the dead past. Its home
> Is in oblivion. There let it rest.[60]

Similar overcrowding concerns were later featured in a humorous *Chicago Tribune* vignette "Not Enough Room." The scene opens with a woman named Mrs. Crinoline grumbling that the "selfishness of men in street cars is disgusting." When her husband asks her to elaborate, she explains, "I entered a crowded street car today and only two men got up."[61] Although Mrs. Crinoline casts herself as the victim, readers would have recognized that she had been the one to discommode the other riders with her oversized skirt.

Yet even Mrs. Crinoline's most ardent critics conceded that fashionable women were not solely to blame for the coming plague. "The story has always been as to a new fashion men devise it purely in the interest of trade," explained one opponent.[62] To be sure, anyone connected with the fashion industry—designers, retailers, manufacturers, seamstresses—stood to benefit from a hoopskirt revival. The style required additional fabric, labor, and supplies to construct. "It will take just about four times as much cloth to make a dress that will cover a crinoline," observed one Chicago woman, "and that is what the dealers and dressmakers want, but it is hard on the husbands who have to foot the bills."[63] Gaston Worth, too, acknowledged the potential profits. "It might even benefit us materially," the designer confessed, "for our silk and other accessories are our own, and crinolines would mean more stuff and more money spent."[64] Gesturing to these financial motivations, one Chicago hoopskirt detractor insisted, "Lovely woman must be made to understand that hoopskirts are not ordained by fashion, but by a lot of manufacturers of dress goods who have become persuaded that womankind can be led into any sort of folly if a few leading dressmakers can be bribed to tell them it is fashion."[65]

The apparent ease with which women succumbed to the manipulations of the fashion industry alarmed many male contemporaries. In their view, the potential revival of such an obviously inconvenient and

obtrusive style called into question women's very fitness for full citizenship and "capability to use the ballot."[66] As one outraged Chicagoan
asserted, "It is an indication of woman's servility and lack of independence that she bows to the mandate [of fashion] without questioning
the authority or disputing its good taste and propriety. . . . So long as the
sex exhibits this servile spirit it is questionable whether it is prepared to
enjoy those rights which so many of its members are demanding."[67] Similar concerns were raised in a more lighthearted manner by a *Chicago
Tribune* parody featuring a woman who demands personal autonomy
while slavishly following fashion trends:

> Husband—"You were not so late as usual today."
> Wife—"No, the meeting of the Society for the Emancipation of
> Women from the Thralldom of Men had to be postponed."
> Husband—"What was the matter?"
> Wife—"One of the members came in with a crinoline on, and we all
> rushed out to buy one."[68]

The crinoline's awkward dimensions were also used to portray women
as out of place in public life. In the *Inter Ocean,* for example, one writer
jested that the "advent of the hoopskirt will present another obstacle to
woman suffrage" because as the recently adopted Australian, or secret,
ballot booths were "not built on the balloon plan."[69]

Gauging the potential for women to act with civic virtue seemed urgent to many Americans in a decade marked by significant developments
in the push for women's suffrage. In 1890, Wyoming, which had allowed
women to vote since the territory was first organized in 1869, finally
became a state, the first to provide full voting rights to women. Three
years later, Colorado adopted the first state amendment enfranchising
women.[70] Meanwhile, the organized women's suffrage movement, dominated by moneyed white women, was gaining national strength and
visibility. The two major arms of the movement—the National Woman
Suffrage Association and the American Woman Suffrage Association—had
recently reunited under the banner of the National American Woman
Suffrage Association after a quarter century of estrangement.[71] Suffrage was also expected to be a major topic at the World's Congress of
Representative Women, to be held in Chicago during the Columbian Exposition, and many prominent female suffragists—including Elizabeth
Cady Stanton, Susan B. Anthony, Julia Ward Howe, and Anna Howard
Shaw—were slated to speak.[72]

In the eyes of many critics, any woman who adopted hoops justified her exclusion from the polity by placing her consumer desires before common sense and good citizenship. Yet opposition to the crinoline was more than a screen for anxieties about women's voting rights; it marked unease with women's growing presence in urban public life. The looming hoopskirt invasion threatened to undermine ideals of feminine privacy and male dominion over public space that had ordered metropolitan existence for the last century. The problem was at once material and moral, reaching beyond the ballot box.

No one could dispute that hoopskirts occupied more space than the sheath dresses in vogue in the early 1890s—a style that, according to Worth, made women resemble "arrows in their quivers."[73] But Americans had endured the reign of cage crinoline before, without much complaint. As a writer for the *Youth's Companion* reminded his readers, "The hoopskirt in its day was not universally detested, and found some defenders even among men." In 1893, by contrast, the hoopskirt "called forth many protests" from individuals "who ordinarily concern themselves but little with the changes of fashion."[74] As one Chicago reporter reflected, "Never before in all its history has the odious thing ever received such an amount of antagonism or brought on such a bloodless war."[75] This shift in reception owed not to any modifications in the hoopskirt's appearance or size. On the contrary, early reports suggested the revived crinoline was more compact than its mid-century counterpart. Instead, the outcry found root in women's growing public presence in the turn-of-the-century metropolis.

When the crinoline last held sway, moneyed white women had not been a conspicuous component of urban public life. In fact, at least one visitor to Chicago had difficulty discerning any ladies at all in the city center. "The streets are very peculiar in not having a lady walking in them," Caroline Kirkland wrote in the *Atlantic* in 1858. "Day after day I traversed them, meeting crowds of men. . . . Yet one lady walking in the streets I saw not."[76] Kirkland made clear that she encountered female domestics on her excursions in the Loop but never women of a higher status. This variance is not surprising, given that working-class women were regularly forced to navigate city streets and public transit for their employment, whereas Chicago ladies spent much of their time within private homes, private clubs, and private religious institutions.[77]

As described by the social secretary of a prominent widow, the typical lady of "early Chicago" organized her life around domestic cares, charity work, and participation in literary organizations and social clubs. She was "devoted to her church; a good housekeeper; a careful mother," and although she did sometimes venture out to the dressmaker or milliner, most of her apparel was fitted at home by a seamstress who "came early and toiled all day." In short, the Chicago lady's domain was the private realm, where the "miles and miles of pleatings and ruffles" that bedecked her skirts could not easily inconvenience others.[78]

Moneyed women did not spend all their time in private, of course. Even at mid-century, they could be found engaged in marketing activities, pursing charity work, attending church, watching parades, enjoying city parks, and lobbying for the vote.[79] Still, their presence in public was rarely prolonged or undertaken solo. Standards for ladies' public behavior were outlined in mid-century etiquette guides. These sources, although sometimes outdated and rarely followed with perfect precision, captured the intense cultural pressure constraining moneyed women's movements. On city streets, ladies were expected to obtain escorts, especially after dark. "Be careful not to be alone in the streets after night fall. It exposes you to insult," warned Florence Hartley, author of *The Ladies' Book of Etiquette.* "If you are obliged to go out, have a servant, or another lady, if you cannot procure the escort of a gentleman, which is, of course, the best."[80] Similar advice echoed through countless etiquette books. In at least five separate guides, the authors supplied the same warning: "After twilight, a young lady would not be conducting herself in a becoming manner, by walking alone."[81] Failure to adhere to such conventions exposed a woman to charges of immorality, even prostitution.[82]

When a lady did venture out into the city alone, she was expected to move efficiently and inconspicuously, minimizing her visual and vocal presence. "Let your conduct be modest and quiet. . . . Walk slowly, do not turn your head to the right or left, unless you wish to walk that way, and avoid any gesture or word that will attract attention," instructed Hartley.[83] Ladies in public were further discouraged from wearing bright colors, swinging their arms, occupying too much space on the sidewalk, speaking to strangers, stopping unnecessarily, or otherwise drawing attention to themselves.[84] "A lady walks quietly through the streets, seeing and hearing nothing," counseled an 1877 deportment manual. "She is always unobtrusive. She never talks loudly or laughs boisterously, or does anything to attract the attention of passers-by."[85] Through careful bodily management, lack of expression, and sedate clothing, the true lady created "a symbolic shield of privacy."[86]

Such standards were not always scrupulously upheld. Nonetheless, respectable women of the mid-nineteenth century experienced public space primarily as something to move through, not to linger in or enjoy. They were discouraged from engaging in the very practices that sustained a culture of consumption. This conflict—between Victorian propriety and commercial desire—was especially obvious in warnings against window shopping. As late as 1889, for example, one etiquette writer cautioned, "In moving along the street it is inelegant for a lady to be gadding into windows and hotel doorways. . . . She should go about her business quietly and for her own sake, attracting as little publicity as possible."[87] Many Chicago ladies appear to have adhered to this expectation. As an *Inter Ocean* reporter observed of women of "wealth, culture, and importance" on State Street in the 1880s, "They never carry bundles, rarely look in windows, and never, never stop, no matter what the attraction or hindrance."[88]

Restrictions on moneyed women's public movements eased over the course of the nineteenth century. Still, ladies did not enjoy the same freedom available to moneyed white men, who were permitted to roam and savor all that the metropolis had to offer. This spirit of exploration was embodied in the figure of the flâneur, who strolled through the streets and mingled with the crowd as a way of knowing the city.[89] In his 1895 novel, *With the Procession*, Henry Blake Fuller provides a Chicago example of this modern urban type in the character of Richard Truesdale Marshall, the dissolute son of a wealthy grocery wholesaler. Marshall spends his days exploring the city's cafés, theaters, artists' studios, and "places of general and promiscuous resort." His sisters, by contrast, are discouraged from going into "bad" neighborhoods and venturing into the streets without an escort.[90] This gendered divide in urban access was also reflected in the spate of Chicago guidebooks and travel literature published in advance of the World's Fair. Invariably, the authors of these texts advised female readers to visit only State Street and the fairgrounds, while male readers were encouraged to sample the sights and sounds of outlying neighborhoods, the stockyards, and even the city's vice district. Rand, McNally's *Handy Guide to Chicago and World's*

Columbian Exposition, for example, offered male readers a "slumming" itinerary that led the sightseer from the gambling dens of the "Bad Lands" to the Chinese restaurants of South Clark Street to the dance halls of the North Side's German quarter.[91]

Standards of public comportment at century's end remained particularly exacting for women who ventured forth without escorts. Bertie Patterson, the country cousin of Fuller's novel, alludes to these constraints when discussing her unfulfilled desire to promenade in the lobby of the elegant Auditorium Theater. She explains, "I wanted to walk in the foy—in the place where they promenade . . . ; such a lovely place, and such a grand crush under all those yellow arches! But we didn't have any gentleman."[92] Without a male protector, the young lady and her aunt could not expose themselves to promiscuous mingling and public view—even in one of Chicago's finest theaters. In her journal, Frances Glessner corroborated such conventions, describing a social world in which men freely roamed public space and ladies waited to be approached. Glessner, who regularly attended plays and musical performances, made a habit of recording the names of those who called on her box. These visitors were almost always male. During one intermission of the Chicago Symphony Orchestra, for instance, Glessner welcomed ten male callers, presumably on their rounds to several boxes. By contrast, her sole female caller remained in Glessner's box throughout the first half of the program before returning to her own party.[93] Glessner herself never made calls during intermission, although she did occasionally join other women in their boxes for portions of a performance.

Even women visiting Chicago from out of town were expected to obtain escorts or chaperones when exploring the city. Contemporary guidebooks and travel literature often provided detailed instructions on how to secure appropriate companions. In its *Handy Guide to Chicago* (1893), for example, Rand, McNally informed readers that telegraph boys could be hired not only for delivering messages but also for "escorting ladies to the theater or to a railway station." For longer engagements, ladies were advised to employ the services of an organization such as the Woman's Directory, Purchasing and Chaperoning Society, which provided chaperones at "a moderate rate."[94] According to the society's 1893 brochure, "reliable" escorts to afternoon matinees could be obtained for $1.00 to $1.50, while guides for miscellaneous errands ran $1 for the first hour and 75 cents for each additional hour.[95] Similar services were advertised in the newspapers of other cities in the months leading up to the World's Fair. In April 1893, the *New York Times* alerted its readers to a program offered through the Women's Exchange that provided "unprotected women or parties of women desiring to go to Chicago" with travel chaperones and local escorts.[96]

So ingrained were conventions governing moneyed white women's mobility that many assumed they would need an escort to gain admittance to the World's Fair. To encourage women's attendance, Ellen Martin Henrotin, vice president of the fair's Board of Lady Managers, issued a statement several months before the exposition reassuring visitors that "young women may come to the World's Fair without male escorts or chaperons."[97] Henrotin and her consorts nevertheless feared that many women would simply stay at home if unaccompanied. Accordingly, early in its planning, the Board of Lady Managers endorsed the use of chaperoning services. "It offers many advantages to women," asserted one supporter. "They want to see the Fair, and many of them will come here with husbands who are on business that will occupy most of their time. Why should they remain in their rooms at the hotels?"[98] For ladies who did venture out alone, the fair offered an opportunity to explore the city on their own terms. In an 1893 article penned for the *Inter Ocean*, reporter Teresa Dean recounted overhearing one woman tell her companion of the pleasure she derived from attending the exposition without an escort: "I've just had the loveliest time I ever had in my life. I came alone to-day. The other day when I came with Sam, he wouldn't let me do this or do that, but to-day I've done 'em all."[99]

Although many restraints on women's public movements persisted, new possibilities arose in the 1890s for respectable women to explore and enjoy urban public spaces. For a brief time, the World's Fair offered a font of such opportunities. More enduring was the access provided by the expanding consumer economy. As department stores, grand hotels, restaurants, theaters, and cafés proliferated in the city center, moneyed women achieved unprecedented mobility in the public realm. Far from urging ladies to avoid downtown streets and public spaces, merchants and entrepreneurs beckoned female customers into the central business district, where their purchasing power fueled commercial growth. Invitations to "visit our store" or "inspect our latest wares" called out to moneyed ladies from the pages of local newspapers. Typical was the sedate advertising used by department store Siegel-Cooper & Co.: "We are displaying an elegant line of Ladies' Street Dresses and House Gowns. All this season's best styles, which it will pay you to inspect."[100] Specialty shops, restaurants, and theaters relied on similar tactics to signal welcome to female shoppers. "Bring in your family and we will fit you out in fine style," declared an advertisement for Showers & Miller, a State Street retailer offering women's ready-to-wear garments. Like countless other advertisements during this period, the notice concluded with a simple invitation: "We invite you to call."[101]

And call they did. For the fin de siècle lady, "going downtown" on shopping excursions became a regular feature of daily life.[102] In her journal, Frances Glessner chronicled the new rhythm of consumption. Each week, she recorded at least three or four (and often five or six) trips to the retail district. On occasion, she detailed a specific errand that brought her downtown, such as selecting table linens at Marshall Field's or ordering flowers for a birthday dinner.[103] More often than not, however, she described her excursions as simply going "down town to do some shopping" or even just "shopping."[104] Glessner's practices were far from atypical among the city's moneyed women. As the *Chicago Tribune* observed, the expanding State Street retail corridor was "where fashionable and unfashionable women meet every day, rain or shine. They come in their swell carriages, in cabs, in omnibuses, in streetcars, on foot."[105]

Most of these shopping ladies were unattended by male escorts. Indeed, shopping provided opportunities for women such as Glessner to move about the city on their own, experiencing a small taste of the peripatetic pleasures of flânerie.[106] When not joined by her children, female relatives, or friends, Glessner shopped alone—never with her husband or other adult men. In recording these solo excursions, Glessner sometimes assumed a tone of adventure, especially when contrasted with her domestic life. "Tuesday I had calls at home. I went down town prowling in the morning and found some excellent Japanese vases which I bargained for and bought," she wrote of one exploratory shopping mission.[107] Fuller, too, highlighted the autonomy moneyed white women enjoyed as shoppers. Respectable ladies such as Bertie Patterson and her aunt could not promenade alone at the theater, but they could circulate unaccompanied through the retail district. "Aunt Lydia and I go shopping almost every day," Bertie boasts to her cousin shortly after arriving in Chicago. Through these excursions, she learns "where the shops are . . . and the theaters, and the post-office, perhaps, and the hotels, and what all besides," knowledge that gives her a sense of familiarity and belonging to the city center.[108]

To be clear, all women did not have equal access to Chicago's blossoming consumer realm. Patronizing these spaces required the ability to pay. Accordingly, moneyed white women predominated among the shoppers and pleasure seekers who strolled the elegant State Street retail district. Working-class women fulfilled much of their shopping in small neighborhood stores, supplemented by the rare trip to a bargain basement in one of the more affordable department stores.[109] Meanwhile, discrimination prevented African American women of any income bracket from freely patronizing downtown businesses. Black consumers in the State Street retail district were often ignored or treated with contempt. "The discrimination is not made openly," journalist Ray Stannard Baker said of the "color line" drawn by consumer institutions in northern cities, "but a Negro who goes to such places is informed that there are no accommodations, or he is overlooked and otherwise slighted, so that he does not come again."[110]

Despite such racial and class barriers, the number of women who crowded downtown each day continued to grow in the years before the World's Fair. This escalating female presence did not escape the notice of Chicago men. In newspaper articles and travel guides, they invoked terms such as "swarm" and "throng" to describe the shoppers who daily crowded onto State Street, nicknamed the "ladies' half mile."[111] As early as 1888, the *Chicago Tribune* marveled at shoppers' impressive ranks. "The 'after-dinner' shoppers are coming now, and their name is legion," the newspaper declared. "Between 1 and 2 o'clock the crowds surging past your corner are so thick they cannot be counted."[112] Three years later, Louis Schick warned his readers that the retail district was packed with "a dense throng of femininity" from ten o'clock to four o'clock each day. Hinting at an emerging sense of male displacement, Schick observed, "There is a steady stream of ladies, almost always in parties of two or three, passing along Adams street in either direction, and, as they meet the throng on State street, there is a good humored crush in which the male pedestrian feels that he is sadly out of place."[113] A similar sentiment marks John J. Flinn's 1891 guidebook, *Chicago: The Marvelous City of the West*, in which the author leads his readers (assumed to be male) on a fictional excursion through the Loop. After pausing in front of the "great retail houses," Flinn urges caution: "We will have to stand close to the edge of the sidewalk or we will be carried along by the crowd."[114]

Circulating through Chicago's burgeoning consumer landscape, moneyed ladies exposed themselves to unprecedented public scrutiny. As Thorstein Veblen explained in *The Theory of the Leisure Class*, the modern metropolis provided more "large gatherings of people to whom one's everyday life is unknown." In recently erected "theaters, ballrooms, hotels, parks, shops, and the like," men and women both confronted the gaze of "transient observers."[115] But it was women, according to Veblen, who performed "the great, peculiar, and almost the sole function" of signaling and reinforcing their families' "pecuniary strength."[116] Clothing served as their primary means of communicating status. "The first principle of dress, therefore, is conspicuous expensiveness," Veblen claimed.[117] For this reason, women donned intricately decorated gowns and exaggerated shapes that required additional fabric—such as balloon sleeves and, potentially, hoopskirts—to signal extravagance and waste. "I cannot tell you how glad I am over the introduction of the crinolines," enthused fashion columnist Augusta Prescott. "It gives the modistes such a fine opportunity to display costly laces and artistic draping."[118]

Americans had long used clothing to signal status, belonging, or taste. But fashion emerged as a national obsession in the 1890s. This preoccupation was reinforced by new retailing and marketing strategies devised to sell a growing array of ready-to-wear goods.[119] The primary targets of these efforts were women with money to spend. As an editorial in the *Dry Goods Economist* noted, "The way out of overproduction must lie in finding out what the woman at the counter is going to want; *make it; then* promptly drop it and go onto something else to which fickle fashion is turning her attention."[120] Interest in fashion also increased due to the rapid new pace of change within the garment industry. The rise of steamships, telegraphs, and telephones at century's end had enabled faster cross-Atlantic communication and, in turn, hastened the rate at which style innovations from Paris couture houses reached American wardrobes. Veblen himself perfectly articulated the spirit of the times: "flux and change and novelty."[121]

For many observers, the increasingly conspicuous presence of fashionable ladies in the city center portended the colonization and, indeed, feminization of urban public life. Such fears were reinforced by two physical marks etched onto the Chicago landscape by women in the early 1890s: the Woman's Temple at Monroe and LaSalle Streets and the Woman's Building at the World's Fair. Construction began on the first of these projects in 1890, when the Woman's Christian Temperance Union (WCTU), then led by Frances Willard, secured financing to erect a downtown office building. The clubwomen hoped the new structure would provide both rental income and permanent meeting facilities. The latter objective had thus far proved elusive for the organization, which had repeatedly been pressured to leave male-owned office spaces. Designed by architect John Root, Daniel Burnham's partner, the Woman's Temple numbered among Chicago's first skyscrapers (fig. 2.3).[122] As described in 1893 by Rand, McNally's *Bird's-Eye Views and Guide to Chicago*, the "colossal" building was "second or third in size" among the city's commercial structures and "the most conspicuous office building" in the western part of the Loop. Its edifice, the guide insisted, "dominates that region of the city."[123]

The Woman's Temple served as a highly visible indication of the new claims women exercised over urban space. From the moment of its initial groundbreaking, which took place while two thousand children sang hymns, such as "The Saloon Must Go," the ornate French Gothic building asserted a decidedly feminine presence downtown.[124] Root's design was said to embody the qualities of the women who founded the building—strength, grace, and beauty.[125] As the author of *Chicago by Day and Night* declared shortly before the building's completion in April 1892, the Woman's Temple stood as "an everlasting monument to the influence of good women upon the existence of mankind."[126] This influence later extended to the street in front of the building, where a bronze statue commissioned by the WCTU of a girl with outstretched hands holding a small cup invited passers-by to drink from the fountain below—and, it was hoped, avoid the temptations of the saloon.[127] In her 1893 novel *Samantha at the World's Fair*, Marietta Holley underscores the significance of the building to women at the time. Reflecting on the sights she hopes to see when visiting Chicago, one character exclaims, "And then that temple there in Chicago, dreamed out and built by a woman—the nicest office buildin' in the world! jest think of that—*in the World.* . . . I wouldn't miss the chance of seein' wimmen swing right out, and act as if their souls wuz their own, not for the mines of Golconda."[128] For the speaker, the existence of a skyscraper constructed by women and dedicated to

Figure 2.3 The Woman's Temple, built by the Woman's Christian Temperance Union, was completed in 1892. Located at Monroe and LaSalle Streets, the twelve-story office building numbered among Chicago's first skyscrapers. It was demolished in 1926. Courtesy of the Ryerson & Burnham Archives, School of the Art Institute of Chicago.

Figure 2.4 The Board of Lady Managers of the World's Columbian Exposition oversaw construction of the Woman's Building. The building was designed by a female architect, Sophia Hayden, and contained a grand exhibit hall showcasing women's achievements in art, industry, and design. It was completed in 1892, then destroyed, along with most of the exposition's buildings, in 1894.   Prints and Photographs Division, LC-USZ62-74119, Library of Congress.

their public work as reformers provides evidence—more valuable than a diamond mine—of women's growing independence and belonging in the public realm.

As WCTU clubwomen raised the Woman's Temple, members of the Board of Lady Managers of the Columbian Exposition were occupied with another construction project demonstrating that women's "souls were their own": the Woman's Building (fig. 2.4). Led by Bertha Palmer, the Board of Lady Managers provided women with a greater organizational role than they had attained at any previous World's Fair.[129] As one of their earliest undertakings, the board held a national competition to select a female architect to design its exhibition hall. The winner, recent MIT graduate Sophia Hayden, submitted an Italian Renaissance–

inspired design, which, according to fair organizer Maud Howe Elliott, was "essentially feminine in character," with "qualities of reserve, delicacy, and refinement."[130] Completed in October 1892, the Woman's Building housed a library; a model hospital; a model kindergarten; and a grand exhibit hall showcasing women's achievements in art, industry, and science.[131] By all accounts, the Woman's Building was a triumph for the Board of Lady Managers. In the words of John J. Flinn's *Hand-Book of the World's Columbian Exposition*, the building offered irrefutable proof that "the sex so long neglected or relegated to a minor or obscure position in the affairs of mankind is fully capable of maintaining the position attained." It was, he contended, "one of the noblest buildings of the Exposition, and pronounced one of the finest specimens of modern architecture."[132] Countless other contemporary observers echoed Flinn's praise, helping to ensure that the Woman's Building was among the most heavily trafficked destinations at the fair.[133]

Both the Woman's Building and the Woman's Temple were demolished not long after completion—one along with most of the fairgrounds after the close of the exposition, the other three decades later.[134] But during their shared lifetimes in the early 1890s, the two buildings attracted substantial public interest and media attention. Together, they stood as salient physical markers of moneyed women's new claims to commercial and civic space, as well as their growing participation in public life. The two organizations behind the buildings—the WCTU and the Board of Lady Managers—offered Chicago women unprecedented opportunities to engage in public activism and reform. Admittedly, the very existence of a "woman's" office building and a "woman's" exhibition hall indicated that Chicago women had more ground to cover to achieve parity with men. Nevertheless, these high-profile buildings—and the female leaders who developed them—marked Chicago women's advance into public life and foretold the further erosion of male sovereignty over the public realm.

By seizing new opportunities for civic engagement in the early 1890s, Chicago ladies also opened themselves to greater public scrutiny. As the president of the Board of Lady Managers, Bertha Palmer, for example, became an internationally known figure. According to the Parisian publication *Le Figaro*, Palmer occupied "more space in the public eye to-day than any other woman in America."[135] Indeed, Palmer herself was said to be among the most popular exhibits at the Columbian Exposition. In her private journal, Frances Glessner noted Palmer's growing celebrity after attending a fundraising bazaar for the fair. "We had a talk with Mrs. Palmer and when we turned to go found we were the centre of a ring of people gazing at her," Glessner wrote.[136] Even women who did not helm prominent civic projects could find themselves objects of public interest. Society reporting blossomed in the late nineteenth century and transformed many moneyed women into local celebrities.[137] In *With the Procession,* Fuller alludes to this emerging culture of publicity when wealthy patriarch David Marshall confesses that he is troubled to see "five or six lines" in the paper describing his daughter's gown at a recent social function. "Ten years ago this would have brought a protest, and twenty a flogging," observes one of Marshall's friends before concluding, "Well, times change."[138] The truth of his claim was reflected in the society pages of newspapers. Each day, they recounted the fashions, marriages, vacations, club meetings, visitors, teas, and receptions of women of wealth. More than ever before, the doings of Chicago ladies were thrust into the public consciousness.

When the crinoline crisis erupted in 1893, moneyed women were a growing presence in the commercial and civic life of the metropolis. Yet their claims to participation and belonging, which often hinged on access to financial capital accumulated by their menfolk, were far from secure. As they moved into spaces and areas of activity previously coded as male, Chicago ladies faced new efforts to regulate their consuming practices as well as the terms on which they accessed the public realm. It was here that the hoopskirt war found its roots.

By early February 1893, the first cage crinolines could be seen in department store fashion previews and on leading stage actresses—known for pioneering new trends—in cities across the United States.[139] The hoopskirt made its debut in Chicago at an operatic concert in the Auditorium Theater, where famed dramatic soprano Lillian Nordica appeared in "fluffy, flaring pink skirts." The women in the audience that night were said to be enamored with Nordica's silhouette. According to the *Chicago Tribune,* "The long breath of mingled anxiety and expectancy that the feminine portion of the gathering had drawn as the singer appeared at the back of the stage changed to a murmur of relief and approbation as she approached the footlights, a radiant pink vision, who looked as if she might have stepped out of an old print."[140] A week later,

Chicago ladies greeted with similar enthusiasm the hoopskirts featured in a new production at the Schiller Theater. In her review of the performance, Amy Leslie, a theater critic for the *Chicago Daily News,* pronounced the gowns "quaint and airy and tremendously swell." Leslie also maintained that the play's title, *Surrender,* should inform the actions of "the scoffing sex which rises in wrath at the mention of a hoop-skirt invasion."[141]

But surrender they would not. On the contrary, as the hoopskirt transformed from a Parisian abstraction to an American reality, its detractors among the "scoffing sex" intensified their efforts to thwart the style's revival. From New York to San Francisco, Minneapolis to Atlanta, journalists, legislators, businessmen, and reformers denounced the crinoline as a public nuisance and an affront to common sense and good citizenship. In Chicago, men and women alike closely followed the battles unfolding in other cities, even as they debated the hoopskirt's fate in their own hometown.

The first anti-crinoline measure to capture public interest in Chicago came from Minnesota. On February 3, 1893, Democrat George M. Bleecker, a "doughty little lawyer" from Minneapolis, introduced a bill to the Minnesota House of Representatives prohibiting the manufacture, sale, and use of "any hoop skirt or hoop skirts, or anything like thereunto."[142] Bleecker, who had been elected only three months earlier, claimed to be sincere in his attempt to stamp out the dreaded hoopskirt.[143] "If we sit idly by," he warned his colleagues, "[hoopskirts] will come into use here. We can prevent this nuisance, and let us do it." The bill called for any persons violating the crinoline ban to pay a fine of at least $25 for each offense or serve up to thirty days in jail.[144]

In statements to the House and the press, Bleecker clarified that his primary objective in proposing the new sumptuary measure was to prevent fashionable ladies from unduly congesting public space. "The streetcars and sidewalks of Minnesota are not wide enough to permit our putting our wives and daughters into hoopskirts," he declared. The overcrowding caused by a crinoline revival, according to Bleecker, would especially inconvenience men. As he predicted when first announcing the bill, the "introduction into this State of [the hoopskirt] . . . would drive the male population out."[145] With behooped ladies mobbing the sidewalks and "already over-crowded street cars," Bleecker argued, male pedestrians would be forced "to take the middle of the road."[146] To avoid this calamitous fate and preserve male access to the city center, the crinoline invasion had to be stopped.

Bleecker's bold stroke captured national press attention, including front-page headlines in the *Chicago Tribune* and the *New York Times*.[147] His actions also inspired imitation. Within weeks, similar bills appeared on the floor of state legislatures in California, New York, Pennsylvania, Missouri, Iowa, Kentucky, and Indiana.[148] Some of these measures were chuckled over and quickly dismissed, as was the case in Missouri, where Representative Charles D. Boisseau proposed to make public enemies of anyone who sold or wore hoopskirts. Boisseau, a Republican from the Kansas City area, introduced his resolution with dramatic flourish, warning that although the recent cholera epidemic had passed, "Another and greater pestilence is now raging . . . which if not checked will engulf our State in ruin and gather within its meshes the fairest daughters of our great State." Those daughters could not resist this pestilence on their own, Boisseau contended. Instead, the "people of the State are expecting the Legislature to arrest the further spread of the said plague."[149] A majority of Boisseau's colleagues disagreed, however. After another House member proposed to amend the bill such that Boisseau himself would be compelled to wear a hoopskirt, the resolution was tabled "amidst roars of laughter."[150]

Elsewhere, crinoline legislation inspired serious consideration and debate. In Indiana, for example, a hoopskirt ban proposed by Republican state senator Fred C. Boord was identified as "one of the most popular measures which have come before the House this session."[151] Boord claimed to have introduced the bill so that "mankind in general and womanhood in particular may be protected from those who are trying to foist an article of this kind upon our ladies." Like Boisseau before him, Boord implied that only male intervention could save women from the manipulation of retailers. In this instance, however, the resolution received broad support and was enthusiastically referred to the Judiciary Committee.[152]

In New York State, anti-crinoline measures were introduced by Democrat Frank D. Smith, who dropped his bill into the state assembly box with a rousing cry of "Hoop-La!"[153] Smith insisted he "did not introduce the bill in any spirit of levity, but to call the attention of women of common sense to the silly demands of fashion."[154] As written by Smith, the measure highlighted the spatial problems that hoopskirts would inflict on the public. "Whereas, It is reported in the public press that the fashion of hoopskirts is about to be established in this country which will result in a great deal of annoyance and inconvenience to the public travel, and especially at church, theater, and other public gatherings," the bill's preamble proclaimed. Notably, Smith's vision extended all the way to Chicago. The introductory section of the bill concluded by suggesting that a crinoline ban would "save additional space which would be required at the World's Fair in Chicago."[155] Smith's overcrowding concerns were echoed by some of his colleagues, who focused particularly on male pedestrians. "In view of the narrow streets in the lower part of New York city, the use of crinoline by women would make it almost impossible for a man to navigate," protested one state representative. After some initial debate, the bill was referred to the Committee on Commerce and Navigation.[156]

Chicagoans watched these legislative maneuverings with keen interest. But no local lawmakers stepped forward to sponsor similar measures. In fact, some Chicagoans spoke out against crinoline prohibitions—not because they welcomed hoops but because they viewed legislative action as counterproductive. "It is the height of folly to forbid a woman to do a certain thing and to threaten her with penalties if she does it," declared a *Chicago Tribune* editorial published after the Minnesota bill debuted. "Mr. Bleecker has little knowledge of the female nature," the author insisted. Although "all the arguments are on [Bleecker's] side," every woman would "appear in a hoopskirt of the largest dimensions possible" if the bill passed. Bleecker's actions, the author predicted, would cause women everywhere to adopt hoopskirts as a protest against "the cruelty and injustice of the Tyrant Man" in "an expression of sympathy" with the ladies of Minnesota. "Bleecker has put his foot in it," the editorial concluded.[157] Other lawmakers involved in the conflict did not escape censure. As more states contemplated crinoline bans, criticism became more barbed, invoking epithets such as "fool" and "clown."[158]

Yet lack of support for crinoline legislation by no means indicated enthusiasm for or acceptance of hoopskirts. On the contrary, the ranks of the city's crinoline detractors grew as the opening of the World's Fair drew closer. "It is highly important that organization should be effected before the World's Fair opens," argued one outspoken opponent. Not only would hoops make transportation to the exposition more dangerous and inconvenient, but overcrowding would hamper public enjoyment of the fairgrounds themselves.[159] Already journalists visiting Chicago to witness preparations for the fair were hinting at congestion problems. Some questioned whether the fair's organizers had done enough to ensure the public's comfort. "The stores, little and big, the cars and the elevators are as packed as if the stranger were already within the gates," observed a reporter from the *Los Angeles Times*. Although the Bureau of Public Comfort for the exposition may have accounted for sufficient hotel and restaurant accommodations, the reporter warned, "no remedy can be found" for the "terrific friction" of "hoop-skirt against hoop-skirt" on the city streets.[160]

Instead of complaining to lawmakers in Springfield, Chicagoans relied on social pressure to combat the coming of hoops. Article after article appeared in the local press denouncing those who donned hoopskirts as foolish and self-centered. Meanwhile, men and women alike called for the creation of an anti-crinoline league, which would agitate for the elimination of the crinoline threat.[161] Similar leagues had been organized in London, where thousands of women were said to have signed anti-crinoline pledges.[162] Local advocates hoped to inspire comparable enthusiasm in Chicago. Another creative anti-crinoline tactic took the form of an exhibit at Kohl & Middleton's Dime Museum, Chicago's answer to Barnum's American Museum (fig. 2.5). Advertised as the "Latest, Greatest, Neatest, Sweetest and Funniest Show of the Season," the Great Crinoline Show invited Chicagoans to "judge of the results of a crinoline craze by seeing how it looks on tall girls and short girls, fat girls and lean girls."[163] Observing the style on women of extraordinary size, hoopskirt critics hoped, would deter other women from adopting the trend. As detailed in a review for the *Inter Ocean*, the "fat girls in their enormous crinolines make a great display, and their hourly march down the center of the curio hall is highly amusing and instructive to those who view the proposed new fashion with questioning eyes." Dubbed a "howling success," the Great Crinoline Show reportedly attracted such large crowds that its run was extended an additional week.[164]

Such tactics demonstrated to ladies that adopting the crinoline would mean inviting public ridicule and scorn. Among the most effective of these efforts was a "test of public feeling" orchestrated by the *Chicago Tribune*. On a bustling Friday afternoon, the newspaper enlisted a female reporter to "saunter leisurely" along State Street wearing a "modishly

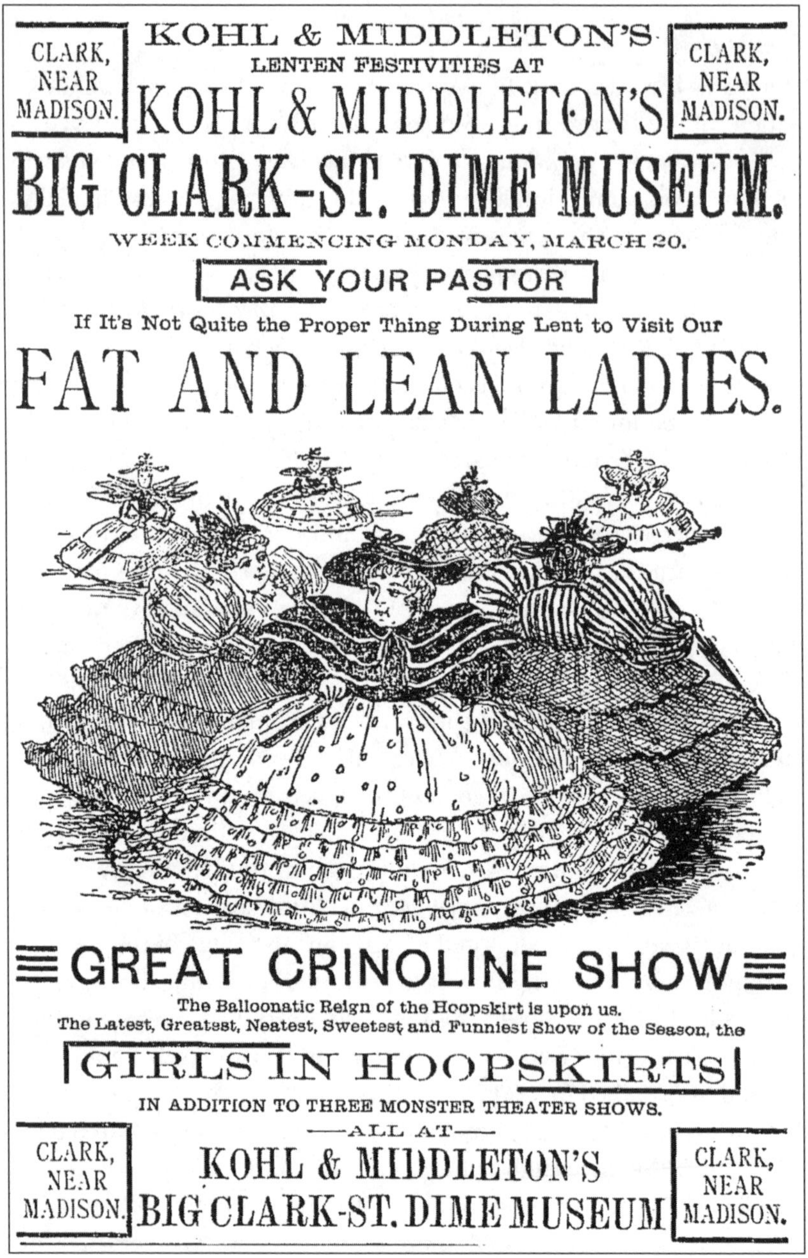

Figure 2.5 The Great Crinoline Show at Kohl & Middleton's Dime Museum featured hoopskirt-wearing "fat and lean ladies," who hourly paraded throughout the museum displaying their attire. Advertisements for the show, which ran in several Chicago newspapers, depicted full-figured models whose bodies were comically enlarged by hoopskirts. *Chicago Daily Tribune,* March 19, 1893, 37.

made gown" that "stood out at least two feet from the wearer's feet all around." As she swept "a four-foot passageway through the hurrying multitude," her hoopskirt attracted gasps, stares, and shouts of derision. Wherever she went, she met "men scowling and swearing." After her skirt brushed the shins of a male bystander near McVicker's Theater, his companion "hurled a few explosive expletives" at her retreating form. "If there's any idiot thing a woman won't do I should like to know what it is," called out another onlooker. Even within the *Tribune*'s own office building, the reporter provoked hostile whispers as she boarded an elevator:

> The elevator man gasped as she engineered her voluminous draperies through the door, and the men in it muttered unpleasant things under their breath as they made room for her or tried. Their attempts at compression weren't altogether successful.
>   "One of you gents'll have to git out," remarked the elevator man finally. "Tain't no use to crowd."

Later, as the reporter attempted to exit the office building, her skirt swept against a young man who "murmured words that have no standing in the revised edition of society's manual of conversation."[165]

Throughout her journey, the hoopskirted reporter expressed discomfort in public space. The street, she recounted, "became as one large eye" fixed on her "offending attire." Mere moments into her walk, she had to check her "inclination to make a frantic dive for the first friendly doorway that promised shelter" from public scrutiny. "Be brave," she told herself when contemplating the "mob at [her] heels." Her feelings of apprehension were likely compounded when a streetcar driver refused to let her board. "Next car, please," he shouted to her, as another onlooker murmured, "If I was running a street car line I'd put up signs reading something like this: 'Gents with smallpox symptoms and ladies with hoops are requested not to ride on this line.'" These confrontations combined with the "cold, critical, in some cases horrified, glances" of critics to render the streets and public spaces of the Loop inhospitable to the reporter.[166]

The exertions of male crinoline opponents—on the street, in newspapers, and within the halls of distant state legislatures—did not go unnoticed by Chicago women. "One would think to read the papers and see all the stir and consternation there are on the hoopskirt question that some strange calamity was impending which could only be averted by the prompt and energetic action of legislators, editors, and other public men," exclaimed a female writer in an anonymous *Chicago Tribune* opinion piece. Like many of her peers, the writer saw in the campaign against crinoline an attempt to restrict women's freedom. She explained,

> It is not the hoopskirt that we fly to defend so much as the principle of the thing; it is millions for defense but not a cent for tribute. Were no attack made we might ourselves discard hoops as stiff and ungraceful, but when it becomes a question of right and privilege we fling the hoopskirt to the breeze as our oriflamme, and call upon all women to rally to its rescue.

The writer acknowledged the hoopskirt's defects but balked at the prospect of male legislators dictating her apparel. "There is nothing in the Constitution of the United States . . . to prohibit a woman wearing hoops if she chooses," the author observed. She then insisted that ladies would continue to dress as they pleased without regard for male opinion—or the law. "Make all the laws you wish against crinoline," she announced disdainfully. "[Women] will pay no attention to them, unless it be to take the newspapers in which they are printed and make bustles of them."[167] For the author, the cumbersome crinoline had come to embody personal autonomy.

Some men, too, viewed the campaign against hoopskirts as an assault on women's rights. In an article for *Current Literature,* one male author denounced anti-crinoline agitation as a dangerous precedent. He admitted that hoops posed many practical problems and that, "at first blush," their prohibition might seem desirable. "Calm reflection, however, brings the thought that the remedy may be worse than the disease," he continued. "For if the tyrant man once establishes his supremacy in the matter of woman's dress it is not easy to say where he will stop." The author then speculated that if hoopskirt opponents prevailed, men would soon dictate other aspects of woman's dress. They could, he argued, "dethrone the long and sweeping skirt, the theater hat and a good many of what seem to the masculine sense the abominations of woman's apparel. Would this be well?" For the author, the answer was a resounding no. "Of the possibilities which lie behind the appareling of woman in accordance with man's requirements or taste we know nothing and can only guess. Shall we not rather bear the ills we have?" he concluded.[168]

Yet for many women, the potential restrictions imposed by sumptuary legislation were less concerning than those presented by the crinoline itself. However enticing its aesthetic and hygienic qualities, the style's ungainly shape limited the mobility of women who now frequently navigated the city center. "Most of the girls and women who are trying to do something out in the world to-day were in their infancy or had not come into existence at the last crinoline epoch," pointed out journalist Marie Evelyn. But women's place had since evolved, making hoops more impractical. "Weighted by the crinoline," Evelyn cautioned, "there is danger that we may sink out of sight altogether." Ordinary activities, from walking to riding public transit to attending the theater, would be made more difficult. In a crinoline, the modern woman "would always be late," Evelyn insisted, because "it would be practically impossible for her to make her way through a crowd."[169] Even shopping would "become a burden to the soul of woman," predicted New York journalist Mary McGuire. "Surround a Friday bargain counter with fifty hoop-skirted ladies and the tangle would never be unraveled in season to shut the doors at 6 o'clock," McGuire wrote, adding that "every woman's life would be a nuisance if those abominations prevail again."[170]

Such considerations prevented many fashionable women from embracing a crinoline revival. Still, most ladies did not want to be labeled radical dress reformers and, as a result, did not publicly denounce the style. According to the *Chicago Herald,* women who privately opposed the hoopskirt refused to publicize their views for fear "that their husbands would ridicule them for becoming dress reformers, which [was] the habit of husbands in the brief intervals they . . . reserve[d] from denunciation of hoops."[171] Accordingly, Chicago women expressed their limited enthusiasm for hoops not through public statements but through their consumption—or, rather, lack thereof. Few women asked retailers to stock the style. By mid-February, employees at several State Street department stores acknowledged that demand was light. "We haven't bought them yet," confessed a forewoman of the undergarment department at Marshall Field's, "and I am not trying to force them because I think they will be so awkward and uncomfortable. One month more will probably decide the matter."[172]

The forewoman's prediction was not far off. As March faded into April and still no hoopskirts graced the figures of Chicago ladies, its detractors breathed a sigh of relief. "The crinoline scare has somewhat abated," observed the *Chicago Tribune* in early April.[173] Other publications corroborated the paper's findings. "Although it is certain that skirts will be made fuller, it is equally certain that the crinoline will not be adopted," affirmed columnist Isabel A. Mallon in the *Ladies' Home Journal*.[174] Similar assertions appeared in *Godey's Lady's Book*, *Harper's Bazaar*, and other fashion publications.[175] By the end of April, the routing of the hoopskirt was regarded as inevitable. "It seems now a settled matter that crinoline will be entirely unnecessary," declared a fashion writer in the *Inter Ocean*.[176] The crisis had passed.

The crinoline's defeat came at the hands of women who rejected the style's uncomfortable dimensions. But the "open antagonism" aroused in men exposed their discomfort with moneyed women's growing presence in urban public life.[177] In opposing hoops, they revealed their hyperawareness of women's new claims to the downtown and women's mounting influence as consumers. For these anxious male onlookers, the waning of the crinoline threat could not quell their suspicions that women might again place their commercial desires before the common good. What did seem certain, however, was that moneyed women's consuming practices would continue to spark conflict as the expansion of the consumer economy brought the sexes into more frequent contact in downtown commercial spaces, such as the elegant new theaters then spreading across Chicago's Loop.

3

Consumer Rights and the Theater Hat Problem

O N THE OPENING NIGHT of John Philip Sousa's *El Capitan*, a rowdy "tumult" erupted among the "highly-respectable" audience members of the Columbia Theater, one of Chicago's elegant playhouses. Less than two weeks earlier, in the first week of January 1897, the city council had approved an ordinance prohibiting hats and bonnets in theaters. Before the curtain rose on Sousa's operetta, hundreds of men enforced the new ordinance by shouting, hissing, catcalling, and booing at ladies in hats. As each female patron entered the auditorium, she was verbally assaulted until she had removed her headgear. "Never did hats come off so quickly from feminine heads," reported the *Chicago Tribune*. "Women came down the aisle with hair disordered from the quick withdrawal of hat pins, and with faces more red than the plush upholstery of the seats." The "noisy demonstration" continued after the show began, drowning out the music and threatening to break up the performance. Even after the theater's ushers had subdued the crowd, several men remained hanging over the balcony throughout the night "to make sure no woman put her hat on again." Only one woman, in a broad-brimmed cap trimmed with duck feathers, dared to do so.[1] The disorder had disciplined the women in the audience. The "high hat problem" plagued theaters not just in Chicago but in cities across the nation. At issue were the rights and duties of men and women in sharing public places of consumption.

Before the fracas at the Columbia, Chicago women had resisted all efforts to restrain their millinery exuberance. Since the early 1890s, theater critics and social observers had denounced female playgoers in high hats as selfish public nuisances and called for more modest headwear. Yet the high hat problem persisted and, in fact, grew worse as theater audiences became increasingly female over the course of the decade. Indeed, as theater managers bolstered ticket sales by courting more women patrons, the possibility of finding a seat unobstructed by ladies' headgear grew ever more remote. By 1895, the problem appeared so dire that the Illinois legislature, at the appeal of an exasperated Chicago representative, joined several other states in considering a ban on theater hats.[2] These measures soon failed, however, amid fears that women's opposition would render them unenforceable.

In Illinois, many ladies at the time had objected to the "impertinent" restrictions on their individual freedom and vowed to protect their right to dress as they pleased.[3] Nonetheless, two years later, in 1897, Chicago became the first city to pass a high hat ordinance. Most observers familiar with the state law's history predicted that the new measure would also fail, that Chicago ladies would once again rise up to defend their liberty. "The new woman will not be coerced," affirmed one male editor. "Her hat will not down."[4]

But a new conception of rights was then emerging that proved the high hat's demise. Its logic undergirded the city's new sumptuary ordinance and fueled the disturbance at the Columbia. The assumption was that anyone who paid for a good or a service deserved full enjoyment of its use. The right of consumption conflicted with older codes of genteel sociability that called for deference to ladies in public—even ladies wearing exasperatingly high hats. No longer need men suffer silently behind enormous chapeaus merely to uphold outdated standards of etiquette, the argument went. The purchase of a ticket had secured all spectators a right to view the stage—a right that trumped the claims of Victorian politesse. The uproar over theater hats contributed to a reordering of public culture in spaces where men and women increasingly mingled as paying customers, lending force to new assertions of consumer rights.

In constraining one mode of ladies' conspicuous consumption, Chicago lawmakers demonstrated, paradoxically, a new commitment to protecting the consuming public. Only a decade earlier, the notion that the state could compel ladies to remove their hats in places of public amusement would have been considered outlandish. Since the late

1880s, however, Progressive reformers and muckraking journalists had successfully agitated for new legal protections for consumers, breathing life into a distinct new constituency with unique rights and interests.[5] Chicago stood at the epicenter of this consumer awakening, even before Upton Sinclair's *The Jungle* (1906) captivated the nation. The pressure for theater hat legislation in Chicago reflected a growing popular awareness of the rights owed to consumers, as well as a cultural climate favorable to state action on behalf of consumer interests. Newly imbued with a sense of themselves as consumers, Chicagoans endeavored to "get what they paid for" at the theater—to ensure that the price of admission guaranteed an unobstructed view of the stage. But in securing the rights of consumers, lawmakers restricted the personal liberty of women adorned in sumptuous goods. They expanded the role of the state in maintaining a commercial public realm that both sexes could occupy together.

The debate over Chicago's theater hat ordinance illuminates the evolving relationship between consumption and citizenship in the late nineteenth century. The ability to enjoy public accommodations, such as theaters, hotels, and restaurants, became entwined with definitions of freedom and equality in the age of Jim Crow.[6] In 1885, Illinois codified this link at the state level by passing civil rights legislation that guaranteed all citizens "full and equal enjoyment" of public accommodations.[7] But the equal enjoyment lawmakers envisioned in theaters did not extend to the self-fashioning of men and women. The bodies and apparel of women were regulated to assure the rights of the consuming public—a public protected by male guardians. In resisting the new sumptuary measures, high-hatted ladies asserted claims to civic equality and belonging in public space. Those claims, however, were overcome by the rights of other members of the audience. The practices of consumer society thus brought new civic obligations, as well as freedoms, to women of the moneyed classes.

"The patience of men has reached its limit," insisted renowned musical critic Henry T. Finck in an 1896 opinion piece for the *Looker-On*. As a regular contributor to the magazine, Finck focused on reviewing musical productions and the work of composers and singers. That summer, however, he turned his critical eye to ladies' "offensive habit" of wearing large hats to public performances. With "disheartening discouragement,"

Finck noted that the practice had persisted for nearly a decade. Since the mid-1880s, he explained, women in voluminous hats had been plaguing theaters and making it "quite impossible for those sitting behind them to see the scenery and enjoy the play."[8] The problem, warned Finck, could no longer be ignored—the high theater hat must be toppled.

The rise of the big hat reflected a broader trend toward more conspicuous styles in the late nineteenth century. According to fashion scholars, the sartorial excesses of the period marked the culmination of a long pendulum swing away from the simplicity and austerity of the age of revolution.[9] No one millinery style predominated. Rather, ladies chose from an array of shapes, fabrics, and trimmings (fig. 3.1). The Gainsborough, or picture, hat featured an expansive brim and was often trimmed with ostrich tips or other large plumes.[10] The round felt hat boasted a more moderate brim and was topped with flowers, ribbons, fur, fruits, vegetables, or any number of bird parts—feathers, heads, even entire bodies.[11] Bonnets, which were distinguished by ribbons that tied under the chin, incorporated a fluffy profusion of feathers, flowers, or lace. Straw boaters had low, flat crowns and were often adorned with sprays of feathers or flowers. Turbans and capotes had the smallest frames, but even these styles typically featured feather aigrettes that substantially extended their vertical lines. Certain styles were recommended for specific activities; however, these guidelines were constantly changing and far from universal. As a result, most women wore whatever they deemed becoming.[12]

The pleasures of large hats were not reserved for any single class of women. Up and down the socioeconomic spectrum, women embraced elaborate millinery. Wealthy ladies, such as Bertha Palmer and Frances Glessner, were often photographed wearing large hats ornamented with costly baubles and trimmings. In February 1897, mere days after Chicago's theater hat law was enacted, Glessner posed for a "multigraph" (a photographic portrait taken from five different angles) in a bonnet topped by a full-sized bird.[13] Palmer was often shown sporting even more ample styles—from a bejeweled chapeau decked with velvet bows to a wide-brimmed Gainsborough laden with white ostrich plumes.[14] Working-class women, too, wore large, profusely decorated hats. The materials and artisanship that went into these styles was, of course, less expensive. To save money, many workingwomen trimmed their own millinery. After adorning her hat with paper roses purchased from a pushcart,

Figure 3.1 Millinery styles in the 1890s were profusely ornamented with feathers, flowers, ribbons, and bows, as in this 1896 illustration from the women's magazine the *Delineator*. Even the most restrained of these looks had the potential to obstruct sightlines in a crowded theater.

"Winter Millinery," *Delineator* 48 (Dec. 1896): 779.

Mashah—one of four sisters in Anzia Yezierska's novel of Jewish immigrant life in New York—exclaims, "Like a lady from Fifth Avenue I look, and for only ten cents."[15] Yet women such as Mashah did not merely mimic the tastes of fashionable socialites. Young working-class women favored brighter, bolder colors to "emphasize the element of display." They also tended to mix hues with abandon, while their wealthier counterparts generally restricted themselves to one or two sedate shades at a time.[16]

The market for women's hats, much like the market for dresses, was divided between custom-made and ready-to-wear options. Whereas workingwomen tended to attach their own embellishments to cheap, untrimmed hat bases, moneyed women typically purchased their millinery pre-trimmed, leaving design and construction to the experts. For an entirely custom-made hat from a skilled milliner, more than $20 (roughly $500 today) was not an uncommon expense, and many customers gladly paid more.[17] Affluent ladies supplemented their wardrobes with more affordable ready-to-wear designs from department stores, mail-order catalogs, and millinery shops.[18] In 1895, for example, Marshall Field & Co. offered "fine trimmed hats and bonnets" reflecting the "high-art designing which characterizes all trimmed millinery from our own workrooms" for reduced prices of between $7.50 and $12 (roughly $188 and $300 today).[19] Two years later, Siegel-Cooper & Co. advertised "the most exquisite styles—designed by our own artists" as well as "imported models from Paris and London"—for between $2.95 and $12.50 (roughly $74 and $312 today).[20]

Regardless of price, a woman's hat was an indispensable component of her wardrobe. Social convention dictated that respectable women covered their heads in public. Accordingly, it was de rigueur for women to wear headgear not only on the street but also inside restaurants, stores, offices, schools, galleries, libraries, and churches.[21] The theater was yet another place where women were discouraged from appearing bareheaded. "Here you must wear your bonnet," instructed etiquette expert Florence Hartley. This dictum was slightly revised for the opera, where patrons generally wore full evening dress. In that case, Hartley advised ladies to adopt "a head-dress or dressy bonnet of some thin material."[22] Exceptions did exist. In her etiquette manual, Abby Buchanan Longstreet noted that ladies in private boxes—where they were somewhat removed from public intercourse—could appear "unbonneted" as long as they covered their heads when traveling to and from their seats.[23] Elsewhere in the theater, ladies were expected to retain their hats at all times. Some experts encouraged women seated on the main floor to avoid particularly voluminous styles. Agnes Morton, for example, wrote in her 1893 guide that "it certainly shows a gross disregard of civility to wear to the theatre the very *largest* hat one possesses." Yet even Morton insisted that female theatergoers keep their heads covered, as most "pretty styles of bonnet and hats" posed "no serious source of annoyance or imposition to other people."[24]

Gentlemen abided by different rules of decorum. Although most men wore hats in public, they were expected to remove their headgear in the presence of ladies. Indeed, etiquette held that women in public deserved courtly deference from men as well as accommodations to preserve their feminine privacy. As such, a gentleman was expected to give up his seat to a woman on public transit, to offer his inside arm to a female companion when walking in a crowd, and to avoid greeting any lady on the street without first obtaining her recognition.[25] Simply put, ladies in public were to be treated much like guests.

Guided by these standards, men appeared sans chapeau in many spaces where women did not, including the theater. As Eliza Bisbee Duffey succinctly explained in *Ladies' and Gentlemen's Etiquette* (1877), "A gentleman never retains his hat in a theatre."[26] The divergent practices of men and women were evident in contemporary illustrations of Chicago theaters. In an 1889 *Harper's Weekly* sketch of an opera performance at the Auditorium Theater, for example, the men in the elegantly dressed audience were depicted without hats, as were the ladies in the theater's private boxes. By contrast, the women seated on the main floor were all shown wearing bonnets or toques.[27] These conventions applied beyond the confines of the main auditorium, as shown in an 1891 drawing of the lobby of McVicker's Theater (fig. 3.2). Once again, the men were shown without head coverings, many with exposed bald patches or receding hairlines, whereas the women all appeared in millinery trimmed with feathers and flowers.[28] As such images made clear, only female patrons wore headgear at the theater. Consequently, only female patrons could be criticized for obstructing sightlines to the stage.

Before the debate over theater hats reached the Chicago City Council, the controversy unfolded in print. In magazines, newspaper editorials, cartoons, interviews, and speeches throughout the 1890s, critics expressed

Figure 3.2 Nineteenth-century etiquette demanded that men doff their caps in the presence of women, whereas women were expected to retain their millinery in public spaces, including theaters. These gendered conventions were evident in contemporary illustrations, such as this detail of an 1891 sketch of the grand foyer of McVicker's Theater *McVicker's Observanda* (Chicago: W. J. Jefferson Press, 1891), 20–21. Courtesy of the Chicago History Museum.

a rising disdain for the millinery worn by women theatergoers. Complaints focused on the theater hat's tendency to obscure the stage. As renowned author William Dean Howells observed in *Harper's Weekly*, even small hats could interfere with the enjoyment of others. "The most exiguous aigrette in the simplest toque can blot out a heroine at the most important moment," he lamented.[29] In an essay in the *Argonaut*, another man described how a hat "garnished with flowers, with vegetables, with shrubs" had ruined his own recent trip to the theater. "As she had cocked her cocked hat over her eyes," he recounted, "it resulted that the rear of this vegetable garden towered above the top of her blonde chignon, so that I could see no more of the stage than if I had been in far Cathay." Though the man "leaned to the right, then to the left," he could still see nothing of the play.[30] Henry Finck claimed to have endured several similarly frustrating experiences. In his view, "Five dollars for an opera seat commanding a close view of a woman's back hair and feathered erection on top of it, with little else to be seen, is rather too expensive an amusement."[31]

High hat opponents sometimes expressed their discontent through humorous vignettes and illustrations. With biting sarcasm, for example, the author of the 1895 article "The Theater Hat: Some Apologies for Its Existence" suggested that men had not fully considered the high hat's advantages. "A canopy of lace and feathers over the seat in front of me often shields me from many things I do not care to see," he jested, adding that a large hat had recently prevented him from viewing a mediocre drama. "As I left the theater," he continued, "I heard people saying they did not like the play. I had no objections to give vent to, for I had not seen it—thanks to the hat."[32] Other critics took a less subtle approach. In a comic published by *Life* magazine, for example, the artist depicts three men in enormous feathered hats blocking the view of the women seated behind them. The ladies' unhappy frowns underscore the sentiment expressed in the caption: "Revenge Is Sweet."[33] A sketch from the *Chicago Tribune* focused specifically on the selfishness of high-hatted women. After a gentleman politely asks a woman seated in front of him to remove her hat, she refuses emphatically: "Certainly not. How do you suppose I should be able to see if I held it in my lap in front of me? You men are just utterly selfish!"[34]

The high-hatted lady provided rich fodder for the funny pages. But when humor failed to diminish her visibility, criticism adopted a more somber tone. "Seriously, though—and good-humored appeals have been made so often and so fruitlessly that it is time to treat the matter seriously—the high hat must go," argued a writer for *Munsey's*. The woman "who destroys the enjoyment of others who have, like herself paid for their seats in a place of amusement," the writer claimed, "is not only guilty of indecent selfishness and signal bad taste; she is positively dishonest, she makes herself a crying public nuisance."[35] A reporter for the *Chicago Tribune* similarly underscored the problem's gravity, noting that the outcry was "regarded at first by many women as a bit of fun at their expense, but later appreciated as a serious protest." According to the reporter, the trouble persisted because most women felt no obligation to heed the rights of other audience members. "Certain women have required only a suggestion that their theater hats were encroaching on the rights and privileges of the other sex to cause them to remove them always when in a theater," he observed. "The large majority, however, have refused to consider the proposition as anything but impertinent."[36] Notably, the reporter referred only to the rights of the "other sex." Although men and women shared theatrical spaces, objections to the high hat were most often articulated as a violation of men's rights—rights owed to them as paying customers.

Yet ladies, too, could be inconvenienced by theater hats. In 1893, for example, Frances Glessner recorded her frustration at being seated behind two especially large hats at a performance of the drama *Camille* at Hooley's Theater. The famed Italian dramatic actress Eleonora Duse was starring, and Hooley's had increased its base ticket prices to $3 (roughly $81 today).[37] After Glessner and her husband took their "very good seats" on the main floor, two women sat in front of them "with great towering hats which cut off the stage almost entirely." John Glessner complained in vain to the management. As his wife later wrote in her journal, "There is no rule—so we changed our seats for some in the balcony."[38] The problem was even more acute at matinees, where female patrons predominated. "At the evening performance," one young woman told the *Chicago Tribune,* "there are spaces over and about men's heads through which vistas of the stage may be seen even by the women themselves. In the afternoon the hats loom up in a solid phalanx, ever shifting and shimmering, with plumes waving, and flowers nodding. She hears the sound of distant voices, the applause of those in the front rows . . . but she sees only a plateau of felt or velvet."[39]

Whether male or female, ticketholders whose views were impeded by high hats were, according to critics, being stripped of an entitlement for which they had paid. "Patrons of the theater pay to see as well as to hear what is going on upon the stage; anything that interferes with their ability to do this in comfort defrauds them of a right inalienably theirs," asserted one opponent in early 1893.[40] Three years later, a writer for the *Chicago Tribune* suggested that high-hatted ladies did not understand the financial implications of their choices: "They must be convinced that they are taking from a man something of pecuniary worth when they deprive him of the opportunity to view a performance for which he has paid $1 or $2 at the box-office."[41] Here, again, the rights of men and consumers were intimately linked. Indeed, the figure of the beleaguered male theatergoer repeatedly surfaced in the press. Invoking this figure, Howells protested: "He has bought his seat for the purpose of seeing the play and the person who prevents him from seeing it plunders him and oppresses him, however unwillingly and unwittingly."[42]

Yet even if critics agreed *why* the theater hat posed a problem, they struggled to identify *who* was responsible. Ladies in high hats were selfish and ungracious, many argued. But did not theater managers have an obligation to provide paying customers with an unobstructed view? "I have sometimes imagined asking at the ticket office, when I buy my seat: 'Does this coupon guarantee me against the eclipse of the stage by a woman with a large hat in the seat before me?'" confessed Howells.[43] Many believed such a guarantee was implicit in the act of purchase. "The purchaser of a ticket to any *performa* hands over his money with the understanding that he is going to be permitted to see the stage and those who appear on it," reasoned one opponent. "He would hardly take the trouble to go to the box office and pay for a reserved seat to look at a milliner's window. . . . Why, then, should the company that accepts his money fail to guarantee him that which he paid for?"[44]

The notion that a ticket effectively served as a contract—and that theater owners had to uphold that contract—was reinforced by rumors in the Chicago press that some high hat victims in other cities were suing for damages. In late 1891, for example, a Pennsylvania man allegedly filed a suit for 50 cents against a theater wherein two large hats prevented him from viewing the play. The plaintiff maintained that he had "paid to see the people on the stage" and that in "selling him the seat for this performance the management guaranteed him that right." In its account of the proceedings, the *Inter Ocean* declared that the management had "failed in its obligations" and that "the case will be watched with interest from every theater town on the continent."[45]

One Chicagoan likely paying attention was Will J. Davis, the manager of the Columbia Theater. Davis spied in the high theater hat a "destroying blight" that not only inconvenienced customers but also diminished his profits by forcing him to reseat any patrons who complained. In early 1893, Davis resolved to take matters into his own hands by initiating a "crusade" against the theater hat. His strategy was to announce his opposition to high hats in the local press and recommend that ladies adorn their heads with jeweled combs instead of millinery. Davis did not suggest that women in hats would be unwelcome at the Columbia. Instead, he expressed his wish that "some recognized social leader among the ladies" would begin "frequenting the theaters wearing no hat" and set an example for others. Davis hoped the press, following his lead, would sustain its own campaign against the theater hat. "There is scarcely a month passes by that the entire conservative press of the country does not concentrate its power against some crying evil, political, social, or moral," he pointed out. "So I feel sure that if a crusade against the big hat in a theater is begun by the daily press of the country, just so sure will the high hat have to go."[46] For a short time, Davis printed notices in the Columbia's theatrical programs asking women to remove their headwear.[47]

In the coming weeks, Davis claimed to receive many letters from Chicagoans who endorsed his actions and similarly opposed the theater hat. "If you have started something that will even modify the fashion," wrote one supporter, "you are a benefactor to the theater-going public." Others urged him to stay resolute in the face of women's indifference. "If you will persevere . . . you will gradually gain sympathy and one day you will succeed," another exhorted. In one laudatory missive, a male correspondent revealed his hope that Davis's efforts would enable the author to start visiting the theater again. "Until a few years ago," he recalled, "I went to the theater regularly once or twice a week. I became so annoyed by having my view of the stage completely shut out by large hats worn by thoughtless women that I gave up going to plays in disgust." The author insisted that "crusades against high hats" were commencing in various other cities. Yet Davis's efforts in Chicago were of particular importance because of the city's unusual place as an arbiter of national taste and social customs. "Chicago sets the pace for all the cities in the United States," he contended. "Why not then in matters of common courtesy in the theaters."[48]

Chicago's ability to "set the pace" depended on the compliance of women patrons. That compliance remained elusive, however. While some ladies "assented to [Davis's] wishes and removed their head covering," many more ignored his pleas, citing the inconvenience of taking off their elaborate millinery in public. "Theater Hats Were There Galore," announced a front-page *Chicago Tribune* article surveying the state of affairs at the Columbia two days after Davis's pronouncement. "There was the same garden scene of roses and lilies and violets, with birds and feathers, on greater or less expanses of felt when the curtain went up on the first act. There was the same dodging of theater hats, the same craning of necks," observed a reporter tasked with monitoring the display.[49] Two years later, the *Tribune* suggested that the number of high hats had actually increased since Davis began his campaign.[50] Among those who declined to support his efforts were the "society leaders" to whom he had appealed for aid. According to the *Inter Ocean,* these unnamed women were "united in declaring that the managers must provide good dressing-rooms for their lady patrons first."[51] Only with such facilities in place, they argued, could ladies attend to the pinning and redressing that accompanied the removal of headgear. Until these needs could be met, women would resist taking off their hats.

Moral suasion had brought limited results. Indeed, most women theater patrons seemed uninterested in, even actively opposed to, hat reform. One journalist made note of the standoff: "It is a large subject—the theater hat—and somewhat timeworn, but with each recurring year comes the old rivalry between its colors and the jeers which it excites as to which shall be louder."[52] The conflict between high-hatted women and their detractors prompted serious discussion of the rights of consumers and the place of women in commercial public life. So, too, did it lay bare how traditional manners and codes of civility conflicted with the new practices of a consumer society.

The waving plumes and abundant flora of 1890s millinery aroused the ire of many a theatergoer. But fashion had smiled on large hats before. As one journalist said of the average hat adorning the lady theater patron, "It may be big, but it is well to remember that those of her grandmothers and great-grandmothers have been bigger." To be sure, large hats had interfered with the sightlines of audience members in playhouses and concert halls in decades past. "Turning back only to the beginning of the century," the journalist remarked, "one finds evidence that the eccentricities of the fashionable headgear did not escape caustic comment of the men who were inconvenienced by it."[53] Harry Germaine, a columnist for the *Inter Ocean,* took an even longer view when he proposed that women's hats had blighted public performances for as long as theaters had existed. Germaine unearthed supporting evidence from as far back as the early 1700s, when British dramatist Joseph Addison denounced "'the wearing of unseemly toppings' to 'obstruct the vision.'"[54]

No longer, however, was the theater hat simply an object of droll protest; the nuisance was becoming an object of legislative action. It has
"made its way in to politics," a writer for *Munsey's* noted sardonically in
early 1895 as several state legislatures began to contemplate enacting
high hat prohibitions. "It may yet become a tremendous party issue like
the tariff or the silver question."[55] The concern owed not to any increase
in the size of ladies' hats but to the growth of the consumer economy.
As theater managers endeavored to capitalize on an expanding market
of women shoppers, playhouses aggressively catered to female tastes and
expectations and, in turn, pushed male preferences to the margins. The
outcry against high hats arose from discomfort with ladies' growing
dominance in the world of the theater. It was sustained by a newly acute
awareness of the rights owed to paying customers. While the theater hat
itself was a storied institution, the conflict that it generated emerged
from the cultural practices of the consumer city.

For most of the century, the presence of ladies had rarely obstructed
the pleasure of men during theatrical performances. Not since the colonial era, when the theater was primarily an aristocratic institution, had
women constituted a significant portion of the audience. With the
democratization of American theater in the early republic, the playhouse
had emerged as an overwhelmingly male space. It was the domain of
actresses and prostitutes—not respectable women.[56] In his 1912 account
of Chicago's early history, J. Seymour Currey underscored the unruly
masculine atmosphere of the city's first theaters: "The audiences were
made up almost entirely of men, and the presence of policemen was necessary to keep order, for frequent and violent quarrels arose in the
audience." The aesthetic environment reinforced the manly atmosphere.
According to Joseph Jefferson, an actor who traveled through Chicago
during its early days, the theater where he performed featured "a large,
painted, brick-red drapery . . . showing an arena with a large number
of gladiators hacking away at one another in the distance to a delighted
Roman public."[57] The plays themselves aided in defining the mid-century
theater as a male space. To appeal to male patrons, managers selected
works featuring manly heroes, such as Richard III or Macbeth, played
by actors known for their masculine "vigor" and "muscular" presence.[58]

The theater, then, was not a key site for women to display their millinery. When a lady did attend the theater, she obtained a male escort
and confined herself to a private box, away from the rowdy male crowds

that occupied the wooden benches of the main floor "pit" and balcony.[59] Without these protections in place, she was thought to expose herself to the dangers and insults of the promiscuous crowd. In his 1860 guide to gentlemen's etiquette, Cecil B. Hartley hinted at these evils when underscoring the importance of the escort's role. "When you are with a lady at a place of amusement," he wrote, "you must not leave your seat until you rise to escort her home." Should the escort fail in this duty, Hartley cautioned, he "deprives [a lady] of his protection, and gives her the appearance of having come alone."[60] The unspoken implication, of course, was that the unattended lady would be mistaken for a prostitute.

Respectable women were never entirely excluded from the nineteenth-century theater. But their presence was suspect and carefully scrutinized. Accordingly, they were advised not to attract undue notice. "A lady's deportment should be very modest in a theatre," warned the author of *The Ladies' Book of Etiquette*. "Avoid carefully every motion or gesture that will attract attention. To flirt a fan, converse in whispers, indulge in extravagant gestures of merriment or admiration, laugh loudly, or clap your hands together are all excessively vulgar and unladylike."[61] Such restraint was necessary, etiquette experts maintained, because theaters exposed ladies to the gaze of strangers. In the words of author Agnes Morton, the theater was one of many spaces "where the general public is our observant critic."[62] Gentlemen, too, were to act with decorum. But ladies were held to standards designed to diminish their visual and vocal presence.

The American theater began to open to respectable women in the second half of the nineteenth century, as theater managers sought to enhance their profit margins by catering to moneyed patrons. It was in this era that "legitimate theater," including plays and operas, came to be distinguished from the lighter, less expensive fare of vaudeville, variety houses, and concert saloons.[63] As part of this sorting, legitimate theaters eliminated many of the more disreputable—and masculine— aspects of earlier playhouse culture. Their efforts included barring prostitutes, eliminating alcohol sales, prohibiting shouting and other unruly audience behavior, charging higher ticket prices, and often segregating the races.[64] In addition, they redesigned interior spaces to create an atmosphere of luxury and refinement. Thus, the "pit" was renamed the "parquet," and its wooden benches and boisterous working-class patrons were replaced with upholstered armchairs and a more affluent clientele.[65] In 1870, *Harper's New Monthly Magazine* noted the transformation: "Where the noisy crowd of men were massed, upon hard, backless benches, there is the luminous cloud of lovely toilets mingled with the darker dress of the *jeunesse dorée*."[66]

Hooley's Theater in Chicago offered a vivid illustration of the material changes that accompanied the rise of legitimate theater. In 1877, Hooley's new management endeavored to increase its appeal to "all the better classes of the theater-going public." To accomplish this goal, its operators abandoned variety shows in favor of serious drama and completely "renovated, cleansed, refurnished, and beautified the theater to make it an appropriate resort for ladies and gentlemen." That summer, the *Inter Ocean* admired the remodeling effort, which included installing frescoes, chandeliers, luxuriously upholstered seats, and an ornamental dome:

> The entire establishment, from the entrance on Randolph to the back of the stage, and from the basement to the dome, has undergone a thorough transformation, the dingy and worn decorations of the house as it was being replaced by a brightly and elaborately decorated interior. The other evening the theater was lighted up to test the effect of the decorator's work, and it gave an agreeable foretaste of the brilliant appearance the auditorium will present with an elegant audience to complete the charm.

The renovations sanitized the theater, removing the "dingy" decorations along with the less affluent customers who favored variety shows. In this way, the management rendered all spaces—not just the private boxes—suitable for ladies. Crucially, in assessing the overall effect of the renovations, the *Inter Ocean* concluded that Hooley's "looks prettier and more home-like to cultivated folks than it ever did before."[67] In other words, the atmosphere was decidedly more feminine.

Chicago's newest and largest theater, the Auditorium, was equally elegant. Completed in 1889, the building was designed by the architectural firm of Adler and Sullivan. In addition to theatrical performances, the Auditorium hosted the grand opera season of the Chicago Opera Association, as well as the programs of the celebrated Theodore Thomas Orchestra.[68] The design of the Auditorium was remarkable for its limited number of private boxes. Unlike theaters in New York, which were dominated by private boxes for the city's elite, the Auditorium reflected the belief of its financier, Ferdinand W. Peck, that opera and high culture should be open to all.[69] Despite this commitment to cultural democracy, the Auditorium's high ticket prices and sumptuous interior ensured that its audiences were dominated by moneyed patrons. When visiting Chicago for the World's Fair, French traveler Marie Lédier Grandin described the grandeur of both the theater and its guests on the night of a ball: "Lush flowers, green plants, and velvet wall hangings decorated the long marble staircase; bright lights shimmered in mirrors and in the polished gold décor. . . . The ladies' ravishing gowns were literally blinding with their sparkling constellations of precious stones and diamonds."[70] Of course, by providing these fashionably dressed ladies with fewer private boxes, the Auditorium generated more opportunities for female guests to obstruct the view of other patrons.

By 1893, Chicago boasted more than a half dozen legitimate theaters, which clustered together around the city's booming retail district. Travel guides aimed at fairgoers offered a glimpse into their opulent interiors. In *Chicago by Day and Night*, Harold Richard Vynne clarified that these establishments were "known as the 'down-town' or high-priced theaters, the scale of prices ranging from 25 cents to $1.50 per seat." They should not be confused, Vynne warned, with the "'second class' or 'provincial' theaters" that resided in the outlying neighborhoods and attracted a "mercurial" working-class clientele who enjoyed "more sensational types of plays."[71] The second-tier playhouses were far from suitable for ladies, who were confined to downtown theaters offering high-minded "art" in a staid, luxurious atmosphere. At the Columbia Theater, for example, ladies enjoyed "only the higher grade of performances" in an "elaborately finished and furnished" environment. According to the *Marquis' Hand-Book of Chicago*, this "first-class play-house," which had been renovated in 1884, was decorated with mosaics, bronzed papier-mâché, and illustrated scenes from Shakespeare, as well as "thirty oil paintings of the modern school, and other works of art including several pieces of statuary."[72] Down the street at McVicker's Theater, ticketholders encountered "the better English drama and comedy" in a beautifully renovated space that travel writer Louis Schick deemed "one of the finest" in Chicago, "with its rich, but harmonious decoration."[73]

Audiences at the downtown theaters were drawn chiefly from Chicago's moneyed classes. Working-class patrons sometimes purchased the least expensive tickets, typically for the uppermost balcony. There, as promotional material for McVicker's stated in 1891, "people of humble means" could enjoy, "for twenty-five cents, precisely the same privilege as the man who can afford to pay for a private box."[74] Yet even at twenty-five cents, a theater ticket was a rare treat for most Chicagoans. As Dreiser wrote of the working-class household where Sister Carrie began her stay in Chicago, "going to the theatre was poorly advocated here." Carrie's pleas to attend a show were met by her sister and brother-in-law with "the unspoken shade of disapproval to the doing of things which involved the expenditure of money."[75] Carrie's family was not alone in their hesitation to pay for theater tickets, especially when neighborhood variety houses offered more affordable spectacles without the expectation of refined dress or manners.[76] Accordingly, legitimate theater remained the preserve of moneyed patrons.

Chicago's legitimate theaters were not only financially exclusive but racially exclusive as well. Despite the guarantee of equal access to public accommodations afforded by the Illinois Civil Rights Act of 1885, black patrons were invariably restricted to the house's cheapest seats, usually in a separate corner of the upper balcony. As interpreted by most theater managers, the law simply prohibited outright exclusion from, not segregation within, public accommodations. Even after Josephine Curry, an African American woman married to a Chicago doctor, successfully sued People's Theater in 1888 for refusing to seat her on the main floor, the practice of segregating black patrons continued unabated.[77] Mere days after the verdict was handed down in Curry's case, the Columbia Theater refused to seat the Reverend Birdie Wilkins on the main floor parquet, instead ushering him to balcony seats reserved for African Americans.[78] Notably, only black consumers were unwelcome on the first floor of Chicago's theaters. Black workers constituted more than 25 percent of the city's theater employees, a staggering number given that African Americans at that time accounted for less than 2 percent of the total population.[79]

Bounded by race and class, and designed to appeal to affluent guests, downtown theaters were increasingly recognized as leisure spaces suitable for ladies. As such, theater managers sought new ways to capitalize on female consumption.[80] The matinee, or daytime performance, had first been introduced in the 1850s, but its popularity grew dramatically as the rise of new consumer institutions—especially department stores—drew more women into the city center. In the 1897 short story "A Pair of Silk Stockings," set in an unnamed city, Kate Chopin highlights the link between shopping and theatergoing. After discovering a small windfall, the main character, "little Mrs. Sommers," goes to a department store and purchases a few small luxuries, including silk stockings and magazines, before "her next temptation presents itself in the shape of a matinee poster." Enticed into the theater, Mrs. Sommers soon discovers that it is packed with women. "But there were vacant seats here and there, and into one of them she was ushered, between brilliantly dressed women who had gone there to kill time and eat candy and display their gaudy attire."[81] In this story, the leisured, feminine atmosphere of the department store extends into the confines of the theater.

Shopping and theatergoing reinforced each other.[82] In Chicago, the first-class playhouses were all located near the great department stores. The Columbia Theater, for example, was situated around the corner from the Fair, while McVicker's was across the street from the Boston Store and a half block from Schlesinger & Mayer. The proximity of these institutions encouraged ladies to go from one to the other. In her journal, Frances Glessner regularly recorded combining shopping with a matinee. Typical was an entry from March 1893:

> Yesterday I did some shopping in the morning. In the afternoon I went to the orchestral matinee where beside a magnificent program we had Paderewski, who played his concerto with the orchestra and in the second part played three solos.
>
> I sat in the parquet with Fanny Zeisler. Mrs. von Holst, Mary, Mrs. Hale, Mrs. Lawrence were in the box with Fanny [Glessner's daughter] and Miss Scharff.[83]

As Glessner's account illustrates, male escorts were not required at daytime performances. Typically, Glessner attended matinees with female relatives or friends. Other women also embraced the sociability of matinees. "As a rule," noted one observer, "the girls attend the matinees in pairs, and sometimes they go in groups."[84]

By the early 1890s, Chicago's downtown theaters all offered regular matinees on Wednesdays and Saturdays. These performances, in the words of one theater manager, "always attract[ed] women."[85] The vast majority were moneyed women, who could afford the high ticket prices and felt at ease in the sumptuous surroundings. Moreover, they possessed the leisure time to attend midday shows in an era when the work week still stretched into Saturday. Many of the women were young and unmarried, free from the obligations of running their own households. Their pursuit of amusement soon inspired a new urban type—the matinee girl. She was impulsive, autonomous, and, above all, devoted to pleasure.[86] In 1897, *Munsey's* offered an account of her origins:

> The matinee girl is unquestionably a product of the end of the century. That she is *fin de siècle* does not need to be proved, for it is well known that only in recent years has the privilege of attending theaters been allowed to young women unescorted by brother or father, or the creature known by the elastic and accommodating term "cousin." This last decade of the nineteenth century has brought to girlhood the inestimable joy of going wherever her own sweet will dictates, unescorted and unprotected.

Munsey's overestimated the freedoms afforded the matinee girl. After all, social convention still prevented her "sweet will" from carrying her unaccompanied to second-tier theaters and variety shows. Nevertheless, matinees granted women from "the cultured and highly respectable ranks of society" new opportunities to savor commercial recreation without the constraints of a male escort.[87]

This very freedom unsettled many observers, who feared the matinee girl would abandon herself to sensuous pleasures. Invariably, her critics highlighted the sociability and emotional enjoyment women derived from theater attendance. *Munsey's*, for example, complained that matinee audiences too often burst into tears because they allowed their feelings to "have full sway when the sterner and more practical sex is away."[88] In an article on the "Best Known Matinee Girl in Chicago," the *Chicago Tribune* expressed concern about women who went to the theater to "whisper and laugh and cry and giggle, and just have a 'perfectly heavenly time' together" while enjoying "all the bonbons they can eat."[89] Whereas female patrons had once been expected to minimize their presence at playhouses—not daring to laugh, clap, or eat candy—matinee girls now brazenly savored all that the theater had to offer.

Newly aware of this lucrative female market, managers began to court female audiences for evening performances as well as matinees. In addition to crafting a luxurious atmosphere, they appealed to women consumers by staging lighthearted musical comedies and sentimental melodramas showcasing female leads in the latest fashions.[90] During a typical week, Chicago's first-class theaters were dominated by such fare. One week in June 1893, for example, the Grand Theater staged the drama *April Weather* by renowned playwright Clyde Fitch, while the Auditorium hosted a troupe of magicians; the Columbia presented an operetta starring Lillian Russell; the Chicago Opera House introduced a new ballet "executed by seven coryphées"; Hooley's offered a romantic comedy titled *The Professor's Love Story*; the Schiller Theater continued a run of the musical *The Girl I Left Behind Me*; and McVicker's celebrated the 101st night of *The Black Crook*, a musical comedy featuring an enormous female corps de ballet and tunes such as "You Naughty, Naughty Men."[91] The shift in focus disturbed many theater critics, who called for more cerebral, morality-driven drama. But managers were acutely aware that women—and not theater critics—filled the house seats. To further entice female customers, managers introduced new services, such as women ushers and elegantly appointed retiring rooms, staffed with matrons dedicated to helping guests readjust their gowns and coiffure.[92] The results helped transform the theater from a rowdy, male-dominated clubhouse into a refined preserve for moneyed women.[93]

By the final decade of the century, contemporary reports held that between two-thirds and three-quarters of theater audiences were composed of women.[94] "It is an admitted fact," noted *Munsey's* in 1897, "that woman is the mainstay of the amusement business."[95] Once a masculine domain frequented by prostitutes, the theater now relied on the patronage of respectable women for its financial health.[96] "The theater lives by ladies and for them," announced one Chicago observer in 1895.[97] Women wielded tremendous influence over the operational choices made by managers. "All theatrical managers try to produce plays which please the women. . . . They have got to please the women or starve," insisted theater critic Walter Prichard Eaton.[98] Fellow critic Clayton Hamilton similarly apprised the situation. "For, nowadays at least, it is most essential that the drama should appeal to a mob of women," Hamilton argued. "Practically speaking, our matinee audiences are composed entirely of women, and our evening audiences are composed chiefly of women and the men that they have brought with them. Very few men go to the theater unattached."[99] Unsurprisingly, the tastes and predilections of female patrons were increasingly privileged over those of men. *Munsey's* described the phenomenon as the "business of pandering" to the modern girl.[100]

The theater thus joined the department store as a commercial institution devoted to women's consumption. In both spaces, managers promoted a culture of fashion, desire, and display. In particular, managers sought to ensure that leading actresses were richly garbed in the latest styles.[101] These fashions sometimes proved more alluring than the productions themselves. In 1896, for example, a writer for the *Chicago Tribune*'s entertainment section suggested that the greatest attraction of Lillian Russell's new operetta at the Great Northern Theater was her stylish gowns. "It is not inapropos to give homage to the dressmaker at the outset, for the dressmaker has done more than either the librettist or the composer in this latest production of Miss Russell's," the writer declared.[102] Russell had many of her tour costumes fashioned by a dressmaker in Chicago, a detail covered extensively by the press. Such reportage was hardly unusual. Women's magazines and newspaper articles were filled with details concerning the modishly made gowns of theatrical stars, reinforcing the emergent culture of consumer desire.[103]

Yet the commodity spectacle presented at the theater extended far beyond the footlights. In his *Theory of the Leisure Class*, Veblen identified the theater as one of the critical spaces wherein women were able to showcase their "pecuniary strength."[104] The promenade, which occurred between acts, offered a crucial vehicle for exhibition. "The lady goes to the opera not only to see but to be seen," stated Eliza Bisbee Duffey, "and her dress must be adopted with a full realization of the . . . hundred lorgnettes which will be no less spying."[105] As Veblen and Duffey were aware, the grand interiors and crush of affluent patrons promoted an atmosphere of conspicuous—and competitive—display. Galleries designated for promenading proliferated in the second half of the nineteenth century. "In our new opera houses," explained etiquette writer Florence Hartley, "there are rooms for promenade, and between the acts your escort may invite you to walk there." When promenading, ladies and their male escorts circled the room, exhibiting their finery and greeting acquaintances. "In walking up and down in the promenading saloon, you may pass and repass friends," Hartley warned.[106] The repetition and ritual of this practice heightened the sense of pageantry.[107]

Contemporary novelists captured the air of feminine display and conspicuous consumption that pervaded fin de siècle theaters. In his classic Chicago novel *The Pit*, for example, Frank Norris offers a vivid account of the lobby of the Auditorium Theater on the evening of an opera performance: "Everywhere the eye was arrested by the luxury of stuffs, the brilliance and delicacy of fabrics, laces as white and soft as

froth, crisp, shining silks, suave satins, heavy gleaming velvets, and bro-
cades and plushes, nearly all of them white—violently so—dazzling
and splendid under the blaze of the electrics." According to Norris, the
spectacle was amplified between acts, when "everybody was promenading" and the "air was filled with the staccato chatter of a multitude
of women."[108] Many of these sights also arrest the interest of the main
character in Hamlin Garland's 1895 novel, *Rose of Dutcher's Coolly*. Upon
attending her first performance at a Chicago theater, Rose, an aspiring
writer, is overcome by "the beauty and grandeur" of the scene. "Around
her the boxes filled with girls in gowns of pink, and rose, and blue, and
faint green. Human flowers they seemed, dewed with diamonds," Garland wrote. The spectacle of the crowd—"the beautiful dresses! the
dainty bonnets! the flow of perfumed drapery! the movement of strong,
clean, supple limbs!"—all kindle Rose's desire for more luxuries.[109]

The feminization of the American theater, which began slowly in the
mid-nineteenth century and culminated in the 1890s, set the stage for
the high hat crisis. By the time the city council approved the hat bill in
1897, Chicago ladies had become the mainstay of the theatrical business,
and managers were ever more reluctant to alienate their fair patrons.
In light of this shift, the answer to the puzzle posed by *Munsey's* the preceding year required little explanation. "It seems odd," a writer for the
magazine had mused, "that we have no manager who is bold enough to
take decisive steps against this big hat nuisance."[110] The financial stakes
were simply too high. Even Will Davis, who had initiated his own crusade against the high hat at the Columbia Theater, had reversed his position after encountering staunch resistance from his lady patrons.[111] In
1896, three years after his initial anti-hat efforts, Davis announced his
"gallant resignation" and insisted that "it is altogether useless to agitate
the subject further." When pressed for a statement, Davis alluded to financial motivation. "Women are all so beautiful," he proposed, "that
men cannot afford to cavil at what they wear."[112] Those who could least
afford to cavil, of course, were managers such as Davis.

As theater managers grew more resistant to constraining their lady patrons, many other Chicagoans were increasingly insistent on the rights
owed to them as consumers. The final decade of the nineteenth century
saw a wave of consumer activism, driven by Progressive reformers and
their allies in journalism and academe. The signal achievements of this

effort were the enactment of the Pure Food and Drug Act and the Meat
Inspection Act, both in 1906, which set minimum standards for food
safety and quality.[113] Yet long before attaining these national measures,
consumer advocates had won numerous state and local reforms in a
range of industries—from meatpacking and brewing to streetcar service
and retail sales.[114] These victories helped promote public awareness of
the rights of paying customers—and, crucially, an expectation that the
state would intervene in private commercial affairs to safeguard those
rights. Ultimately, this emergent reform movement encouraged ordinary
Americans to think of themselves as consumers and to entertain legal
and legislative remedies to abuses encountered in the marketplace.

Much like Progressivism itself, consumer activism established a
stronghold in Chicago. Throughout the 1890s, the city was awash in
consumer rights claims, as reformers and activists agitated for new consumer protections.[115] Among their earliest efforts were campaigns to
prevent the adulteration of milk, bread, and meat products.[116] Indeed, a
decade before muckraker Upton Sinclair began working undercover in
the city's slaughterhouses to research his 1906 novel, *The Jungle,* Chicago
reformers were demanding—and receiving—new food safety regulations and increased transparency in product labeling.[117] In 1897, for
example, shortly after Mayor Swift signed the theater hat bill into law,
he approved another city ordinance that prohibited makers of butterine,
or margarine, from tinting their products yellow and mandated the use
of "imitation butter" labels. The ordinance's objective was to prevent the
"deceiving of customers" who might purchase butterine assuming it was
real butter.[118] A similar measure had been introduced to the state legislature two years earlier by a senator from Chicago. "This is a fraud on
the consumer," the senator had claimed at the time. "He is not getting
what he paid for."[119]

Services, too, captured the interest of consumer advocates. Most notably, Chicago hosted a pitched battle over the regulation of streetcars.
At the center of this conflict was Charles T. Yerkes, the notorious "Goliath
of Graft."[120] Since the early 1890s, Yerkes had attempted to gain a monopoly over the city's street railways, and as his control grew, customer
satisfaction declined. Other streetcar lines also suffered from service
problems, but Yerkes lived in the press as the source of all consumer
woes: poorly heated and ventilated cars, unreliable schedules, insufficient rush-hour coverage, and, above all, overcrowding. These frustra-

tions converged in the figure of the "straphanger"—a rider forced to stand holding one of the leather straps transit operators had installed to expand streetcar capacity. Denied the very seat for which his fare had supposedly paid, the straphanger came to embody consumer exploitation in the popular imagination. As the "straphanger evil" grew, many Chicagoans began to call for state regulation, fueling a broad-based movement for municipal ownership of transit companies.[121] Strikingly, on the same day the city council approved the high hat ordinance, they also debated a new law requiring streetcar companies to provide all paying customers with seats.[122]

Theaters were hardly streetcars. Still, many of the questions raised by the "traction problem" were echoed in the debate over theater hats. What rights did the purchase of a car fare or theater ticket grant the consumer? And what role should the state play in protecting those rights? By the mid-1890s, a growing number of theatergoers had come to believe not only that ticketholders were entitled to an unobstructed view of the stage but that government regulation offered a viable means of safeguarding this view. "Anybody who goes to the theater is liable to the exasperation and loss of being seated behind a huge hat," observed one journalist. "That it is an outrage, since it deprives persons of a right for which they pay, is beyond all question." To protect the rights of paying customers, the journalist saw a clear path forward: "There appears to be no remedy except in a legislative enactment."[123] *Munsey's* came to the same conclusion, stressing that the rights of paying customers trumped those of conspicuously adorned ladies. "We are opposed on principle to unnecessary legislative interference with individual liberties," the magazine assured its readers, "but the strong arm of the law is an effective remedy when milder methods have been tried in vain." According to *Munsey's*, protecting those who "paid for their seats in a place of public amusement" from the high-hatted lady was a legitimate use of state power. "If she cannot be suppressed without legislation," argued *Munsey's*, "let there be a statute severe enough to meet the necessities of the case."[124]

On the surface, theater hat legislation seemed to share more in common with familiar constraints on women's consumption than with consumer protection laws. But unlike efforts to regulate dance halls or other spaces of cheap amusement, high hat regulations were advanced as a means of protecting *other consumers*—not women themselves, or their morality.[125] Accordingly, theater managers were increasingly identified alongside high-hatted women as the parties responsible for the problem. Ladies in large hats were still viewed as selfish and vain, but managers who permitted these women to obstruct other patrons' views were charged with violating the rights of ticketholders. "The only persons who can abate the big hat nuisance are the managers of the theaters," contended an 1895 editorial in the *Chicago Tribune*. "Sail into the managers and make life a burden to them." If the problem persisted, the author added, the "fault is with the theater-going people who are annoyed by big hats, and who, instead of making a row with the manager and telling him they will stay away if he does not protect them, will work off their wrath writing letters."[126]

By the mid-1890s, many Chicagoans agreed that the high hat nuisance marked a failure of consumer protection. And, indeed, many indicted theater managers for indulging women's selfishness while neglecting to safeguard the rights of paying customers. In the summer of 1896, one Chicago man sought to illustrate this point in a protest that concluded with his arrest. Thomas Lavender, an official in the city's water department, purchased a ticket to a performance at the Chicago Opera House, where his view was obscured by a woman "with a hat of the cartwheel style." Incensed, Lavender resolved to retain his own high hat. When two police officers approached him and requested he remove his headgear, Lavender refused. According to the *Chicago Tribune*'s report, "Lavender could not see why he did not have as much right to wear his hat as the woman, because he had paid the same price of admission." The officers apparently disagreed. As they ejected him, Lavender "grew abusive" and was then escorted to the Central Station jail.[127] The incident highlighted the gendered etiquette that made the high hat problem so intractable. A growing number of Chicagoans, however, were unwilling to continue to defer to the high-hatted lady. Instead, they sought to enlist state action to protect the broader consuming public.

In January 1895, at the start of the new theatrical season, Alexander J. Jones, a Democrat from Chicago, introduced to the Illinois General Assembly a bill making it a misdemeanor to "obstruct the vision of any other patron" in a commercial amusement space by wearing "any hat, bonnet, or other unsightly head covering." Framed as a defense of consumer interests, Jones's bill promised to "protect the rights and secure the comfort of patrons of theaters, opera houses, lecture halls, concert halls, and other places of amusement."[128] Penalties of up to $25 fell on those who persisted in wearing their hats as well as on any managers who failed to enforce the provisions of the law. According to Jones, a recent violation of his own consumer rights at the Auditorium Theater had spurred him to action. "I had a seat near the front which cost one of my friends $2," he revealed. "A dude from Blue Island with his girl sat in front of me and she had on a hat 7 feet in circumference and 2 feet in diameter. That ended all hope of seeing anything." The frustration and disappointment of that evening, Jones insisted, served as "the hair which broke the camel's back."[129] No longer would he sit idly by while large hats destroyed the pleasure and trampled on the rights of the consuming public.

Although many Chicagoans viewed Jones as a pioneering crusader, his anti–theater hat efforts aligned with similar initiatives arising in other states. In January, when Jones introduced his bill, state legislators from New York and Missouri proposed their own anti–theater hat laws. The following month, comparable measures were put forward by lawmakers from Massachusetts and California.[130] In each instance, the sponsor characterized sight-obstructing headgear as a threat to consumer rights. The legislator behind the New York bill, for example, reported he was moved to act after spending an evening at a theater where the managers claimed they were "unable to regulate [their] patrons' dress" and, as such, could not compel the woman seated in front of him to remove her hat. Much like Jones, this lawmaker hoped his bill would guarantee paying customers an "unobstructed view" and "unimpaired enjoyment" of theatrical performances.[131]

When Jones took office in the fall of 1894, just three months before introducing his theater hat legislation, he identified as a reformer. Since 1893, the journalist-turned-lawyer had been a member of the Civic Federation, an organization founded in the wake of British reformer William T. Stead's lecture series "If Christ Came to Chicago" and devoted to improving "the material, social and moral conditions of our municipal life." Under the leadership of such prominent citizens as Jane Addams, Bertha Palmer, and Lyman Gage, the Civic Federation became one of Chicago's leading reform agencies, addressing issues ranging from sanitation and education to tax reform and labor arbitration.[132] Mere weeks before introducing the high hat bill, Jones underscored the influence this organization had on his legislative goals. "I am a member of the Civic Federation of the City of Chicago," he explained, "and as such am prepared to favor the legislative action necessary to secure a thorough and non-partisan investigation of the municipal government of the County of Cook." Jones also hoped to increase public oversight of commercial relations, especially disputes between corporations and their employees.[133]

Upon initiating his anti–theater hat efforts, Jones made clear that his bill had neither been prepared nor endorsed by the Civic Federation. Nevertheless, he touted the act as a "reform measure . . . in the interests of a long-suffering people."[134] Those long-suffering people were, of course, male theater patrons. "My bill will fill an aching void in the heart of every male lover of the play," Jones predicted.[135] He maintained that public sentiment was "overwhelmingly" in his favor and that the bill would quickly become law.[136] Early reports seemed to corroborate this view. According to the *Chicago Tribune*, the Committee on the Judiciary—the body to which the bill had been referred—unanimously supported the measure and would soon usher it through the House.[137] Ordinary male citizens were also thought to be squarely in Jones's corner. "When Representative Alexander J. Jones framed a bill for the Illinois Legislature to regulate woman's high hat," the *Tribune* alleged, "thousands of masculine sufferers sent up a loud and long shout."[138]

But not all Chicagoans endorsed Jones's bill. The first to object were the managers charged with enforcing its provisions. "Chicago Managers Doubt the Wisdom of an Anti–High Hat Law," announced the *Chicago Herald* the morning after the bill was introduced. The city's theater managers, according to the *Herald*, had grave reservations about the law's enforceability and believed women would simply refuse to comply. "The bill doesn't interest me," declared the co-manager of the Grand Opera House. "I am not in sympathy with any special legislation, and should be the last one to legislate against ladies on matters concerning their apparel. If a high hat is becoming to a woman she is going to wear it whether she goes to a theater or to a funeral." At Hooley's Theater, manager Harry Powers was no less skeptical. "It would be impossible to enforce such a law as Mr. Jones has introduced. Managers have a right to stop the wearers of high hats at the door if they choose, but they will scarcely adopt such a plan." These concerns were echoed by Tom Prior of the Schiller Theater and Will Davis of the Columbia, both of whom insisted that ladies' millinery could never be regulated. "I fail to see the utility of the law as long as hats are hats and women are women," Prior quipped. Davis, perhaps reflecting on his own failed crusade, was even more fatalistic. "The women," he concluded, "will wear what ever fancy and fashion decrees, regardless of Mr. Jones or any other legislator."[139]

While theater managers queried enforcement, other Chicagoans were alarmed by the potential restrictions on individual freedom. An editorial in the *Chicago Tribune* observed that the measure seemed "to trample ruthlessly on the platform of the Illinois Democracy, of which Mr. Jones is a member." According to the author, "that platform declares that 'sumptuary laws infringing upon the individual rights of the citizens are not to be countenanced.'" If such an obvious violation of personal freedom could become law, the author warned, legislators might also prohibit coughing, whispering, and applauding at inappropriate times. To further underscore the bill's absurdity, the author proposed an amendment such that "any man who goes to a show and is cheated out of any part of it by reason of the misconduct of any of the misdemeanants mentioned above shall be entitled to a proper rebate."[140] Jones's former employer, the *Chicago Times,* offered a similar perspective in an article penned by a New York critic. "The anti-hat bill besides being too sumptuary for our taste, represents too spasmodic an attempt to regulate the habits of women through state legislation," the writer asserted. "If it should be enacted we believe that a great many women would refuse to go to the theater."[141]

Chicago ladies greeted the bill with mixed emotions. Many acknowledged that large hats posed a problem and advocated smaller styles. "There is but one thing to be said," opined Kate Huddleston, secretary of the Chicago Woman's Club and the Illinois Federation of Women's Clubs—"that is, that the theater hat should not be of such proportions that it will obstruct the view. It is in keeping with the principle that we should never intrude on rights of others." Mary Ellis, an early supporter of the Art Institute of Chicago and widow of a leading Chicago divine, agreed: "It is not right for any one to do anything to take away the rights of others. Out of the principle grows the fact that it is not right for a woman to wear a large theater hat, inasmuch as it imposes on the rights of others." After noting that European women did not wear hats to the theater, Jennie Gunther, wife of candy manufacturer Charles Gunther, stated simply, "The large hat at a place of amusement is an imposition."[142]

Yet even ladies who objected to oversized theater hats tended to look unfavorably on Jones's bill. In their view, women themselves, not lawmakers, should act as agents of change. "It seems exceedingly ridiculous to introduce a bill against any article of dress," remarked Mary Plummer, a prominent clubwoman and wife of a corporate lawyer. Reform, she argued, "must come through women of wealth and culture, who can start an innovation." These sentiments were echoed by numerous other women. "The measure is to be regretted," commented Ellen Martin Henrotin, "because women should make the decision themselves." Marion Foster Washburne, a writer and suffragist, recommended that women's clubs take charge of the matter, as she did "not believe any bill can effect the reform."[143] In a letter to the editor of the *Chicago Tribune*, a woman identified only as J. W. H. went so far as to advocate creating a new women's group devoted to eliminating theater hats. "We have an Audubon Society, a Humane Society, a Society of the King's Daughters, societies of all kinds and degrees," she wrote. "Will not our cultivated, considerate, broad-minded women and girls, as a society array themselves against this indefensible, shameful, alas, purely American custom."[144]

More than ineffective or unnecessary, some women viewed Jones's bill as downright discriminatory. The bill was "purely sex legislation—one of the most odious of all forms of class legislation," according to Mary H. Krout, a journalist who covered political and social issues for the *Inter Ocean*.[145] In her view, the proposed law unfairly targeted women, who, as non-voters, were "without means of defense or redress."[146] Both sexes, she suggested, indulged in habits that could annoy other theatergoers. "The man who goes out between every act, who treads on your toes, thrusts his elbows in your face . . . is quite as unbearable a nuisance as the wearer of the cart-wheel hat," Krout contended.[147] Yet the freedom of men to move about the theater was not at risk—lawmakers intended only to regulate women's practices. "[Men] themselves have no pleasure in wearing broad-brimmed hats blazing with flowers," Krout observed. If they had, "it goes without saying that there would be no legislation against it."[148]

Jones's colleagues in Springfield approached the bill with less gravity. Despite Jones's insistence that he had introduced the measure "in all seriousness," many fellow legislators viewed the issue as a joke. According to the *Inter Ocean*, when the bill finally came up for discussion in the

House Judiciary Committee, "There was considerable levity."[149] After another member proposed an amendment prohibiting theater patrons from leaving their seats between acts, the bill was referred to a subcommittee charged with evaluating its merits. From the start, the prospect of Jones's bill making it out of the subcommittee seemed bleak. The very announcement of the committee's formation was reportedly "received with an outburst of laughter."[150] Reflecting on the legislature's next move, the *Chicago Tribune* articulated what many lawmakers were likely already thinking: "It is not the business of a State to regulate clothing."[151] A month later, the five-member subcommittee issued an unfavorable report.[152]

Jones's bill was dead. But the outcry against theater hats persisted—and, indeed, grew louder. In early 1896, Chicagoans were stunned to learn Ohio's state legislature had succeeded in passing a theater hat regulation. Many had expected the measure to fail, as had its predecessors in Illinois, New York, Massachusetts, Missouri, and California. But the Ohio bill's sponsor, Cincinnati Republican Philip C. Fosdick, triumphed after amending the bill to direct penalties solely at theater managers—and not at women who wore high hats.[153] With this revision, Fosdick secured the sympathy of many theater-loving ladies across the state. In Columbus, efforts to rally support were so successful that when the measure finally made its way to the Ohio Senate, "prominent society women" filled the galleries of the statehouse to applaud the legislators who voted in its favor.[154]

Despite early enthusiasm, the Fosdick law proved an "empty victor[y]" for theater hat opponents.[155] The measure was never enforced by the state, ensuring that most women openly defied its provisions. On the first evening after the bill went into effect, female patrons of several of Cincinnati's first-class theaters refused to remove their headgear. At the Grand Theater, for example, the "auditorium looked like a small conservatory when the curtain went up, and several men changed their seats perforce to get a glimpse of the performance."[156] Nearly a year later, compliance had not improved. "Instead of any perceptible diminishment in the size of these hanging vistas of horticulture," noted one observer, "there has been a marked determination to aggravate their floral splendor."[157] Toledo capitalist S. C. Schenck offered a similar appraisal, insisting "the big hat still flaunts its tantalizing feathers in the parquet circle." In Schenck's view, the law had been a "dead letter" from the start. "There were a few spasmodic efforts [by managers] to enforce the statute," he explained, "but theaters are run on business principles, and the managers of them dislike to offend their patrons as much as men in other lines of business do."[158]

In nearby Chicago, Ohio's enforcement woes were quickly glossed over, and news of Fosdick's legislative success was met with congratulations and support. "Hats off to the peerless buckeye state!" exclaimed the *Chicago Times-Herald*. "It was taken for granted that Representative Fosdick's bill was merely a bit of legislative frivolity," the paper reported. "But Mr. Fosdick is sincere in the belief that a man who pays $3 for a seat at a theater and has to sit behind a hanging garden of roses, waving plumes and gayley pinioned birds should have some means of redress."[159] The *Chicago Tribune*, which only a year earlier had dismissed Jones's bill as absurd, was also enthusiastic. "The anti–theater hat crusade has passed beyond the humorous stage," the paper conceded before praising Fosdick's strategy of penalizing only managers. "Who cares if the manager of a theater is fined?" the *Tribune* queried. "Besides, the idea is a rational one. . . . The man who harbors on his premises a nuisance is responsible therefore."[160] The shift in tone was notable. By late 1896, many Chicagoans had ceased to regard with mirth the suggestion that the state regulate theater hats. The time had come to act.

In the wake of these legislative failures, the high hat's persistence seemed notable. "The Theater Hat has been an object of so much discussion, derision, and denunciation that it might have been expected to shrink into insignificance and retire into innocuous desuetude long ago," argued a writer for *Munsey's* not long after Jones's bill was defeated. "As a matter of fact, however, its vitality and exuberance seem to be greater than ever."[161] For many observers, the style's tenacity was especially puzzling given that European women had long since ceased to wear hats in the theater.[162] Although some American women had adopted the habit of removing their headgear, many more clung tightly to their millinery.[163] "For all that has been said and written about it," noted Harry Powers of Hooley's Theater in late 1896, "there seem to be as many [large hats] now in the theaters as ever before." Louis Sharpe of McVicker's agreed: "We have given the women every encouragement in the way of retiring-rooms and matrons, with no success whatsoever."[164] The intractability of the problem raised a key question: Why, in the face of strong public opposition, did high-hatted ladies fail to heed calls for reform?

Searching for an explanation, Will Davis of the Columbia Theater foregrounded the habits not of women but of men. In contrast to Europe, where leisured aristocrats filled the theaters, the male theater-going public of the United States, Davis observed, was composed mostly of businessmen. European elites often lived "entirely on their incomes" and therefore possessed "plenty of time to devote to dressing for the theater." But American businessmen kept regular hours, ensuring that their theater outings were appended to the end of a workday, when changing into formalwear was inconvenient. Men's clothing choices determined the options available to the ladies whom they escorted. If a man wore street clothes, his female companion would be obligated to avoid eveningwear, thereby ceding her option to appear bareheaded, a style reserved solely for formal dress. The result, according to Davis, was that in most cities in the United States, "the major portion of the audience is in the ordinary street and commercial dress of the day."[165]

More obviously, women kept their millinery firmly on their heads for practical reasons. Unlike men's hats, which could be quickly doffed, women's hats were secured by extensive pinning, tying, and tucking. To keep hairstyles neat and hats on straight, ladies often required the aid of a mirror and, in some cases, another set of hands. Women who did take off their hats struggled to store them. "[Women's hats] are not like men's hats," asserted one woman. "You can't roll 'em up in your mackintosh with your galoshes and have 'em come out all right or put 'em under the seat in the frame, or have them stuffed into little pigeon-holes of boxes and checked like storm cloaks." To sit with a three-foot-wide hat in one's lap was hardly comfortable. Nor did it guarantee the hat's safety, as the same commentator emphasized: "Of course she can hold [a hat] in her lap and have one more thing to drop when every man in the row between every act of the play promenaded out over her feet."[166] Some ladies attempted to avoid this conundrum by wearing jeweled combs or headdresses. But these styles, like going bareheaded, were reserved for formal dress, which remained uncommon at evening performances and entirely inappropriate for matinees.

More than practicality hung on the feathery brims of theater hats, however. A hat carried tremendous social significance and communicated a lady's status.[167] In his analysis of women's dress, Veblen claimed that large hats helped underscore the leisured station of the wearer. "The more elegant styles of feminine bonnets go even farther towards making work impossible than does the man's high hat," he noted.[168] At the same time, heavy ornamentation exhibited conspicuous waste. An 1894 illustration from *Life* magazine captured this spirit of display. Titled "A Woman's Reason," the drawing reveals an elegantly dressed woman seated in a theater, where her stylish millinery obstructs the stage. In the accompanying text, her husband asks why she insists on wearing her high hat. "For the same reason that you wear a Knox hat on the street," the woman responds; "because it's stylish, becoming and attracts attention."[169] Readers would have identified the Knox hat, made by one of the nation's premier hatters, as a status symbol. The Knox Company highlighted the signaling function of headgear in its own advertising: "No one can observe the careful tailoring of your clothes when you sink into the cushions of a lounge in a lobby or the seat of a railroad train. Your hat is then the most conspicuous article of your dress."[170] The same argument held true for ladies at the theater.

For most women, hats were not only status markers but a source of great personal pleasure and pride. In an 1890 column outlining new fall styles, one Chicago fashion commentator reflected on the large hat's particular appeal. "Yes, large hats are not only to be worn but they are to be exceedingly stylish, despite the fact that they are accursed of mankind," she wrote. "This is a bit of news to be deplored by theatergoers, but welcomed by the woman who knows in her secret heart that the large hat gives her a stylish and queenly air, and who knows furthermore and best of all that a large brim throws a soft shadow over the face, which lends the charm of distance and is to imperfections wondrous kind."[171] Several years later, another "well known woman" offered a similar perspective in defending the large theater hat. "[A woman] does not wear a hat because it is necessary," she declared, "but because it is part of her costume. She thinks that her hat is a pretty one and becoming, or else she would not have bought it, and to ask her to leave in a cloakroom or hide in her lap something which she admires and which she thinks adds to her beauty when she has it on her head is preposterous and unreasonable."[172] Self-gratification, then, motivated some women to resist hat reform.

For others, hats took on special political resonance at a moment when women were seizing new opportunities to participate in public life. In donning a hat, a woman staked a claim to the public realm where hats were worn. The more visual space her headgear occupied, the bolder her claim. "Through the huge hat, with its wilderness of bedraggled feathers, the girl announces to the world that she is here. She demands attention to the fact of her existence, she states that she is ready to live, to take her place in the world," observed Jane Addams of young workingwomen in Chicago.[173] Moneyed women, too, used their hats to affirm their presence in public. As one fashion editor explained, when the Chicago lady left the "bosom of her family" and entered the public realm, "she asserted her rights abroad, through her millinery, firmly and determinedly." In describing one historic style, the journalist captured the attitude of women who wore it: "It is flaunting and assertive; impudent and shameless. Towering above the head, flaring at the sides, adorned with waving plumes and fluttering ends of ribbons, it is as hopeless, as far as the man who thinks he has a right to an unobstructed view of the ballet is concerned, as the biggest Gainsborough."[174] Such capacious styles provided a subtle means of claiming belonging in public life.

At least one female theatergoer made explicit this link when she suggested that large hats offered women recompense for their lack of full citizenship. "Women may be denied the right of suffrage by the men that make the laws," she proclaimed, "but they possess a counter-irritant in the theater hat, of whose power they are too fully conscious to give it up easily."[175] In a letter to the editor of the *Chicago Tribune* penned a month after Jones's bill had failed, another woman, who signed her missive "A Woman Fond of Large Hats," attempted to leverage the theater hat to obtain access to the ballot:

> Now surely men know how hard we worked for our small allowance of politics during the last campaign, and how grateful we should have been for more, which same was denied us, possibly by the very men who are now crying out that we are defrauding them of their rights because we persist in wearing (to us) the exceedingly becoming but to them nerve destroying "fiery, untamed theater hat."

The writer proposed a trade: women would support a high hat law and men would grant them "full suffrage at our next Presidential campaign." Should her proposition be accepted, Illinois women would "rise up and bless the name" of any man who had supported it. "Otherwise the fight is on," she warned. "This weapon has been placed at our disposal to do battle with those who seek to deprive us of that which is of far greater importance than a 'Passing Show.'"[176] Her threat, even if exaggerated, revealed the hostility many Chicago women felt toward those who would infringe on their personal freedoms.

None of the reasons ladies refused to relinquish their high hats appeared to interest lawmakers when, on January 5, 1897, the city council unanimously approved an ordinance prohibiting "any hat or bonnet" in licensed theaters.[177] Its author, Alderman Nathan M. Plotke, a German immigrant, had practiced law in Chicago since 1871, had served briefly in the state legislature, and was elected to the city council in 1896 as a Republican. In proposing the ordinance, he claimed to have been inspired by public sentiment: "I heard so much complaint upon all sides about the high hat that I made up my mind to see if something could not be done to give every man who pays a dollar or two a chance to see the stage." The alderman counted himself among the men whose rights had been compromised by the high hat. According to Plotke, the "last straw" had come that Sunday when he was seated behind a "solid wall of feathers and velvet" at a downtown theater. "Two women were in front of me, and when they brought their heads together," he recalled, "I could not see any part of the stage." After the performance, without conferring with his wife, he prepared the ordinance "alone with his conscience" and steeled himself for the coming storm.[178]

Plotke knew that should the law pass, Chicago would be at the forefront of theater hat reform. "Some city had to make a test," he told the press, "and we might as well make a start." But success was not guaranteed, even after all sixty-two aldermen present that day approved the measure.[179] "[The ordinance] was passed with a celerity that would have frightened any woman in the chamber, if one had been present," reported the *Chicago Times-Herald*. "But there was not a woman in attendance. No black eyes could look reproachfully at the aldermen."[180] Early reports predicted Chicago ladies would resist the measure and, ultimately, render it useless. In its account of the proceedings, the *Chicago Tribune* alleged that most women would view the ordinance as "a piece of impudence" and "scorn" its provisions.[181] Meanwhile, the *Inter Ocean* foretold that Alderman Plotke would soon be "the most disliked man in the city council by the ladies who are in the habit of attending theaters."[182] After years of anti–high hat agitation, few observers actually expected Chicago women to relinquish their millinery.

Yet it was the city's theater managers who first stepped forward to oppose the ordinance. As initially penned by Plotke, the measure made it "unlawful for any person, firm or corporation . . . to permit or tolerate the wearing of any hat or other headgear by any person while in the theater or place of amusement during the performance."[183] Penalties of $10 to $25 per hat awaited managers who failed to enforce the ordinance's provisions. The proposed measure thus held theater managers responsible for surveilling female patrons, an obligation that aroused the managers' ire. "How can [the ordinance] be enforced without doing injustice to the manager," asked Milward Adams of the Auditorium Theater. Echoing this concern, Harry Powers of Hooley's Theater insisted, "It is putting it a little strong to say managers must be fined if they do not compel women to remove their hats."[184]

Chicago's theater proprietors argued that the state had no power to intervene in private relations with customers. Their position foreshadowed the argument made by white business owners who opposed the desegregation of public accommodations by race in the mid-twentieth century.[185] At issue in both instances was the state's authority to regulate access to consumer spaces. David Henderson, co-manager of the Columbia Theater, voiced the opinion of many of his colleagues when he denounced the high hat law as unconstitutional. "The theater is not a public institution, and no one has any business to dictate how the manager shall run his house," contended Henderson. "If a woman comes into the place with a hat ten feet high," he continued, "it is the manager's business and the woman's business, and no one's else."[186] Will Davis agreed the state should stay out of the matter. "The Aldermen must, indeed, be suffering from a lack of wise measures to try to regulate such a matter as high hats," he scoffed.[187]

As the city's theater men railed against the ordinance, its author attracted a growing number of supporters. In the days following its introduction, Plotke was reportedly "busy receiving cards of thanks from the long-suffering public."[188] These missives, he claimed, expressed overwhelming support. "All the letters favored it," Plotke told the *Chicago Record*. "Everybody seems to favor it. It looks so much nicer to see pretty, well-dressed hair than a millinery display. We can look at millinery in the stores."[189] One letter, from a correspondent named J. S. Corbin, urged the alderman to stay the course: "For man's sake, keep up the fight to a finish."[190] The *Chicago Chronicle* offered a favorable assessment in a cartoon depicting a man of small stature at the theater. In a panel labeled "Before the Reform Measure," the man is shown craning his neck while seated behind a row of large, feathery hats. In the next panel, "Plotke's Ordinance a Law," the same man is clapping with delight as he enjoys a clear view to the stage (fig. 3.3).[191]

Plotke also won crucial support from city officials. Mayor George B. Swift immediately endorsed the ordinance and announced his determination to sign it. When outlining his motives, Swift invoked the rights of consumers: "When a person buys a ticket and goes to a theater he wants to see the show, and not have his view obstructed by a large piece of millinery on some woman's head in front of him." Chief of police John J. Badenoch likewise backed the measure, informing the press that he would "take pleasure in enforcing its provisions."[192]

The question remained, however, as to how women themselves would respond. Reflecting the public's growing comfort with consumer regulations, some women expressed enthusiasm for the proposed law. "I approve of the ordinance in toto, for even a small hat, with a feather on the side, may be an annoyance to the one sitting behind," reasoned Cornelia Baker, wife of prominent real estate broker Wilson G. Baker.[193] Also favoring the measure was Nellie Pullman Stewart, daughter of railroad magnate George Pullman and wife of wholesale grocer Graeme Stewart. "I think the council has passed one of the best ordinances that ever came before it," she asserted, "and I am glad theatergoers will have an opportunity to see a play without having to dodge some flower-laden or plume-adorned hat."[194]

Many women were less sanguine, however. Mrs. Ferdinand W. Peck, wife of the real estate investor who established the Auditorium Theater, questioned if the law would be obeyed and predicted that "many women would be afraid to leave the head entirely unprotected." Although Joan P. Chalmers, wife of manufacturer W. J. Chalmers, assented that persons "who buy tickets to the theater certainly have a right to an unobstructed view of the stage," she did not believe managers should be "compelled to enforce this rule." Meanwhile, Mrs. H. O. Stone, whose husband had made his fortune in real estate, commended the purpose of the ordi-

THE ANTI-THEATER HAT LAW IN CHICAGO.

BEFORE THE REFORM MEASURE.   PLOTKE'S ORDINANCE A LAW.
                                              —Chicago Chronicle.

Figure 3.3 In this comic reprinted from the *Chicago Chronicle*, a frustrated male theatergoer is initially denied a view of the stage due to the large headgear of the women seated in front of him. After the passage of Alderman Nathan Plotke's ordinance prohibiting theater hats, the same man delights in having a clear view of the performance.   "The Anti-Theater Hat Law in Chicago," *St. Louis Republic*, Jan. 7, 1897, 6.

nance but challenged the "propriety of saying that women should be compelled to remove their hats."[195]

Some women went so far as to denounce Plotke's ordinance as a violation of personal liberty. In accounting for these critics, the *Chicago Tribune* noted that those who "defend the wearing of hats do so for the reason that a woman has rights of her own, and they belong to the type of new woman who have no use for the ordinary courtesies of their sex."[196] One such "new woman" was Mary E. Miller, a practicing attorney and suffrage advocate. In an interview with the *Chicago Times-Herald*, Miller suggested that the city council had recklessly disregarded women's rights by attempting to regulate theater hats. "These stalwart councilmen of ours, headed by their own Plotke and applauded by our reform mayor, in a matter like this, where only the personal liberty of women is concerned, not only do not hesitate, but indeed madly rush to pass most unjust and illegal acts," Miller declared. In her view, the council had overstepped its authority. It was "reviving pagan practices and sumptuary laws that have long been considered too savage and tyrannical for semi-enlightened people such as we, behaving, indeed, as if it were the prerogative of any legislature in our land to dictate the time and place where particular raiment should be worn."[197]

According to Miller, in passing the ordinance, Chicago lawmakers had started down a slippery slope leading to further restrictions on women's freedom and, ultimately, a denial of their self-sovereignty. "Who knows but that the next act of this council may prescribe that women shall wear pink knitted hoods, both summer and winter, whenever they have occasion to appear in the street," she reflected, "and this might lead to another act which is much desired by some of our husbands and brothers and uncles, and that is that all women shall finish shopping and go home before 5 P.M." Miller was not far off the mark, as the campaign for shopping time limits demonstrated a decade later. But in 1897, she could only speculate. Miller advised Chicago women to resist the theater hat law in order to prevent the further erosion of their rights. "If this ordinance is meant seriously," she argued, "then must women meet it so, and by united resistance exert what strength their anomalous position affords."[198] Their anomalous position, of course, was their status as non-voters governed by an all-male city council.

Other "new women" joined Miller in her opposition. Mary Krout, the *Inter Ocean* journalist who had protested the proposed 1895 state law, identified Plotke's ordinance as a flagrant instance of "the voting sex outrageously discriminating against the disfranchised."[199] Adopting a similar framework, Catherine Waugh McCulloch, president of the Chicago Political Equality League, labeled the ordinance an exhibition in "tyranny and idiocy."[200] McCulloch had long disapproved of high hats.[201] Nevertheless, she warned Chicago ladies that Plotke's ordinance placed their personal freedom at risk. "This obnoxious ordinance, though apparently directed against the managers of houses of public amusement, still is in reality an ordinance forbidding women to wear certain head adornments," she asserted. In her view, such restraints were the inevitable result of a political system in which "the rights and liberties and privileges of women are left wholly to the caprice of male legislators." So long as women lacked the vote, she claimed, "so long can women expect such sumptuary laws."[202]

Critics such as McCulloch and Krout likely rejoiced when, a week after the measure was approved, reports began circulating that the mayor planned to exercise his veto power. "Mayor Swift's veto will doubtless suffice to put a quietus on theater hat legislation for some time to come," predicted a reporter for the *Chicago Times-Herald*.[203] But Swift's initial rejection did not spell the end of Plotke's law. The mayor sent the bill back to the city council with two proposed changes that laid bare the gendered inequities at the measure's core. First, Swift called for exemptions for skullcaps and close-fitting knit hats of the type worn by bald men, such as the mayor himself. Second, he recommended that wearers of high hats, and not merely theater managers, face penalties for noncompliance.[204] "The wearer [of a high hat] will be taken in custody after the performance by a policeman and be given the privilege of going to jail or giving up $3 as a guarantee of appearance at trial," explained the *Chicago Tribune*.[205] With these revisions in place, Plotke once again ushered the ordinance through the city council—this time by a vote of 47 to 6.[206]

Even before Mayor Swift could sign the revised ordinance, Chicagoans wondered if Plotke's law would join Fosdick's as a toothless empty victory. Early reports suggested Chicago ladies were poised to resist enforcement. "WOMEN DEFY THE HAT ORDINANCE," announced a *Chicago Tribune* headline in early January. Shortly after the ordinance's proposal, reporters for that paper "made a careful survey of several leading theaters" to appraise women's compliance. Their results revealed a "preponderance of hats." At the Columbia Theater, for example, 126 women appeared in hats, while only 31 went bareheaded. At McVicker's, the numbers were similar: 128 women in hats to 36 sans chapeau. Across the downtown theaters, reporters observed nearly twice as many women in headgear as without. The display, they concluded, sent a clear message: "The conspicuous exhibition must be regarded as a declaration to the world that the new woman doesn't intend to allow herself to be regulated by man in his capacity as Alderman or any other capacity."[207]

Both the ordinance and Chicago women's responses to it captured the attention of newspapers across the country. "Every community has felt the desolating touch of the high theater hat. . . . Every community has writhed under it, every community has been lashed into frantic if abortive rebellion against it," noted a journalist for the *Washington Post* days after Plotke proposed the law. The crux of the high hat war, according to the author, was the unwillingness of both women and men to modify their customs in order to coexist in an increasingly mixed-sex public realm. "Curiously enough, it is in Chicago that this conflict has attained its most violent manifestation," insisted the *Post*. "On the one hand men are appealing to their sex for better manners toward women in public places," the author continued, "while women are systematically frustrating those appeals by calculated rudeness so offensive and so shocking as to elicit from the City Council a rebuke almost brutal in its severity." The article closed with a simple question: "Will it end this side of rioting, we wonder?"[208]

Nine days later, the uproar at the Columbia Theater appeared to provide an answer. Galled by Chicago women's noncompliance with an ordinance that had still yet to be signed by the city's chief executive, "hundreds of excited and indignant theatergoers took the high hat question into their own hands" and aggressively policed women in hats. "Nobody knows who started the demonstration," reported the *Chicago Tribune*. "From the suddenness of the outburst it might have suggested itself to a hundred persons at the same instant. It began with yells of 'Hats off,' that were interspersed with hisses and groans as some of the women showed a disposition not to obey."[209] The scene called to mind the unrest that had troubled another elegant theater, New York's Astor Place Opera House, in the summer of 1849. In that instance, the competing claims of working-class and affluent theater patrons fueled a bloody "struggle for power and cultural authority within theatrical space."[210] But in 1890s Chicago, it was the competing claims of male and female consumers that provoked the disturbance.

The disorder of an evening helped seal the fate of the theater hat. As one woman in the audience later contended, "The managers need never be afraid now of being fined for having high hats in their theaters. Since the gallery has joined hands with the Aldermen and enlisted in the high hat crusade the war is over."[211] DeWolf Hopper, the star of *El Capitan*, offered a similar view. "It must be admitted," he claimed, "that in a few stirring and excited moments they were able to accomplish with decision and dispatch what ordinances, ridicule, and crusading have so far failed to do—the hats came off with punctilious and beautiful regularity." Although Hopper fell short of condoning the riotous behavior, he maintained that "it has done a good work, hard, harsh and distasteful as were its methods."[212] His perspective was shared by many of the city's theater managers, who predicted the incident would "have the effect of causing the women to remove their hats in the other playhouses."[213] Will Davis, longtime manager of the Columbia, also beheld in the uproar the high hat's demise. The episode prompted him to withdraw his opposition to Plotke's ordinance. "I have no doubt," he declared, "that there is now a strong public sentiment against large hats in theaters. I intend to encourage the women as much as possible in leaving their hats in the check-rooms."[214]

One week after the scene at the Columbia, Mayor Swift fixed his signature to the ordinance, noting that "the agitation of the question" had already ensured that 85 percent of women now removed their hats in the city's downtown theaters. According to the *Chicago Times-Herald,* on the first night that the law was in effect, ladies "quite generally removed their headgear or wore small bonnets."[215] The *Chicago Tribune* offered a similar account. Indeed, as documented by the reporters dispatched to tally the number of high hats, "in not a single theater were there more than two or three big hats, and these were almost invariably confined to the rear rows." This was a stunning reversal. Where women in broad-brimmed hats once sat in "lofty contempt," they now "bundled [their hats] off in a hurry."[216] Not a single arrest had been made. The threat of public shaming alone seemed to have subdued the large hat.

Of course, the success of the law was not total. Some women reportedly only removed their headgear if "some one especially requests them to do so."[217] Still, the lady who refused quickly became an aberration. Many women were said to embrace the bareheaded look, and local hairdressers allegedly enjoyed a surge in business.[218] Meanwhile, theaters expanded their hat-checking services and used their printed programs to remind patrons to remove their headgear.[219] Sketches of theater promenades, once peopled by high-hatted ladies and their male escorts, began to depict women sans chapeau with beautifully coiffed hair (fig. 3.4).[220] To keep abreast of the change, Chicago etiquette writers updated their manuals. As Annie Randall White, who had earlier discouraged only exceptionally large hats, advised in 1900, "Custom now wisely prohibits the wearing of bonnets or hats at the theater."[221] Confirming the trend, the *Inter Ocean* mentioned offhandedly in a fashion column from the same year that Chicago women had "recognized that the theater hat was a nuisance and they have cheerfully discarded it."[222]

Figure 3.4 This 1902 portrayal of intermission at Chicago's Iroquois Theater highlights ladies' new practice of removing their millinery when attending the theater.
Iroquois Theater Souvenir Program (Chicago: Rand, McNally, 1903), 6. Courtesy of the Newberry Library.

Whether or not women truly surrendered their hats with cheer, Chicago lawmakers had seemingly resolved the high hat nuisance. Plotke's approach inspired other cities to act. Within months, lawmakers in Pittsburgh, Indianapolis, Baltimore, Madison, and San Francisco had all proposed to "imitate Chicago" and enact their own theater hat legislation.[223] Even Chicago's longtime rival St. Louis admired the new legislation. "It is not often that Chicago evolves anything worthy to serve as a model for St. Louis," sneered the *St. Louis Post-Dispatch* shortly before the municipal assembly of that city passed a theater hat law.[224] By late February, the *Chicago Tribune* observed that such measures could no longer be considered out of the ordinary: "The theater hat regulation, though at first regarded by many people as almost an absurdity, has had so general a spread as to bring it almost within the limits of the commonplace." Nonetheless, the *Tribune* added, "the regulation of these things by legislation is a new and decidedly 'freakish' method of procedure."[225]

The transformations that produced Chicago's "freakish" theater hat ordinance were material as well as moral. As theater managers courted more women patrons, ladies' heightened presence in downtown playhouses provoked a millinery crisis. But male outrage at sight-obstructing headgear alone did not account for the new sumptuary regulations. The legislation also found root in Chicagoans' growing commitment to consumer rights as well as their more expansive view of the state's role in mediating relations between businesses and consumers. Together, these developments produced legislation that protected consumers while constraining the self-fashioning of moneyed women. As this history makes clear, consumer society did not always privilege women's desires. Within commercial spaces where men and women mingled as paying customers, ladies would be held to the same standards as men in upholding the rights of the consuming public. Yet access to such spaces brought more than new obligations. It also brought new pleasures that drew Chicago ladies into the restaurants, tearooms, and cafés of the downtown.

4

Tippling Ladies and Public Pleasure

ON THE SECOND DAY of September 1907, the Reverend Frederick E. Hopkins nailed a large placard to a tree standing just beyond the doors of his church, the affluent Pilgrim Congregational Church on Chicago's South Side. The placard announced the pastor's upcoming sermon "The Growing Habit of Women Drinking Booze in Public." No latter-day Martin Luther posting revolutionary theological doctrine on his church doors, Hopkins instead summoned congregants to protest the public consumption of alcohol by moneyed women in the dining establishments located within the city's new department stores, skyscrapers, and grand hotels. That Sunday the pews of the Pilgrim Church were overflowing as Hopkins declared, "When I see the girls and women of our city, as no one can help but see, going into restaurants and cafés where booze is freely served and sitting at the tables ordering and drinking cocktails and highballs with the same ease and nonchalance of manner with which they would order a cup of tea, I wonder what the society of our time is coming to and what kind of a nation we are going to become." The sermon initiated Hopkins's monthlong crusade against ladies' drinking that culminated with the pastor raiding seventeen of Chicago's "first-class" restaurants in search of women tipplers. His sensational tactics drew national press attention. Yet he was hardly unique among Chicago reformers in claiming that moneyed women were learning to become "drunkards and moral outcasts" in fashionable new consumer spaces.[1]

As Chicago emerged as a hub of capitalist development, its downtown transformed by an expanding consumer economy, local newspapers and reform tracts brimmed with concern over the rise of the "lady tippler"—a woman of good family and comfortable circumstances who publicly quaffed spirits. This troubling new metropolitan figure evoked myriad evils, from the decay of home life to the spread of drunken hedonism. Allegedly, by indulging in improper public pleasures, the tippling lady revealed herself as unwomanly, selfish, and reckless with her purse and her body.[2]

Censure of drinking and drunkenness was certainly nothing new. Since the early nineteenth century, temperance reformers had aimed to regulate access to public houses and saloons while deploring the drinking customs of workers.[3] At the turn of the twentieth century, however, Chicagoans newly targeted the public drinking of moneyed women in the tearooms, cafés, confectioneries, and clubs spreading across the city's downtown. As one Hopkins enthusiast remarked, "It is no longer just the women of the red light district—stylish demimondes or ragged street walkers who 'booze,' but intelligent women from homes of wealth and culture."[4] Of course, even women from wealthy homes had been known to sometimes take a private nip too many. Still, until this era, ladies had been advocates rather than objects of temperance reform.

What accounted for the sudden outcry over tippling ladies? At stake was the legitimacy of emerging forms of female pleasure seeking in the city's new commercial public spaces, which were designed to entice the consuming woman with pleasures that intoxicated—spaces such as Berry's Candy Shop, the tearoom of Marshall Field & Co., and the Pompeian Room of the luxurious Congress Hotel. Seated at white-clothed tables and marble soda fountains provided by enterprising businessmen, Chicago ladies savored alcohol, leisure, and sociability. They also pressed against the social and spatial boundaries that ordered Victorian women's lives. For much of the nineteenth century, respectable ladies had consumed alcohol only in private, often for medicinal reasons or alongside their husbands. Public drinking was a male privilege and a vital component of masculine camaraderie; a woman who so imbibed was thought to be a "public woman," her body available for sale.[5] With the emergence of commercial establishments that catered to downtown shoppers, however, moneyed women began to experiment with new modes of recreational public drinking. They evoked alarm by disrupting conventions of female respectability and challenging the notion that men alone could pursue sensuous pleasure in public.

The conflict over tippling illuminates a crucial moment in the making of consumer society: when public space and public culture accommodated the female pleasure seeker. Existing scholarship has highlighted moral contestation over workingwomen's pursuit of commercial pleasure in turn-of-the-century dance halls, cabarets, and nickelodeons, and addressed the advent of a democratized heterosocial drinking and dining culture on the eve of World War I.[6] So, too, has it documented the entry of female reformers and temperance advocates into the public realm, tracing their influence in the politics of progressivism and the achievement of Prohibition.[7] Moneyed women's movement into refined and feminized commercial public spaces, where their purchasing power fueled economic growth, has also been noted.[8] Yet the conflict over ladies' conspicuous tippling concerned more than spatial boundaries; it pivoted on the right of women to pursue individual pleasure in public—a right most brazenly expressed by drinking.[9] Involving sensory gratification, fulfillment of personal taste, and release from self-restraint, the experience of tippling held the attractions that propelled modern consumerism. The rise of the lady tippler marked the creation of a moral climate that sustained the expansion of consumer society.

This new female figure offers insight into the reorientation of American culture at the turn of the century, when codes of gender separation and privacy gave way to customs of heterosociability and female autonomy. Unruly working-class women were bearers of this transformation.[10] But so were moneyed women. By drinking in public, Chicago ladies did not simply imitate and appropriate the ways of the working classes; rather, as they lingered over liqueur at Marshall Field's, lady tipplers ushered in new forms of urban pleasure and standards of respectability. They enacted a female subjectivity, rooted in consumer culture, which affirmed self-indulgence, self-fulfillment, and self-determination. Other consuming practices, from shopping to theatergoing, spurred the transformation as well. To anxious spectators, however, it was tippling that epitomized the "sublime selfishness" and "careless irresponsibilities" that psychologist G. Stanley Hall would soon identify as characteristic of the flapper. The lady tippler rarely vindicated her drinking. But her debut hastened the emergence of the new metropolitan woman who laid claim to public amusements, individual pleasure, and the possibilities of urban consumption.[11]

By the time Reverend Hopkins began his crusade in 1907, Chicago had established its position not only as a commercial leader but as a center of progressive reform. Home to a burgeoning consumer rights movement, the midwestern metropolis was the hub of organized temperance. Since 1884, the Woman's Christian Temperance Union, the most popular women's association of the nineteenth century, had maintained its headquarters in nearby Evanston. Chicago-area temperance leaders, notably Frances Willard, commanded a national audience and shaped the contours of the country's escalating debate over drink.[12]

To be sure, ladies defied convention and began to drink in public in places other than Chicago. But the tippling skirmish there—sensationalized in the national press—distilled the clash between the ethos of temperance and new customs of female consumption. It revealed on a large stage the uneasy shift from a culture of restraint to one of accumulation and desire.

"Do Our 'Best' Women Drink?" asked Jane Brookshire, a writer for the Chicago-based literary magazine *Wayside Tales*. The question, which Brookshire addressed in a four-page spread in 1906, had interested Chicagoans since the mid-1890s, when the press first began to speculate that respectable ladies were drinking more.[13] Since then, articles with suggestive headlines such as "Increasing Habits of Intoxication," "The Drink Habit among Women," and "Women Drinkers Are on Increase" peppered newspapers and invited Chicagoans to reflect on female tippling trends.[14] For her article, Brookshire purportedly interviewed several citizens familiar with the drinking customs of ladies. After speaking to the proprietor of a French restaurant on Monroe Street, she concluded, "Those who believe that the talk about the increase of this habit among women is all sensationalism should drop in there some afternoon—any afternoon about four o'clock when there is no matinee or after the theater has closed."[15] Had Brookshire's readers carried out her suggestion and visited any of the fashionable candy stores, cafés, restaurants, or tearooms she referenced, they would have observed new practices of public recreational drinking flourishing among respectable moneyed women.

The turn to public drinking by Chicago ladies was the product, in part, of the city's distinctive social structure. Unlike their counterparts in New York or Boston, the rich families who dominated Chicago society had amassed, rather than inherited, their fortunes, and a persistently high rate of upward mobility ensured that a steady stream of new faces and new money flowed into their ranks.[16] Many of these upwardly mobile families came from Chicago's thriving old-immigrant communities, particularly German, Irish, and Swedish enclaves. As women from these groups ascended the socioeconomic ladder, they carried with them cultural attitudes toward alcohol and its public consumption; whereas Swedes were known as "avowedly temperate," Irish and German women often consumed alcohol in public at social events and holidays.[17] This infusion of pro-drink sentiment into Chicago society helped transform respectable drinking practices.

More significant as a catalyst for change, however, was the expansion of a consumer economy that invited moneyed women's presence in the city center. Indeed, "going downtown" to shop or attend matinees occupied an increasing amount of Chicago ladies' time at the turn of the century. In his 1903 novel *The Pit*, Frank Norris described the daily crush on State Street: "From each street doorway was pouring an army of 'shoppers,' women for the most part . . . fashionably dressed. Many of them stood for a moment on the threshold of the storm-doorways, turning up the collars of their sealskins, settling their hands in their muffs, and searching the street for their coupés and carriages."[18]

Initially, the women who composed this "army" had difficulty finding respectable places to eat, drink, and rest. The Loop's dining facilities had been a male preserve throughout the nineteenth century, and few public or private institutions welcomed female patrons. Downtown merchants offered few amenities to retail customers, and the saloons and private clubs in which men dined closed their doors to ladies. Even most restaurants and cafés refused to admit unescorted women.[19] Accordingly, respectable women rarely dined in public. As the *Chicago Tribune* explained in 1896, "Many women of a generation or two back, and well informed ones at that—have lived and died without ever seeing the inside of a restaurant. Such a thing, indeed, as a modest wife and mother dining unattended in a public restaurant would have been considered highly improper."[20] With limited accommodations open to them, most ladies were forced to return home for sustenance.

To avoid interrupting their downtown excursions, some ladies patronized the only respectable enterprises that offered unaccompanied women any refreshment—drugstores. The chief allure of these establishments was the soda fountain, where clerks dispensed carbonated water mixed with homemade tonics and patent medicines, such as Coca-Cola and Lydia Pinkham's Vegetable Compound.[21] These nostrums contained between 7 and 50 percent alcohol by volume and were said to appeal to shoppers seeking an afternoon pick-me-up.[22] "It would surprise you to see the number and class of women who drink milk punches here," one druggist disclosed of a popular brandy-based remedy. "It is a great bracer for a woman who has been shopping all day," he concluded, "and the habit is easily acquired."[23] In addition to tinctures, many druggists also combined soda water with boozy blends of crushed fruit and hard liquor. "Nearly all," insisted one observer, "of the soda fountains, large and small, use mixed flavoring with alcohol in some form or another."[24]

The drugstore's brisk trade in alcohol did not long escape the notice of Chicago saloonkeepers, who, unlike druggists, were required to hold expensive dram-shop licenses.[25] As one disgruntled saloon owner observed, "The soda water fountain is the ladies' saloon. The ladies know quickly enough what quack medicines contain alcohol. They say to the clerk: 'My nerves are shattered. Give me a little coca.' Or, 'I have felt a weakness all day. They tell me safronine is an excellent tonic.' And the result is no worse than if they came to my saloon and soaked themselves in rum."[26] Despite saloonkeepers' protests, drugstores continued to serve alcohol without licenses, and their numbers multiplied on State Street. In 1881, four drugstores were located on the eight-block stretch between South Water Street and Van Buren Street. By 1907, that number had nearly quadrupled.[27] These establishments, according to the *Chicago Tribune,* became especially crowded at lunchtime, "when the shopping girl is feeling the effects of the crushing she received at the bargain counter."[28]

As other entrepreneurs recognized the profitability of catering to unescorted shoppers, countless new commercial spaces boasting "ladies' menus" and stimulating drinks sprouted across the retail district. In 1890, Marshall Field & Co. helped pioneer this trend by opening a tea-room attached to the ladies' fur department in his State Street store.[29] Along with such favorites as chicken salad and chicken pot pie, the initial bill of fare included rose punch—a blend of rose cordial and vanilla ice cream, served with a rose on the side.[30] Both the Schlesinger & Mayer and Carson Pirie Scott & Co. department stores followed suit, and, within five years, dining rooms had become standard fixtures in downtown retail establishments.[31] "There is not a store of any pretensions," one observer declared in 1896, "which has not its restaurant."[32] Visitors to these establishments could expect to find wine, champagne, and various mixed drinks. The tearoom at Fish, Joseph & Co., for example, advertised a menu that included Roman punch and frozen milk punch, while Siegel-Cooper offered a *table d'hôte* (a multicourse meal at a fixed price) featuring two varieties of wine.[33]

Numerous independent cafés, confectioneries, and restaurants courted downtown shoppers by providing separate quarters for unescorted women.[34] H. M. Kinsley's, then considered Chicago's finest restaurant, established one of the first dining rooms for ladies when the business moved into an enormous new four-story building on Adams Street in 1885.[35] Many more female-friendly dining spaces opened over the course of the next decade. "In the line of cafés the Chicago woman is well catered to," observed the *Inter Ocean* in 1898. "Every establishment on State street that has space to give them devotes a section to the hungry shoppers. By the way the tables are filled it is safe to say that the shoppers appreciate it all."[36] The trade of women theatergoers was likewise sought by restaurateurs. "After the Performance Go to Vogelsang's" to enjoy "a new room for Ladies" with its own "separate entrance" urged a 1901 advertisement in a program for Powers' Theater, previously Hooley's.[37] Often such spaces preserved gender separation in name only, as men were permitted when accompanied by women—and often even when not. The problem of men invading women's dining spaces became so acute that in 1904, Chicago ladies complained that male diners would soon entirely "crowd out" female patrons at popular ladies' cafés and tearooms.[38]

Rarely did any of the tearooms, restaurants, or candy stores that served women fail to provide alcohol. Indeed, as competition increased, the range of boozy beverages available to female customers also grew. Ladies no longer needed to limit their consumption to tonics found at drugstore counters—not when new cocktails and mixed drinks could be had. "Among the many fancy drinks now popular in Chicago," one soda jerk reported, "are lime juice champagne, French currant, cusinniere, creme de cassis, grape milk, malted milk, cocoa sirup, orgeat, nectar, checkerberry, calisaya bitters . . . and 'you know,' the latter a combination of spirits of some sort with bitters and sugar."[39] At the Congress Hotel, ladies could savor liqueurs such as crème de menthe and

SELL FAIR SHOPPERS STRONG DRINK.

Figure 4.1 An 1897 sketch from the *Chicago Tribune* depicts fashionably dressed shoppers imbibing spirits at one of the many large soda fountains that spread across the retail district in the 1890s. Soda fountain operators endeavored to cater to ladies' tastes by purveying sweet or colorful mixed drinks, such as those posted on the menu here. "Sell Fair Shoppers Strong Drink," *Chicago Tribune*, Jan. 17, 1897, 25.

mixed drinks such as punch lalla rookh, while patrons of the ladies' ice cream parlor at Berry's Candy Store could choose from dozens of alcohol options, such as mint julep, Bordeaux flip, and claret lemonade.[40] In an 1897 article on soda fountains, the *Chicago Tribune* highlighted the new diversity in ladies' drinks: "Some of the city candy stores patronized almost exclusively by shopping girls have lists of drinks on their walls varied enough and strong enough to answer the purpose of a mixed drink bill-of-fare for any saloon in town." In the illustration accompanying the article, a crowd of "fair shoppers" was shown gathered at a soda fountain to sample "golden punch" and "sherry flip" (fig. 4.1).[41] The whimsical names often disguised potent brews. In one liquor license investigation, officials reported that two prominent confectioneries were selling drinks called yum yum and Roman punch that contained 13 and 20 percent alcohol, respectively.[42]

Downtown tearooms, cafés, and restaurants relied on more than glamorous menus to entice female customers. To put moneyed women at ease in commercial public space, proprietors drew on strategies first used to preserve women's respectability in theaters and department stores.[43] In particular, they employed sumptuous décor and equipage to communicate an atmosphere of safety and refinement. In the tearoom of Schlesinger & Mayer, for instance, guests enjoyed white linens, mosaic marble floors, onyx columns, and mahogany furnishings, while patrons of Marshall Field's tearoom found "surroundings that harmonize with wealth and fashion" (fig. 4.2).[44] Several restaurants catering to lady tipplers featured lavish European themes. The Hofbrau House, for example, had vaulted ceilings decorated with "flowing ribbons bearing mottoes and shields" and "old Germanic heraldic devices"; the Pompeian Room boasted Italian murals and stylized Greek columns; and the Hotel Bismarck's Ladies' Café was embellished with scenes of Renaissance and Bavarian architecture.[45]

Candy stores offered similarly grand interiors. On her first trip to Chicago, French traveler Marie Lédier Grandin marveled at the "luxurious" appointments of the large State Street confectioneries. They were, according to Grandin, "temples of feminine desire that bring together the delicacies of the palate and visual pleasure."[46] In a 1901 advertisement, Berry's Candy detailed some of the features that helped create this pleasurable effect: "Beautiful mosaic floors in fancy panels with marble borders. The ceilings and walls have been decorated and painted by the best artists from Marshall Field Company. . . . It is like a dream to see the angels and cherubs soaring through the clouds in the beautiful decorated panels on the ceilings above."[47] At Gunther's Confectionery, patrons entered a "palatial" mirror-lined café featuring rose-colored marble counters, velvet upholstery, stained-glass windows, and a custom-made soda fountain of onyx inlaid with gold (fig. 4.3).[48] Because fountain beverages, priced between ten and fifteen cents per glass, were a rare treat for working-class consumers, even modest drugstore fountains courted moneyed patrons by striving for an air of refinement.[49] "Now every drug store . . . must have a marble and nickel fountain," one reporter ob-

Figure 4.2 Marshall Field & Co. established its first tearoom in 1890. Two decades later, the store operated seven separate dining facilities. The South Grill Room, seen here in 1909, featured Circassian walnut paneling, crystal chandeliers, and a marble fountain. It was later renamed the Walnut Room and still operates today.　Chicago Daily News Negatives Collection, DN-0007502. Courtesy of the Chicago History Museum.

served. "And the big places are satisfied only with a glittering construction half as high as the room and twelve or fifteen feet long."[50]

Within these elegant new spaces, ladies with money to spend could indulge their appetite for drink without compromising their respectability—but ability to pay did not grant all women that privilege. The tearooms and cafés that catered to well-heeled shoppers often denied service to African Americans. In 1905, Florence Jones and Jessica Morris, wife of a prominent African American attorney, brought charges against Berry's Candy for violating the Illinois Civil Rights Act of 1885. According to Jones, her party was seated and then ignored for nearly an hour. Such treatment was far from extraordinary. Jones and

Figure 4.3 This 1907 postcard offers a glimpse into the elegant interior of Gunther's Confectionery, one of the most prominent candy stores in Chicago. Gunther's served fountain beverages in a mirror-lined café featuring rose-colored marble counters, velvet upholstery, stained-glass windows, and a custom-built soda fountain of onyx inlaid with gold.   1907 Postcard, Chicago, Author's Private Collection.

Morris's case captured public interest not because Berry's practices were unusual but because the two women dared to protest the color line that prevailed in downtown restaurants. As Morris's husband later noted, legal efforts to hold Chicago proprietors accountable for racial discrimination "nearly always are failures." This case was no exception. Although one Berry's waitress faced a grand jury, the store's owners and managers escaped without consequences, free to resume their discriminatory practices.[51]

For the moneyed white women who could enjoy Chicago's commercial drinking spaces, the move from drugstore counters to elegantly appointed tearooms and cafés promoted a more recreational, gregarious tone. "The positive delight of the ladies' café is its ease," argued a correspondent for the *Inter Ocean*. "Men have always had lounging places," the writer noted, but women were just discovering the pleasures of having a space in which to drink and chat without "being stared at or thought unconventional." "The something to drink is anything from a ginger ale to a cocktail," the reporter continued, "and the chat may be about anything from a club meeting to a scandal."[52] In 1907, Anita de Campi, wife of a distinguished civil engineer, similarly contended that Chicago ladies had come to relish meeting friends downtown "for the purpose of attending a matinee and going 'somewhere' afterwards for a jolly little chat over a 'glass of something.'"[53] Two years later, Bonnie Royal, a well-known writer and illustrator, remarked on the atmosphere of conviviality in downtown candy stores, where "streams of variously flavored deliciousness" flowed. Upon visiting a "veritable palace on State street," Royal observed ladies lingering together, "each indulging in her favorite drink and enjoying on the side a bonbon or two of the choicest gossip."[54]

While many ladies were attracted to its sociability, tippling also won devotees because it was chic and cosmopolitan. The practice appears to have been inspired by similar trends in Europe. Chicago newspapers printed several pieces on women's public drinking in Paris and London before noting similar patterns locally.[55] In 1892, for example, the *Inter Ocean* reported that all Parisian women consumed "aperitifs, bitters, vermouths, absinthe, and similar liquors" at cafés and restaurants. "[Parisian] women have a particular taste for this kind of drink," the article continued, "and are frequently the victims of these pretty colored cordials."[56] Five years later, one observant Chicagoan reported that shoppers were ordering cocktails and liqueurs with "Frenchy names" in downtown candy stores.[57]

Many contemporaries credited an uptick in foreign travel and the influence of the 1893 World's Fair with fostering a new era of respectable public drinking. "It is well known that the women of foreign countries have for centuries been more accustomed to these practices than Americans," noted James S. Stone, rector of the exclusive St. James Episcopal Church. Contact with "foreign parts," he proposed, encouraged women to "demand other, more exciting amusements," such as tippling.[58] At the World's Fair, many Chicago women were introduced to European drinking practices by patronizing the restaurants of the Midway Plaisance. At the Polish café, for example, guests could order wine and champagne, while beer flowed freely at the German Village and at its Austro-Hungarian counterpart, Old Vienna. According to Teresa Dean, a columnist for the

Inter Ocean, the restaurants of the Midway encouraged Chicago "society leaders" to mix with the "miscellaneous crowd" and experiment with drinking.[59] Among these adventurous ladies was Frances Glessner, who recorded in her journal having a "fine dinner" at the German Village and spending an evening at the "beer garden" of Old Vienna.[60]

Yet even as the lady tippler embraced excitement and pleasure, her drinking practices continued to diverge from those in the male saloon. Most obviously, ladies avoided the hard liquors and malt beverages characteristic of masculine drinking. They enjoyed instead wine, liqueurs, cocktails, and mixed drinks. "What they want is a drink with a cherry or a piece of orange in it, and they don't care particularly how strong it is," declared one observer.[61] "They aren't strong for beer or ale," confirmed a restaurateur. "They want wine or cocktails."[62] Though reports varied as to how much alcohol ladies consumed, outright drunkenness was said to be rare. According to de Campi, this moderation owed to the fact that ladies had not adopted the custom of "treating," or buying rounds, which was widely associated with saloon culture. "A dozen men are not satisfied that each one has done his part until each one has 'stood treat' for the dozen," de Campi stated. "There is no such nonsense among women. They all sit down together, and it is understood beforehand that the treat is 'Dutch.'"[63] But even ladies who imbibed moderately could enjoy the heady sensations of strong drink. "Few of the women who come here ever drink too much," confessed the head waiter of one fashionable restaurant. "Every night we have one or two who might find it hard to walk a straight chalk line," he revealed. "The rest take just enough to make 'em feel good and let it go at that."[64]

By 1907, the year of Reverend Hopkins's crusade, respectable ladies enjoying stimulants had become a familiar, if not always welcome, sight in downtown Chicago. The *Inter Ocean* labeled these women "the cocktail brigade." In a 1901 article, the paper recounted an imagined conversation between two workingmen who observed several "richly dressed women" enter nearby cafés. One of the men explained to his friend that the women

> are participants in a function that takes place in Chicago every afternoon. I come here every day about 4 o'clock, and at the same time the brigade begins to advance on the cocktail supply. They have been shopping, most of them. Their husbands think they go to some State street confectioner's for a cup of cocoa when they become tired. They don't do

anything of the kind. They go to some restaurant for their cocktail. The habit has reached proportions in this town that amount almost to an epidemic.[65]

This brief vignette highlights an important strain in public discourse at the turn of the century as many Chicagoans noted with alarm a surge in ladies' public drinking. Whether or not that surge amounted to an "epidemic," as the newspaper suggested, the tippling trend raised new questions about women's morality and standards of public behavior. By entering commercial leisure spaces where alcohol was served, Chicago ladies challenged ideals of female virtue and masculine dominance that had framed American social life and drinking customs for the last half century.

In March 1874, more than three decades before Hopkins and his allies stormed the Loop's eateries, a different group of reformers invaded commercial drinking sites across Chicago as part of the Women's Temperance Crusade, which began in Ohio the preceding year.[66] The ladies who carried out these raids disrupted business in dozens of "whisky joints" and "gin palaces" by reciting scripture and confronting patrons. The presence of moneyed women within these masculine spaces was a decided curiosity. In the first saloon that the crusaders entered—an Irish-owned establishment on bustling Halsted Street—the ladies attracted a crowd of more than two hundred onlookers. After nine crusaders knelt on the sawdusted floor in a circle of prayer, one bystander jeered, "Why don't you set up the drinks for the gals?"[67] The wisecrack, which merited a mention in the *Inter Ocean*, underscored the absurdity of respectable women consuming alcohol in public. Such behavior, most Chicagoans agreed, befitted only prostitutes or immigrants—not ladies.

The incident brings to light a code of respectability that governed moneyed women's drinking practices and public presence in the decades following the Great Chicago Fire, as the city set about rebuilding. The ladies who aided in that task did not patronize commercial drinking establishments. Yet they did consume alcohol at private events and at home—practices omitted from many accounts of the period.[68] Although their exploits as temperance activists have tended to overshadow their drinking practices, Chicago ladies were far from teetotalers. Even many women involved in the temperance movement imbibed alcohol throughout the 1870s and 1880s. Unlike the male drinkers whom the crusades targeted, however, moneyed women drank exclusively within the private sphere, where their consumption was carefully regulated and served to reinforce established class and gender norms.

Throughout this era, alcohol played an important role in conspicuous consumption and genteel sociability. Most spirits—except domestically produced beer and whiskey—carried heavy import duties that greatly inflated their price.[69] "Even poor wine is, compared with European prices, exceedingly dear," British traveler George Makepeace Towle reported in 1870.[70] As a result, alcohol was often used to signal and re-inforce status. On New Year's Day, for example, women from leading families would open their doors and lavish gentlemen callers with wine and eggnog as well as "apple toddy, milk punch, brandy smash, [and] Tom-and-Jerry."[71] The drinking and socializing that accompanied this annual ritual helped establish group ties and strengthen common ideals.[72] Private dinner parties offered further opportunities to reinforce shared values while allowing hosts to showcase the quality and diversity of their liquor cabinets. A sample menu from a Chicago etiquette guide outlined a formal dinner that included a separate alcohol pairing for each course: sherry with soup, white wine with oysters, claret with game.[73] Even simple dinners and lunches called for at least a few alcohol options. These customs ensured that ladies encountered spirits during the course of their ordinary social obligations. In *The Art of Entertaining* (1893), Mary Elizabeth Sherwood assured readers of "moderate means" that a dinner "good enough for anybody" could be achieved with only one servant and sherry, claret, or champagne.[74]

Ladies were expected to imbibe temperately at social occasions. "To drink to excess is worse than ill-bred," advised etiquette writer Annie Randall White.[75] At formal dinners, when the range of alcohol offerings was greatest, the practice of separating the sexes after the meal, before male guests began to drink heavily, minimized opportunities for ladies to overindulge. Once the final course had been cleared, "gentlemen are left to wine and cigars, *liqueurs* and cognac, and the ladies retire to the drawing room to chat and take their coffee."[76] This gendered segregation could last anywhere from a few minutes to more than an hour and was designed to shield women from alcoholic excess. In her journal, Glessner recalled "the odor of whiskey" that assaulted her senses when the menfolk invaded the ladies' drawing room after being "served liquors" at the home of banker John Wesley Doane.[77] Doane and his male companions could savor the pleasures of sociable after-dinner drinking, but ladies such as Glessner were expected to indulge only within the context of the meal.

The mere suggestion that women violated the rules of appropriate drinking conduct could provoke grave indignation, as Julian Ralph discovered while visiting Chicago in 1893. On this occasion, Ralph penned "Chicago's Gentle Side," his essay for *Harper's New Monthly Magazine* detailing the social and political world of the city's moneyed women. Ralph noted an astonishing "freedom of intercourse between the sexes." In no other city, he asserted, did women of "very nice social circles" violate the custom of withdrawing from the dining room after a formal dinner. Recounting one such instance, Ralph wrote, "When the coffee was brought on . . . there was no movement on the part of the women towards leaving the table. No suggestion was made that they do so; there was no apology offered for their not doing so; the subject was not mentioned. There were glasses of 'green mint' [liqueur] for all and cigars for the men." Ralph's accusation that Chicago women tippled after-dinner drinks incensed several "ladies in society," who voiced their concerns to the *Chicago Tribune*. Such behavior, the ladies alleged, occurred only in "less conventional and more bohemian" circles. Their protestations prompted Ralph to "correct the impression" that he claimed to have seen women indulging in after-dinner drinking, contending, "I never saw anything of the sort." Still, Ralph maintained that he had seen ladies linger after dinner while their menfolk drank. The *Tribune* dismissed Ralph's allegations as reflective of a rare lapse in decorum, an "excrescence" unworthy of mention.[78]

Outside carefully monitored social gatherings, ladies most often consumed spirits in pursuit of health and well-being. The medicinal use of alcohol peaked in the mid- to late nineteenth century, and even teetotalers found they could not avoid imbibing. In this era before antibiotics, most doctors endorsed the therapeutic qualities of alcohol and liberally prescribed spirits for injury or illness. Whiskey, for example, was often indicated for consumption, brandies and wines for fevers, and sherry for digestive complaints.[79] In one instance in 1886, the *Inter Ocean* celebrated the "wonderful cure" of a New York merchant's daughter who contracted tetanus and was then treated with "morphine, large quantities of rye, whisky, brandy, champagne, sherry, egg-nog, milk punch, and other stimulants."[80] In the words of one physician, most practitioners "would rather dispense with the use of salicyl, quinine, or antipyrine than with good wine or brandy."[81]

While men and women from every social class consumed medicinal alcohol, doctors most often prescribed the daily use of "bracers" to moneyed women, who had gained a reputation for frailty due to their high rates of invalidism.[82] Whether their complaints were physiological or psychogenic, they were regularly prescribed liquors and fortified wines as restorative tonics.[83] "Ladies who are in good health," one physician suggested, "should take one glass of sherry or claret at lunch; one and a half ordinarily at dinner." By contrast, ladies in "delicate health who are going to ride in the park" should "take a glass of dry sherry and a biscuit."[84] In his popular text *The Practitioner's Handbook of Treatment* (1887), Dr. John Milner Fothergill recommended that female patients drink "sound malt liquor or some generous wine" with every meal and before retiring at night.[85]

Far from disrupting gendered expectations, ladies' use of therapeutic bracers reinforced traditional notions of female delicacy and dependence. Unlike men, women allegedly needed the restorative power of alcohol to face the pressures of modern life. Chicago novelist Amelia E. Barr argued that the weariness caused by "numerous social engagements following one another in ceaseless routine" compelled many ladies to resort to the use of stimulants. "A glass of wine or a tablespoon of brandy," she explained, "is privately taken some day to meet the social strain, and is found to be apparently restorative. The stimulant makes the taker feel that the dance or the dinner which seemed to be impossible is possible."[86] At the 1876 Centennial Temperance Conference, Chicago reformer Helen Brown suggested that many husbands actually goaded their wives into using bracers. "You are not as well as usual, wife, to-day; you must drink a glass of champagne," she mimicked.[87] In his handbook, Fothergill echoed these sentiments and proposed that officious spouses often drove women to overuse medicinal alcohol. He lamented that the phrase "'You had better have a glass of wine, dear, before you go out; you are not strong yet,' has laid the foundation of many a ruined life."[88]

In the hope of further bolstering their health, many women supplemented their daily bracers with patent medicines. These intoxicating remedies, which later could be found at soda fountains, were initially sold through the mail or in grocery stores and consumed at home.[89] Most purported to cure a long list of ailments peculiar to women. Lydia

Pinkham's Vegetable Compound, for example, promised relief from "Painful Complaints and Weaknesses so common to our best female population," including "Bloating, Headache, Nervous Prostration, General Debility, Sleeplessness, Depression, and Indigestion."[90] Industry advertisers often took special aim at moneyed women. An advertisement for Dr. Pierce's Favorite Prescription, for example, pictured a bejeweled woman resting on a divan in a crowded ballroom. The accompanying text announced that Pierce's tonic would cure the deleterious effects of "over-rich and indigestible food, late suppers, the fatigue of the ballroom, and the bad air of the illy-ventilated, overcrowded theater."[91] In a Pinkham advertisement, a smartly dressed woman was shown fainting into the arms of a mustachioed man. "She is taken with that 'all-gone' or faint feeling while calling or shopping," the caption declared.[92]

By connecting female discomfort and fatigue to pastimes such as shopping or theatergoing, patent medicine advertisements reinforced the notion that ladies needed stimulants to fulfill their daily routines, which, in turn, strengthened the link between medicinal alcohol and refined femininity. As Helen Brown observed in 1876, many "educated and cultured" individuals believed that women needed to use alcohol-based tonics "to keep up [their] strength for the busy round of duty at home and abroad."[93] Paradoxically, the popularity of medicinal alcohol grew just as the temperance movement was gaining momentum.[94] Many professed teetotalers and temperance women were said to use bracers and patent medicines. In his handbook of treatment, Fothergill alleged that patent medicines were "largely consumed by people who fondly believe[d] themselves to be total abstainers."[95] Later, in an exposé in the *Ladies' Home Journal*, Edward Bok, the magazine's editor, claimed that nearly 75 percent of WCTU members were "regular buyers and partakers of 'patent medicines.'"[96] While Bok and Fothergill likely exaggerated, few women viewed temperance values as conflicting with the medicinal use of alcohol.[97] Even Lydia Pinkham, whose patent medicine contained over 20 percent alcohol by volume, was a lifelong supporter of temperance.[98]

As patent medicine use increased, temperance advocates stepped forward to condemn ladies' reliance on medicinal alcohol. Rarely did these critics censure women drinkers, however. Instead, they condemned the fraudulent claims and boozy foundation of the patent medicine industry. The WCTU initiated the effort in 1900 by publishing

Martha Meir Allen's *Alcohol: A Dangerous and Unnecessary Medicine*. Four years later, Edward Bok ran two editorials in the *Ladies' Home Journal* on the evils of patent medicines. Both authors charged patent medicine manufacturers and unethical doctors with hoodwinking naïve women into consuming alcohol. After dubbing America "the Paradise of Quacks," Allen insisted that most women did not know that patent medicines contained stimulants and that many "accepted with amazing credulity their startling claims to miraculous cures."[99] Bok similarly argued that women were easily manipulated by patent medicine advertisements. "Their eye catches some advertisements in a newspaper," he explained, "and from the cleverly-worded descriptions of symptoms they are convinced that this man's 'bitters,' or that man's 'sarsaparilla,' or that 'doctor's' (!) 'vegetable compound,' or So-and-so's 'pills' is exactly the thing they need as a tonic." Bok feared that most ladies did not possess the medical knowledge to use tonics safely, concluding, "There is nothing so dangerous as drugs used without intelligence or taken without advice."[100]

While reformers such as Bok and Allen were critical of ladies' drinking practices, they cast women drinkers not as transgressors but as victims, whose natural innocence made them easy prey for unscrupulous advertisers and doctors. Ultimately, the campaign against medicinal drinking fueled popular anger against the patent medicine industry, and the women who privately used these products evoked more sympathy than censure. But as Chicago's tippling ladies began to adopt new modes of public recreational drinking, this balance began to shift.

When Carrie Nation arrived at Chicago's luxurious Congress Hotel, then called the Auditorium Annex, in the summer of 1908, she needed no introduction. The fiery temperance advocate had gained notoriety a decade earlier, when, armed with bricks and stones, she destroyed several saloons across the dry state of Kansas. Since then, Nation had set aside her "smashers" in favor of a hatchet and had also widened her sights. No longer did the self-appointed "home defender" agitate solely against illegal dive bars and their working-class patrons—she also took aim at the moneyed men and women who drank spirits in upscale restaurants, cafés, and candy stores. Shortly after arriving at the Auditorium Annex, Nation took up her cause at the famed Pompeian Room, where Chicago ladies tippled cocktails to the sounds of a bubbling Tiffany fountain (fig. 4.4). Clutching her hatchet, Nation faced the crowd of diners en-

Figure 4.4 This 1911 advertisement for the Pompeian Room at the Congress Hotel, initially called the Auditorium Annex, depicts an "aristocratic" mixed-sex crowd drinking beside the restaurant's Tiffany fountain. The Pompeian Room was among the first-class dining establishments that the Reverend Frederick E. Hopkins stormed in his 1907 booze crusade. Garrick Theater Playbill, Playbill and Broadside Collection, box 10, folder 9. Courtesy of the University of Chicago's Special Collections Research Center.

joying "queer drinks with trees planted in them" and bellowed, "You sinners, sitting here drinking this filthy stuff. . . . This is a h—hole . . . which if you don't break away from will —— you the rest of your lives."[101]

Nation was exceptional in many ways, but her message and tactics on this occasion were not unique. A year earlier, Reverend Hopkins had visited the Pompeian Room as part of his campaign against women's public drinking and similarly decried the debauchery of the restaurant's patrons. While their theatrical styles differed, both reformers were engaged in the same battle against dissipation and in defense of home life. Other moralists and religious leaders joined them in this fight. In newspapers, reform tracts, and public speeches, Chicago reformers accused respectable women of endangering their marriages, families, and virtue by imbibing alcohol in public spaces. Unlike the campaign against patent medicines, this new wave of temperance reform did not cast women drinkers as unwitting dupes of the liquor trade. On the contrary, critics now condemned ladies who drank in public as wanton "sinners" who put personal enjoyment before domestic and familial obligations. These attacks concerned more than the boundaries of woman's sphere; at stake were new anxieties about moneyed women's pursuit of self-gratification and commercial pleasure.

Outcry against tippling ladies rang out from select voices across Chicago. Few women, however, stepped forward to take up the cause. Although the WCTU occasionally warned of the dangers posed to women by medicinal alcohol, the organization primarily concentrated on battling saloons and male inebriety. Tellingly, the Chicago branch adopted only one resolution that addressed women drinking in public. "It has come to our notice," the 1897 resolution declared, "that drinks mixed with liquor are dispensed to young women at soda fountains in our city." The statement made clear that the WCTU continued to view women drinkers as victims, tricked by liquor dealers into imbibing intoxicants that "masquerade under the alluring names of 'velvets,' 'sherry flip,' 'crème de menthe' and the like." To combat the evil, the clubwomen pledged to warn women so that they would not "partake of these drinks unknowingly." In a follow-up editorial, the *Chicago Tribune* mocked the WCTU's efforts as ineffectual and belated.[102]

Several years later, a small group of Irish Catholic women attempted to rouse female opposition to public tippling trends. They established the

Catholic Daughters of Temperance in 1905 to oppose alcohol in all its forms, and they called on members to socially ostracize any woman who served or imbibed intoxicants. In an outline of the club's founding principles, Mrs. W. C. H. Keough, the club's president and the wife of a prominent lawyer, explained,

> When a candy store, patronized almost wholly by women and young girls finds it profitable to sell cocktails in cups it is high time for the good women and mothers of Chicago who still cling to a few high ideals of womanhood to lend a hand in defending the home against one of the greatest perils that can face it. Drinking among women is increasing in Chicago at such an alarming rate that every organization interested in the improvement and stability of the institution called the "home" should undertake to check the spread of the evil.[103]

For moneyed Irish Catholic women such as Keough, reform work was essential to asserting and maintaining status and respectability. By advocating total abstinence, the group's members distanced themselves from working-class Irish, who had gained a reputation for drunkenness. At the same time, the organization's emphasis on motherhood and domesticity highlighted their commitment to traditional markers of respectability.[104] Despite their zeal, the Catholic Daughters of Temperance failed to attract a significant following and soon faded from public view. No other women's groups stepped forward to take their place in protesting public tippling. The dearth of critical female voices suggests that few women were interested in attacking their peers for consuming alcohol in respectable public venues.

While Chicago clubwomen shied away from crusades against public tippling, many men embraced this new arm of the temperance cause. Their enthusiasm coincided with a trend of heightened male participation in the broader temperance movement. In 1898, the male-dominated Anti-Saloon League opened a Chicago branch that soon eclipsed the WCTU as the city's most powerful temperance organization. The group's orientation toward political action attracted many of Chicago's leading men, while its focus on attacking commercial liquor traffic appealed to those who wanted to close working-class saloons without sacrificing their personal liquor stock.[105] A sudden shift in the city's political climate in 1906 may have further stimulated male interest in temperance. That year, Mayor Edward Dunne, an Irish Catholic Democrat, surprised his constituents by endorsing a high license law that doubled liquor license fees. He also proposed to enforce defunct Sunday saloon-closing laws. The latter decision in particular met staunch resistance from working-class and immigrant communities, but many moneyed Chicagoans embraced the mayor's reform spirit.[106] These initiatives, as well as the work of the Anti-Saloon League, ensured that more Chicago men were engaged in temperance than ever before.

Yet increased male involvement in the war on working-class saloons does not alone account for the vigor with which many men attacked ladies who consumed alcohol in public. These assaults revealed discomfort specifically related to the lady tippler. At once more menacing and more confusing than the working-class drunk, the respectable lady who indulged her appetites in public defied traditional ideals of women as passionless and passive. By appropriating the cultural prerogatives of the saloon and insisting on her right to pursue sensuous pleasures in public, she unsettled the boundaries of respectability while appearing to place individual wants before obligations to husband and home. Hoping to stem this tide, male critics denounced tippling as selfish and unwomanly, and advocated a return to traditional domestic values.

In September 1903, the Reverend William B. Leach initiated the first large-scale assault on ladies' public drinking. From his pulpit at the Wicker Park Methodist Episcopal Church, Reverend Leach denounced women who drank in the dining rooms of downtown women's clubs. Many of the city's largest clubs had facilities that boasted restaurants and tearooms, and these dining spaces often competed with commercial eateries for customers. According to Leach, they also "smack[ed] of the high ball" and promoted "drinking and drunkenness." The clergyman warned that nine out of ten women's clubs served alcohol and, in so doing, drove members to forget "babies and home comforts for the intoxicants of club life." For Leach, public drinking and club involvement were entwined problems; both promoted self-indulgence and destroyed domestic happiness. "The homecoming of the husband from work means little to the wife in these days of club life and social endeavor," he mourned.[107]

Leach's attack on "drunken" clubwomen occurred as women's clubs were blossoming across the city. These institutions proliferated rapidly after the 1893 World's Fair and the 1894 Pullman Strike, events that provided women opportunities to develop their own voluntary organizations and build networks of like-minded peers.[108] In 1885, the city's social directory—the *Chicago Blue Book*—recorded only eight women's clubs, most of which met at members' homes. Two decades later, the number of women's clubs had increased to ninety-nine; nearly a third had their own downtown facilities, while the rest often met in hotels or concert halls.[109] Within these clubs, Chicago ladies blended leisure and sociability with education, politics, and reform. They hosted speakers, staged debates, developed philanthropic programs, and lobbied for municipal improvements. They also lunched, chatted, and relaxed together. Much like department stores or fashionable cafés, women's clubs sold entertainment and services that allowed women to enjoy themselves outside the domestic sphere.

For men such as Leach, however, women's clubs appeared to promote hedonism and to create the potential for women to lose control in public. In their search "for cards, for drinks, for excitement," the clergyman warned, "maidens are selling themselves to desire, appetite, passion, gambling, and so-called pleasures—selling themselves to remorse, to pain."[110] Disguised as venues for intellectual and moral development, he claimed, women's clubs instead nurtured improper pleasures such as recreational tippling. "In most of the clubs[,] not the programs but the side issues are the attractive features—the wine and cigarets," he advised a hostile audience at a meeting of the prominent Women's Social Economics Club.[111] Such accusations met staunch resistance from club-women, many of whom regarded Leach's efforts as an assault on their right to pursue interests and pleasures outside their homes. One club-woman explained, "Critics of women's clubs, the Rev. Mr. Leach including, may be chagrined to know that several hundreds of women, housewives, will spend Monday discussing live topics, reading papers, and enjoying musical programs, instead of superintending the washing of their husbands' shirts."[112] While Leach connected club life to the decline of traditional values, club members saw its pleasures as a release from domestic tedium. Without denying that they drank alcohol, the clubwomen disputed charges of drunkenness and demanded that Leach recant. Yet Leach stood by his claims, insisting that he had broad support among men. "Only yesterday," he declared, "a man in my church came to me and said: 'Leach, give me your hand. You are the hero of the northwest side.'"[113]

Although Leach gained many followers, the press eventually sided with the clubwomen and dropped the story. Leach's message failed to sustain public interest at least in part because many Chicagoans regarded clubs—which required membership and were inaccessible to outsiders—as private spaces governed by the rules of decorum that applied at home, where ladies could drink moderately. In his own anti-drinking efforts, Reverend Hopkins later gave credence to this distinction by contrasting illicit drinking in "public places" with respectable consumption "in homes or in private clubs."[114] Leach's message also missed the mark by exclusively targeting clubwomen, a group most contemporaries associated with public service, not debauchery. "The most reasonable and certainly the most charitable assumption," argued the *Chicago Daily News,* "is that Dr. Leach has failed to watch the work of the women's clubs in Chicago or to study the effects of their work as reflected in important social and economic reforms."[115] Club life did offer new possibilities for individual pleasure, yet most Chicagoans believed that women's clubs did more to promote civic welfare than reckless self-indulgence.

Four years later, Hopkins succeeded in arousing the level of widespread public interest to which Leach had aspired. Hopkins, who later spoke on the famed Chautauqua circuit, had a history of denouncing urban trends, including ice cream, dancing, and the custom of moving to a different rental home each spring.[116] Yet none of the pastor's other causes achieved the visibility of his "booze" crusade. Like Leach before him, Hopkins linked women's public alcohol consumption to decadence and the decay of home life:

> There is not one man here who would want that woman for his wife who would go into a restaurant and sip her cocktail or highball as nonchalantly as though it were tea. . . . This is the sort of woman who thinks it is more laudable to possess the expert knowledge to make a gin rickey than to fry a beefsteak and who thinks babies and housekeeping a drudge and a nuisance.[117]

Hopkins did not stop at sermonizing, however. He also coordinated a muckraker-style investigation that brought him to seventeen downtown restaurants. Accompanied by representatives from the local dailies, Hopkins hunted "women who booze" in establishments ranging from swanky after-theater haunts, such as the Tip Top Inn and the Pompeian Room, to quiet lunch spots with "reasonable" prices, such as the Boston Oyster House and Stillson's Café. All of these spaces, according to the *Inter Ocean,* attracted "women regarded as entirely reputable in the respectable neighborhoods where they live and by the decent society in which they move." Yet more than 50 percent of the ladies encountered were imbibing alcohol, a circumstance Hopkins believed should "arouse the energy of every man and woman in this city."[118]

Hopkins's crusade captured front-page headlines and drew hundreds of curious listeners to his sermons. But support for his cause divided along gender lines. Helen Hale, a writer for the Evangelical newspaper the *Advance*, reported that "only one woman in the vast city has publicly defended him."[119] Notably, the WCTU refused to endorse Hopkins, which provoked accusations that the organization failed to "apply to the goose the sauce with which they have so freely basted the gander."[120] In a series of letters to the *Inter Ocean*, a woman writing pseudonymously as Anna Freiheit ("freedom" in German) made clear the reason for Chicago ladies' "antipathy" to the pastor:

> No especial criticisms would have been made by women had Mr. Hopkins stopped at restaurants and noted that he saw so many "persons" consuming fancy drinks, but this reformer did not, so far as has been recorded, step up to any gentlemen and say: "Excuse me sir, but let me ask if you take claret in your lemonade, or pray inform me why you prefer the cocktail to a nice iced tea?" He counted only the women.[121]

Freiheit proposed that women should not be ashamed "to drink moderately at the table" and that the real offense was "being shadowed by a clergyman."[122] In her eyes, Hopkins's antics undermined "social equality between the sexes" by impinging on women's claims to public pleasure and the possibilities of urban life.[123] "Individualism is not a virtue in one sex and a sin for another," she had earlier reasoned.[124]

While Chicago women scorned Hopkins, many men rallied to his defense. "To any sane minded man," asserted one supporter, "the facts of Dr. Hopkins' sermons are undeniably true." In a letter to the *Inter Ocean*, James Truscott invited skeptics to "drop into some of the fashionable hotel cafés" to witness "the truth." Mustering even greater enthusiasm, Henry Mitchell, an insurance executive, insisted that Hopkins was "engaged in a noble work and . . . will find thousands upon thousands of supporters." Hopkins did purportedly receive a "flood of correspondence" endorsing his work. According to the *Chicago Tribune*, these letters demonstrated a sharp split between men and women. "As a rule those [letters] written by women, many of them anonymous, criticize him . . .

while the letters from men, all of sincere nature, extol his action and say all his charges are true." Hopkins claimed to be surprised by the censure he received from women but pleased that "in the hundreds of letters that I have received . . . there has been no word of criticism of my attitude toward women and booze that was written by a man." Nor did he receive significant criticism from the male-dominated press. On the contrary, the *Chicago Record-Herald* lauded his restaurant investigation as "one of the most remarkable bits of detective work ever carried on by a Chicago divine."[125]

The enthusiasm Hopkins inspired reflected broader apprehensions about the changing place of moneyed women in urban public life. In the year of the crusade, 1907, Chicago women made their first significant push into city politics by battling a newly proposed municipal charter. After being denied representation at the Chicago Charter Convention and then disappointed in their hopes for municipal suffrage, local clubwomen organized broad-based opposition that demanded a greater voice for women in city affairs. In the same month that Hopkins initiated his anti-booze effort, clubwomen helped defeat the charter referendum.[126] This activism undoubtedly unsettled many Chicagoans, including Hopkins. Indeed, amid his fight against public drinking, Hopkins denounced as a drunkard Catherine Waugh McCulloch, the president of the Chicago Political Equality League and a principal figure in the anti-charter movement.[127] He also underscored his belief that clubwomen had no place in politics. In a phone call with Emily Hill, head of the Chicago WCTU, he excoriated the organization for publicly campaigning on behalf of the Prohibition party ticket. "The minute [the WCTU] took up politics," he declared, "it lost its prestige."[128]

Yet the agitation against public drinking did not simply channel concerns about women's political engagement. At base, it reflected anxieties about women who dared to indulge their desires in public. According to Hopkins, his uneasiness over public drinking was first aroused when he witnessed a woman order a Manhattan: "Then she drank it with evident relish and murmured under her breath 'that was fine.'" Her obvious pleasure rankled the preacher and inspired him to investigate. In his sermons, Hopkins emphasized that he was not "meddling with people's business in their own homes." Rather, his concern was for ladies who made themselves vulnerable to public disgrace. As one supporter explained, "the disgust and horror" of women's public drinking was only fully apparent "when the eye rests on some woman of seeming culture, staggering or stammering under the influence of drink." Again and again, Hopkins raised the specter of the lady uncontrolled. He pointed to a Chicago woman who drank herself into "such a condition" at her club that she paid her account three times, as well as to a woman who became so intoxicated at a downtown hotel that she ripped her gown, ruined her hat, and required the attention of a doctor. Unlike men, the minister suggested, women could not control their own appetites. Light wine soon became "something stronger," and one drink turned into two, three, or even four. "Even if a woman is moderate in her drinking," maintained another supporter, "there is always the temptation for the weaker members of her sex to be less so." Hopkins argued that "the colored lights, the sensuous music, the careless and well dressed crowds" lulled the moral senses and led to "other and worse avenues of vice."[129]

Some tippling women reportedly did take up other vices, such as smoking and gambling.[130] But even those who enjoyed less daring amusements embraced the new focus on pleasure and excitement. In her discussion of café culture, Anita de Campi observed that many women paired alcohol consumption with club activity, trips to the theater, eating out, and card playing. "There is a tendency among women to flock together and entertain themselves without depending upon the men for their amusement—to have a jolly good time patterned after the fashion that men have enjoyed for so many years," she reflected. By thus "throwing themselves into the vortex of pleasure," ladies rejected the expectation that women "sat at home" while their menfolk enjoyed the possibilities of urban consumption. "Escort or no escort," de Campi claimed, tippling women were taking up new public pleasures and seizing "the spirit of enjoying oneself in one's own way."[131] That spirit invited ladies to consider their own wants—and to find fulfillment outside their roles as wives and mothers.

The self-indulgence of public drinking emerged as a theme in women's literature. In Kate Chopin's 1897 short story "A Pair of Silk Stockings," for example, the main character, a housewife on a tight budget, delights in drinking alcohol at a fashionable restaurant in an unnamed city. Rather than devoting an unexpected windfall to her family's needs, the protagonist purchases consumer luxuries for herself, such as silk stockings and a glass of Rhine wine. "She sipped the amber wine and wiggled her toes in the silk stockings," Chopin wrote. "The price of it made no difference."[132] Agnes Surbridge's 1904 novel about a Chicago clubwoman similarly connects the pleasures of public drinking with a release from domestic obligations. After attending a reception at a downtown hotel, the main character recalls, "there was music, and gay chatter, and laughter, and the excitement of strong coffee, and the fragrant punch from another dainty stand nearby, and I scarcely thought of my baby or the mother who was faithfully filling my place at home."[133] Surbridge's clubwoman joined Chopin's housewife and other lady tipplers in finding satisfaction and fulfillment outside their homes.

This shift toward individual pleasure troubled many Chicago men and inspired at least one husband to take legal action. In April 1910, Sidney J. Hamilton, a prosperous manufacturer, demanded that the proprietors of Chicago's downtown drinking establishments refrain from selling alcohol to his wife, Susan. According to Hamilton, Susan had grown overfond of "the dazzling glitter" of hotel cafés, where she liked to meet friends and "show her clothes." Invoking Illinois's dramshop law, which allowed spouses harmed by a person's drinking to recover damages from whomever sold that person alcohol, Hamilton "posted" his wife's name with the city's café owners. He then outlined his grievances to the press: "These dress display drinking places are the cause of more misery than any other places in Chicago. They are the places where wives spend their time seeking admiration, while the husband is slaving away at the office." Hamilton called on other men to join him in forming a "Husbands' Protective association" to safeguard "vain women" from the lure of tippling establishments. His appeal appears to have gone unanswered.[134]

Hamilton's efforts to halt the rise of the lady tippler came too late. The conventions governing ladies' presence in commercial drinking spaces were already evolving. Campaigns such as Hopkins's resonated precisely because men felt the cultural landscape shifting under their feet. By the time Hamilton brought his concerns to the press, the lady tippler had staked a place in urban life—and would not retreat. In a syndicated opinion piece published in 1910, noted Baptist author Rev. Madison Peters reflected on this revolution in manners. "That women drink as freely and frequently as the men is a sight that you can see for yourself in the fashionable cafés of our great cities," he averred. "Scenes that shocked us ten years ago are now passed by without comment.

Indeed, so common is drinking that the situation is often a source of embarrassment to the woman who does not drink." While covering the Hamilton affair that year, the editor of the metropolitan section of the *Chicago Tribune* echoed many of these sentiments and disparaged Hamilton's efforts to reverse the public tippling trend. "The modern woman," he declared, "insists that she shall have all the rights of man. If man can drink, says she, then she is entitled to the same privileges. . . . In short, mankind no longer need fancy that drinking in public is his prerogative."[135]

Not all ladies claimed that prerogative. But enough moneyed women drank in public to call into question standard historical accounts of Prohibition, which present ladies' support of repeal in the 1920s as a "startling" reversal.[136] Untiring dry advocates they all were not. In the metropolitan scene of fin de siècle Chicago, moneyed women reveled in the leisure, sociability, and sophistication of consuming spirits in commercial public spaces. They may not have objected to restricting working-men's alcohol use in cheap saloons and gin joints, but they did challenge constraints placed on their own public drinking. Sipping cocktails in elegant cafés and tearooms, they laid claim to new personal freedoms in the city center as they asserted that "women may do what men do."[137] Rejecting the old double standards of Victorian morality, they belonged to a new generation of women—no less than shop girls and factory operatives—who found autonomy, meaning, and even limited opportunities for political expression through consumption. The tippling lady was the flapper's progenitor, resisting the restraints on personal liberty later embodied in the Eighteenth Amendment and seizing the ideals that defined the Jazz Age: public amusement, self-indulgence, and female autonomy.

Of course, freedoms rooted in consumer capitalism had peculiar limits. Their enjoyment required access to financial resources and tended to reinscribe women's economic dependence on husbands or fathers. Moreover, these freedoms were exploited by businessmen aiming to capitalize on women's consuming desires, to induce new wants by promoting a vision of the good life as marked by luxury, spending, and acquisition.[138] The emergent culture thrived in no small measure because moneyed women were invited to drink fully of the delights offered by new commercial institutions—that is, to enter openly into a public arena of pleasure. But in serving the aims of entrepreneurs, tippling ladies also laid claim to new possibilities for self-fulfillment and revised the moral boundaries of urban public life. In the rise of the lady tippler lies the making of new standards of female respectability and the burgeoning of America's culture of consumption. As this culture flourished, however, the conflict over ladies' consuming practices spilled out of restaurants, cafés, department stores, and theaters and onto the city streets, where respectable women were increasingly crossing paths with less reputable denizens of the downtown.

5

Mashers, Prostitutes, and Shopping Ladies

"THE WOMEN of Chicago—the women who stand for things, see things and do things—are growing tired of running the gantlet of staring looks every time they go shopping." So declared a 1906 news report on the growing outcry against mashers, or sexually aggressive men, who made a hunting ground of the retail district. Following a wave of violent crimes against women, Chicago's "leading" female citizens, the report claimed, were seeking to improve the "civic conditions" that permitted mashers to accost unaccompanied women in public. "It has become so that a young woman cannot stand at any State street show window without being approached by one of these so-called 'mashers,'" lamented a member of the West End Woman's Club. "The minute you stop at a window one will walk up and stand there beside you hoping to get some encouragement."[1] The time had come, argued clubwomen, to "demand protection from the city against the men who hunt down helpless women on the public streets."[2] By calling on city officials to expand police protection for unescorted women and purge mashers from the downtown, Chicago women asserted a right to occupy and move freely in urban public space.[3] At the same time, they helped establish the "civic conditions" that enabled a culture of consumption to thrive.

Street harassment has, of course, existed as long as have streets. But the growth of the consumer economy generated new opportunities for predatory men to press their attentions on unescorted women. In Chicago, complaints first arose in the 1880s that gentlemen of dubious morals had taken to loitering outside theaters, department stores, hotels, and other commercial establishments that catered to female customers. These mashers only became more conspicuous as the retail district flourished.

By the early twentieth century, at nearly every street corner and shop counter along State Street they could be found ogling, insulting, following, and even fondling unaccompanied women. The "annoying masher" thus emerged as "the bane of many a modest girl's existence."[4]

But so, too, was he the bane of many a merchant's and entrepreneur's existence. Indeed, the capitalists who operated the very institutions that sustained the masher regarded him as a threat to their financial well-being. By harassing ladies, mashers rendered the downtown inhospitable to women and drove away valuable trade. As one observer noted in 1903, "The masher has become so rampant on State street that many women and girls avoid the thoroughfare as much as possible."[5] In short, the masher's unwelcome advances obstructed shoppers' mobility, stifling the flow of urban commerce.

To protect their interests, retailers, hoteliers, and theater owners joined Chicago clubwomen in demanding that city officials address the mashing problem. Their calls for municipal action affirmed an urban public realm where women—and their money—could circulate freely without compromising their respectability. It was a vision that state actors had not previously been charged with upholding. Public opinion had long maintained that virtuous women could easily repulse the average masher, while private business owners might drive away the most tenacious harassers. Yet shortly after the turn of the century, in the wake of high-profile assaults on unescorted women, demand for civic intervention in the mashing problem surged. Guided by clubwomen and capitalists, this popular outrage soon provoked official action. By early 1907, substantial municipal resources had been raised and redirected to curtail street harassment. Once considered a private problem, mashing came to fall squarely under the purview of Chicago police and city officials.

A city center where ladies traveled freely without male escorts departed from earlier models of urban public space. The nineteenth-century downtown had been dominated by men, and unattended women were often assumed to be prostitutes. Since Chicago's 1871 fire, brothels and saloons had lined south State Street, allowing the commercial sex industry to thrive. Yet as the retail district expanded, pressing south into the vice district by century's end, reputable and disreputable commerce collided. The proximity of the shopping district to the city's brothels called into question the virtue of any woman who ventured onto State Street in the early twentieth century without an escort. As a result, to enable the traffic of respectable ladies at a crucial moment in Chicago's development, city officials and business leaders drove traffickers in sex from the central business district into a segregated red-light zone.

Intimately connected, the efforts to contain prostitution and mashing redrew the social boundaries of Chicago's downtown. They also dramatically expanded the role of the state in maintaining an environment that facilitated consumption.[6] Existing scholarship has tended to link progressive campaigns against street harassment to an increase in women's public authority and the rise of a more self-reliant female ideal.[7] This account upholds that framework, yet it also demonstrates that such efforts did not merely erode male dominion over public space. The campaigns to purge mashers and prostitutes from the downtown helped establish a sanitized commercial sphere, where ladies could linger and feel at ease pursuing consumer pleasures. By curbing both streetwalking and street harassment, city officials and law enforcement agents facilitated commercial growth. Indeed, the modern consumer city was erected on a foundation of police power.

The masher first emerged as a problem of social order in the late nineteenth century, as unescorted women gained greater access to the public realm. In *Sister Carrie,* which opens in Chicago in 1889, Dreiser introduces readers to this "order of individual" by way of Charles Drouet, a traveling salesman who approaches the unaccompanied Carrie on a train. As Dreiser wrote, "He came within the meaning of a still newer term, which had sprung into general use among Americans in 1880, and which concisely expressed the thought of one whose dress or manners are calculated to elicit the admiration of susceptible young women—a 'masher.'"[8] The label derived from *mash,* slang for "flirt" or "crush," and had first been linked to actresses and their male admirers.[9] Its use, as Dreiser estimated, had indeed become common in the early 1880s.[10] By then, according to the *Oxford English Dictionary, masher* described a man who made indecent sexual advances to women, especially in public.[11] Drouet confines his mashing activities to initiating a conversation with Carrie and, later, beguiling her into a romantic relationship. But mashing could involve any unwanted sexual attention, from catcalling and making "goo goo eyes" to stalking and sexual assault.[12]

Women could be harassed in this manner by any man with ill intentions and access to public space, from a laborer on his lunch break to a millionaire on his way to the theater. Yet as represented in the press and reform discourse, the masher was most often identified as a native-born white man of financial means. Rarely did mainstream publications depict the masher as a racial or ethnic minority. In part, this bias owed to the racialization of rape, which cast nonwhites, especially African Americans, as brutish sex offenders. Accordingly, any advances made by nonwhite men to white women on the street were viewed as violent assaults rather than mere harassment.[13] Affluent white males also predominated in popular portrayals because the masher's activities were rooted in a sense of entitlement to urban public space that only men of that demographic fully enjoyed. In the tradition of the flâneur, who roamed the city as a way of consuming it, the masher depended on the privileges of race and class, as well as gender, in pursuing his targets.

Characterized as having "more money than sense," the masher was especially known for his dapper dress.[14] In *Street Types of Chicago* (1892), photographer Sigmund Krausz offered a typical portrait (fig. 5.1). Attired "according to the latest fashion plate," in a top hat and fitted suit, Krausz's masher was "every inch a dude" as he twirled his mustache and leered from the page. "Wherever we meet him," Krausz wrote, "he is trying to attract the attention of the fair sex" with his smart apparel and "winning smile."[15] Dreiser, too, noted the significance of the sartorial to the masher's activities. "Good clothes, of course, were the first essential, the things without which he was nothing," stressed the novelist. Notably, it was Drouet's stylish appearance that first kindled Carrie's interest. "There was something satisfactory," she mused, "in the attention of this individual with his good clothes."[16]

Carrie personified the white workingwomen who were objects of the masher's unsolicited devotions. But this new male figure appeared especially alarming because he also pursued moneyed ladies who entered the city center as pleasure seekers. Describing the masher's prey, club-woman and etiquette writer Mary Elizabeth Sherwood warned that "refined young women, belonging to the best families, had been followed for hours through the downtown district by some of these vain and villainous creatures."[17] In an illustrative case from 1904, a pair of mashers shadowed two affluent young wives along State Street before seizing one of the ladies from behind and saying, "Hello, Belle, what's

Figure 5.1 In *Street Types of Chicago—Character Studies* (1892), photographer
Sigmund Krausz provided a characteristic portrait of the masher. "We see
him every day, we see him everywhere, we meet him on the streets, in the
parks, in hotels, theaters," Krausz said of the man who was constantly "trying
to attract the attention of the fair sex." In accord with most contemporary
renderings, Krausz's masher was a dapper dresser who used his stylish clothes
to draw women's notice.   Sigmund Krausz, *Street Types of Chicago—Character Studies* (Chicago:
Max Stern, 1892), 10. Courtesy of the Chicago History Museum.

your hurry?"[18] As such accounts made clear, neither fortune nor family shielded women from harassment. Mashers, moaned the Reverend William T. Meloy of the First United Presbyterian Church, "go so far as to insult our wives and daughters."[19]

Although men accosted women of all racial and class backgrounds, public outcry concentrated on the moneyed white woman as victim. This focus owed, at least in part, to the widespread assumption that less privileged women courted male attention. African American women in particular were denied sexual respectability. Cast as lascivious sirens, black women rarely figured as victims of mashing in mainstream discourse.[20] White working-class women, by contrast, were occasionally recognized as objects of harassment. Still, they were often accused of inviting the male gaze by dressing or behaving immodestly—a perception rooted in class bias as well as in the fact that working-class courtship rituals left more room for public flirtation than did those of the moneyed classes.[21] Women commuting to work were just as vulnerable to street harassment as were moneyed ladies out shopping, but only the latter group was believed to possess the moral virtue that made a masher's advances unwelcome.

The exposure of moneyed women to harassment had grown with a consumer economy that drew them sans escort into the city center. Before the late nineteenth century, ladies had passed much of their time within the private realm, where their interactions were most often with men whom they or their families already knew. Whereas working-class women had long been forced to traverse the downtown on their own, moneyed women typically avoided appearing solo on city streets and public transit, where they might encounter male strangers. Failure to obtain a proper escort or chaperone in such places exposed a lady to charges of impropriety, even prostitution. Chicago's moneyed women gained new opportunities to explore the downtown alone—and to encounter unfamiliar men—as department stores, theaters, restaurants, and confectioneries proliferated on State Street at century's end. The novelty of seeing crowds of unattended ladies circulating in the city center, mixing with strangers, aroused the interest of many male Chicagoans. For at least some of these men, the leap from looking to harassing was easily made. Accordingly, mashing became ever more prevalent as the retail district thrived.

The masher arose wherever unaccompanied women congregated. Initially, he attracted attention for lurking near one of the first venues that catered to ladies without escorts: the matinee. In Chicago, mashers reportedly "turned out in force" on Wednesdays and Saturdays (when matinees were held) to gawk at the ladies as they exited downtown theaters. "As the hour for the ending of the matinees approaches," observed an *Inter Ocean* reporter, "these abnormal creatures begin thronging the corners in the vicinity of several theaters. Some plant themselves upon either side the entrance of a theater, and stare with their impudent eyes into the faces of ladies and young girls coming out." The boldest matinee mashers carried their pursuit indoors: "They often go inside, 'spot' their prey, and when the curtain falls secure a position behind the victim or victims."[22]

The dangers awaiting unescorted women outside Chicago's theaters in the late nineteenth century were briefly highlighted in Willa Cather's *Song of the Lark* (1915). The novel follows the career of Thea Kronborg, a young woman from Colorado who moves to Chicago in the 1890s to study music. After enjoying her first orchestral matinee at the Auditorium Theater, Thea emerges from the show only to be accosted by mashers. One young man, who had exited a nearby saloon, eyes her "questioningly" before inquiring, "Looking for a friend tonight?" When Thea offers no response, he walks away. A second masher proves more persistent:

> He wore an overcoat with a black fur collar, his gray mustache was waxed into little points, and his eyes were watery. He kept thrusting his face up near hers. Her hat blew off and he ran after it—a stiff, pitiful skip he had—and brought it back to her. Then, while she was pinning her hat on, her cape blew up, and he held it down for her, looking at her intently. His face worked as if he were going to cry or were frightened. He leaned over and whispered something to her. . . . "Oh, let me alone!" she cried miserably between her teeth.

The mashers' intrusions render the street a hostile, unwelcoming space to Thea. Their actions also rob her of the joy she had experienced at the performance. "There was some power abroad in the world bent upon taking away from her that feeling with which she had come out of the concert hall," Cather wrote. "Why did these men torment her?"[23]

The "torment" of mashers, initially confined to the vicinity of the theaters, soon spread to nearly every corner of the downtown. "They loiter about the theater entrances, the hotels, and cafés. But most of them will be found in the State street promenade, where our wives and daughters and sisters go shopping," remarked a city official.[24] Even beyond State Street, mashers forced their attentions on unaccompanied women. "It is impossible for a woman to walk along a street in the downtown district without being almost openly insulted," protested one young woman. "We hear comments on our dress, are told whether or not we are good looking, and are compelled to suffer other disagreeable things."[25] By the early twentieth century, the masher seemed omnipresent. "At the theater, in the restaurant, on the street, the street cars, everywhere, the masher is waiting for her, ready to tip his hat and utter the odious, 'How are you, sweetheart?'"[26] His actions, asserted one victim, transformed the downtown into an unpleasant "sea of eyes."[27]

When navigating this sea, ladies approached with special caution the many grand hotels that had sprung up over the last quarter century. Their lobbies and entryways were often thick with mashers, attracted by female guests as well as by ladies passing through for club meetings and other events.[28] A favorite haunt was the Palmer House, at State and Monroe Streets. On any given day, mashers were said to fill the lobby's armchairs and line the sidewalk out front so that "there was hardly room for pedestrians to pass."[29] The Palmer House was far from the only hotel troubled by mashers, but its position on State Street—within two blocks of most of the major department stores—made it a notorious "headquarters" for mashing.[30] In a 1903 piece on street harassment, the *Chicago Tribune* vividly detailed the scene outside. "The sidewalk in front of the Palmer house is the Mecca of the curbstone flirt," the paper explained. "From early morning to late evening feminine pedestrians in State street pass in constant review before those connoisseurs of their charms. The flirts line up some dozen deep at times, and their effrontery of manner and speech makes it a real ordeal for any woman who has to pass."[31] And many women did, indeed, have to pass due to the hotel's position "in the heart of the busiest shopping thoroughfare in the United States." By one account, "thousands of women" were insulted in front of the Palmer House "between the hours of 10 A.M. and 11 P.M. each day."[32]

Even if exaggerated, such estimates underscored the discomfort many women experienced in front of the Palmer House. According to Jane Brown, a reporter for *Inter Ocean*, the block near the hotel was "a space dreaded by every right-minded woman in Chicago." The men who gathered there relentlessly ogled passersby. "In winter they watch the women as the wind tosses their skirts and hats," Brown claimed. "In summer they are not dismayed by the heat; even rain does not frighten them away. For mustn't a woman lift her skirt in rainy weather, and do not these mashers have the supremest joy in the sight of a woman's ankle?"[33] To avoid such unwelcome scrutiny, many ladies chose to navigate around the Palmer House block. One young woman declared that she "made it a rule never to walk past this corner."[34] Others adopted a similar regimen. "So notorious is the corner as the lounging place of the masher," reported the *Chicago Tribune*, that women often "cross to the other side of the street to escape insults from the loungers."[35]

Many Chicago mashers made a habit of lingering inside State Street department stores, where female customers were rarely accompanied by male escorts. Detailing a popular tactic, a 1901 report on mashers stated, "They follow a woman into a store and interest themselves in articles or goods at which she is looking. If encouraged, they will assist her in making a selection."[36] Dreiser's masher, Drouet, employed this technique. "In the great department stores he was at his ease," the novelist wrote. "If he caught the attention of some young woman while waiting for the cash boy to come back with his change, he would find out her name, her favourite flower, where a note would reach her, and perhaps pursue the delicate task of friendship until it proved unpromising."[37] Not all department store mashers limited their strategies to unsolicited conversation, as Drouet did. Some took advantage of crowded stores to grope, pinch, and fondle unsuspecting female shoppers.[38]

Out on the street, mashers found a fertile hunting ground near display windows, where ladies paused to admire the latest wares. Speaking to the *Chicago Tribune*, Mary Elizabeth Sherwood recounted the experience of her friend, "an extremely sweet, refined young woman," who paused to look at a shop window. "She had been standing there but a moment," Sherwood narrated, "when an elegantly dressed young man took a place beside her at the window. He presented himself to her by remarking about several of the articles displayed. The young woman turned away from the window and started to the corner when she discovered the man was following her." The man "slunk away" as soon as the young woman confronted him. But other mashers were not as easily deterred. Ella E. Lane Bowes, founder of the Chicago Culture Club, told of a friend who had been shadowed up and down State Street while window shopping. A jewelry display first caught the friend's attention. "She had been there only an instant when a man edged in beside her and pressed up against her elbow," Bowes began. "She thought perhaps he was a pickpocket and turned to look at him only to find him smiling pleasantly in her face." The woman hastened away and did not stop again for several blocks. When she finally did pause at another store window, the masher reappeared at her side.[39]

Such reports underscored many women's reluctance to detail their own experiences with harassment and their desire to avoid embarrassment by relating the encounters of friends. Yet mashing was becoming so common that many women wondered if *any* woman could go shopping without being "subjected to a humiliating experience." To test this theory, reporter Jane Brown walked north along State Street, stopping only "to look at the pretty things displayed." She traveled the first block without incident. But upon reaching the corner of Jackson and State, two men approached her. The first, a gray-haired man with a pink carnation, "leered" and "grinned in an insinuating way." The second, a younger man in a Panama hat, touched her elbow and said, "Well, well . . . where now?" Both followed her to a nearby store and waited outside until she exited several minutes later. At State and Madison, a man with a "big diamond" and a "fierce black mustache" accosted her as she admired a corset display. "He stood facing the corsets when I first went to the window, then he turned, looked serious for a second, got closer," she recalled. "I moved, so did he. I side-stepped and went on. So did he, and whenever I stopped in that block he stopped also." By day's end, the reporter claimed to have endured several similarly trying interactions.[40]

In Brown's view, the experiment proved that even a woman who "attends absolutely to her own business" could not "shop in State Street and be unmolested in any way." The only means of combating unwanted advances, she contended, was to move with ruthless efficiency. It was a lesson the average female commuter had already learned, according to Brown. A workingwoman "knows that if she stays away from shop windows, if she looks neither to the right nor the left, is mindful of only the street crossings, she rarely knows what is going on in the faces of the men who pass-by," Brown explained. By contrast, the average shopper made herself vulnerable by pausing at store windows. "Frequently when she turns to a display," the reporter observed, "she encounters a pair of man's eyes looking down into hers." Engaged in an act of consumption, the shopping lady was often herself consumed.[41]

Brown's descriptions, even if embellished, made plain the potential for harassment to hinder women's freedom of movement on State Street. And, indeed, many Chicago ladies cited mashing as an impediment to using that thoroughfare. "It's simply disgusting!" asserted one shopper. "This street is getting so that I hate to come down here alone."[42] Sadie T. Wald, a housing reformer and organizer of the juvenile court, informed the *Chicago Tribune* that she had forbidden her daughter from visiting State Street alone "for the sole reason that . . . no young girl is safe from insulting looks and insulting remarks on the downtown streets." Evelyn Frake, a leading clubwoman and pure food activist, had adopted a similar policy for her daughter, then a student at the University of Chicago. "I am positively afraid to have my daughter come through the downtown district during the late winter afternoons," Frake confessed.[43]

Chicago retailers were acutely aware of the harmful effect mashing had on trade. Yet few openly discussed the problem for fear of tarnishing their stores' reputations. Speaking anonymously to the *Inter Ocean* in 1902, one State Street merchant offered a rare account of the difficulties posed by mashers. "We have numerous complaints from our women customers, but what can we do?" he lamented. "[A masher] is told to move on, and he moves on. But inside of ten minutes he is back at his post again, like a fly on your nose on a hot day." Several mashers, according to the merchant, had become fixtures on State Street, or "what we call curbstone habitués." "There's one old chap," he revealed, "who stands near the entrance to the Palmer house at least two afternoons every week. He wears the best fitting clothes that money and tailor's skill can produce." This particular masher often lifted his hat to a female passerby, commented on the weather, and then grabbed his target's arm. "Every shopkeeper on this side of State street on this block has had complaints against him from women customers," admitted the merchant, "but we have never managed to get him arrested."[44]

The behavior of "curbstone habitués" vexed shoppers and retailers alike. "There is not a merchant anywhere who does not look upon [mashers] as one of the deterrents to his business," declared a 1906 *Chicago Tribune* exposé. The favorite hangouts of these pests, such as the "lair" near the Palmer House, worked "against the best interests of nearly every business which lies within the block." The masher's antics, according to most merchants, interfered with everyday commerce. As such, his movements were carefully tracked. "Some of the professional mashers in State street have been known to business men so long," noted the *Tribune*, "that names may be given by some of the business victims of mashing."[45]

By the early twentieth century, many Chicagoans recognized that mashing threatened both the mobility of shoppers and the success of retailers. Yet what could be done about the problem? And who should take action? Were women alone responsible for their safety, as some moralists suggested, or did business owners have a role to play in protecting their female patrons? Further, what obligation, if any, did police and city officials have to women in public? At issue were notions of morality, public rights, and state power. The debate over these questions shaped commercial development in the early twentieth century. But the discussion had commenced many years earlier, in the 1880s, when the matinee masher first intruded into public consciousness.

"If there is one shallow-brained libertine more than another deserving of excoriation it is the 'masher,' the 'matinee masher.' He has become a bane to the city," announced an 1880 *Inter Ocean* profile of this disturbing new figure. At the time, only four "legitimate" theaters operated in Chicago.[46] But each of these elegant playhouses had begun to encourage female attendance by holding matinees. As these performances became more popular, complaints of mashing grew. On matinee afternoons, crowds of "well-dressed, and sometimes good-looking, dastards" lined both sides of downtown theater entrances to ogle and proposition female patrons. "Respectable ladies are helpless," insisted the *Inter Ocean*, "because no woman with an escort is ever molested."[47] To protect unaccompanied ladies from harassment, the *Inter Ocean* initiated Chicago's first anti-masher campaign. The plan did not call for more policing or stricter laws; instead, it focused on transforming public morals.

The *Inter Ocean* was then helmed by William Penn Nixon, a former Ohio legislator and staunch Republican with Quaker roots. Nixon managed both the business and editorial arms of the paper, dictating each issue's content and tone. Although no bylines were ever associated with the anti-mashing effort, Nixon was undoubtedly the unnamed "masher editor" responsible for the *Inter Ocean*'s coverage. In this capacity, he wrote, or at least oversaw, the relevant articles. Nixon's contempt for mashers likely owed to his commitment to civic reform as well as the influence of his progressive wife, Elizabeth Duffield Nixon. A member of the Fortnightly and the Chicago Woman's Club, Elizabeth helped found both the Woman's Exchange—a cooperative for female artisans—and the Illinois Training School for Nurses.[48]

To purge mashers from Chicago, Nixon and his *Inter Ocean* collaborators proposed to use one simple tool: public shaming. According to the paper's first article on the subject, "If certain familiar faces are hereafter found among the corner loafers, who make ladies afraid to attend theatrical matinees, their owners may expect to find their names published among the 'Directory of Mashers' this paper will establish." The plan was to surveil downtown theaters and then "minutely and unmistakably" describe any mashers. "It is the only method that now suggests itself for abating the nuisance, unless the male relatives of the ladies insulted hunt out and shoot down these harpies," the masher editor claimed.[49]

On the afternoon of the next matinee, three *Inter Ocean* representatives watched the four theaters holding performances. When few mashers were found, Nixon supposed that the paper's warning had encouraged them "to betake their slimy bodies to obscure hiding places until the commotion excited by the article might subside." The *Inter Ocean* thus delayed the release of its masher list. "But let no one be deceived into the belief that this paper will abandon the reform set about," the editor avowed. "Too much interest has been aroused in the matter to permit of retreat." Should mashers again descend on the theaters, the paper would publish its directory. "Threats will not avail to protect any of these mashers, be they high or low degree," the editor alleged. Even a libel suit would not deter the paper. "The pert little dandy who declared, in a party of his confreres, that he would 'make it hot for the *Inter Ocean*' if his name was ever published as a 'masher' will find his dire threat laughed to ridicule if he does not keep out of the way," the editor cautioned. "Fair warning has been given and repeated."[50]

The *Inter Ocean*'s actions elicited a wave of supportive letters from Chicago women. "Allow me, in behalf of the entire respectable community, as I am sure, to thank you for your plain words of exposure of those unmitigated nuisances who infest the precincts of our theaters

Wednesday and Saturday afternoons," asserted one characteristic epistle. The letter's author, identified only as an "Indignant Wife," stressed the need for decisive action. "The gauntlet of insinuating, indecent oglings, and attitudes, not to speak of more open shamelessness of speech, cannot much longer be run by any women of respectability," she wrote. Several missives conveyed a similar tone of exasperation. "I have more than once suffered annoyance from men who hang about theaters to insult ladies after performances," recounted another woman. "Matinees are for ladies and children, yet we often are afraid to go." Several correspondents urged Nixon to publish the directory. "Many citizens now wait to see the *Inter Ocean* break the ice and publish the names of these men," purported one letter writer. "Give us their names that we may know them."[51]

Perhaps emboldened by this outpouring of support, the *Inter Ocean* published its first masher list on October 14, 1880. The list was prefaced with a florid defense of the newspaper's actions. "Warnings and intimations seem only to have driven [the mashers] into less conspicuous places, but have not served to prevent them insulting ladies unfortunate enough to pass them," Nixon explained before providing brief descriptions of fourteen men. "One of these was a county employ, whose name is at this moment unknown. Another is known by the name of Kalloch," the report began. It was hardly the detailed catalog Nixon had promised. Still, the editor hoped the list would demonstrate that "the paper is in earnest in what it threatens." The report concluded by warning that more details—names, addresses, and employment information—would be released if the mashers did not reform their ways.[52]

This final threat proved hollow, however. The *Inter Ocean* never added to its directory. Fear of a libel suit may have deterred the paper from publishing more details. More likely, the sheer inefficacy of the campaign had spelled its doom. Surveillance of the theaters merely drove mashers to other parts of the retail district. "In fear of the 'masher editor,'" noted an article published later that year, the masher "has, of late, retreated from the immediate vicinity of the theaters after the matinees, and now ensconces himself at various convenient corners not far distant, where ladies must pass him on their way to the stores to attend to their shopping."[53]

With mashers resuming old practices—and, indeed, spreading to new corners of the Loop—the *Inter Ocean* acknowledged that private action alone could not eradicate street harassment. Police intervention was needed. Under Mayor Carter Harrison's administration, observed an *Inter Ocean* editorial, male harassers "are free from the frowns of the police, and are evidently 'solid' with the Mayor." A drastic policy shift was needed to contain the mashing evil and rid Chicago of "its danger and its shame." To ensure this outcome, the *Inter Ocean* exhorted readers to consider the mashing problem when casting their votes. "There is a way to stop this downward course and put the ban of criminality on all these practices," the paper maintained. "That way is to rebuke the men who have fostered and encouraged such demoralization by voting them out of office to-day."[54] As a Republican-leaning newspaper, the *Inter Ocean*'s criticism obviously aligned with a desire to undermine a Democratic mayor. Nevertheless, the paper's demand for police intervention marked a novel shift away from private solutions.

Until that point, city officials and police had paid little heed to harassment. This inattention owed, in part, to a simple lack of legal infrastructure. As the *Inter Ocean* emphasized in 1878, there was "no clause or section in the ordinances to cover [mashing], save that referring to disorderly conduct."[55] Further impeding action was the fact that police discretion alone determined what constituted disorderly conduct—and many police officers simply did not view street harassment as a criminal problem. In 1880, for example, one frustrated citizen wrote to the *Chicago Tribune* to report that a police officer had recently ignored the complaint of a "perfect lady" who was being harassed by a masher at the corner of State and Madison. "A policeman standing by was told of it, and the offender was pointed out to him," recounted the letter's author. The officer "indifferently replied, 'He's only a loafer,' and he continued to enjoy the chew of tobacco which he had deliberately taken while the lady was addressing him."[56]

Harrison was reelected in April 1881, but the *Inter Ocean*'s pleas for action against street harassment seemed not to have fallen on deaf ears. A month after his reelection, as part of a broader anti-vice effort, Harrison ordered chief of police William J. McGarigle to arrest mashers under the city's existing vagrancy law. In a directive to his captains, McGarigle explained, "You will instruct your patrolmen that it will be their duty to keep their respective posts clear" of "loafers and idlers, who habitually congregate on prominent street corners and in front of public places, using vile language and staring and often insulting women who have occasion to pass by." These men, the mayor indicated in his order, should be "classed as vagrants, and should be arrested and prosecuted as such."[57]

For the first time, city officials assumed some responsibility for regulating street harassment. Marking the change, the *Inter Ocean* jested: "And so [Harrison] is down on the 'mashers.' Oh, if the 'mashers' had known that before election."[58] A week later, the paper turned its attention to assessing the mandate's progress. "The fashionably dressed gang who make attendance upon matinees on the part of ladies a trying ordeal was not found distributed about its customary stands," the account began. The author claimed to have surveyed the scene in front of the matinee theaters. No sign of the pests could be found near McVicker's, Hooley's, or the Grand Opera House. "Ladies passed to and from the theater with impunity, safe from the shafts and ogling glances and obscene remarks so long and so disgracefully kept up in times past," the author affirmed. Meanwhile, outside Haverly's, only a few persistent mashers "obtruded themselves upon the notice of lady passers-by."[59]

The results excited Chicago's theater managers. Shortly after Harrison issued his order, Harry Hamlin, the manager of the Grand Opera House, stated that he took "great pleasure at the relief from [mashers'] presence." Hamlin had "repeatedly tried to drive [mashers] away without success" and had "begun to despair of ever getting rid of them." As a result, he welcomed police intervention. So, too, did the proprietor of Hooley's Theater, Richard Hooley, who wished to see even more police patrolling the theater district "in the interest of the people." Summing up the popular response, the *Inter Ocean* struck an optimistic note: "A feeling found expression also that the theater-going public were under obligations to Mayor Harrison for his prompt action in the matter, and it was hoped that the nuisance having been once put down would be kept down."[60]

But the masher was not kept down. No new police patrols were added to the theater district, and nearly half as many vagrancy arrests were made in 1881 as in 1879.[61] By the fall of 1882, the *Inter Ocean* admitted that the problem of street harassment not only continued but had grown worse. Once again, a "rowdy brigade of 'mashers'" could be found "loafing in the neighborhood of the theaters after the matinee," the paper lamented. "These vermin, driven away once by the power of public censure, are back at their old haunts in increased numbers."[62] And, once again, the paper called on police to intervene. "All over the city men are to be found ready to insult any lady whom they find unprotected," averred the *Inter Ocean*. "What do the Mayor and city officials generally propose to do about it? Nothing?"[63]

Nothing was precisely the course of action pursued by the city. Police and municipal authorities seemingly lost interest in street harassment. In 1887, the *Inter Ocean* observed that the vagrancy act had "long been in a state of desuetude," unused in the war on mashers.[64] A year later, Chicago's theater managers acknowledged that despite their best efforts, their establishments were still beset by mashers. "The nuisance is now greater than the oldest settler can remember," reported the *Chicago Tribune*. "The result is that . . . many ladies are abjuring the theater altogether."[65] Still, city officials took no further steps to prevent mashing.

The indifference of authorities, as well as many Chicago residents, toward the mashing problem would not be easily overcome. It found root, in no small part, in the belief that women alone, and not any outside authority, were responsible for their own safety. Any woman pursued by mashers, most contemporaries assumed, had somehow provoked the attention. In 1884, Mayor Harrison gave voice to this perspective at a benefit for a young woman who had been raped and murdered while walking home from work.[66] In his speech, Harrison admonished women "to stop flirting on the streets."[67] Failure to do so, he warned, would have dire consequences: "A young man lifts his hat and smiles to a young lady and she smiles in return—that smile in return was . . . the death-knell to that young girl's hopes." Harrison concluded by urging female listeners to "shun mashers as they would shun lepers."[68] His views were shared by many women as well as men. Actress Maude Waldemar, for example, asserted in an 1887 interview, "If you see a man following a girl, you may be sure that by a word or look she is leading him on." To ask police to intervene would be "absurd," the actress claimed, since a "woman is protected by her native modesty, and nobody knows it better than a masher."[69]

In the decade following the *Inter Ocean*'s failed mashing crusade, Chicago's retail district continued to expand, pressing south into the vice district. As a result, moneyed white women, who were typically credited with "native modesty," were brought into closer contact with women assumed to lack any such virtue: prostitutes. In plying their trade, streetwalkers allegedly encouraged inappropriate public expressions of male desire and, in turn, helped sustain the mashing problem. Moreover, the proximity of the vice district to the shopping district raised the alarming possibility that respectable shoppers might be mistaken for sex workers who welcomed the advances of strange men. To protect shopping ladies and facilitate the continued growth of the retail district, civic and business leaders resolved to drive female prostitutes, not male harassers, from the downtown.

For much of the nineteenth century, the women who most often moved unescorted in public space were prostitutes. Any woman who appeared on the streets unattended, or unowned, by a male companion was thought to be a "public woman," selling her body.[70] This assumption, according to British moral reformer William T. Stead, still guided Chicago's police force at century's end. In his best-selling exposé *If Christ Came to Chicago* (1894), Stead, who spent several months investigating the city's moral conditions, observed that anti-vice measures in Chicago involved indiscriminately arresting unescorted women in public. "The question as to whether a woman is a street walker or not is decided according to the arbitrary caprice of the policeman," he explained. "A woman sauntering or gossiping with a friend in the streets of Chicago at night is liable to be arrested by the police, in virtue of no ordinance, for the law is singularly weak, but in virtue of the high and singular power with which every police officer in Chicago seems to be invested to arrest anybody." Open solicitation was minimized as a result, Stead acknowledged. But that victory came at a terrible price: "sacrificing the liberty of the single woman in the streets of Chicago at night."[71]

The "arbitrary" power of Chicago police to arrest women on the street did not extinguish prostitution; it did, however, help restrict the "social evil" to a segregated red-light district known as the Levee. Since the era of the Great Chicago Fire, the Levee had operated just south of the business district, extending west from State Street to Clark Street, and south from Van Buren Street to Twelfth Street (Map 2). The first of two Chicago vice districts to bear this name, the Levee had gained an international reputation amid the World's Fair, when pleasure seekers as well as visiting reformers, such as Stead, toured the district's many brothels, bawdy saloons, and gambling halls.[72] Describing the nightly scene, Clifton Wooldridge—a police detective who patrolled the Levee in the 1890s—wrote, "At all hours after dark painted females, half-clad in

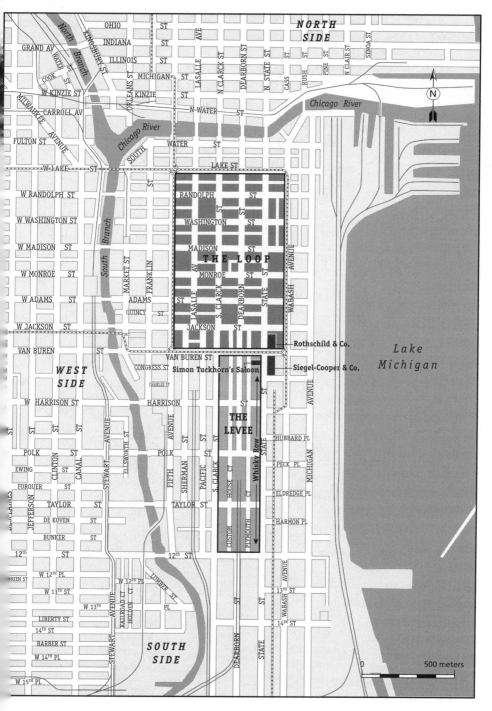

Map 2 The Levee Vice District at the Turn of the Century

finery, walked around in company with their low male escorts and held high carnival in the little dens called 'private wine rooms.' . . . They went from house to house in this awful locality, singing and yelling coarse jests and investing their money in cheap champagne." A sketch accompanying Wooldridge's text, captioned "Night Scenes on the Levee," depicted women in saloons and carousing on the street (fig. 5.2).[73]

For the unescorted woman, Van Buren Street, where the Levee met the business district, marked the "boundary line between decency and indecency."[74] Above Van Buren, retail stores, offices, banks, restaurants, grand hotels, and theaters competed for space in sleek new skyscrapers. Below Van Buren, dilapidated wooden buildings sheltered the industry of vice that had made the district famous. Since the 1870s, these two commercial spheres had operated side by side. But as the city prospered and demand for real estate grew, the business district strained against the Levee's northern border. The problem was vividly illustrated in a May 1901 *Chicago Tribune* photograph in which steel-framed high-rises stood opposite "old dives" (fig. 5.3).[75] As one real estate expert commented at the time, "The congestion at the central part of the city, the low prices prevailing outside of the older business district, and other things tempt the investor to cross over the line and build in what had been disreputable territory."[76]

The crunch for real estate was especially acute on State Street, where retailers paid top dollar for space on Chicago's preeminent shopping corridor. With inventory on the northern blocks of State Street evaporating, merchants and investors began to eye the rundown lots south of Van Buren, known as "Whisky Row." This strip harbored a nearly unbroken line of cheap saloons that spanned the full length of the Levee. As Mayor Carter Harrison Jr., son of the previous Mayor Harrison, recalled in his autobiography, Whisky Row then "duplicated a wild and wooly frontier town of cowboy days."[77] Prostitution and gambling were conducted openly, even flagrantly, along this street. "The conditions which exist elsewhere are to be observed here in an exaggerated degree," affirmed a 1901 *Chicago Record-Herald* editorial. "The 'joints' are strung along one after another, they thrust themselves upon the attention of the people, and . . . they keep up a perennial parade of vice and disorder."[78]

The first attempt to annex part of Whisky Row to the business district had occurred a decade earlier, amid the construction boom of the World's Fair. In 1892, Siegel-Cooper & Co. initiated the movement south

Figure 5.2 The nightly scene in Chicago's red-light district, known as the Levee, is depicted in this 1901 illustration from an account published by former police detective Clifton R. Wooldridge. According to Wooldridge, female prostitutes openly walked the Levee's streets and caroused in saloons and brothels.   Clifton R. Wooldridge, *Hands Up! In the World of Crime* (Chicago: Thompson & Thomas, 1901), 245. Courtesy of the Newberry Library.

Figure 5.3 The southern edge of Chicago's business district pressed against the northern border of the Levee in the early twentieth century. The result, as shown in this 1901 photograph, was an incongruous mix of skyscrapers and dilapidated "old dives."
"Where Levee and Business District Mingle," *Chicago Tribune*, May 26, 1901, 29.

by opening a grand new store at the southeast corner of Van Buren and State Streets.[79] Built by Levi Leiter, a former partner of Marshall Field, the block-long building stood eight stories high and contained a massive 553,500 square feet of floor space. When construction began in 1889, many Chicagoans doubted Leiter would find a tenant willing to locate so far south.[80] "His temerity," critics insisted, was "greater than his judgement."[81] As soon as news broke, however, that Siegel-Cooper had leased the space, Leiter was heralded as a visionary who had dared to reimagine the traditional boundaries of the business district.[82] When the store finally opened in March 1892, the *Inter Ocean* declared that "the retail trade center of Chicago had been moved south."[83]

Siegel-Cooper's relocation pressed the shopping district into closer contact with the Levee, a juxtaposition that inspired some concern. "State street yesterday evening to an observant man presented a problem in evolution," one reporter wrote the morning after the store's grand opening. "The sidewalks were filled with well-dressed prosperous men and women, come to inspect the locality where they would in the future do their trading." Yet the business of vice had carried on. "Between Van Buren and Harrison streets the old element still lingered," lamented the reporter. Evidence of Whisky Row's continued vitality was manifest in "the open doors of bar-rooms, or in occasional loungers at corner lamp posts." The reporter predicted, however, that State Street's evolutionary problem would soon be resolved. "The days of the old regime are practically ended," he argued, "and the business house will replace the saloon."[84]

This prophesy proved unduly optimistic. Whisky Row demonstrated considerable resilience in the decade that followed. Despite the relocation of stores such as Siegel-Cooper and Spaulding's Jewelry south of Van Buren, most of the old dives endured. The notorious saloon of Simon Tuckhorn, for example, carried on its trade directly opposite the main entrance of Siegel-Cooper. Within the very shadow of one of Chicago's largest commercial palaces, "Tuck's" peddled a heady blend of sex, booze, and gaming.[85] The boundary line between the Levee and the shopping district remained indistinct. "It is difficult to say," confessed one observer, "how much of State street is in the levee and how much has been annexed to the mercantile district."[86]

The proximity of the vice district to the central business district troubled Mayor Harrison. Since taking office in 1897, Harrison, like his father before him, had maintained a "liberal attitude" toward "necessary evils, such as alcohol, gambling, and prostitution." But Harrison also believed that these evils should be kept out from "under the noses of decent women" and contained "where no one saw it who did not wish to see."[87] He was, at base, a civic reformer, committed to economic growth and honest government. He had famously battled the monopoly of streetcar baron Charles T. Yerkes and helped fight graft in the city council.[88] In April 1901, at the start of his third term, Harrison further bolstered his reform credentials by replacing an unpopular and politically divisive police chief with a thirty-year veteran of the force, Francis O'Neill. The new chief, an Irish immigrant, had distinguished himself as a captain by shuttering several disorderly gambling houses in his precinct.[89] Upon accepting the nomination, O'Neill insisted that his actions "would be guided largely by what the Mayor considered desirable."[90]

Chief among the mayor's desires at that time was the expansion of the central business district, which was bursting at the seams amid a national economic boom that had begun at century's end. In the spring of 1901, rental prices across the Loop were surging to unprecedented heights. Unsurprisingly, the market was especially tight on State Street. As W. B. Frankenstein, partner in the real estate firm Willis & Frankenstein, observed, "Space in the retail quarter is practically all absorbed, and at rental in excess of those of 1900, with a demand for stores which the brokers cannot fill, and the retailer, wishing to enter the field, finds that he must . . . get outside of the 'Charmed Circle.'"[91] With the river providing a boundary to the north, the only space to move beyond the Loop's "charmed circle" lay to the south, on Whisky Row.

The potential of Whisky Row as a site of commercial expansion had not escaped the notice of Chicago's chief executive. Initially, Harrison claimed that "the steady pressure of business towards the south" would gradually cleanse the area.[92] But calls to accelerate this transformation were intensifying. According to business and property owners, "the fact that the territory south of Van Buren street had been turned over to disreputables of all classes made their property valueless for reputable business purposes." By June, their entreaties had swayed Harrison. "Whisky row on State street will have to go," he declared.[93] The "moral sweeping-out" began with the mayor revoking the license of the establishment that Chief O'Neill had labeled the "worst in Chicago"—Simon Tuckhorn's saloon. The immediate justification for the mayor's action was the suicide of seventeen-year-old Edith Smith, whose husband had allegedly forced her into prostitution at Tuck's.[94] Yet the commercial motives of the mayor's actions were not far beneath the surface. As a reporter for the *Chicago Tribune* surmised, "Tuckhorn's license was revoked because of the Mayor's desire to redeem the State street block." Tuck's was merely the first Whisky Row joint targeted for removal. "There are other places close to Tuckhorn's saloon which bear about the same repute," explained the reporter, "and to these Chief O'Neill has given warning."[95]

Warnings soon evolved into action. "Police Declare War against State Street's 'Whisky Row,'" proclaimed the *Inter Ocean* one week later. On

June 28, at Harrison's directive, O'Neill issued a police order designed to cripple the dives of Whisky Row. The order took aim at their core business—prostitution. "No women will be permitted in the saloons in this neighborhood," announced O'Neill.[96] The hope was that without profits from prostitution, Whisky Row saloons would suffer financially and eventually close or relocate. "Every saloonkeeper expects to shut up within a week," asserted one State Street patrol officer. "All know they are doomed."[97] Enforcement began exclusively on the block between Van Buren and Congress Streets—directly across from Siegel-Cooper. Saloons lying farther south on Whisky Row would have until August 31 to expel women. Reflecting on this timeline, O'Neill cautioned, "I want to say that the 'levee' has been downtown since the days of the Chicago fire. It is no light job to lift it up and throw it back a distance."[98]

Yet it did turn out to be a "light job" to regulate the traffic of women on Whisky Row. On the first evening the ban went into effect on the Siegel-Cooper block, O'Neill stationed several police officers on the street. They were instructed to surveil the saloons and raid any that defied the chief's edict. No raids were needed, however, as few women appeared north of Congress. "The few who did venture over the 'dead line,'" according to the *Chicago Chronicle*, "were stopped by the officers and told they would have to seek some other district."[99] When the ban was extended farther south on August 31, several saloons tried to resist enforcement. But once again police had little difficulty expelling women from State Street. "Promptly at midnight hundreds of women characters of the 'levee' were told that their presence was no more desired and they were forced to depart from the saloons," the *Chronicle* recounted. "Several detectives were on hand to see that no efforts were made to evade the new order, and at 1 o'clock this morning they reported that all the women had been driven into the street."[100] Herded like cattle, the women of Whisky Row moved south, deeper into the Levee.

Some observers questioned the legality of prohibiting women from entering Whisky Row establishments. The editor of the *Chicago Record-Herald*, for example, opined that "it is difficult to see upon what legal grounds the privilege of drinking can be denied to a woman."[101] Judge P. L. Palmer of the Denver district court agreed. While passing through Chicago, he argued that "city authorities have the right to compel good order" but could not "draw a line which takes from woman any privilege enjoyed by man." Palmer had devoted considerable thought to the subject, having recently issued an injunction preventing Denver police from barring women from a bawdy saloon there. "A woman has as much right, under the constitution of the United States, to enter a barroom or wineroom to take a drink as a man has," Palmer had stated in his decision.[102] Chicago officials disagreed. Harrison had taken the precaution of clearing the Whisky Row ban with Charles M. Walker, the city's corporation counsel. "There is no doubt that a reputable woman has a right to go into a saloon," Walker noted. "But in the downtown resorts the probability is that any woman found in a saloon is disorderly and could legitimately be excluded. Of course, the police have control over disorderly houses."[103] In short, simply by appearing in a Whisky Row saloon, a woman could be deemed disorderly and driven away.

And many women were, in fact, driven away. As the *Chicago Tribune* observed in mid-July, "Women are leaving the territory in large numbers."[104] Saloonkeepers on Whisky Row soon felt the effect, with their average receipts falling from $100 a day to less than $10. Faced with dwindling profits, several saloons, including Tuck's, moved south. The exodus transformed Whisky Row from "one of the worst pestholes of the city" to an area as orderly "as the main street of a country town."[105] In his annual report for 1901, O'Neill highlighted this achievement. "Lewd Women and street walkers so-called finding the new conditions unfavorable and repressive, have practically disappeared from the business district," he wrote. "The 'Levee' district has been considerably curtailed and the opportunities for the extension of the business district have been correspondingly increased."[106] By 1905, the Levee's boundaries had been pushed even farther south, to a region between Eighteenth and Twenty-Second Streets, leaving much of the district's former home open to commercial development.[107]

That Harrison's purge had succeeded seemed obvious to real estate men, who soon reported rising retailer interest in property on Whisky Row. "The order of Chief O'Neill to move the levee district south of Harrison street has already shown good results," claimed Edward F. Keebler, head of commercial real estate firm E. F. Keebler & Co., in early September 1901. "Only a few days ago we made an offer for one of our customers, a large retail house, of $12,000 a year for a sixty-foot building on State, south of Van Buren street."[108] Three years later, Keebler remained bullish on Whisky Row. "Since Mayor Harrison ordered the levee district in State street to move farther south, a number of desirable tenants have located south of Van Buren street and there have been a number of important sales," he revealed. "State street south of Van Buren will be an important factor as a retail district."[109]

Retail establishments had indeed begun moving to south State Street. The millinery house of Baumgarden & Littman, for example, leased space on State Street just north of Tuck's former location. Before moving into the new space, previously a cheap hotel, the merchants modernized the building, adding electric lighting, steam heat, and elevators.[110] Retailer Henry Friend, who dealt primarily in cloaks, signed a five-year lease for a large storefront a few doors down.[111] Both additions were just above Van Buren. Still, real estate experts believed the rental market south of that critical avenue would continue to strengthen. "The condition on State street, south of Van Buren, is improving every day," insisted the *Inter Ocean*'s real estate columnist in the summer of 1905. "The cleaning of this locality from disreputable resorts has had a wonderfully stimulating effect on real estate values."[112]

The crusade to purify Whisky Row—and open south State Street to retail development—hinged on the ability of city officials to control the movement of unescorted women in public space. The objects of reform in this instance were not women in hoopskirts or high hats, nor even lady tipplers, but sex workers in the Levee's dives. To enable moneyed women to circulate as consumers in the city center, the freedom of movement of disorderly women was constrained. "The time is past," one observer later declared, "when the citizens of Chicago will permit the dissolute denizens of Whisky row to rub elbows with the respectable shoppers."[113] In the next decade, as the emphasis of vice reform pivoted from segregation to abolition, prostitution would cease to be countenanced in any region of the city.[114] In the meantime, by corralling prostitutes into a bounded area far from the downtown, Harrison, O'Neill, and their allies had secured a purified commercial realm, where unescorted shoppers could roam freely without compromising their respectability.

With "dissolute" women thus purged from State Street, only respectable women remained to absorb the interest of male predators. As the retail district thrived, reports multiplied of mashers harassing moneyed white shoppers. In response, many Chicagoans demanded coordinated action against mashing. Only a minority, however, believed that the mashing problem fell within the purview of the state. Instead, as Chicagoans had many times in the past, they turned to the private sector for solutions.

In May 1901, mere days after Francis O'Neill began his tenure as Chicago's new chief of police, the Lakeview precinct headquarters received a call from the proprietor of a corner drugstore. Since warmer weather had arrived, the storeowner complained, a group of mashers had been gathering out front to insult "every woman that passed."[115] Captain Herman F. Schuettler, who led the district, promptly dispatched a police wagon to break up the scene. Eight men were arrested. For the next two days, the *Chicago Tribune* splashed stories touting a new anti-mashing "crusade" across its front page. "Police Aim to Check Mashers," one headline declared. "New Chief Ready to Extend Crusade." The accompanying sketch, titled "Trouble for a Chicago Pest," depicts a courtroom in which Lady Justice is shown spanking a masher. Several other mashers, flashily dressed, anxiously observe the proceedings, while a judge and police officer look on with approval (fig. 5.4).[116] Finally, it seemed as if city officials were taking steps to abate the mashing problem.

Yet evidence that police or city officials had any intention of sustaining a "crusade" against mashing was thin. Not only was the *Tribune* the only paper to announce the start of the alleged crusade, but its coverage revealed little more than indifferent commitments from police. "While of course I know that the masher is more or less annoying to women, no complaints have been made to me," the new chief told the paper. O'Neill pledged to respond to any reports of harassment but offered no "radical action" to address the problem. In his estimation, the police department did not have the resources to "carry on the work successfully" and had to prioritize other issues. "After the pickpocket, the thug, the holdup man, and the 'con' man comes the 'professional masher,'" he specified. Such indifference extended down the chain of command. As one officer noted, "We are busy with the 'con,' thug, and holdup men, but I guess we are able to take any steps needed to shield our girls."[117]

No new steps were taken by police, however. This inaction met most Chicagoans' expectations. Even those who decried mashing rarely advocated police intervention, calling instead for private solutions. "I would leave the matter to the men of the city instead of asking the police force

TROUBLE FOR A CHICAGO PEST.

Figure 5.4 This 1901 cartoon, which portrays Lady Justice spanking a masher, implied that police and city officials would address street harassment and hold mashers accountable for their actions in court. The vision was overly optimistic, as substantial municipal resources would not be devoted to the mashing problem for another five years.   "Trouble for a Chicago Pest," *Chicago Tribune,* May 7, 1901, 1.

to take it up," advised clubwoman and suffragist Dr. Julia Holmes Smith. "The best remedy, to my mind, would be for the men to take it upon themselves to thrash the street masher."[118] Among those echoing her call for vigilante justice were Charles Atkins and Walter Williams of the Christian Endeavor Society, a nondenominational youth group. The two friends proposed organizing an "Anti-Mashers League" to defend women "on the streets, in public buildings and stores, in railroad trains, and in street cars."[119] The goal was to enlist "athletic young men" to "smash the mashers." Members were to "wear little emblems on their lapels" and physically restrain anyone caught mashing.[120] The plan reportedly won the "sympathy" of O'Neill and his men.[121] Yet despite initial enthusiasm, the league quickly disappeared from the media spotlight, leaving no evidence of having ever successfully "smashed" a masher.

That Chicagoans would favor applying private resources to a public problem was hardly surprising. Private organizations and funds had often been used to accomplish civic goals in the midwestern metropolis. Since the 1893 World's Columbian Exposition—a substantial portion of which was financed by local business leaders—private capital had been tapped to pave roads, create parks, found schools, shelter the homeless, and build streetcar lines. Regulating mashers might have easily been another item added to the list. And, indeed, at least one group had already begun devoting its own resources to street harassment—State Street business owners.

Hotels were the first to invest in anti-mashing efforts, likely due to their frequent use as waystations for male flirts. At the Palmer House, for example, driving away mashers had been a priority of its private police force since the late 1890s. A hotel security team targeted the "smirking, mustache-twirling" masher and aimed to ensure that he "will be made to move on and no longer will be allowed to smile at impressionable passers-by."[122] The hotel's managers later made several changes to the physical environment to discourage loitering, removing the billiard room from the ground floor as well as the armchairs that lined the entrance hallways. Both features had attracted male idlers "who ma[de] it a pastime to force their attentions on women," and their elimination, it was hoped, would render the space "much less inviting" to these men. Other grand hotels, such as the Great Northern and the Sherman House, experimented with similar tactics to discourage harassment.[123] The head house detective at the Auditorium Hotel went so far as to entrap mashers by disguising a "good-looking maid" as a female guest and placing her as bait in the hotel's parlor.[124]

State Street department stores, too, developed methods for deterring harassment. For retailers, the stakes of the mashing problem were even higher than for hoteliers, as women constituted a majority of department store customers. Within the store, the floorwalker became the first line of defense. Floorwalkers, many of whom were men, oversaw operations in an assigned department or zone. Among their responsibilities was ejecting any unwelcome individuals, including mashers. "O, those men and boys—some of them nothing but boys—give us much trouble," disclosed one floorwalker from a State Street department store. "We have to drive them out of here every day."[125] The protection provided by floorwalkers sometimes drew women into the store. For example, when a strange man "shadowed her from one end of the shopping district to the other," an unnamed member of the Young Fortnightly Club entered a department store so that a floorwalker could "aid her in getting rid of the masher."[126] In another instance, a woman who had been followed for hours by a masher found relief only when she appealed for help at a department store lace counter.[127]

But floorwalkers could not patrol downtown streets, where mashers preyed on window shoppers, promenaders, and women waiting for public transit. There, in the domain of the police, retailers were "powerless to cope."[128] For years, State Street business owners had been issuing "vain appeals" for police officers to purge well-known masher hangouts, such as the block in front of the Palmer House. These requests had largely gone "unheeded," however.[129] On the rare occasions when patrol officers were moved to act, their assistance was marginally effective, according to merchants. As one retailer explained, "We report the matter to the police, who sometimes succeed in identifying their man and arrest him. But there the matter ends."[130] The arresting officers often failed to follow up on the charges in court, and offenders soon returned to the streets.

With police unable—or simply unwilling—to "drive [the masher] away," State Street merchants resolved in October 1904 to "band together" in a "systematic crusade for the protection of women customers."[131] "A war of extermination on the masher has been declared by the State street department and dry goods stores," announced the *Inter Ocean*. "The insults offered to respectable women who come down town on shopping trips have become so frequent and so gross that the merchants have been forced to act, in the absence of any willingness on the part of the police, to rid the street of the pests who ogle women at every turn." In addition to driving away known offenders, the merchants planned to maintain jointly a "system of detectives, privately working in the crowds, even outside of the stores."[132] Their efforts attracted national press attention. "'Mashers' have become such a nuisance on State street that all the dry goods stores have entered into an alliance to prosecute and drive them off the street," proclaimed one characteristic report.[133] From New York City to Washington, D.C., Minneapolis to Charlotte, the press lauded Chicago merchants' novel approach to protecting their customers.[134]

The scheme's principal champion was Edward Hillman of Hillman's & Co. department store. Hillman had begun his career as a cash boy at the Boston Store and had worked his way up to general manager of that establishment before opening his own retail house in 1898.[135] Located at the southwest corner of State and Washington Streets, in the former home of Carson Pirie Scott & Co., Hillman's & Co. stood within a block of four other department stores—in other words, at the nexus of the mashing problem. To drive away mashers, Hillman sought to enlist the cooperation of not only other store owners but also private citizens. "Every man who passes along State or any other street should assist in the maintenance of good order by assisting the store owners in their prosecution of mashers," he contended.[136] In Hillman's view, the problem of street harassment touched everyone who traversed the city center.

Hillman did not undertake this "war" alone. Six of Chicago's largest retail houses supported the initiative, and others were expected to join. "I am surprised that nothing has been done officially in this matter long ago," confessed Robert M. Fair, a partner at Marshall Field & Co. "Our firm will certainly do everything in its power to protect shoppers—our customers or others." Jacob L. Kesner, general manager of the Fair, indicated that he would personally devote as much time as possible to the initiative "until any woman can patronize the State street stores without constant fear of molestation." Executives from Mandel Bros., Rothschild & Co., and Siegel-Cooper pledged "vigilant participation" in the fight. "Not only our own customers, but others," avowed the head of Rothschild & Co., "will find ready refuge and assistance from us."[137]

The amount of resources that retailers ultimately invested in the scheme remains unclear. Nevertheless, their conviction that the "vultures of State street" could no longer be permitted to harass female shoppers was apparent. Notably, their concern focused on the safety of customers—not the female clerks or cash girls who staffed their stores. For these businessmen, the stakes of the "War against the Mashers" were unambiguous: street harassment discouraged potential customers from spending time and money in the retail district.[138] Reportedly, the merchants had been compelled to act because only "the most courageous of women" had "dared to venture of late into the shopping district without escort." When asked for comment on the retailers' efforts, even Chief O'Neill underscored their financial motivation. "I am told that this annoyance materially cuts down the business of some stores," O'Neill responded before noting that the volume of mashing complaints had accelerated in recent years. "We are receiving hundreds of complaints every day," he admitted.[139]

State Street business owners demonstrated no comparable interest in protecting female employees. Yet these women were often harassed when commuting to and from work, especially at night. The problem, ignored by retailers, became a focus of activism for reformers. Since its founding in 1885, the Protective Agency for Women and Children had provided aid to women victimized by sexual violence. Among its members were moneyed ladies from organizations such as the Chicago Woman's Club, the WCTU, and the Cook County Woman's Suffrage Association. Its clients, by contrast, were primarily working-class women.[140] According to the agency's class-biased view, State Street mashers promoted the "demoralization" of workingwomen and made them vulnerable to prostitution. To protect female workers, the agency's leaders demanded the "immediate enactment of more stringent laws vesting greater rights of punishment." They also called for better police protection. "If the chief of police wants to ingratiate himself in the hearts of the self-respecting women," argued Alice J. Sterling, the agency's corresponding secretary, "and at the same time rescue hundreds of poorly paid shop girls from the pitfalls opened to them by this class of grinning, idiotic criminals, he will send a squad of policemen to State street and arrest every masher on sight."[141]

But law enforcement demonstrated even less interest in protecting laboring women than it did in protecting shoppers. State Street patrol officers maintained that in the absence of any complaint, mashing was "too delicate for their attention." Often young working-class women welcomed street flirtation, officers insisted. As such, unless explicitly appealed to for help, police "wouldn't for the world interfere with an incipient flirtation if the young woman appears to be in a receptive mood."[142] Several officers claimed to have embarrassed themselves attempting to rescue workingwomen from mashers. "Sometimes we think we are pretty sure that someone is getting insulted," alleged William Dooley, who patrolled the corner of State and Adams Streets, "but if we interfere nine times out of ten the girl will say she has no complaint to make or that she knows the fellow." Dooley recounted his own ill-fated attempt to arrest a man who had been showering a woman on the street with "sweet smiles and bows." When Dooley ordered him to desist, the woman curtly replied, "What concern is it of yours how much he bows to me?"[143]

Despite growing demand from business owners and reformers, anti-mashing efforts remained firmly within the private realm. The city's failure to act was partially the result of a shortage of manpower. Chicago had the least police officers per resident and per square mile out of the country's five largest cities.[144] But an even greater obstacle to state action was the widely held belief that mashing was only a nuisance. "Too much importance has been given to the question of suppressing the mild 'masher' evil," the *Chicago Chronicle* asserted. "It is seldom, indeed, that a woman or girl on the street at timely hours, modest, circumspect and careful in her deportment, meets interference from men who are sober."[145] Few Chicagoans departed from this view and advocated using public resources to combat mashing—that is, until the death of one unescorted woman placed a spotlight on the problem of street harassment.

In January 1906, the lifeless body of a woman was found lying face down in a manure heap on Chicago's Near North Side. Around her neck was coiled a fifty-inch copper wire. The wife of an executive at a large printing firm, Bessie Hollister was affluent, socially prominent, and a leading figure in her church. On the morning of her death, Hollister had left home to perform several routine errands—purchase a bouquet at the florist, place an order with the grocer, take a clock to the jeweler's, visit her dressmaker, and sing with her church choir. She never completed these tasks, however. At some point during the day, Hollister was dragged from the street into the stables of a carpentry shop, raped, and strangled to death.[146]

The grisly fate of the "beautiful and accomplished" young white woman captivated and enraged the city.[147] "Probably no murder of a private citizen who was unknown to the public at large, ever anywhere created so much widespread indignation," observed a psychologist studying the case.[148] Many commentators at the time interpreted Hollister's death as an "atrocious" climax to a "crime wave" targeting unescorted women.[149] This wave, which purportedly included at least three additional homicides, was "imperiling the lives of women who venture on the streets alone."[150] In mass meetings convened across the city after Hollister's slaying, Chicagoans resolved that official action must finally be taken to protect women in public.[151]

From the outset, Hollister's murder was linked to the problem of street harassment. "The masher and the murderer of Mrs. Hollister belong to the same species," explained Evelyn Frake, then president of the Illinois Federation of Women's Clubs, to the *Chicago Tribune*. She continued:

> The question, "What shall be done with our mashers?" is a serious one at the present time. Chicago literally is infested with them. At no time in my memory have the streets of Chicago been so unsafe as now. The situation positively is serious. . . . It is positively dangerous for a woman to go on the street nowadays.[152]

Other Chicagoans voiced similar concerns. As a writer for the *Inter Ocean* noted, it was from the "ranks" of mashers, those "dangerous human pests," that men who murdered women developed.[153] Four days after Hollister's death, the peril posed by mashing was highlighted by Ralph Wilder, an artist for the *Chicago Record-Herald*. In a sketch titled "Chicago's Foremost Duty," Wilder depicts a well-dressed white woman walking alone as two men trail menacingly behind her. An enormous fist, imprinted with the word "Chicago," halts the men's pursuit by pummeling the first man while the second man, helpfully labeled "Masher," watches with dismay (fig. 5.5).[154] The implication was that Chicago must take action against mashers to protect women in public.

Ogling, catcalling, following, and even grabbing a woman on the street were a far cry from murder. Still, many contemporaries believed that mashing fostered an environment where violent crime—particularly against women—flourished. This perspective was illustrated in comments made by Justice John F. Boyer, of nearby Evanston, when faced

Figure 5.5 "Chicago's Foremost Duty," as depicted in this 1906 illustration by Ralph Wilder, was to protect unescorted women from harassment by mashers on the street. Wilder's drawing portrays a masher being pummeled by a large "Chicago" fist, while another man, with the label "masher" attached to his lapel, watches in dismay.   "Chicago's Foremost Duty," *Chicago Record-Herald,* Jan. 16, 1906, 1.

with two mashers who had been arrested for "insulting" women at a train station. "It is just such scenes as this one," Boyer said of the men's behavior, "which leads to the crimes which are committed in Chicago, where women are held up and robbed and even murdered."[155] Reverend John Norris Hall, of the Wesley Methodist Episcopal Church, where Hollister had been a parishioner, shared this outlook.[156] Addressing an anti-crime meeting, the pastor described a recent incident in which a masher—"blonde and well-dressed"—accosted a member of Hall's congregation and, after trying to take the woman's arm, followed her about the city. Had the woman not found refuge in Hall's home, the pastor claimed, she would have faced the same fate as Hollister.[157] For Hall and many other concerned citizens, the progression from harassing women on the street to slaying them in cold blood seemed inevitable.

To halt the "carnival of crime," Chicagoans agreed that police resources had to be devoted to mashing.[158] But this feat would not be easily accomplished. The Chicago Police Department was then struggling with unprecedented levels of understaffing and underfunding. As Chief John M. Collins, who had replaced O'Neill the summer before Hollister's death, acknowledged in his annual report for 1905, "The numerical strength of the department has been inversely proportioned to the city's growth in population."[159] Since 1899, Chicago had gained nearly 400,000 residents, but the size of the police force had actually declined by almost 700 men.[160] In comparison to other large cities, Chicago's force was diminutive at best, with only 68 patrolmen for every 100 miles of streets. By contrast, New York City had 304 patrolmen for the same area; Boston had 186; and St. Louis had 128.[161] Following Hollister's murder, Collins—facing sharp criticism of his leadership—insisted that an insufficient number of officers was the primary obstacle to his ability to protect women on the street. "With an adequate force," he contended, "adequate protection would be possible." To enable this work, Collins requested an additional one thousand men.[162]

Many Chicagoans rallied to the cause of expanding the police force. Still, financing proved a sticking point. "The city is without funds—we cannot go into debt for the men, but we must get them," admitted Mayor Edward F. Dunne, who had succeeded Harrison in 1905.[163] Several funding proposals emerged.[164] The most popular called for doubling the city's liquor license fees—a move that would add $1 million in annual revenue and, as a supplementary benefit, drive out of business some of the most disreputable drinking establishments.[165] Yet the success of a "high license" law was anything but certain in a city where saloon and liquor interests had long held substantial political influence.[166] A heated battle over license reform commenced.

In the months that followed, as the city council debated and revised the high license ordinance, Chicago women's clubs, led by the Cook County League of Women's Clubs, emerged as outspoken advocates of the reform. Composed of hundreds of distinct women's organizations from across the city, the league represented nearly ten thousand clubwomen and held "the pulse of the woman's clubs of Chicago."[167] At a league meeting in February, license reform emerged as a key issue. "It is high time for the women of Chicago to demand that the streets of Chicago be made safe for the women and children," declared Mrs. Frederick K. Tracy, president of the West End Woman's Club, which was hosting that month's gathering. Tracy introduced a resolution recommending that clubs belonging to the league endorse and work to pass the high license law for "the protection of the women of our city." All but one woman present voted to support the measure.[168]

Collaborating across league organizations, Chicago clubwomen drafted petitions, lobbied aldermen, and spoke out for high license reform. The most prominent groups to join the effort included the Chicago Woman's Club, the Fortnightly, the Friday Club, the Daughters of the American Revolution, the Catholic Woman's League, the National Council of Jewish Women, the Lake View Woman's Club, the Chicago South Side Club, and the Englewood Woman's Club. Even many organizations whose missions had no obvious connection to civic welfare, such as the Amateur Musical Club and the art-focused Arché Club, provided support. "Every member of the Arché Club is anxious that something be done at once to check the crime wave that is imperiling the lives of women," proclaimed the club's president, Mrs. Charles F. Adams. "I believe every woman's club in Chicago has been aroused."[169]

In agitating for high license reform, Chicago clubwomen stressed the need for "relief from conditions which make it unsafe for women to go on the streets alone."[170] This relief, they maintained, could be achieved if the city devoted more attention and resources to street harassment. Providing a characteristic view, Emily Hill, president of the Chicago branch of the WCTU, stated, "I would suggest that more policemen be put into the downtown district and that every uniformed police officer and every plain clothes officer should be instructed to watch for mashers and arrest them as unhesitatingly as they would pickpockets or criminals of any other kind." Others recommended expanding police powers to make apprehension easier. "The interpretation of the police power to arrest suspicious characters might be enlarged to reach the mashers," proposed Gertrude Blackwelder, a vice president in the Chicago Woman's Club. In her view, police officers must "be given the power to arrest the masher on sight or on complaint without the issuance of a formal warrant." This suggestion was echoed by several other clubwomen, including Marion Burton Upton, who further recommended harsher punishments for mashing offenses. "A fine is not a heavy enough penalty," Burton emphasized. "Severe measures should be resorted to."[171]

At least one Chicagoan had a strikingly different view of how best to secure women's public safety. Persuaded that additional officers could never entirely extinguish the mashing problem, Chief Collins advised women simply to "stay at home," especially at night.[172] It was an opinion shared by other male commentators. "No man," suggested the editor of the *Chicago Chronicle*, "can feel that his wife can go for an afternoon with a sister or friend with any confidence that she will be permitted to return in safety."[173] Unless the streets could be made "reasonably safe," the editor argued, it was "unwise in the last degree, for women especially, to try to use them."[174] This perspective was later reinforced in a *Chronicle* cartoon titled "Four Ways in Which Women May Protect Themselves from Holdups." Composed of four separate panels, the drawing depicts a woman fending off an attacker with jiu-jitsu, a hatpin, and a police whistle. "But the fourth and best way," the sketch concludes, "is to stay at home at night."[175]

The suggestion that women limit their public movements aroused immediate opposition. Among the first to voice disapproval was Dr. William A. Quayle of the St. James Methodist Episcopal Church. From his pulpit, Quayle implored Chicagoans to apply "serious thought" to the police chief's advice that women "stay at home." "I think this is the most humiliating circumstance I have ever known to occur to city life, that the authorities responsible for the maintenance of public order should feel themselves compelled to refuse the right of the road to any of the city's citizens," remarked the pastor.[176] For Quayle, safe access to city streets was a basic right of citizenship.

His outlook was shared by many Chicago women, who likewise found little to appreciate in Collins's advice. In the words of Mrs. W. C. H. Keough, who had earlier founded the short-lived Catholic Daughters of Temperance, "Every woman should turn a deaf ear" to the suggestion that she "should not go unaccompanied along the streets." As Keough wrote in an opinion piece for the *Chicago Tribune*, women had a "Right to Be on Streets" and should refuse to stay at home. "It is time for Chicago women to arouse themselves from their lethargy and demand protection from the city," she asserted. Keough called on her peers, other moneyed white women, to persevere in the fight against mashing—for their own benefit as well as for the benefit of workingwomen who were compelled to use the streets. "It is an easy matter for the woman of leisure to stay at home when her husband cannot go out with her," Keough noted. But "the woman in comfortable circumstances must outreach a helping hand to the less fortunate sister who cannot afford to stay at home, no matter at what peril or at what cost she ventures out."[177] In this view, city officials must be forced to ensure that all women could travel the streets without fear of harm or harassment.

Clubwomen had, of course, previously demanded municipal intervention in the mashing problem. But in the wake of Hollister's murder, they saw an opportunity to stimulate broader support. Clara Millspaugh, of the Chicago Woman's Club, detailed the basic plan: "The public should be aroused, and, through the public, the city officials."[178] One method was to appeal to business leaders, a tactic Keough employed in her writing. "The carnival of crime is costing Chicago thousands of dollars annually," Keough argued, highlighting in particular women's fear of moving alone through the streets. "When Chicago begins to realize the fact that the sport of hunting women is emptying its pocketbook," she insisted, "then Chicago will wake up and find that it is able to support an adequate and efficient police force."[179]

Retailers did not take long to "wake up" to the threat posed by a perception that Chicago's streets were unsafe for a woman to travel alone. They joined clubwomen in calling for the expansion of the police force. They also challenged the safety advice of Chief Collins, especially after he urged women not to "linger about the counters of the stores" or "wait too long before starting for home."[180] The police chief's suggestions, they believed, not only discouraged leisurely shopping but also reinforced concerns about the safety of unescorted women. Already merchants had noticed a drop in trade since Hollister's murder. As Reverend Hall, of Hollister's church, reported, "Business men whose stores are open in the evening told me that the people venture out after nightfall only in the case of absolute necessity."[181] With one eye on the bottom line, retailers joined clubwomen in lobbying for the high license ordinance. Reflecting on their motivations, R. C. Mangold, of the Boston Store, later said, "An efficient police force will mean dollars and cents to Chicago. It will be the cause of restoring confidence in the safety of Chicago's streets."[182]

In advocating enhanced police protection, retailers considered more than the mobility of Chicago women; they also gave weight to the safety concerns of tourists. Across the country, potential visitors had learned of Hollister's murder and absorbed headlines such as "Women in Peril in Lawless City."[183] Many worried that the bad press would reduce tourism. "The feeling has gone abroad that inadequate police protection has rendered the streets unsafe," explained Edward Hillman. These reports circulated to "the detriment of the commercial interests."[184] Such fears were not unfounded. At least one female traveler had already stated that safety concerns were prompting her to leave the city. "I have been visiting in Chicago," Mrs. Z. Dexter informed an audience of three hundred people gathered at the Auditorium Hotel to discuss public safety, "but I am afraid to remain longer. I am returning to my home in New York to-night because of the conditions here."[185] Retailers hoped that travelers such as Dexter could be persuaded to stay if the city devoted more resources to policing. "Visitors will be attracted to Chicago," Ernst J. Lehmann, founder of the Fair department store, later agued, "and they will not regret that they came if they find that the city has an efficient police department prepared to protect its citizens and visitors alike."[186]

In the weeks following Hollister's murder, interest spread from retailers to business owners in other industries who likewise feared the financial consequences of street crime and harassment. In an interview with the *Chicago Record-Herald,* for example, Frank J. Shead, president of the Shead Lumber Association, claimed that business was "kept away" from Chicago due to the belief that women were being assaulted there. The streets must be "made safe for commerce and travel," Shead maintained.[187] In letters to the newly organized Anti-Crime League, several real estate men chimed in, claiming that since Hollister's death, "persons out of town absolutely refused to invest in Chicago property or business." As one of the writers revealed, "One deal, in which almost half a million dollars was involved . . . was called off the day after Mrs. Hollister was murdered."[188]

With the financial stakes laid bare, numerous business and professional associations threw their support behind the high license ordinance. Among the most prominent were the Board of Trade, the Union League Club, the Commercial Club, the Chicago Bar Association, the Chicago Athletic Club, the Hamilton Club, the Illinois Club, and the Lincoln Club.[189] The influential Chicago Commercial Association considered the high license ordinance "absolutely imperative for the welfare of the city" and appointed a four-person committee, led by banker David Forgan, to lobby the mayor.[190] Meanwhile, the owners of Hibbard, Spencer, Bartlett & Co.—a leading hardware company and antecedent to True Value—went so far as to send letters to all employees urging them to ask their aldermen to support the high license law.[191]

The bill came up for a final vote in the city council on March 5, 1906. A robust opposition campaign led by saloon and liquor men had ensured that the fate of the ordinance remained uncertain to the last. One thousand curious citizens attended the proceedings, filling the council chambers and spilling out into the hallways.[192] "Judging by the crowds that flocked to the city hall," observed a reporter for the *Chicago Record-Herald,* "the popular interest in the $1,000 ordinance was greater than that shown in any previous measure that has come up in years."[193] Women were unusually prominent in the audience. "On the sides of the chamber were rows of women," recounted the reporter, "while the floor itself was sprinkled with the wives and daughters of aldermen." When the ordinance finally passed by a vote of 47 to 20, the hall erupted in applause. Joining the celebration, several ladies allegedly clapped "until some of them split their gloves."[194]

Chicago was now assured a larger police force—one capable, it was hoped, of securing women's public safety. "Mrs. Bessie Hollister died," pronounced one commentator, "that we might have safer streets and better police protection. This sensitive woman's death has stirred the city as nothing ever has stirred it before."[195] In the next several months, 1,010 patrol officers were added to the police force, practically doubling its size.[196] Moreover, curbing mashing became a priority of law enforcement. Mayor Dunne signaled the shift even before the high license ordinance passed by ordering Collins to "do better work" protecting women. "There is no reason," Dunne contended, "why the men on beat should not get after the youths who hang around alleys and dark corners for women."[197] Guided by the mayor's advice, Collins instructed his men to "make special efforts" to arrest any mashers loitering on the streets.[198] The changes were greeted enthusiastically by clubwomen and businessmen alike. "I feel safe in saying that in several weeks' time," remarked Willard Parker Stearns, president of a large chemical company, "we can permit our women folk to go upon the street."[199]

Yet popular concern for women's safety did not simply evaporate with the expansion of the police force. On the contrary, the issue helped determine the outcome of the 1907 mayoral election. Throughout the campaign, Dunne faced sharp criticism for having allowed public safety to languish while he focused on an improbable quest for the municipal ownership of utilities.[200] After a single term as mayor, Dunne was ousted by Republican Fred A. Busse, a career politician promising "businesslike" efficiency.[201] Even before taking office, Busse dismissed Chief Collins and appointed as his successor George M. Shippy, a Chicago native and twenty-year member of the police force.[202]

As chief of police, Shippy demonstrated the city's new commitment to stopping street harassment. "I hate a masher worse than any other form of human being," he announced. "I am after the State street masher from now on."[203] Shippy paired this rhetoric with aggressive new strategies for deterring mashing. With Busse's support, the new chief successfully lobbied the state legislature to revise the vagrancy law to permit police to make arrests without warrants.[204] He also requested that judges be empowered to punish vagrants with hard labor instead of mere fines.[205] Notably, both reforms had first been advocated by Chicago clubwomen. In July 1907, when the revised vagrancy law went into effect, Shippy immediately applied it to mashers. "From now on mashers must go," he affirmed.[206] His determination bore fruit. In 1908, Shippy's first full year as chief, vagrancy arrests reached a new high, increasing by more than 300 percent from Collins's final year in office.[207]

However, neither an expanded police force nor a stronger vagrancy law could eliminate all mashers from Chicago's streets. Women in public remained vulnerable to harassment and assault, yet one crucial transformation had taken place since the masher first elicited public interest. Civic and business leaders now acknowledged that the state had an obligation to ensure that streets and public spaces were accessible and safe for unescorted women. The change was manifest two years later, when Chicago actresses objected to harassment from "stage door johnnies" lurking outside the downtown theaters. Shippy responded by organizing a "Mashers' Squad" to patrol State Street in plainclothes. On their first day in May 1909, officers in the unit arrested four mashers.[208] The squad outlived its founder and, by 1916, had appointed its first female officers.[209]

With the expectation set that the state would protect women on the street, the focus of anti-harassment activists quickly shifted to persuading victims to report and testify against mashers. This work was not easily accomplished, however, as many women remained reluctant to appear in court, especially to discuss sexual offenses. Offering encouragement to victims, a writer for the *Inter Ocean* declared, "Whenever a young woman displays sufficient courage to face the discomfort and notoriety attendant upon causing the arrest and assisting in the conviction of a 'masher' she assists mightily in cleaning up the city and making it livable for her sex."[210]

That a city should be "livable" for unescorted women, and not merely for men, was an unprecedented conception that flourished with Chicago's retail district. Yet just as novel was the notion that the state had an obligation to establish and maintain that environment. This idea, forged amid agitation over mashing and public safety, took root as Chicago evolved to meet the demands of consumer capitalism. With sexual aggressors and dissolute women contained by law enforcement, virtuous women could now circulate throughout the central business district without compromising their respectability. Still, their presence was not universally welcomed; their movements animated debate over the purpose of downtown space and the appropriate use of city streets.

6

The Traffic of Women

WOMEN WERE A NUISANCE to Walter D. Moody. The Chicago booster made plain this view to an audience of 150 women at a civics symposium organized by the Illinois Federation of Women's Clubs in March 1908. Moody was there to address one of the most urgent problems facing the modern metropolis—traffic congestion. Speaking in his capacity as head of the Chicago Association of Commerce, a prominent business group, Moody advised his listeners that they might easily diminish congestion in the Loop by modifying their consuming practices. Chicago women sharpened traffic woes, he contended, by lingering until rush hour in State Street department stores and specialty shops. To ease congestion, he recommended a shopping curfew:

> Gather up your bundles and baby carriages and go home at 3 o'clock in the afternoons and the working girls and men will have some chance to get a seat in the cars. . . . Heed this advice, tell fifty other women, and induce each one of them to tell fifty others, and we will come fairly close to solving the transportation problem.

The proposal provoked indignation among audience members but found favor in the local press, which joined in condemning women shoppers as a significant source of downtown congestion. The burden on sidewalks and streetcars could be reduced, critics argued, if shoppers vacated the Loop before workers and businessmen began making their way home. With the reform of women shoppers upheld as a salve for the growing congestion crisis, Chicagoans faced new questions about the place of women and consumption in urban life.[1]

As manager of the Chicago Association of Commerce and, later, director of the Chicago Plan Commission, Moody played a significant role in shaping the city's congestion relief strategy. But he was hardly alone in these efforts. For nearly a decade, business leaders, city officials, and planning experts had puzzled over and debated different means of combating a sharp rise in Loop congestion. Nearly all of these men recognized the need for long-term infrastructural improvements, such as new bridge and subway construction. Still, many also echoed Moody's call to achieve some immediate relief by modifying the flow of people and goods through the city streets.

At the center of such traffic proposals invariably stood State Street— Chicago's widest and most heavily traveled north–south artery, as well as the spine of its downtown shopping district. On any given day, State Street hosted a throng of store clerks, office workers, businessmen, freight wagons, streetcars, carriages, and shopping ladies that together produced seemingly unending chaos and delay. According to proponents of new traffic regulations, these crowds could be tamed and overall circulation improved if State Street were reserved for those with legitimate claim to its use. But what constituted a legitimate claim? Who belonged on State Street?

In debating the answers to these questions, Chicagoans advanced two opposing views of the metropolis, each grounded in a different understanding of urban commerce and women's place within it. Those calling for a shopping time limit favored a civic ideal in which the streets served primarily as conduits for the movement of workers and freight. Upheld by businessmen who made their fortunes in manufacturing, finance, and wholesale, this vision cast the city as a rationalized industrial entrepôt, where the needs of production and distribution outstripped those of consumption. In such a world, women consumers played a marginal role at best. Chicago retailers subscribed to a second model of the metropolis. One year before Moody spoke to the Illinois Federation of Women's Clubs, the city's leading merchants formulated their own congestion relief plan, calling for a ban of all freight traffic from State Street. Far from treating State Street as an efficient artery, the retailers advocated the creation of a "Shoppers' Paradise," where the streets served as a stage for urban consumption and ladies could circulate freely.[2] Unlike the industrialists' model, this view of the city foregrounded consumer institutions and cast shopping ladies as key players.

The conflict between Chicago capitalists' two metropolitan visions played out over the bodies of moneyed women shoppers—where they could be, and when. Efforts to regulate female bodies in public were, of course, nothing new.[3] Just a few years earlier, Carter Harrison Jr. had purged the northern reaches of Chicago's red-light district by issuing a police order prohibiting women from entering Whisky Row saloons. Yet the problematic female bodies at the center of Chicago's traffic debate were not prostitutes or working-class women adrift but moneyed ladies on a respectable retail thoroughfare.

The sudden flurry of concern over the traffic of shopping ladies arose not only from a surge in street congestion but from a revolution in consumption. The rise of a new retailing ethos of service and spectacle at century's end had transformed shopping from burden to pleasure and encouraged consumers to use the city streets for social purposes. As a result, women shoppers were increasingly viewed as idle pleasure seekers, ladies of leisure who obstructed efficient circulation. Responding to this shift, Chicago industrialists and their allies demanded new restrictions on shoppers' movements. The uproar over traffic reveals the vexing presence of moneyed women in a downtown slowly adapting to the demands of consumer capitalism.

The traffic debate also casts new light on how ideas about gender and consumption shaped the urban landscape in the early twentieth century. After the triumph of the World's Fair, Chicago stood as a site of international urban planning interest and a hub of the City Beautiful movement.[4] Yet as the world looked to Chicago for solutions to the crises of modern urban living, the men guiding the city's growth were preoccupied with women—that is, they clashed over whether to regulate or accommodate the consuming practices of ladies. This conflict framed the debate over civic and commercial development in the early twentieth century and, ultimately, left its imprint on Daniel H. Burnham's *Plan of Chicago* (1909). Simply put, moneyed women's presence on State Street, their everyday practices as consumers, and their vision of the city streets shaped the choices made by those who steered the city's future. The battle over traffic laid bare the gendered underpinnings of Chicago's blueprint for development.

Nearly every major city struggled with congestion in the early twentieth century, yet Chicago's problem was especially acute. The population had practically doubled each decade over the previous thirty years, reaching 1.7 million in 1900. Meanwhile, the annexation of suburban lands had expanded the city's boundaries to almost two hundred square miles without alleviating pressure in the downtown. Surrounded by water on three sides, the Loop remained concentrated in an area of one and a half square miles. With nowhere to build but up, Chicago developers erected dozens of skyscrapers in the 1890s. These mammoth towers sprang up in all corners of the business district. Little functional segregation prevailed; retail, wholesale, financial, and manufacturing concerns operated side by side.[5] As a writer for *Harper's Bazaar* explained, "There is no quarter in Chicago given over entirely to shopping. The banks and the shops are nearer together than in New York, and men and women mingle more upon the crowded streets."[6] Certain industries did tend to cluster in particular areas. LaSalle Street, for example, had attracted many financial institutions; Dearborn Street was home to several publishing houses; and South Water Street brought together the city's wholesale grocers. Nevertheless, the Loop's compactness ensured that workers, capitalists, and shoppers regularly crossed paths on streets, sidewalks, and transit lines.

Chicago's rapid concentrated growth produced, in the words of one real estate investor, "congestion in the street, congestion in the store, congestion in the office building, congestion in the theater, and hall, and hotel."[7] Street congestion attracted the most attention and critical inquiry. As defined by planning expert and Chicago City Club secretary George E. Hooker, street congestion reflected an "undue density" that operated on three levels: the crowding of passengers in public conveyances, the crowding of vehicles and pedestrians on the roadway or sidewalks, and the crowding of transit lines on the street surface.[8] All three of these factors combined to generate gridlock that threatened to strangle the city's economic growth. With Chicago's future seemingly in peril, the problem of street congestion emerged as "one of the most serious with which the city has to deal."[9]

By all accounts, street congestion peaked on State Street. At 120 feet wide, it was the broadest street in the Loop and, as such, particularly attractive to freight wagons and other large vehicles.[10] State Street was also a major public transit hub. Cable lines from the South Side ran down the middle of the street, while the West Side line, which operated on Madison Street, made its turnaround on State Street. After 1897, when the Union Elevated Loop was completed, ridership on the elevated lines surged and, with it, the crowds who poured onto State Street from "L" terminals at Lake Street to the north and Van Buren Street to the south.[11] In addition to its arterial functions, State Street hosted Chicago's largest retail houses—nearly all of which were then expanding their facilities to accommodate more customers. The Fair completed construction of its new building in 1897; Mandel Brothers in 1898; Siegel-Cooper & Co. in 1902; Schlesinger & Mayer in 1904; the Boston Store in 1905; and Marshall Field & Co. in 1907. In less than ten years, State Street department stores had practically doubled their floor space and were attracting ever larger crowds from across the city and region. "Every day the whole corn-belt sends in people and people and people to shop on State street," exclaimed a writer for the *Chicago Examiner.* "Ten times as many visiting shoppers throng Chicago now as did ten years ago."[12]

Along the half-mile stretch from the river to Van Buren Street, State Street stores mingled with other businesses—including banks, medical offices, hotels, restaurants, and theaters—to generate an unprecedented volume of vehicle and pedestrian traffic. As early as 1890, seventy-five hundred people every hour traversed the block between Madison and Monroe Streets—nearly quadruple the count for 2016.[13] This traffic intensified as new transit lines were created and existing lines were extended. In the words of novelist Henry Blake Fuller, the street was a "seething flood of carts, carriages, omnibuses, cabs, cars, messengers, shoppers, clerks, and capitalists, which surges with increasing violence for every passing day."[14] The chaos was captured in turn-of-the-century photographs, postcards, and stereographs (figs. 6.1–6.2). Visitors to Chicago often emphasized the difficulty of moving through State Street crowds. As one woman wrote to a Wisconsin friend on a postcard of State Street, "Such a mob, had to watch your step, no chance to stop."[15] Others stressed the trials of crossing the wide, busy roadway. "With your eyes peppered with dust, with your ears full of the clatter of the Elevated Road . . . ," observed a British writer in 1900, "you take your life in your hand when you attempt the crossing of State Street, with its endless stream of rattling wagons and clanging trolley-cars."[16]

The contest for space carried onto public transit. With routes designed by privately owned transit companies to maximize class segregation, even the "nice class of people" rode public conveyances.[17] Frances Glessner often took the State Street cable line when traveling from her Prairie Avenue home into the Loop.[18] She was not alone in that practice. As journalist Annette Reid noted in 1910, "Chicago women all take

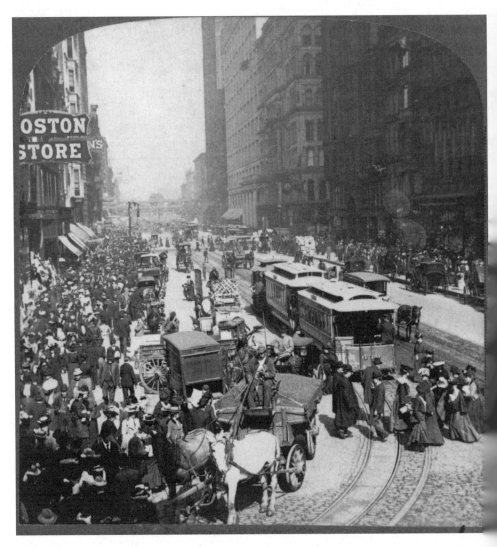

Figure 6.1 This 1903 photograph of the corner of State and Madison Streets reveals the intense traffic congestion that plagued Chicago's downtown in the early twentieth century. The problem was most acute on State Street, the city's widest and most heavily trafficked north–south artery. Shoppers, commuters, streetcars, and carriages all competed for limited space on that thoroughfare. Prints and Photographs Division, LC-USZ62-101148, Library of Congress.

Figure 6.2 State Street's crowds, as shown in this 1908 photograph in front of Marshall Field & Co., astonished visitors, who often commented on the difficulty of moving along the sidewalks. The pedestrian throng sometimes spilled into the roadway, inhibiting the flow of vehicular traffic.   1908 Postcard, Suhling Company, Chicago, Author's Private Collection.

the streetcars for shopping."[19] Shoppers thus joined workers and businessmen in squeezing onto crowded cars and clinging to the leather straps provided to supplement the insufficient number of seats. A 1901 poem captured the agony of the Chicago straphanger: "You're forced each day on close-pack'd cars to ride, / Whereon, for weary miles, you jerk and grind, / Hanging to straps, squeezed, trampled, unresigned."[20]

In responding to the chaos, planning experts underscored the need to address the Loop's infrastructural inadequacies. New tunnels, more bridges, wider streets, and the first passenger subways were all heralded as Chicago's salvation. But such large-scale construction projects required substantial time and money to complete. In the short term, Chicagoans frustrated by traffic looked beyond the built environment to consider other sources of congestion with potentially quicker remedies.

Shoppers soon emerged as an object of blame. In newspaper editorials, interviews, guidebooks, and even fiction, they stood accused of promoting unnecessary obstructions and delays. In 1902, for example, an irate journalist denounced shoppers "strung along the curbstone over the crosswalk" and "loaded down with bundles" as "one of the most distressful forms of street blockading."[21] That same year, a State Street police crossing guard alleged that nine out of ten collisions between vehicles and pedestrians on his beat were caused by shoppers "rubbernecking," or turning to admire another woman's apparel.[22] A fellow officer, stationed near State and Madison, insisted that shoppers promoted congestion by "rushing across the street" before police could stop traffic. "They like to show how cleverly they can manage to go it alone," he claimed. "Sometimes one of these smart ones gets stuck right in the middle of the road. . . . Of course, this delays traffic considerably, but what can you do?"[23] In addition to causing accidents and blockades, shoppers were charged with creating a general atmosphere of inefficiency. "The shopping district," declared one observer, "is a vast hopper of which State and Madison is the middle point, and into this hopper all those shoppers are thrown, there to circle and eddy about. Most of these shoppers are women, and are slow in their motions. This makes the congestion all the more acute."[24]

Complaints linking shoppers to congestion were often hyperbolic. Still, shoppers did tend to move through the streets in a manner distinct from most urban commuters. Their pace was at once more leisurely and more erratic. Most notably, shoppers were more likely than other pedestrians to pause mid-sidewalk to peer into store windows. The development of cast iron architecture in the mid-nineteenth century had first permitted retailers to use plate glass.[25] But in the 1890s, manufacturers honed new production methods that made plate glass cheaper, clearer, and much grander in scale. At the same time, the rise of steel-frame construction allowed for buildings with nearly unbroken surfaces of glass. The result was the rapid proliferation of display windows at century's end.[26] Unprecedented in their size and clarity, these windows transformed downtown streets into glittering display cases that beckoned to shoppers. Highlighting the shift, Theodore Dreiser dwelt on Sister Carrie's fascination with plate glass when she initially arrived in Chicago. Later, the young heroine's thoughts of finding work were

Figure 6.3 Window design emerged as a professional field at the turn of the century. Experts such as Arthur Fraser of Marshall Field & Co. developed new visual merchandising tactics that used color, light, and glass to attract the attention of passersby. Their creations were "essentially artistic," as evidenced in this 1906 Fraser design. *Merchants Record and Show Window* 19 (Nov. 1906): 22.

"readily changed" by the "long window display" of the Fair, which drew her, "lured by desire," into the store to shop for jackets.[27]

Merchants had certainly displayed goods to passersby in decades past, but most had piled together random items in cramped, poorly lit windows. Not until the 1890s did retailers adopt modern visual merchandising tactics that attracted potential customers through the use of color, light, and glass.[28] Window trimming emerged as a distinct professional field, with Chicago at its center. It was in the midwestern metropolis that L. Frank Baum, future author of *The Wonderful Wizard of Oz* (1900), founded the National Association of Window Trimmers and began publishing the *Show Window*, the first journal dedicated to the craft of window display.[29] In this same era in Chicago, Arthur Fraser of Marshall Field & Co. began his ascent as the nation's foremost window designer. Fraser, who had a background in theater, became known for elaborate themed windows that transformed merchandise displays into entertainment (fig. 6.3).[30] Speaking to the *Dry Goods Reporter* in 1903, he explained

Figure 6.4 Enormous show windows proliferated at the turn of the century, when glass manufacturers honed production methods that made plate glass cheaper, clearer, and larger in scale. The displays were typically designed to appeal to female shoppers, who accounted for a majority of department store purchases. As a result, women, not men, tended to linger in front of store windows, as seen in this detail of a 1907 photograph of the exterior of Marshall Field & Co. Prints and Photographs Division, LC-D4-34698, Library of Congress.

that while "old fashioned" displays treated the window as a "veritable stock room," "modern displays are essentially artistic."[31]

Other Chicago retailers competed with Fraser and Marshall Field & Co. to produce the most spectacular crowd-drawing show windows. More often than not, these displays were designed to appeal to the women customers who were said to account for the vast majority of State Street purchases.[32] "The most numerous displays," remarked one contemporary observer, "are those of women's dress, dress fabrics, millinery, hats and bonnets, laces, and ribbons."[33] With feminine finery dominating show windows, it was ladies, not men, who tended to collect on State Street sidewalks. In his guidebook, Louis Schick described the perpetual crush near State and Madison, where dress-good displays were "constantly surrounded by an admiring gathering of ladies, young and old."[34] Photographs of State Street from the period confirm his assertion, revealing sidewalks lined with women surveying artfully arranged goods as male pedestrians hurry past (fig. 6.4). In order to generate even larger crowds, some retailers went so far as to employ female "window gazers," who stood outside the stores and stared admiringly at displays to attract the interest of passersby.[35]

As window design and, in turn, window shopping blossomed in the early twentieth century, many Chicagoans began to view women gaping on sidewalks as deterrents to efficient circulation. These perceptions were reinforced by the still unfamiliar rhythms of window shopping, which often contradicted basic traffic principles. In particular, critics fretted that window shopping violated that immutable rule of the road: keep to the right. Instead of staying in their lane of movement, window shoppers often cut across sidewalks to observe displays. In a 1905 discourse appropriately titled "Keep to the Right," one Chicagoan lamented, "Those who should keep near the curb hug the shop windows so as to see their contents, and elbow aside others who have the right of way. The result is confusion, delay, and ill temper."[36] Another observer concluded, "'Walk to the right and pass to the left' is not as well understood in Chicago as it might be."[37]

When not zigzagging across walkways, window shoppers were known to stop abruptly or, worse still, walk without taking their eyes off the displays. Chicago satirist George Ade highlighted the latter problem in his 1898 novel *Artie: A Story of the Streets and Town*. When Artie first ventures onto State Street, the young man struggles to escape "a bevy of women who were carrying bundles and looking at show windows at the same time, thus contriving to mow down anything and anybody that happened in their way."[38] The erratic movements of window shoppers were assumed to particularly inconvenience male pedestrians. As one frustrated Chicagoan asserted in 1903, "A woman knows by instinct when another woman ahead of her will stop suddenly in her tracks, right about face, and march for a shop window. A man never does. . . . Before he can sidetrack himself he has run into her."[39] Four years later, John Newcomer, a judge in the municipal court, advised "inoffensive males" to avoid sidewalk collisions—and accusations of mashing—by walking in the middle of the street. The average window shopper, he warned, "seems unaware of her surroundings until she is bumped into by a man, and then she is highly insulted."[40]

Women shoppers also differed from other pedestrians in their tendency to walk in groups. Unlike most commuters, who rushed solo to and from work, shoppers often used the streets as sites of social intercourse—places to meet acquaintances, show off purchases, or stroll with friends. As Schick observed, women "in the heart of the shopping district" were "almost always in parties of two or three."[41] Indeed, shopping had become a social activity. "Mother says to daughter, sister to sister, friend to friend: 'Let's go out shopping,' in the manner of saying: 'Let's go out for a walk," revealed one Chicago woman.[42] In his 1895 novel *With the Procession,* Henry Blake Fuller similarly emphasized the sociability of shopping when noting that heroine Jane Marshall "always accompanied" her friend Susan Bates on retail excursions. "They priced things, debated things, and tried on things—on themselves, on each other, on the attendants," Fuller wrote.[43]

The social aspects of shopping are readily apparent in photographs of State Street from the early twentieth century. In a 1909 snapshot of the exterior of Marshall Field's, for example, several ladies are shown walking together in small groups, some with arms linked or hands clasped. At least one group, anchored by a woman with a fur muff, appears to be engaged in conversation, mouths agape as they scurry across the street.[44] An early *Chicago Daily News* photograph portrays Christmas shoppers walking together in pairs, some with small children in their arms, with a larger group of ladies moving together in a row across the background (fig. 6.5).[45] In contrast to women shoppers, the men in these scenes are typically walking alone, sometimes with legs blurred from hurrying past the photographer's lens. A 1905 photograph taken in front of Siegel-Cooper & Co. underscores these divergent styles as three women, walking abreast with packages in hand, are passed by individual men.[46]

Shoppers' sidewalk sociability increasingly came under fire as Chicago's traffic problems intensified. In 1904, for example, John A. Howland, a self-identified "business man," alleged that women "unconsciously infringe[d] on the rights of others" by walking "three or four abreast" and "block[ing] up doors and passageways."[47] An individual identified only as C. S. R. conveyed a similar sense of exasperation in an opinion piece titled "State Street Pedestrianism," published by the *Chicago Tri-*

Figure 6.5 Shopping had become a social activity by the early twentieth century. Female shoppers, as shown in this 1905 photograph of State Street, typically walked in groups, sometimes with small children in tow. Their pace conflicted with the expectations of commuters, who usually moved expeditiously and alone.   Chicago Daily News Negatives Collection, N-0002541. Courtesy of the Chicago History Museum.

bune. "One shopper may meet a small group of friends in the middle of the sidewalk. They stop and occupy twelve square feet of space in a path which is just big enough for the people who are walking," he lamented. According to C. S. R., these gatherings caused accidents and delays, particularly for male pedestrians. "Men never can avoid the group. Soon three or four men have pushed their way directly through the bunch and have scattered it over the sidewalk and possibly landed part of it in the gutter," he claimed.[48] In a follow-up essay, C. S. R. contrasted the shopper's leisurely stroll with the "hurrying," "hustling," and "running" gait of the average businessman.[49]

With congestion mounting in the early twentieth century, many frustrated Chicagoans were eager to assign blame for downtown problems.

They found easy targets in shopping ladies, whose distinctive way of traversing the Loop highlighted social uses of the street and often seemed at odds with efficient circulation. As the ranks of these shoppers expanded, some business and civic leaders began to fear that, in pursuing the delights of consumption, moneyed ladies were obstructing the flow of urban industrial commerce.

Shoppers may have traversed the streets in a distinctive manner, but blaming them for downtown congestion involved more than a little exaggeration. Ultimately, these complaints were undergirded less by actual conditions on the street than by new ideas about consumers and consumption. Indeed, as shopping came to be redefined as a form of leisure at century's end, shoppers—who had once been thought to perform necessary, if not important, work—were increasingly viewed as idle pleasure seekers disengaged from the real business of the metropolis and incapable of understanding the need for efficiency or the value of other people's time. Within this new framework, those who supported the industrialists' view of the city came to see women shoppers as obstacles to the productive use of the city streets.

Shopping had not always fallen into the category of leisure. For much of the previous century, shopping was seen as a crucial aspect of running a household, and a trip to the dry goods store was only one of many errands. To "shop" meant to compare prices on similar goods in different stores, an activity that required significant patience and skill. Accounts of shopping from the mid-nineteenth century often portrayed a round at the stores as onerous and dull. An 1859 etiquette book, for example, labeled shopping an "irksome fatigue" best conducted alone and reminded readers that "a store is not the place for social intercourse."[50] In 1873, the *Woman's Journal* similarly characterized shopping as "a most bewildering and exhausting business."[51] Two decades later, many American women still regarded shopping as an unpleasant undertaking. Highlighting this view, a columnist for the *Inter Ocean* spoke hopefully of a time when mail-order purchasing could replace shopping, "that hatefullest of all tasks, the one that requires the most useless and extravagant expenditure of time and strength."[52]

Shopping's transformation from burden to pleasure owed primarily to the explosion of new department store services and accommodations at century's end. In preceding decades, dry goods stores had provided few amenities to their customers, and ladies would consider themselves lucky to find even a waiting room. By the mid-1890s, however, nearly all major department stores had opened not only restaurants and tea-rooms but also ticket offices, nurseries, writing rooms, telegraph offices, checkrooms, restrooms, and lounges. Meanwhile, free delivery and generous return policies alleviated some of the more tedious aspects of shopping.[53] Retailers tried to anticipate customers' every need. "The management of the modern department store," observed C. K. Water-house, head buyer at Schlesinger & Mayer, "is exerting itself to serve the public as have no stores in the past history of the country."[54] Their efforts made shopping more enjoyable for many women. A contributor to the *Dry Goods Reporter* put it bluntly: "The shopper who receives slight attention among her acquaintances is treated as a queen in the modern department store."[55]

Stores also sought to attract customers by offering entertaining spectacles. In addition to merchandise displays, retailers introduced fashion shows, live music, parades, floral competitions, and model homes.[56] In her Chicago travel account, Marie Lédier Grandin, a visitor from Paris, marveled at the "great attraction" staged by Siegel-Cooper & Co. to draw the attention of Christmas shoppers. "Children dressed in sumptuous costumes did dances and pantomimes from morning until night," and "two young girls washed fabric that was guaranteed to keep its color," Grandin recalled.[57] Reflecting on the visual attractions of Marshall Field & Co., Thomas W. Goodspeed, an early trustee of the University of Chicago, wrote, "Inside [the shopper] found herself in a fairyland. The scene was one of splendor and of beauty. Everything was invitingly displayed but no one was asked to purchase." The effect, according to Goodspeed, was to create an environment "in which it was a joy to buy."[58]

Retailers' new emphasis on service and spectacle obscured the market relations upholding department store exchanges and, in turn, disguised the work of consumption. As noted in a 1914 Chicago sales manual, stores "spend thousands of dollars yearly for a purpose that has no apparent connection with selling goods" to ensure "the atmosphere of trade is removed and with it the defensive fortifications of the buyer."[59] Once a tedious chore, shopping now seemed to offer endless opportunities for excitement and pleasure. Accordingly, shopping came to be defined as anything *but* legitimate business. In 1908, Delia Austrian, a Chicago clubwoman and poet, explained the transformation:

> Shopping in America has become a habit and pastime, fostered by the many attractions and conveniences to be found in our great stores, such as reading, writing, and rest rooms, cafés, picture galleries, telephone accommodations, the ability to order theater tickets, railroad and steamship transportation, entertain your friends at luncheon or afternoon tea, prepare and post your letters and packages, listen to an entertaining concert, and a hundred and one other interesting things all under one roof.[60]

For other contemporaries, shopping was a "fine art," "a positive obsession," an "agreeable pastime," and a "delectable amusement."[61] As journalist Annette Reid succinctly concluded, "To the Chicago woman [shopping] is an entertainment."[62]

With shopping newly defined as a leisure activity, the work of consumption became increasingly difficult for contemporaries to perceive. Of course, shoppers continued to fulfill the vital task of acquiring clothes, dry goods, and other supplies for their households. Moreover, their purchases helped fuel Chicago's commercial growth. Yet any value provided by women's shopping was obscured by the activity's apparent pleasures. Challenging the new link between consumption and leisure had limited appeal to many moneyed women, whose status, as Thorstein Veblen theorized, hinged on the performance of nonproductivity.[63] By spending time and money in State Street stores, Chicago ladies strengthened their family's social position. They also reinforced perceptions of shoppers as mere pleasure seekers, removed from business and economic life. This view was highlighted in a 1902 article on congestion that described shoppers on State Street as "women and children who are not producers." Tellingly, the article contrasted shoppers' "molasses-like movements" and "infinite leisure" with the "hustle" and "rush" of workers and businessmen.[64]

As the lines between production and consumption, business and pleasure, work and leisure, became more distinct, shoppers were increasingly painted as ladies *of* leisure who wasted precious time. Typical was the perspective of journalist Mira L. Cobbe, writing for the *Inter Ocean:* "One of the resources of women with more time upon their hands than they know how to dispose of is what they term shopping, i.e. visiting the various stores, turning over the goods displayed for sale, and asking for prices upon all articles, without the slightest intention of purchasing a single thing."[65] In a 1908 address, reformer Ellen Martin Henrotin insisted that the average American woman was missing out on new opportunities because "she gives so much time, indeed most of her time," to shopping.[66]

Unsurprisingly, most merchants did not share the opinion that shoppers were wasting time in stores. They encouraged lingering so that the "subtle influences" of the retail environment could "metamorphose visitors into customers."[67] Store employees, by contrast, often resented shoppers' tendency to browse indiscriminately. "Regular shoppers come into the stores in the same cheerful, I-want-to-be-entertained spirit that they wear in going to a card party," protested a saleswoman writing for the *Woman's Home Companion* in 1908.[68] Clerks particularly loathed the "looker," defined by one retail handbook as a "person who spends a great deal of time in the store examining the merchandise without any present intention of buying."[69] As another saleswoman moaned, "[The looker's] visit is timed to that portion of the day when you are most busy and desirous of making your sales. . . . How we hate her."[70] Dubbed the "bane of the shops," the figure of the looker arose in store reports and sales manuals, as well as jokes and short stories, where she would invariably "just saunter around, putting in time."[71]

Outside the store, the looker found her counterpart in the promenading shopper, who strolled casually along the streets in order "to see and be seen."[72] Like the looker, the promenader was thought to have ample time to spare and no definite errands to fulfill. In describing the "veritable parade ground" created on State Street by promenading shoppers, Helen Gale, a fashion columnist for the *Inter Ocean,* underscored the atmosphere of leisure, sociability, and display. "Women of all ages and descriptions saunter about in the delightful consciousness of being strictly 'up to date.' . . . The weather is perfect; the shops are gorgeous; she meets dozens of dear friends, many of whom compliment her on her elegant appearance. She is at peace with the world."[73] The relaxed, gregarious style of the promenader appeared to some Chicagoans to disrupt the flow of downtown traffic. As one critic argued, "There is no room for the promenade gait, in daylight, anywhere between Wabash avenue and Franklin street and Van Buren street and the river."[74]

While shopping ladies were thought to have too much time on their hands, Chicago businessmen clamored for more. For these men, time was money. According to a 1902 investigation, the average Chicagoan—assumed to be male—lost $1,000 per year waiting on blocked streets and closed crossings.[75] A decade later, Charles Wacker, of the Chicago Plan Commission, estimated that the business community lost more than $500,000 per year from delays on one downtown street alone.[76] Although the accuracy of such calculations is questionable, many Chicagoans clearly believed that minutes wasted in commuting to work, delivering goods, or keeping appointments translated directly into lost profits. As a writer for the *Chicago Tribune* warned, "There cannot be much more congestion without serious loss to business interests."[77] Determined to protect their bottom lines, Chicago's business community rushed to solve the traffic crisis. Two competing visions of congestion relief emerged—one backed by the owners and managers of retail houses, the other by manufacturers, wholesalers, and financiers. At the center of each proposal stood the moneyed woman shopper.

On May 17, 1904, representatives of Chicago's largest retail houses assembled at the Palmer House hotel to formulate a plan to address congestion. Among those present were executives from the State Street department stores—Marshall Field's, Schlesinger & Mayer, Siegel-Cooper, Mandel Bros., Pardridge Bros., the Fair, the Hub, and the Boston Store—as well as proprietors of several large specialty shops, such as Gunther's Confectionery, furriers J. T. Shayne & Co., and jeweler C. D. Peacock. Like countless other Chicagoans, these merchants feared that their prospects were being harmed by the city's escalating traffic woes. They resolved to join forces to combat the evils that "rapid growth" and an "overtaxed" municipal government had etched onto the urban landscape. Together, they formed the State Street Improvement Association (SSIA)—a permanent body devoted to devising "ways and means for relieving the traffic congestion" and, more generally, to advancing the interests of State Street property owners. In a statement to the press, the new organization declared its commitment to abetting traffic and transforming State Street into "the best paved, cleanest, and handsomest" thoroughfare in the world—a veritable "Shoppers' Paradise."[78] Chicago's leading retailers thus began developing a vision of congestion relief that prioritized the needs of consumers.

The SSIA's initial agenda focused on infrastructural improvements to facilitate traffic flow and, at the same time, enhance the shopping environment. Within a week of its founding, the group had committed $40,000 to replacing the crumbling granite blocks then paving State Street with bituminous asphalt concrete.[79] Asphalt, a recent and expensive paving innovation, appealed to the merchants for numerous reasons. To begin with, it produced substantially less dust than other paving options. Unlike the stone and wood blocks then lining most Chicago streets, asphalt did not permit dirt and debris to creep up from the earth beneath. As such, the material not only helped retailers avoid damage from dust but also offered pedestrians, especially ladies in skirts, a more hygienic experience. Smooth and easy to clean, asphalt was also considered an aesthetically superior paving option. Further, it absorbed sound, thereby eliminating much of the noise pollution that plagued granite roadways. Not least, asphalt enhanced the comfort and speed of travel by wheel. In contrast to other paving materials, asphalt's even, unbroken surface enabled vehicles to glide along effortlessly. This effect was especially pronounced for the rubber-tired automobiles that were just beginning to gain favor among the city's wealthiest residents.[80]

Asphalt also appealed to the SSIA due to its one major drawback: it was ill-suited for the commercial traffic that many viewed as a threat to pedestrian safety. According to paving experts, asphalt could not withstand the wear and tear caused by the heavy teams used to pull freight wagons. Moreover, its slick, ungrooved surface lacked sufficient footing for horses and, on wet days, could easily produce broken ankles and upended cargo.[81] Chicago merchants would have been well aware of asphalt's incompatibility with commercial traffic. In 1903, nearby Milwaukee had provided a valuable object lesson when, after numerous accidents involving horses skidding on newly laid asphalt, more than one hundred businessmen signed a petition demanding that the material no longer be used to pave city streets.[82] The following year, a mere two weeks before the SSIA's founding, engineer John W. Alvord discouraged the use of asphalt on streets "with a large amount of heavy teaming" in a report on Chicago's street paving problem. Sponsored by the Commercial Club of Chicago, Alvord's report endorsed the use of granite blocks on busy commercial streets while emphasizing asphalt's desirability for "high-class," moderately trafficked roads.[83]

By repaving State Street with asphalt, Chicago merchants sought to discourage heavy teams while enhancing the posh atmosphere that appealed to moneyed shoppers. Since 1891, the number of heavy teams operating in the city had tripled, and throughout the first decade of the twentieth century, freight traffic took up more street space in the Loop than did any other use.[84] State Street, with its broad roadway and direct link to the North Side, bore much of this traffic. Critics of heavy teaming claimed it not only generated more dust and noise than other traffic but also caused more accidents. In 1903, Frank I. Bennett—chair of the Chicago City Council's Local Transportation Committee—identified heavy teams as the gravest danger facing pedestrians. "The teamster goes tearing through the streets without regard to the pedestrians," Bennett protested, "[and when] he causes an accident he either swears at the victim or grins over his shoulder as he gets away."[85] The SSIA merchants shared Bennett's concerns and denounced heavy teaming as especially threatening to women on State Street. "The constant and noisy stream of heavy traffic and street cars have long and seriously interfered with the facility which, it is felt, shoppers in general and women shoppers in particular, should enjoy," noted the *Inter Ocean* in a report on the retailers' asphalt project.[86]

The repaving of State Street concluded in late 1904. Yet instead of curtailing heavy teaming, the well-maintained surface attracted even more through traffic.[87] Within two years, the volume of heavy teams on State Street had tripled, a development that outraged the SSIA and prompted new calls for action. In December 1906, Jacob L. Kesner, the association's president and general manager of the Fair, argued that freight traffic caused "endless congestion" and prevented State Street from becoming "what it should be—a modern metropolitan street."[88] Speaking on behalf of the SSIA's traffic committee, Louis Stumer—who not only owned two large retail millinery shops, a drug store, and two restaurants, but also founded the women's magazine *Red Book*—called for new restrictions on heavy teams:[89]

> We want the street to become absolutely safe for women and children, so that they may cross over in the middle of the block, or anywhere, without fear of being run over by coal wagons. . . . As conditions are now, it is positively dangerous to venture beyond the curb line, even at crossings. This should not be in a shopping street.[90]

Drawing attention to the scene outside, he continued,

> Look out there . . . see the women, children, and even men dodging some "Rube" driver on a coal wagon. What chance have they for life, limb, or conscience. Take these heavy teams off State street and the business interests of the street will be trebled, the lives of shoppers made safer, and the greatest street in the western hemisphere will be a thing of beauty and business.[91]

Stumer and his SSIA associates viewed the public space of the street as an extension of the stores that flanked its sidewalks—a haven where ladies could wander and indulge their desires. Indeed, on Stumer's State Street, shopping ladies would be safe from freight wagons—as well as the working-class "rubes" who drove them—and could satisfy their whims by crossing the street wherever they pleased, even mid-block. In other words, the SSIA merchants sought to transform State Street into a beautiful, well-regulated paradise for consumers.

To achieve this vision, the retailers formulated a new plan in December 1906 to have State Street reclassified as a boulevard. As the special province of an independent parks system, boulevards operated under different traffic regulations than ordinary streets and were off-limits to all vehicles deemed incompatible with a park's alleged purpose—to offer city dwellers a space of refined, bucolic leisure.[92] Accordingly, boulevards were closed to freight wagons and other heavy teams. At the time of the SSIA's proposal, most of Chicago's existing boulevards lay outside the city center and were used to connect far-flung park sites. Within the Loop, portions of only two streets operated as boulevards, and both had been established as such decades prior—the southern end of Michigan Avenue, which connected Grant Park to the South Park System, and Jackson Boulevard, which performed the same function for the West Park System.[93] The SSIA proposed to make State Street the first north–south boulevard to run the full length of the Loop.

The boulevard campaign, which adopted the slogan "Wagons Off State," was backed by twenty-five State Street retail institutions.[94] On the subcommittee directing the scheme were some of the most powerful men in retail, such as John T. Pirie of Carson Pirie Scott and James Simpson of Marshall Field's. The merchants canvassed local property owners and civic leaders with the hope of building enough support to push the plan through the city council.[95] In crafting their appeal, the SSIA men stressed the importance of safety and insisted that heavy teams posed a "constant menace to the lives of women and children."[96] They also maintained that a new boulevard would ease downtown congestion while generating for State Street "an increase in business hundredfold."[97]

The merchants' primary goal was to curb freight traffic. However, their plan also entailed significant aesthetic improvements. Within the street classification system, boulevards were held to higher standards of beauty than were ordinary roadways. In Walter Moody's own words, boulevards "give us places for statues and fountains. . . . We adorn them with flowers and embellish them with rare and beautiful trees and plants. They are important ornamental features of our city, elevating and educational."[98] Accordingly, the merchants' scheme called for several cosmetic upgrades, such as decorative lighting, attractive signposts, and the removal of garish electric signs. The stated desire of the SSIA men was to transform State Street into a "sweeping stretch of grandeur" and "an important part of the city beautiful." In effect, they sought to re-create the luxurious environment of the stores on State Street, making it a rival to Paris's Champs-Élysées as "the greatest of retail thoroughfares."[99]

The success of the boulevard project seemed likely at first. According to the *Chicago Record-Herald,* the SSIA received "only encouragement" from those petitioned, and Bernard H. Snow, of the Committee on Streets and Alleys, pronounced the plan "highly desirable" and worthy of "general support."[100] Opposition soon materialized, however. Property owners on other downtown streets pointed out that closing State Street to freight traffic would exacerbate congestion elsewhere. The most outspoken critics were concentrated in the Loop Protective Association (LPA), an alliance of business and property owners whose interests lay principally on Wabash Avenue and Dearborn Street. Significantly, many LPA members shared backgrounds in manufacturing, wholesale, real estate, and finance, and, as such, saw the city through very different eyes than did the State Street merchants. Less than a week after the SSIA proposed the boulevard plan, LPA president James F. Bowers, of the musical instrument manufacturer Lyon & Healy, denounced the scheme as "nothing short of monstrous."[101] The LPA quickly organized an opposition task force composed of reaper heir R. Hall McCormick, printer H. C. Metcalf, real estate investor LeGrand Burton, publisher Ogden T. McClurg, banker Leverett Sidway, and manufacturer George P. Bent.[102]

In protesting the boulevard, LPA members stressed the importance of circulation while decrying the potential for added congestion. Any new boulevard, they argued, would add to downtown congestion, but State Street's unique position as the Loop's widest and busiest roadway made the prospect of its boulevarding particularly harrowing. "State street and Clark street are about the only through streets we have in the loop district and they must be kept open to traffic," claimed LPA attorney Clarence F. Goodwin. "To close one of them," he reasoned, "would mean intolerable congestion in all the other streets."[103] Echoing these sentiments, real estate investor Daniel F. Crilly considered the proposed boulevard a "great injustice" that would bring traffic "to a standstill by reason of constant blockades."[104] In a memorandum sent to all members, LPA leadership warned that if successful, the SSIA's plans would transform nearby streets into mere "alleys for the traffic sent out by the rear doors of the big State street stores in delivery wagons."[105]

Opponents of the boulevard project viewed city streets, above all, as channels of movement. The LPA demanded that each thoroughfare bear its "fair share" of heavy teams. "I believe that traffic should be evenly distributed, as it is at present," insisted McCormick. "Chicago is well enough supplied now [with boulevards]. In fact, in a business district there can be such a thing as too many boulevards."[106] McCormick's appeal, which dismissed the social uses of the street, revived objections that had been voiced to great effect years earlier against a proposal to extend the Michigan Avenue boulevard. "If you turn any more streets into boulevards," alderman and banker Walter J. Raymer had cautioned in 1905, "you'll have a city that's a thing of beauty and a joy forever, but useless for all that. We're here to earn a living, not to loaf around in a palm garden."[107] Two years later, a *Chicago Tribune* editorial reiterated Raymer's concerns. From "an aesthetic point of view," the piece contended, it would be "delightful to have a park in the center of the business district" in addition to more boulevards, but such schemes were both "selfish" and "impossible." The only solution to the congestion problem, the author concluded, was not more boulevards but "more facilities" and "more bridges" to accommodate even more traffic.[108]

By late January 1907, the anti-boulevard movement had gained enough support among property owners and municipal leaders to thwart the SSIA's plans. The critical blow came when the South Park Board—the entity that would be responsible for the new boulevard—yielded to the

LPA's prodding and refused to endorse the merchants' proposal.[109] Without this support, the boulevard project could not move forward. For the time being, the industrialists' demands for circulation had prevailed. Yet the debate over the boulevard project had exposed key fault lines within Chicago's business community over the appropriate use of the city's streets. This conflict would not be easily resolved. At stake were not only competing visions of urban commerce but different understandings of women's role in commercial life. As would soon become clear, women shoppers occupied only a peripheral place in the industrialists' model of the city.

It was a year after the failure of the boulevard project that Walter Moody recommended a shopping curfew to Chicago clubwomen. His advice built on a conversation that had begun weeks earlier at a meeting of the Chicago Real Estate Board. Founded in 1883 to promote the interests of real estate dealers, the board united many prominent men in the field, such as Crilly and McCormick.[110] At its February 1908 meeting, board members debated familiar proposals for "the relief of Loop congestion" via infrastructural improvements, such as new elevated rail platforms.[111] Midway through the proceedings, however, the conversation took a dramatic turn when Stephen B. Mills, head of an industrial property firm, advocated a new solution rooted in traffic management. According to Mills, "much of the congestion of the loop was due to the fact that women delayed their shopping until late in the afternoon, when they might easily have finished at an earlier hour."[112] To ease congestion, he argued, "women ought to be driven out of the district before the stores close."[113] Over the next several days, his call to regulate shoppers' movements was reported, and debated, in newspapers across the city and country.[114] Chicago's shopping ladies replaced freight wagons as the newest targets of traffic reform.

Up until this point, efforts to relieve Loop congestion through traffic management had focused exclusively on the movement of vehicles. In late 1906, the Chicago City Council passed new "rules of the road," which contained such basic provisions as keep to the right, avoid parking on sidewalks, and never block intersections. In subsequent months, members of the Chicago Association of Commerce, including Moody, collaborated with the Chicago Police Department to implement the new rules and bring about the "expeditious and economical movement of street traffic."[115] They organized traffic education meetings, financed traffic studies, and expanded the mounted police force. By 1908, vehicle flow had marginally improved, but congestion continued to plague downtown sidewalks, streetcars, and intersections. Frustrated by the lack of progress, Chicagoans sought new methods to improve traffic circulation. One such method called for segregating traffic by time, rather than by space, as the SSIA had proposed. This system had already been enacted in New York City, where freight deliveries to the business district were prohibited during business hours.[116] Yet time segregation had never been successfully executed in Chicago, and Mills was now seeking to apply it to the movement of people, not vehicles.

Chicago's consuming ladies, according to Mills, used much of their time unproductively and, as such, could easily adapt to a shopping curfew, which he initially proposed setting at five o'clock. To build his case, Mills invoked popular tropes about consumption as entertainment and shoppers as indolent ladies of leisure. He began by contrasting "lazy women" shoppers with the "poor working girl, who has been worn to a thread by waiting on them all day." He then underscored shoppers' inefficiency and suggested that they shirked their household duties by lingering in commercial leisure spaces. "They fool around all day when they ought to be at home with their babies. They sip chocolate at some shop and gossip or munch chocolate at some matinee," he asserted. "It takes them half an hour to gather up their bundles and get ready to go home and when they do start it is like the march of a conquering army. They are the ones who cause delay and congestion and trouble."[117] In short, they were "pests."[118]

That women shoppers were not essential to Mills's view of the downtown was hardly surprising. At sixty-one years old, the Kentucky-born broker had spent decades buying and selling property for industrial manufacturers. He also claimed to have implemented a shopping curfew in his own home. According to Mills, his wife, Alice, spent much of her time on State Street because she had "no household duties to keep her at home." At day's end, she liked to join her husband on his return commute via the West Side cars. But Mills objected to Alice occupying space that "rightfully" belonged to "some poor girl or man." Instead of traveling with him, Mills insisted that his wife leave the Loop before rush hour. He hoped that "moral suasion and coaxing" could induce other women to adhere to a similar procedure. But should their "selfish hearts" resist, Mills warned, harsher methods could be applied. "You gentlemen all have your beautiful theories of solving [the traffic problem]," he entreated his fellow real estate men, "but here is a practical thing that ought to be enforced."[119]

Mills's proposal generated "merriment" at the Chicago Real Estate Board meeting.[120] Yet his idea was not quickly dismissed. On the contrary, it produced widespread debate and likely influenced Walter Moody, who, a few weeks later, instructed the Illinois Federation of Women's Clubs to adopt an even earlier shopping time limit of three o'clock. Mere months before, Moody had been appointed managing director of the Chicago Association of Commerce (CAC).[121] Founded in 1895 "to get and to hold trade," the association focused on booming Chicago as a hub of manufacturing, processing, and distribution.[122] On the very day Mills proposed his curfew, the CAC had held a meeting in which members touted an uptick in dry goods production and vowed to make Chicago "the center of manufacturing for the whole country, as well as the central point for distributing those manufactures."[123] The organization's members were drawn chiefly from industry, finance, and wholesale trade and included men who had been active in the anti-boulevard campaign. The CAC also shared several members with the Chicago Real Estate Board, and the two groups sometimes collaborated on improvement projects.[124] Both organizations had an interest in enhancing the flow of people and goods through the Loop. For the real estate men, better circulation meant higher densities and higher land values. For CAC members, it meant cheaper transportation costs, faster turnover, and greater profits.[125]

At first glance, Walter Moody seemed an unlikely advocate of shopping restrictions. Before helming the CAC, Moody had spent his entire career as a millinery salesman. He had even recently published a manual on salesmanship, *Men Who Sell Things* (1907). But Moody's background was exclusively in the wholesale end of the millinery trade. He had started as a traveling wholesale salesman in Michigan and later climbed to head of sales for the prominent Chicago-based hatmaker Gage Brothers.[126] Tellingly, Moody referred to customers in his sales manual by masculine pronouns—a move no retailer would dare make. In fact, retail customers and retail salesmen, whom he described as lacking "gumption," held little interest for Moody.[127] As head of the CAC, his primary concern was to preach "the gospel of Chicago, the Great Central Market."[128] Moody knew the city's future hinged on its ability to resolve the congestion crisis, and he agreed a long-term solution would come from massive infrastructural improvements. In the meantime, however, something had to be done to ease the pressure.

This belief guided Moody as he approached the podium at the Illinois Federation of Women's Clubs's "Civics Day" symposium in the rooms of the Chicago Woman's Club in the Fine Arts Building on Michigan Avenue. He began by acknowledging that traffic congestion owed to the "massing together . . . of most of the retail and wholesale mercantile districts and the financial centers of the city."[129] But Moody did not encourage bankers, brokers, or businessmen of any kind to abandon the Loop before rush hour. Instead, he singled out shoppers. "I don't believe you will like me for saying it," he admitted, "but that will not matter, as my wife has many things to forgive me for. I am here to stick by convictions courageously."[130] The CAC director then proposed a three o'clock shopping curfew so that "working people can have a chance to get home when their work is finished for the day." Upon concluding his address, Moody slipped away without answering questions and before the chair of the symposium, Mrs. Frederick K. Tracy, could "say a word for the clubwomen" in their defense.[131]

Five days later, the *Chicago Tribune* took up Moody's plea in an editorial titled "A Shopping Time Limit." "The proposition has come from several sources," the piece began, "that women shoppers might help greatly relieve the congestion and the discomfort of the afternoon crowds by finishing their business in the stores at an earlier hour." In the author's view, a shopping curfew was "well worth consideration." Whereas most Chicagoans needed to travel to and from work at a given time, the author explained, shopping ladies had more control over their schedules and could easily avoid the rush hour crush. Some women might be forced to shop later in the day owing to "the necessary duties of the housekeeper," the author conceded, but most had no such restrictions. He then conjectured that if even a small portion of women shoppers could be induced to overcome their "selfishness" and leave the downtown by four o'clock, the "gain would be great." The piece closed by likening the proposed curfew to the Illinois Consumers' League's annual "shop early" campaigns, which urged women to complete their holiday shopping early to alleviate the strain on sales clerks.[132]

Presented in such a measured tone, the call for restrictions on ladies' consuming practices undoubtedly appealed to many Chicagoans troubled by congestion. After all, as the editorial indicated, the idea of a shopping curfew was not exactly new. The Illinois Consumers' League (ICL) had advocated early shopping every holiday season since its founding in 1897. Like its national counterpart, the ICL sought to use the purchasing power of moneyed women to improve the treatment of workers. While the National Consumers' League, under the direction of Chicagoan Florence Kelley, famously organized "white label" campaigns to encourage women to buy goods made under fair working conditions, the ICL and other state leagues focused on bettering conditions for retail workers in local stores.[133] During the busy holiday season, the ICL attempted to curb employer abuses by asking Chicago ladies to shop early in the season to reduce late-December crowds, early in the week to protect employees' Saturday half days, and early in the day to ensure that clerks were not forced to work late into the night.[134]

On the surface, the ICL's holiday campaigns did appear to share much in common with calls for a new shopping curfew. Both sought to rush shoppers out of the Loop by early evening. Yet each plan was rooted in a very different conception of women's place in civic life. Unlike the men who supported shopping curfews, the ICL joined State Street retailers in viewing women consumers as a primary and powerful force in the urban economy. In the words of ICL cofounder Ellen Martin Henrotin, "Woman's role in the economic world . . . is that of consumer, and in that role she is most important."[135] According to Henrotin, economic "specialization" had redefined woman's place, relieving her of the responsibilities of production while thrusting upon her the burden of consumption. Although many people misunderstood the "importance and dignity" of women's new role, Henrotin argued, the "century of the consumer" was dawning, and women were to be an "all powerful factor."[136] Founded in that same spirit, the ICL's early shopping campaigns were sustained by a belief that consumers could effect political and economic change.

By contrast, advocates of a shopping time limit viewed women consumers as peripheral—even dispensable—parts of the commercial life of the city. While ICL clubwomen regarded consumption as important and necessary economic activity, curfew supporters cast consumption as a mere pastime. Further, while the ICL upheld a vision of a metropolis wherein women had full access to the public realm, Moody and his allies represented the city as something over which women exercised only a qualified claim. Both the ICL and curfew advocates asked Chicago ladies to reform their consuming practices, but only one group challenged woman's right to consume when and where she pleased. Far from a shoppers' paradise, the civic ideal favored by many industrialists made little room for women consumers.

Chicago ladies did not remain silent as the business community debated their claim to the city center. Many spoke out against the proposed curfew as a violation of personal liberty. Lawyer and suffragist Catherine Waugh McCulloch was among the first to object. "I'd like to see them try such a regulation!" she exclaimed shortly after the curfew was suggested. Denouncing the scheme as "outrageous," McCulloch expressed disgust with those who would diminish women's already limited hold on the public realm. She took particular affront to Mills's claim that women shoppers believed space on streetcars and sidewalks belonged to them by "divine right." Such an assumption would be outlandish, McCulloch wryly observed, as every woman knows her rights are limited to "what man, in his chivalrous generosity, deigns to give her."[137]

Other women linked the potential curfew to their lack of full citizenship. "It isn't the women shoppers that crowd the cars," protested Alice B. Young, an affluent sixty-year-old divorcée and fixture of Chicago's elite social directory, the *Blue Book*. "It's the dollar greed of Chicago men that crowds the downtown district into a narrow, confined space." This greed, in her view, spurred investors to build more skyscrapers and transit companies to pack more customers onto streetcars. Young's solution was to place greater political power in the hands of women. "If they would let us women vote," she contended, "we would vote for the Paris regulation that marks a car 'complete' when it is full, and won't let anyone else on." In advocating such a policy, which would have prohibited streetcars from accepting more passengers than available seats, Young prioritized women's comfort on public transit above traffic circulation. If her plan was not adopted, she warned, women would insist on claiming the few rights they had. "If the men won't let us vote—and I am no suffragist—they might at least let us have the seats we can't vote for," she concluded.[138]

Yet more was at stake in the curfew proposition than women's political subordination. The proposal also rested on the assumptions that shopping was inessential to the urban economy and that shoppers were self-indulgent idlers. To counter such beliefs, several curfew opponents highlighted the important contributions of consumers. For example, Esther Falkenstein—founder of the Armitage Avenue Settlement, often referred to as the Esther Falkenstein Settlement—suggested that shoppers were not indolent pleasure seekers but women engaged in the difficult work of maintaining a household. "Let a man try an afternoon of shopping—necessary shopping—once or twice and then see what he thinks of the plan!" she remarked.[139] A Pittsburgh journalist critiquing Chicago's proposed curfew claimed that shopping "is not merely a diversion but more frequently it is a duty and very often a labor." According to the journalist, cities derived great benefits from shopping—no matter when it occurred. "What we need now more than anything else is to encourage shoppers to come out at any old hour of the day that suits their own sweet will," the writer insisted, echoing the views of many retailers. "Let them come, and the more the merrier! Let those who have the cash to spare spend it, no matter what the hour, for at the present stage the great desideratum is that money get into circulation through retail trade."[140]

Most curfew opponents held that shoppers possessed the same right to occupy public space as other citizens. At least one critic, however, declared that shoppers had *more* rights on State Street than other Chicagoans. At a meeting of the Hull House Woman's Club just days after Moody's address, Ella Batcher, the club's recording secretary, outlined a counterproposal calling for a ban on all vehicular traffic on State Street between ten o'clock in the morning and six o'clock at night. Reviving statements made years earlier by SSIA merchants, Batcher, the forty-eight-year-old wife of a civil engineer, argued that State Street should be "a place where shoppers can roam around for hours without the slightest chance of accident."[141] As a retail hub, Batcher maintained, State Street "should not be permitted to become so dangerous that women cannot do their shopping there. There are plenty of other streets to which the traffic could be diverted." In Batcher's view, women had a particular claim to State Street because of its status as a shopping destination. On that thoroughfare, she asserted, women's comfort and safety mattered more than circulation. Although her vision of women's dominion did not extend beyond State Street, Batcher nevertheless advanced a civic model where shoppers played a significant role. Upon hearing her argument, the audience "applauded vigorously," suggesting that many women shared her perspective.[142]

Beyond the clubhouse doors, responses to Batcher's proposal were mixed, although her plan was reportedly "taken more favorably than that of Mr. Mills."[143] Nevertheless, the *Chicago Tribune* ran a cartoon on its front page ridiculing her appeal for a "Shoppers' Paradise" (fig. 6.6).[144] Set at the corner of State and Madison, the drawing highlighted women's social uses of the street, depicting the intersection as a space of sociability, leisure, and consumption. While some women in the image are seen enjoying a tea party, others are working on their embroidery, caring for children, chatting with friends, browsing store windows, and showing off recent purchases. Only a few men appear in the sketch, and all are in some way feminized by the artist: three men hold packages or babies; an African American waiter serves a group of women; and two other men are clearly mashers, attempting to attract women's attention. The sole vehicle in the scene has been brought to a screeching halt just outside the frame by a stodgy police officer. Any other signs of traffic or efficient circulation are absent. Even the women who barrel through the background—heads down, shoulders hunched—forge ahead in a disorderly fashion, moments away from colliding into one another. The scene brought to life the worst fears of those who proposed to make Chicago a rationalized—and masculine—central marketplace. Indeed, as rendered by the artist, the shoppers' paradise was also many a businessman's nightmare.

Though exaggerated, the sketch illustrated many ways in which State Street was already being used by women shoppers. Ladies peeping into windows, mothers holding on to the hands of small children, and pairs engaged in conversation had all become familiar fixtures there in recent years. Even as it rejected the shoppers' paradise, then, the cartoon tacitly acknowledged that space—both physical and ideological—had been made for women consumers in public life. In the years to come, even Moody's CAC began to appreciate the importance of shoppers to Chicago's future. With the hope of drawing conventions and trade shows, the association took new interest in enhancing the city's appeal as "a pleasure place, as well as a business place."[145] The CAC began supporting beautification projects as well as accommodations for women shoppers who might join their husbands on business trips. This new approach was readily apparent in 1912, when the CAC initiated a study of the relationship between congestion and "an increasing number of automobiles used by the legion of downtown shoppers." Before offering any solutions,

Figure 6.6 This 1908 cartoon from the *Chicago Tribune* offered a humorous depiction of State Street's future if vehicles were barred, as some women and retailers desired. Many elements of this feminized shoppers' paradise, while exaggerated in the sketch, had already been achieved on State Street.

"State Street Shoppers' Paradise When Vehicles Are Barred," *Chicago Tribune*, Mar. 20, 1908, 1.

CAC leaders made clear that all proposals must take into account the interest of shoppers and retailers, giving "due regard to their rights."[146] Circulation was still a top priority, but the CAC would no longer dismiss shoppers' claims to the city center.

As the first decade of the twentieth century drew to a close, most Chicagoans, even many industrialists, acknowledged that shoppers had a place in the modern metropolis. Yet tensions still persisted over how best to solve the congestion crisis and make use of the city streets. Ultimately, it was the publication of Daniel H. Burnham's *Plan of Chicago* in 1909 that helped ease the conflict. The *Plan* offered a sweeping blueprint for Chicago's development that reflected the interests of the businessmen who sponsored it—members of the powerful Commercial Club of Chicago. Since its founding in 1877, the Commercial Club had sought to advance "the prosperity and growth of the city of Chicago."[147] Yet unlike other business groups, such as the SSIA, the LPA, or the CAC, the Commercial Club attracted members from across the city's many industries and *both* sides of the traffic debate.[148] Its ranks included merchants such as John G. Shedd, Stanley Field, and John V. Farwell, as well as manufacturers such as John Glessner and Cyrus McCormick.[149] These influential businessmen commissioned Burnham, a longtime club member, to develop a comprehensive plan for Chicago's growth.

Burnham's *Plan*, a result of three years of work, sought to "bring order out of chaos." It was a response, as noted on its first page, to the growing conviction among Chicagoans "that the formless growth of the city is neither economical nor satisfactory; and that overcrowding and congestion of traffic paralyze the vital functions of the city."[150] In short, whatever its other aims, the *Plan* offered yet another proposal for congestion relief. Its chief architect clearly prioritized efficient circulation. "The main problem to be solved," Burnham wrote, "is the disposition of the various streams of traffic, so that people may reach expeditiously the places to which their daily vocations call them."[151] The *Plan* departed from earlier congestion remedies, however, by taking into account "the convenience of both producer and consumer."[152] Indeed, Burnham's *Plan* helped ease tensions between retailers' and industrialists' metropolitan visions by incorporating aspects of both.

The *Plan* achieved this balance chiefly through spatial differentiation and specialization. Its most significant commitment was to improving circulation by routing freight traffic around—instead of through—the Loop's overburdened streets. "No goods should be carried into and out of the congested business center except those needed for construction, for retailing, or for consumption in that territory," Burnham insisted.[153] A new freight center would be constructed outside the central business district, nearer to the major rail and shipyards on the South Side, in order to streamline distribution and cut costs for handling and warehousing. Wider, better paved, and more direct routes around the Loop would connect the new freight depot to manufacturers and merchants on the North and West Sides, eliminating "the congestion in the city [center] caused by bringing in and carrying out goods not to be consumed."[154] Any remaining freight traffic in the Loop was to be diverted to underground tunnels and the lower tiers of new double-decker bridges.[155] These changes, according to Burnham, would make downtown streets cleaner, safer, longer lasting, and less crowded.

At its base, the *Plan* represented the Loop as a hub of commercial activity—one that certainly included women's consumption. Notably, the text referred to the downtown as both a "business district" and a "retail district." Although shoppers were never explicitly mentioned, the importance of their safety was readily apparent. When discussing traffic at a notoriously congested intersection in the retail district, for example, Burnham stated that "104 people, sixty per cent of whom were probably women and children, passed this corner every minute." The architect cited women's presence here to underscore the dangers posed by freight traffic and to build his case for rerouting heavy teams. Their removal from the downtown, Burnham argued, would make streets "safer for pedestrian movement," which, in the retail district, meant the flow of women shoppers.[156]

The *Plan* advocated several other changes first championed by Chicago retailers. On shopping streets, for example, Burnham advised that "the pavement should be smooth and noiseless"—ideal for pedestrians, carriages, and automobiles, not commercial traffic. "There should be frequent islands of safety for the pedestrian crossing from side to side," he wrote, hinting at shoppers' tendency to cross streets mid-block. Further, "the lighting, the signs, and every accessory of the street should be arranged with regard to the dictates of good taste," he suggested.[157] Unlike SSIA merchants, however, Burnham did not envision limiting these improvements to State Street alone. As part of a proposal to boulevard

Figure 6.7 Daniel H. Burnham's *Plan of Chicago* (1909) incorporated women shoppers into development plans for the central business district. In this watercolor painting of proposed improvements to Michigan Avenue, ladies with parasols are shown circulating leisurely under the shade of ornamental trees in close proximity to towering office buildings.   Courtesy of the Newberry Library.

Michigan Avenue—an up-and-coming retail corridor—Burnham called for a divided roadway, with one side for "shopping traffic and carriages waiting for the crowds attending public functions."[158] Watercolor paintings of the proposed boulevard depicted ladies with parasols strolling under the shade of ornamental trees (fig. 6.7). Women shoppers, unlike freight wagons, were clearly welcome in the new downtown.[159]

The *Plan of Chicago* was released to great fanfare on July 4, 1909, by the Commercial Club. Many club members then moved on to positions in the Chicago Plan Commission, the organization charged with evaluating and implementing Burnham's recommendations. As chair of that commission, brewery heir Charles H. Wacker assumed responsibility for hiring a general manager. Wacker knew that the role demanded a man of unusual energy, extensive business contacts, and tremendous sales ability. For that, he turned to the current general manager of the CAC, Walter D. Moody. For the next decade, until his death in 1920, Moody devoted himself to "selling" Burnham's vision of the metropolis—a vision that made room for shoppers, bundles, and baby carriages even as it promoted efficient circulation.[160]

Aspects of Burnham's *Plan* were adopted piecemeal in the decades to come. Between 1912 and 1931, seventeen *Plan*-related projects were completed by the city, for a combined cost of $234 million.[161] None of these projects were undertaken without significant public debate. Yet support came from across earlier divides—from industrialists, retailers, and women's clubs. Together, these groups advanced the civic vision laid out by Burnham—a vision that captured a city in transition, one re-orienting to an emergent mass consumer economy upheld by women's spending. Although shoppers never appeared in the text and only a handful of female names were included on the list of subscribers, women consumers were nevertheless written into Chicago's blueprint for growth. The *Plan* helped establish a built environment that accommo-dated, even welcomed, women's presence in the downtown, enabling the consolidation of a culture of consumption.

Conclusion

I N HER 1907 MEMOIR, celebrated French actress Sarah Bernhardt reflected on the distinctive charms of American cities. By then, she had
toured the United States many times. The Puritan traditions and cultural refinement of Boston intrigued her. In New York, she marveled at
the Brooklyn Bridge. Baltimore left an impression of frigid hotels, and
St. Louis disappointed in being "repulsively dirty." In New Orleans, she
admired the cheerful shops and arcades. Of Chicago, she recalled the
hustle and bustle of the business district, where "men pass each other
without ever stopping, with knitted brows, with one thought in mind,
'the end to attain.'" But it was not only the city's businessmen who
moved with peculiar haste. The ladies of Chicago "do not stroll about
the streets, as in other cities," Bernhardt observed. "They walk quickly;
they also are in a hurry to seek amusement."[1]

Chicago ladies rushed from the plush velvet seats of matinees to the
soda fountains of fashionable confectioneries, and from the ballrooms
of grand hotels to the marble halls of retail palaces. They seemed to glide
easily through the downtown, and yet their right to pursue pleasure in
this manner had not come automatically. Even as Bernhardt was writing,
moneyed women's presence in the Loop was provoking opposition. From
the crucible of conflict, however, a new downtown was beginning to
emerge. Its cultural practices and built environment upheld women's
consumption and affirmed their place in the central business district.
With the aid of merchants, lawmakers, and city planners, the male-
dominated city center gave way to a downtown where women and men
mingled together—and ladies openly indulged their consumer desires.

The creation of this shoppers' paradise assured women's place as the nation's primary "purchasing agents," the essential fuel of a mass consumer economy.[2] In the decades that followed, women's preferences increasingly influenced the design, distribution, and sales of the vast majority of consumer goods. Moreover, their behavior became the focus of the blossoming fields of marketing and consumer research.[3] Even women's foot traffic, once considered a nuisance, came to be highly prized and, by the 1920s, was being used to determine the value of commercial real estate in the downtown.[4]

Yet as the city center opened to consuming ladies, it grew less hospitable to numerous other people and practices. This correlation was no accident. To establish an environment supportive of female consumption, Chicago's business and civic leaders purged from the Loop features that could impede the comfort or circulation of moneyed white women. Mashers, prostitutes, and other morally suspect characters were driven from the downtown. Also pushed to the city's periphery were many of the unsightly remnants of the Loop's industrial past—factories, warehouses, coal wagons, and the workingmen who operated them. No longer would the artifacts of production hold a prominent place at the center of the consumer metropolis, particularly after the publication of Burnham's *Plan*. The Loop was increasingly the province of moneyed shoppers, businessmen, and the service workers who supported their activities.

Bounded by class, the Loop grew more racially exclusive amid the Great Migration that commenced during the First World War. Discrimination had, of course, long prevented African Americans from fully enjoying the fruits of Chicago's blossoming consumer economy. But racial divides became starker and more aggressively patrolled as nearly 200,000 black migrants, many from the rural South, poured into the city in the two decades following the *Plan*'s publication.[5] Drawn by employment opportunities, family connections, and the famous *Chicago Defender* newspaper, these newcomers quintupled Chicago's black population.[6] Since the city's founding, African Americans had constituted little more than 1.5 percent of total residents. By 1930, that number had jumped to 7 percent and would continue to climb, reaching 33 percent by 1970.[7]

This rapid growth unsettled many white Chicagoans and incited more overt racial hostility. One result was the city's notorious 1919 race riot, which lasted seven days and led to the deaths of twenty-three blacks and fifteen whites. The conflict commenced when a black teenager drifted into the waters of a de facto white beach, was struck by a rock, and drowned.[8] Yet beaches were far from the only public spaces where racial boundaries had begun to harden. As the number of black residents increased, so, too, did the exclusionary practices that prevented them from patronizing the Loop's department stores, theaters, restaurants, tearooms, and hotels. In 1916, when the flow of migrants first began to accelerate, the *Chicago Defender* commented on the rising discrimination in downtown stores. Focusing particularly on Marshall Field & Co., the paper reported that although "members of the race" had previously been served there, "of late they find it hard to be waited on." The reason, according to the *Defender,* was that management had issued a new directive "to show Colored patrons 'inattention' and treat them in a manner indicative of the fact that their trade was not desired."[9] Similar policies were adopted by other Loop establishments that had once served black customers.

The discrimination faced by black consumers in downtown Chicago was highlighted in Nella Larsen's *Passing* (1929), a celebrated novel of the Harlem Renaissance. Although much of the story was set in New York City, protagonist Irene Redfield, a fair-skinned African American woman, spent an afternoon early in the book shopping in downtown Chicago. Irene stopped to enjoy a cool drink at the swanky rooftop restaurant in the fictional Drayton Hotel, but she soon worried that someone might discern her race and force her to leave. "It wasn't that she was ashamed of being a Negro, or even of having it declared," Larsen wrote. "It was the idea of being ejected from any place, even in the polite and tactful way in which the Drayton would probably do it, that disturbed her."[10] Neither Irene's affluence nor her social respectability as the wife of a doctor could insulate her from racial prejudice. Unlike the white women Bernhardt had observed hurrying after pleasure, black women were not welcome in many of the Loop's consumer spaces.[11]

The formation of a racially exclusive, class-bounded city center was the product of numerous choices made by retailers, theater owners, restaurateurs, elected officials, policy makers, police officers, city planners, reformers, and moneyed women. Their actions generated stark inequalities, which were then reflected in the landscape. The Loop's broad commercial avenues, towering buildings, and tree-lined parks stood within a short streetcar ride of congested working-class slums, polluted industrial districts, and stockyards thick with the stench of animal waste. At least one Chicagoan, urban planner Jens Jensen, was troubled by the contrast. As he explained in a 1911 article for the *Survey*, he feared that any city that devoted too much attention to its "commercial value" would become "at once a city of palaces and of box-like houses where humanity is packed together like cattle in railroad cars." Such a "show city," Jensen warned, promoted a population of "spendthrifts desirous of a gay life" and was fundamentally "undemocratic."[12]

Yet for many others, especially the owners of retail and service businesses that catered to moneyed white women, the Loop was still a bit *too* democratic. The very qualities that defined metropolitan life—cosmopolitanism, heterogeneity, and openness—made urban space an unreliable business partner, difficult to manage and contain.[13] No matter how much they invested in ordering and controlling commercial environments, these capitalists could never wholly eliminate from the Loop mashers, pickpockets, beggars, or drunks, not to mention African Americans, immigrant workers, or anyone else moneyed white women might find objectionable. Such persons could be driven from, or segregated within, the privately owned interiors of department stores, restaurants, and grand hotels, but they could not be eradicated from the streets, sidewalks, and broader public realm in which those establishments operated.

It was with considerable enthusiasm, then, that many retailers embraced the possibilities of suburban expansion in the 1920s. As automobile ownership came within reach of more Americans, many families elected to leave behind crowded cities for bucolic suburbs.[14] Retailers did not long hesitate to follow. Smaller specialty shops, faced with rising downtown rents, were among the first to relocate. Soon, even department stores were eager to open suburban "branch" locations while leaving intact their downtown flagships. In Chicago, Marshall Field's and the Fair pioneered the trend. Each established two major suburban outposts in 1928 and 1929.[15] Advertising expert Christine Frederick applauded this "decentralizing tendency" in *Selling Mrs. Consumer* (1929). "Women, like men," she warned, "are coming to hate rather than to love 'shopping' under modern crowded city conditions."[16] Branch stores seemed to provide a solution. They offered the same service and selection as their State Street parents but with less congestion, ample parking, and fewer opportunities to interact with anyone not affluent and not white. Even the clerks, as readers of the *Chicago Tribune* were assured after the grand opening of Marshall Field's Oak Park branch, were, "for the most part, residents of the western suburbs."[17]

Still, the early branch locations, located on main streets in growing suburban towns, could not provide retailers with total control over the shopping environment. Such control could only be achieved on privately owned land. The first branch stores thus paved the way for that icon of the postwar era: the shopping center.[18] These carefully manicured and regulated spaces were constructed from scratch to reflect the desires of moneyed white women, especially suburban housewives. Typically located in predominantly white areas, far from public transit and accessible only by car, shopping centers effectively segmented consumers by race and class.[19] They also upheld the family-oriented lifestyles that came to define postwar suburban culture. There were parks and playgrounds to occupy small children; restaurants and cafés for socializing with other mothers; and banks, post offices, and hair salons to make life more convenient. Oversized parking spaces were intended to appeal to the many women who had only recently learned to drive. And, to top it all off, private security forces were hired to patrol the grounds and ensure that any undesirable social elements could be quickly removed.[20]

At first glance, postwar shopping centers seemed vastly different from the heterogeneous urban business districts where women's presence had caused such conflict. In both places, however, moneyed women profoundly shaped public culture and the built environment. Their imprint may have been most obvious in the shopping mall, but traces of their influence could be found on the streets and sidewalks of the downtown as well as within urban restaurants, hotels, theaters, and department stores. Their consumption in the city center sustained American economic growth in the first half of the twentieth century. It also established a new acceptance of women's presence in public—not merely as workers, reformers, or fulfillers of errands but as pleasure seekers, promenaders, and ramblers without specific aims. The pursuits of consuming ladies contributed to the erosion of gender regimes that once distinguished women as intruders in public space, propelling women one step closer to full citizenship and assuring their place in commercial life.

Notes

Introduction

1. Theodore Dreiser, *Sister Carrie* (New York: Doubleday, Page, 1900), 24–25.
2. Dreiser, *Sister Carrie*, 25.
3. "Plan a Shoppers' Paradise," *Chicago Tribune*, May 19, 1904, 12.
4. See, for example, Ellen Hartigan-O'Connor, *The Ties That Buy: Women and Commerce in Revolutionary America* (Philadelphia: University of Pennsylvania Press, 2009); Joanna Cohen, *Luxurious Citizens: The Politics of Consumption in Nineteenth-Century America* (Philadelphia: University of Pennsylvania Press, 2017); Ann Smart Martin, *Buying into the World of Goods: Early Consumers in Backcountry Virginia* (Baltimore: Johns Hopkins University Press, 2008); Kate Haulman, *The Politics of Fashion in Eighteenth-Century America* (Chapel Hill: University of North Carolina Press, 2011); Elizabeth White Nelson, *Market Sentiments: Middle-Class Culture in Nineteenth-Century America* (Washington, D.C.: Smithsonian Books, 2004); Karen Halttunen, *Confidence Men and Painted Women: A Study of Middle-Class Culture in America, 1830–1870* (New Haven, Conn.: Yale University Press, 1982).
5. M. Christine Boyer, *Manhattan Manners: Architecture and Style, 1850–1900* (New York: Rizzoli, 1985), 43–129; Michael P. Conzen and Kathleen Neils Conzen, "Geographical Structure in Nineteenth-Century Urban Retailing: Milwaukee, 1846–1890," *Journal of Historical Geography* 5 (Jan. 1979): 45–66.
6. On postwar consumer society, see especially Lizabeth Cohen, *A Consumers' Republic: The Politics of Mass Consumption in Postwar America* (New York: Vintage Books, 2003).
7. On changes in production and distribution fostering the rise of the department store, see William Leach, *Land of Desire: Merchants, Power, and the Rise of a New American Culture* (New York: Pantheon Books, 1993), xiii–xiv, 15–17.
8. On the development of department stores, see especially Leach, *Land of Desire;* Susan Porter Benson, *Counter Cultures: Saleswomen, Managers, and*

Customers in American Department Stores, 1890–1940 (Urbana: University of Illinois Press, 1986), 12–30; Joseph Siry, *Carson Pirie Scott: Louis Sullivan and the Chicago Department Store* (Chicago: University of Chicago Press, 1988), 13–64; Elaine Abelson, *When Ladies Go A-Thieving: Middle-Class Shoplifters in the Victorian Department Store* (New York: Oxford University Press, 1989), 31–41; Vicki Howard, *From Main Street to Mall: The Rise and Fall of the American Department Store* (Philadelphia: University of Pennsylvania Press, 2015), 9–29; Louisa Iarocci, *The Urban Department Store in America, 1850–1930* (Surrey, U.K.: Ashgate, 2014), 69–126.

9. Dreiser, *Sister Carrie*, 24.

10. On the importance of service and spectacle to department store trade, see especially Leach, "Part I: Strategies of Enticement," in *Land of Desire*, 15–152; Benson, *Counter Cultures*, 82–90; Jan Whitaker, *Service and Style: How the American Department Store Fashioned the Middle Class* (New York: St. Martin's Press, 2006).

11. Asa Briggs, *Victorian Cities* (London: Odhams, 1963), 55–56.

12. Walter Nugent, "Demography: Chicago as a World City," in *The Encyclopedia of Chicago*, ed. James R. Grossman, Ann Durkin Keating, and Janice L. Reiff (Chicago: University of Chicago Press, 2004), 233–235; James Gilbert, *Perfect Cities: Chicago Utopias of 1893* (Chicago: University of Chicago Press, 1991), 27.

13. Homer Hoyt, *One Hundred Years of Land Values in Chicago: The Relationship of the Growth of Chicago to the Rise of Its Land Values, 1830–1933* (Chicago: University of Chicago Press, 1933), 196–207; John F. McDonald, *Chicago: An Economic History* (New York: Routledge, 2016), 24–59; Frederic Cople Jaher, *The Urban Establishment: Upper Strata in Boston, New York, Charleston, Chicago, and Los Angeles* (Urbana: University of Illinois Press, 1982), 472–473; Frederic Cople Jaher and Jocelyn Maynard Ghent, "The Chicago Business Elite, 1830–1930: A Collective Biography," *Business History Review* 50 (Autumn 1976): 288.

14. *Half-Century's Progress of the City of Chicago: The City's Leading Manufacturers and Merchants* (Chicago: International, 1887), 33; George Washington Orear, *Commercial and Architectural Chicago* (Chicago: Donohue & Henneberry, 1887), 32.

15. On Chicago as a manufacturing, wholesale, and distribution center, see William Cronon, *Nature's Metropolis: Chicago and the Great West* (New York: W. W. Norton, 1999), 90–93, 310–312, 327–350; Donald L. Miller, *City of the Century: The Epic of Chicago and the Making of America* (New York: Simon & Schuster, 1996), 240, 243–254; Jaher, *Urban Establishment*, 473–480. For use of "Great Central Market," see, for example, *Chicago: The Great Central Market: A Magazine of Business* (Chicago: Chicago Commercial Association, 1904–1909); *Chicago: The Great Central Market* (Chicago: Marshall Field & Co., 1921).

16. On Chicago department stores, see especially Siry, *Carson Pirie Scott;* Robert W. Twyman, *History of Marshall Field & Co., 1852–1906* (Philadelphia:

University of Pennsylvania Press, 1954); Joel A. Tarr, "The Chicago Anti-Department Store Crusade of 1897," *Journal of the Illinois State Historical Society* 64 (Summer 1971): 161–172; Hugh Dalziel Duncan, *Culture and Democracy: The Struggle for Form in Society and Architecture in Chicago and the Middle West during the Life and Times of Louis H. Sullivan* (Totowa, N.J.: Bedminster Press, 1965), 123–131; Jeffrey A. Brune, "Department Stores," in Grossman, Keating, and Reiff, *Encyclopedia of Chicago,* 238–239.

17. "News about Big Stores," *Dry Goods Reporter,* Apr. 9, 1904, 13.

18. Henry Blake Fuller, *The Cliff-Dwellers* (New York: Harper & Brothers, 1893), 51.

19. Henry Blake Fuller, *With the Procession* (New York: Harper & Brothers, 1895), 25.

20. On the Chicago World's Fair as significant to urban theory and planning, see especially Gilbert, *Perfect Cities;* Thomas S. Hines, *Burnham of Chicago: Architect and Planner,* 2nd ed. (Chicago: University of Chicago Press, 2009).

21. Carl Smith, *The Plan of Chicago: Daniel Burnham and the Remaking of the American City* (Chicago: University of Chicago Press, 2006), 15, 19; Daniel Bluestone, *Constructing Chicago* (New Haven, Conn.: Yale University Press, 1993), 181–204.

22. On the Plan of Chicago, see Smith, *Plan of Chicago;* Hines, *Burnham of Chicago;* Michael P. McCarthy, "Chicago Businessmen and the Burnham Plan," *Journal of the Illinois State Historical Society* 63 (Autumn 1970): 228–256; Robin Bachin, *Building the South Side: Urban Space and Civic Culture in Chicago, 1890–1919* (Chicago: University of Chicago Press, 2004), 169–203; Laura E. Baker, "Civic Ideals, Mass Culture, and the Public: Reconsidering the 1909 Plan of Chicago," *Journal of Urban History* 36 (Nov. 2010): 747–770; Samuel Kling, "Wide Boulevards, Narrow Visions: Burnham's Street System and the Chicago Plan Commission, 1909–1930," *Journal of Planning History* 12 (Aug. 2013): 245–268.

23. "How Boston Sees Chicago," *Chicago: The Great Central Market* 4 (Jan. 1907): 59.

24. Charles Dudley Warner, *Studies in the South and West, with Comments on Canada* (New York: Harper & Brothers, 1889), 196.

25. Jaher, *Urban Establishment,* 495–496. See also Paul DiMaggio, "The Problem of Chicago: Class Authority and Cultural Entrepreneurship," in *The American Bourgeoisie: Distinction and Identity in the Nineteenth Century,* ed. Sven Beckert and Julia Rosenbaum (New York: Palgrave Macmillan, 2010), 209–232.

26. Robert Herrick, *The Gospel of Freedom* (New York: Macmillan, 1898), 111.

27. On rising racial discrimination and the Great Migration, see especially James R. Grossman, *Land of Hope: Chicago, Black Southerners, and the Great Migration* (Chicago: University of Chicago Press, 1989), 164. For demographic information, see Allan H. Spear, *Black Chicago: The Making of a Negro Ghetto, 1890–1920* (Chicago: University of Chicago Press, 1967), 12.

28. "Objects to Color Line," *Chicago Tribune,* Jan. 13, 1899, 8; "Mrs. Henrotin Is Out," *Chicago Tribune,* Jan. 20, 1899, 8.

29. Jaher, *Urban Establishment,* 496–497.

30. Thorstein Veblen, *The Theory of the Leisure Class: An Economic Study of Institutions,* rev. ed (1899; repr., New York: Macmillan, 1912), 84. See also Thorstein Veblen, "The Economic Theory of Woman's Dress," *Popular Science Monthly* 46 (Dec. 1894): 200.

31. Maureen A. Flanagan, *Seeing with Their Hearts: Chicago Women and the Vision of the Good City, 1871–1933* (Princeton, N.J.: Princeton University Press, 2002), 57. On Bertha Palmer's consumption practices, see Kristin Hoganson, *Consumers' Imperium: The Global Production of American Domesticity, 1865–1920* (Chapel Hill: University of North Carolina Press, 2007), 13–56.

32. On Jane Addams, see especially Louise W. Knight, *Citizen Jane Addams and the Struggle for Democracy* (Chicago: University of Chicago Press, 2005); Victoria Bissell Brown, *The Education of Jane Addams* (Philadelphia: University of Pennsylvania Press, 2004). On Frances Willard, see especially Ruth Bordin, *Frances Willard: A Biography* (Chapel Hill: University of North Carolina Press, 1986). On Florence Kelley, see especially Kathryn Kish Sklar, *Florence Kelley and the Nation's Work: The Rise of Women's Political Culture* (New Haven, Conn.: Yale University Press, 1995).

33. Herrick, *Gospel of Freedom,* 115.

34. Veblen, *Theory of the Leisure Class,* 84.

35. See, for example, Mary P. Ryan, *Women in Public: Between Banners and Ballots, 1825–1880* (Baltimore: Johns Hopkins University Press, 1990); Sklar, *Florence Kelley and the Nation's Work;* Sarah Deutsch, *Women and the City: Gender, Space, and Power in Boston, 1870–1940* (New York: Oxford University Press, 2000); Flanagan, *Seeing with Their Hearts;* Barbara Epstein, *The Politics of Domesticity: Women, Evangelism, and Temperance in Nineteenth-Century America* (Middletown, Conn.: Wesleyan University Press, 1981); Lori Ginzberg, *Women and the Work of Benevolence: Morality and Politics in the Northeastern United States, 1820–1885* (New Haven, Conn.: Yale University Press, 1985); Robyn Muncy, *Creating a Female Dominion in American Reform, 1890–1935* (New York: Oxford University Press, 1991); Knight, *Citizen Jane Addams.*

36. Roland Barthes, *Mythologies,* ed. and trans. Annette Lavers (New York: Noonday Press, 1972), 10. First published in 1957 by Editions du Seuil.

37. Simon Patten, *The Theory of Social Forces* (Philadelphia: American Academy of Political and Social Science, 1896), 85.

38. Joyce Appleby, *The Relentless Revolution: A History of Capitalism* (New York: W. W. Norton, 2010), 119. On a favorable moral climate as essential to consumer capitalism, see also T. J. Jackson Lears, "From Salvation to Self-Realization: Advertising and the Therapeutic Roots of the Consumer Culture, 1880–1930," in *The Culture of Consumption: Critical Essays in American History, 1880–1980,* ed. Richard Wightman Fox and T. J. Jackson Lears (New York: Pantheon, 1983), 4; Warren I. Susman, *Culture as History: The Transformation of American Society in the Twentieth Century* (New York: Pantheon Books, 1984), xx–xxi; Jean-Christophe Agnew, "Coming Up for Air:

Consumer Culture in Historical Perspective," in *Consumption and the World of Goods*, ed. John Brewer and Roy Porter (New York: Routledge, 1993), 25–26.

39. Patten, *Theory of Social Forces*, 74, 77.

40. Sven Beckert, "History of American Capitalism," in *American History Now*, ed. Eric Foner and Lisa McGirr (Philadelphia: Temple University Press, 2011), 315.

41. See especially Amy Dru Stanley, "Histories of Capitalism and Sex Difference," *Journal of the Early Republic* 36 (Summer 2016): 343–350. Peter James Hudson points out that the study of black women in particular has not been well-integrated into the field. Hudson, "Interchange: The History of Capitalism," *Journal of American History* 101, no. 2 (Sept. 2014): 505, 515.

42. Christine Frederick, *Selling Mrs. Consumer* (New York: Business Bourse, 1929), 12; William R. Leach, "Transformations in a Culture of Consumption: Women and Department Stores, 1890–1925," *Journal of American History* 71 (Sept. 1984): 333; Benson, *Counter Cultures*, 76; Lizabeth Cohen, "From Town Center to Shopping Center: The Reconfiguration of Community Marketplaces in Postwar America," *American Historical Review* 101 (Oct. 1996): 1072; Alison Isenberg, *Downtown America: A History of the Place and the People Who Made It* (Chicago: University of Chicago Press, 2004), 78.

43. This literature is vast. Some examples include Benson, *Counter Cultures;* Abelson, *When Ladies Go A-Thieving;* Leach, "Transformations in a Culture of Consumption"; Bethany Moreton, *To Serve God and Wal-Mart: The Making of Christian Free Enterprise* (Cambridge, Mass.: Harvard University Press, 2009); Tracey Deutsch, *Building a Housewife's Paradise: Gender, Politics, and American Grocery Stores in the Twentieth Century* (Chapel Hill: University of North Carolina, 2010); Simone Weil Davis, *Living Up to the Ads: Gender Fictions of the 1920s* (Durham, N.C.: Duke University Press, 2000); Jennifer Scanlon, *Inarticulate Longings:* The Ladies' Home Journal, *Gender, and the Promises of Consumer Culture* (New York: Routledge, 1995); Ellen Gruber Garvey, *The Adman in the Parlor: Magazines and the Gendering of Consumer Culture, 1880s to 1910s* (New York: Oxford University Press, 1996).

44. Nancy F. Cott, *The Bonds of Womanhood: "Woman's Sphere" in New England, 1780–1835* (New Haven, Conn.: Yale University Press, 1977); Christine Stansell, *City of Women: Sex and Class in New York, 1789–1860* (New York: Alfred A. Knopf, 1986); Kathy Peiss, *Cheap Amusements: Working Women and Leisure in Turn-of-the-Century New York* (Philadelphia: Temple University Press, 1986); Jeanne Boydston, *Home and Work: Housework, Wages, and the Ideology of Labor in the Early Republic* (New York: Oxford University Press, 1990).

45. See especially Sven Beckert, *The Monied Metropolis: New York City and the Consolidation of the American Bourgeoisie, 1850–1896* (New York: Cambridge University Press, 2001); David M. Scobey, *Empire City: The Making and Meaning of the New York City Landscape* (Philadelphia: Temple University Press, 2002).

46. See, for example, Ryan, *Women in Public;* Deutsch, *Women and the City;* Bachin, *Building the South Side;* Flanagan, *Seeing with Their Hearts;* Lisa Tolbert, *Constructing Townscapes: Space and Society in Antebellum Tennessee* (Chapel Hill: University of North Carolina Press, 1999); Georgina Hickey, *Hope and Danger in the New South City: Working-Class Women and Urban Development in Atlanta, 1890–1940* (Athens: University of Georgia Press, 2003).

47. Isenberg, *Downtown America;* Ryan, *Women in Public;* Jessica Ellen Sewell, *Women and the Everyday City: Public Space in San Francisco, 1890–1915* (Minneapolis: University of Minnesota Press, 2011). On the influence of women shoppers in London, see Erika Rappaport, *Shopping for Pleasure: Women in the Making of London's West End* (Princeton, N.J.: Princeton University Press, 2000).

48. See Isenberg, *Downtown America,* 16. Lizabeth Cohen similarly suggests that women's consuming practices became important to urban development in the mid-twentieth century. See Cohen, *Consumers' Republic,* 278–283; Cohen, "From Town Center to Shopping Center," 1072–1076.

49. Peiss, *Cheap Amusements;* Joanne J. Meyerowitz, *Women Adrift: Independent Wage Earners in Chicago, 1880–1930* (Chicago: University of Chicago Press, 1988); Ruth M. Alexander, *The Girl Problem: Female Sexual Delinquency in New York, 1900–1930* (Ithaca, N.Y.: Cornell University Press, 1995); Nan Enstad, *Ladies of Labor, Girls of Adventure: Working Women, Popular Culture, and Labor Politics at the Turn of the Twentieth Century* (New York: Columbia University Press, 1999); Sharon E. Wood, *The Freedom of the Streets: Work, Citizenship, and Sexuality in a Gilded Age City* (Chapel Hill: University of North Carolina Press, 2005).

50. Walter Benjamin, "The Flâneur," *Charles Baudelaire: A Lyric Poet in the Era of High Capitalism,* trans. Harry Zohn (London: New Left Books, 1973), 35–66; Janet Wolff, "The Invisible Flâneuse: Women and the Literature of Modernity," *Theory, Culture and Society* 2 (Nov. 1985): 40–42; Griselda Pollock, "Modernity and the Spaces of Femininity," in *Vision and Difference: Femininity, Feminism and the Histories of Art* (London: Routledge, 1988), 67–68; Elizabeth Wilson, "The Invisible Flâneur," *New Left Review* 191 (Jan.–Feb. 1992): 93–98.

51. On access to public space facilitating political power, if not actual voting rights, see especially Ryan, *Women in Public;* Sewell, *Women and the Everyday City;* Deutsch, *Women and the City.*

52. See especially Linda McDowell, *Gender, Identity, and Place: Understanding Feminist Geographies* (Minneapolis: University of Minnesota Press, 1999), 56, 148–150; Judith Butler, *Gender Trouble: Feminism and the Subversion of Identity* (New York: Routledge, 1990), 139–141; Elizabeth Wilson, *The Sphinx in the City: Urban Life, the Control of Disorder, and Women* (Berkeley: University of California Press, 1992).

53. On contestation over working-class women's commercial pleasure, see Stansell, *City of Women;* Peiss, *Cheap Amusements;* Meyerowitz, *Women Adrift;*

Enstad, *Ladies of Labor;* Tera W. Hunter, *To 'Joy My Freedom: Southern Black Women's Lives and Labors After the Civil War* (Cambridge, Mass.: Harvard University Press, 1997).

54. On women in commercial public space, see especially Sewell, *Women and the Everyday City;* Abelson, *When Ladies Go A-Thieving;* Benson, *Counter Cultures;* David Scobey, "Nymphs and Satyrs: Sex and the Bourgeois Public Sphere in Victorian New York," *Winterthur Portfolio* 37 (Winter 2002): 43–66; Peter Baldwin, *Domesticating the Street: The Reform of Public Space in Hartford, 1850–1930* (Columbus: Ohio University Press, 1999); Amy G. Richter, *Home on the Rails: Women, the Railroad, and the Rise of Public Domesticity* (Chapel Hill: University of North Carolina Press, 2005); Molly W. Berger, *Hotel Dreams: Luxury, Technology, and Urban Ambition in America, 1829–1929* (Baltimore: Johns Hopkins University Press, 2011); Peter Baldwin, *In the Watches of the Night: Life in the Nocturnal City, 1820–1930* (Chicago: University of Chicago Press, 2012); Maureen E. Montgomery, *Displaying Women: Spectacles of Leisure in Edith Wharton's New York* (New York: Routledge, 1998).

55. See especially Leach, *Land of Desire,* xv.

56. See especially Amy Dru Stanley, "Slave Emancipation and the Revolutionizing of Human Rights," in *The World the Civil War Made,* ed. Gregory Downs and Kate Masur (Chapel Hill: University of North Carolina Press, 2015), 269–303; Jane Dailey, "Deference and Violence in the Postbellum Urban South: Manners and Massacres in Danville, Virginia," *Journal of Southern History* 63 (Aug. 1997): 553–590; A. K. Sandoval-Strausz, "Travelers, Strangers, and Jim Crow: Law, Public Accommodations, and Civil Rights in America," *Law and History Review* 23 (Spring 2005): 53–94; Rebecca J. Scott, "Public Rights, Social Equality, and the Conceptual Roots of the Plessy Challenge," *Michigan Law Review* 106 (Mar. 2008): 777–804.

57. Elizabeth Dale, "'Social Equality Does Not Exist among Themselves, nor among Us': *Baylies vs. Curry* and Civil Rights in Chicago, 1888," *American Historical Review* 102 (Apr. 1997): 312.

58. On codes of civility and etiquette as critical to the social production of space, see John F. Kasson, *Rudeness and Civility: Manners in Nineteenth-Century Urban America* (New York: Hill and Wang, 1990); Mick Smith and Joyce Davidson, "Civility and Etiquette," in *The SAGE Companion to the City,* ed. Tim Hall, Phil Hubbard, and John Rennie Short (London: SAGE, 2008), 231–249; Mona Domosh, "Those 'Gorgeous Incongruities': Polite Politics and Public Space on the Streets of Nineteenth-Century New York City," *Annals of the Association of American Geographers* 88 (June 1988): 209–222.

1. Moneyed Women and the Downtown

1. Julian Ralph, "Chicago—the Main Exhibit," *Harper's New Monthly Magazine* 84 (Feb. 1892): 425. For the collected essays, see Julian Ralph, *Harper's Chicago and the World's Fair* (New York: Harper & Brothers, 1892).

2. Julian Ralph, "Chicago's Gentle Side," *Harper's New Monthly Magazine* 87 (July 1893): 287, 286.

3. Ralph, 287. On Palmer's "praiseworthy interest in civic and national affairs," see also Arthur Meeker, *Chicago, with Love: A Polite and Personal History* (New York: Alfred A. Knopf, 1955), 144–145.

4. Rima Lunin Schultz and Adele Hast, eds., *Women Building Chicago, 1790–1990* (Bloomington: Indiana University Press, 2001), 661–664; Ishbel Ross, *Silhouette in Diamonds: The Life of Mrs. Potter Palmer* (New York: Harper & Brothers, 1960), 58–99; Edward T. James, Janet Wilson James, and Paul S. Boyer, eds., *Notable American Women, 1607–1950: A Biographical Dictionary* (Cambridge, Mass.: Harvard University Press, 1971), 3:8–11. For a fascinating discussion of Palmer's consuming practices, see Hoganson, *Consumers' Imperium*, 13–56.

5. Herrick, *Gospel of Freedom*, 192–193.

6. Emily Wheaton, *The Russells in Chicago* (Boston: L. C. Page, 1902), 59. "The Russells in Chicago" originally appeared in serial form in the *Ladies' Home Journal* in 1901–1902. The collected volume, cited here, was published in 1902.

7. "Books and Men Who Make Them," *Inter Ocean*, June 9, 1902, 6.

8. On Chicago as unusually receptive to women's public service, see especially Duncan, *Culture and Democracy*, 46; Jaher, *Urban Establishment*, 534; Sklar, *Florence Kelley and the Nation's Work*, 207; Flanagan, *Seeing with Their Hearts;* Lana Ruegamer, "Paradise of Exceptional Women: Chicago Women Reformers, 1863–1893" (PhD diss., Indiana University, 1982). On Addams, see especially Knight, *Citizen Jane Addams;* Brown, *Education of Jane Addams.* On Willard, see especially Bordin, *Frances Willard.* On Kelley, see especially Sklar, *Florence Kelley and the Nation's Work.* On Wells, see especially Mia Bay, *To Tell the Truth Freely: The Life of Ida B. Wells* (New York: Hill & Wang, 2010); Kristina DuRocher, *Ida B. Wells: Social Activist and Reformer* (New York: Routledge, 2016).

9. See Frances M. Glessner Journal, Glessner Family Papers, Chicago History Museum, Chicago, Ill. (hereafter cited as Glessner Journal). The journal is organized chronologically, and all citations provided here can be found by date in the transcribed manuscript.

10. John Glessner Lee, "Introduction to the Glessner Journals" (1975), in Glessner Journal, 4–5; Percy Maxim Lee and John Glessner Lee, *Family Reunion: An Incomplete Account of the Maxim-Lee Family History* (Connecticut: privately printed, 1971), 314; Timothy B. Spears, "John and Frances Glessner," *Chicago Dreaming: Midwesterners and the City, 1871–1919* (Chicago: University of Chicago Press, 2005), 24–26, 28–29; Schultz and Hast, *Women Building Chicago*, 320–323.

11. Spears, "John and Frances Glessner," 36; Glessner Journal, entry for Dec. 23, 1874 (written July 13, 1879).

12. On the Glessners' Prairie Avenue house, see especially Spears, "John and Frances Glessner," 36–37, 43, 47–48; John J. Glessner, "The Story of a House" (1923; repr., Chicago: Chicago Architecture Foundation, 1988).

13. Lee, "Introduction to the Glessner Journals," 4.

14. Jaher, *Urban Establishment,* 495–496.

15. Emily Post, *By Motor to the Golden Gate* (New York: D. Appleton, 1916), 55.

16. DiMaggio, "Problem of Chicago," 210; Jaher, *Urban Establishment,* 94, 253.

17. Henry Blake Fuller, "The Upward Movement in Chicago," *Atlantic Monthly* 80 (Oct. 1897): 542.

18. Hamlin Garland, *Rose of Dutcher's Coolly* (Chicago: Stone & Kimball, 1895), 246.

19. Wheaton, *Russells in Chicago,* 25, 30.

20. Robert Shackelton, *The Book of Chicago* (Philadelphia: Penn, 1920), 204.

21. Bessie Louise Pierce, *A History of Chicago,* vol. 3, *The Rise of the Modern City, 1871–1893* (1957; repr., Chicago: University of Chicago Press, 2007), 485.

22. On the transition to "practical work," see "The Practical Work of the Club," in *Tenth Annual Announcement of the Chicago Woman's Club,* 53–55, Chicago Woman's Club Records, box 1, folder 10, Women & Leadership Archives, Loyola University, Chicago, Ill. On the club's history and activities, see Elizabeth J. Clapp, *Mothers of All Children: Women Reformers and the Rise of Juvenile Courts in Progressive Era America* (University Park: Pennsylvania State University Press, 1998), 20–31; Henriette Greenbaum Frank and Amalie Hofer Jerome, *Annals of the Chicago Woman's Club for the First Forty Years of Its Organization, 1876–1916* (Chicago: Chicago Woman's Club, 1916), 9–22; Anne Meis Knupfer, "Clubs, Women's," in Grossman, Keating, and Reiff, *Encyclopedia of Chicago,* 180–181; Pierce, *History of Chicago,* 485–486.

23. Ralph, "Chicago's Gentle Side," 290.

24. Karen J. Blair, *The Clubwoman as Feminist: True Womanhood Redefined, 1868–1914* (New York: Homes and Meier, 1980), 21; Clapp, *Mothers of All Children,* 22, 26.

25. Clapp, *Mothers of All Children,* 35–46; Michael Wilrich, *City of Courts: Socializing Justice in Progressive Era Chicago* (New York: Cambridge University Press, 2003), 81.

26. Ralph, "Chicago's Gentle Side," 290.

27. Glessner Journal, Jan. 31, 1886.

28. Ralph, "Chicago's Gentle Side," 290; Pierce, *History of Chicago,* 486; Clapp, *Mothers of All Children,* 25–26. For a sample annual membership list, see *Thirteenth Annual Announcement of the Chicago Woman's Club* (Chicago: Craig Press, 1890), 5–12.

29. Ralph, "Chicago's Gentle Side," 290.

30. Frank and Jerome, *Annals of the Chicago Woman's Club,* 9, 172. Annual dues were raised from $10 to $12 in 1897.

31. For biographical information on Stevenson, see *History of Medicine and Surgery and Physicians and Surgeons of Chicago* (Chicago: Biographical, 1922), 118–119.

32. Letter from Ellen Mitchell in Glessner Journal, Jan. 30, 1887; May 13, 1888; Jan. 30, 1887; May 2, 1886; Apr. 27, 1888; July 13, 1886. For biographical information, see "Mrs. Mitchell Dead," *Chicago Tribune,* Dec. 17, 1891, 6; "Mrs. Ellen Mitchell," *Inter Ocean,* Dec. 17, 1891, 1. On her husband, Francis M. Mitchell, see "Review," *Chicago Tribune,* Aug. 4, 1891, 10; Charles Randolph, *Twenty-First Annual Report of the Trade and Commerce of Chicago for the Year Ending December 31, 1878* (Chicago: Knight & Leonard, 1879), 179; 1870 United States Federal Census, Chicago Ward 4, Cook, Illinois, Francis Mitchell household, digital image, accessed July 1, 2017, Ancestry.com.

33. Glessner Journal, Mar. 17, 1903. On the Everyday Club, see Jane Addams, *My Friend, Julia Lathrop* (1935; repr., Urbana: University of Illinois Press, 2004), 118–119.

34. Spear, *Black Chicago,* 12.

35. Wheaton, *Russells in Chicago,* 148.

36. Wanda A. Hendricks, *Fannie Barrier Williams: Crossing the Borders of Region and Race* (Urbana: University of Illinois Press, 2014), 76–77, 81–82; Margaret Garb, *Freedom's Ballot: African American Political Struggles in Chicago from Abolition to the Great Migration* (Chicago: University of Chicago Press, 2014), 83, 92–96, 104–105.

37. "Color Line in a Club," *Chicago Tribune,* Nov. 14, 1894, 2. See also Hendricks, *Fannie Barrier Williams,* 86–87; Schultz and Hast, *Women Building Chicago,* 978; Anne Meis Knupfer, *Toward a Tenderer Humanity and a Nobler Womanhood: African American Women's Clubs in Turn-of-the-Century Chicago* (New York: New York University Press, 1996), 163–164.

38. Fannie Barrier Williams, "The Club Movement among Negro Women," in *The Colored American from Slavery to Honorable Citizenship,* ed. J. W. Gibson and W. H. Crogman (Atlanta: J. L. Nichols, 1903), 217.

39. "The Color Line Wiped Out," *Chicago Tribune,* May 20, 1895, 6; "To Wipe Out the Color Line," *Chicago Tribune,* May 17, 1895, 1; "Wiped Out the Color Line," *Chicago Tribune,* Jan. 23, 1896, 10.

40. Schultz and Hast, *Women Building Chicago,* 978.

41. "Scenes in London," *Inter Ocean,* June 20, 1897, 3. On Chicago and the Great Migration, see especially Spear, *Black Chicago;* Grossman, *Land of Hope.*

42. On Curry's suit, see Dale, "'Social Equality Does Not Exist among Themselves, nor among Us,'" 311–312; Cynthia Blair, *I've Got to Make My Livin': Black Women's Sex Work in Turn-of-the-Century Chicago* (Chicago: University of Chicago Press, 2010), 112–113; "A Theater Party Fired," *Chicago Tribune,* Mar. 16, 1888, 1; "Mrs. Curry's Theater Party," *Chicago Tribune,* Mar. 17, 1888, 7; "Recorded of the Courts," *Inter Ocean,* Mar. 16, 1888, 10.

43. On the case as failing to set a precedent, see Dale, "Social Equality Does Not Exist," 312; Christopher Robert Reed, *Black Chicago's First Century*, vol. 1, *1833–1900* (Columbia: University of Missouri Press, 2005), 308.

44. See, for example, "After Damages," *Inter Ocean*, Dec. 11, 1891, 11; "They Want to Know: Restaurant Men Curious about a Novel Crusade," *Chicago Tribune*, Jan. 20, 1893, 1; "Finds for Schiepan," *Chicago Tribune*, Jan. 26, 1893, 1; "Arrested for Not Feeding Him," *Chicago Tribune*, Aug. 3, 1895, 3; "Placed a Screen between Them," *Inter Ocean*, Oct. 22, 1895, 8; "Civil Rights Case," *Inter Ocean*, Oct. 23, 1895, 12; "Civil Rights Law Is Violated," *Chicago Tribune*, Feb. 15, 1898, 12; "Sues under Civil-Rights Act," *Inter Ocean*, Aug. 23, 1899, 6.

45. "Marshall Field & Co. Discharges Saleswoman Who Insults Afro-American," *Chicago Defender*, June 20, 1914, 6.

46. Hyman L. Meites, *History of the Jews of Chicago* (Chicago: Jewish Historical Society of Illinois, 1924), 201; Claudette Tolson, "The Excluded and the Included: Chicago, White Supremacy, and the Clubwomen's Movement, 1873–1915" (PhD diss., Loyola University Chicago, 2008), 93.

47. On the religious backgrounds of the city's wealthiest citizens, see Jaher and Ghent, "Chicago Business Elite," 310. On Chicago's German Jews as compared to eastern European Jews, see Irving Cutler, "Jews," in Grossman, Keating, and Reiff, *Encyclopedia of Chicago*, 436–437; Irving Cutler, *The Jews of Chicago: From Shtetl to Suburb* (Urbana: University of Illinois Press, 1996), 94–98.

48. Glessner Journal, Aug. 9, 1882; Aug. 10, 1882.

49. Solomon, *Fabric of My Life*, 41–42; James, James, and Boyer, *Notable American Women*, 1:324. Henriette G. Frank served as president from 1884 to 1885. Frank and Jerome, *Annals of the Chicago Woman's Club*, 5.

50. Jaher, *Urban Establishment*, 496.

51. Jaher and Ghent, "Chicago Business Elite," 300.

52. Fuller, *The Cliff-Dwellers*, 242.

53. H. C. Chatfield-Taylor, *Chicago* (Boston: Houghton Mifflin, 1917), 127–128.

54. Elias Colbert and Evan Chamberlin, *Chicago and the Great Conflagration* (Cincinnati: C. F. Vent, 1872), 13, 512.

55. "Fredrika Bremer's Visit, 1850," in *The Development of Chicago, 1674–1914, Shown in a Series of Contemporary Original Narratives*, ed. Milo Milton Quaife (Chicago: Caxton Club, 1916), 214.

56. *Picturesque Chicago and Guide to the World's Fair* (Baltimore: R. H. Woodward, 1892), 58–60; Duncan, *Culture and Democracy*, 125–127; Harold M. Mayer and Richard C. Wade, *Chicago: Growth of a Metropolis* (Chicago: University of Chicago Press, 1969), 54; Hoyt, *One Hundred Years of Land Values in Chicago*, 65, 89–90.

57. Duncan, *Culture and Democracy*, 128–129; Gilbert, *Perfect Cities*, 27; Whitaker, *Service and Style*, 8, 13, 79.

58. *Picturesque Chicago*, 60–61.

59. See, for example, Glessner Journal, Feb. 4, 1891; Mar. 22, 1891; June 7, 1891.

60. Glessner Journal, Oct. 30, 1892; Apr. 5, 1881. On the opening of H.M. Kinsley's, see "Notice," *Chicago Tribune,* Nov. 22, 1885, 1.

61. Glessner Journal, Nov. 6, 1892.

62. Glessner Journal, Dec. 23, 1874.

63. Glessner Journal, Mar. 22, 1903; 1880 United States Federal Census, Chicago, Cook, Illinois, Enumeration District 98, 26, John J. Glessner household, digital image, accessed July 1, 2017, Ancestry.com.

64. See, for example, Glessner Journal, June 12, 1891; Oct. 24, 1892.

65. Glessner Journal, June 4, 1881.

66. For rates, see, for example, *Bird's-Eye Views and Guide to Chicago* (Chicago: Rand, McNally, 1893), 41–42; John J. Flinn, *Chicago: The Marvelous City of the West* (Chicago: Flinn & Sheppard, 1891), 561–562.

67. Glessner Journal, June 14, 1885.

68. Glessner Journal, Mar. 11, 1894.

69. Glessner Journal, Mar. 28, 1881; Dec. 15, 1901.

70. Lee, "Introduction to the Glessner Journals," 6.

71. William T. Stead, *If Christ Came to Chicago: A Plea for the Union of All Who Love in the Service of All Who Suffer* (Chicago: Laird & Lee, 1894), 425n.

72. Louise de Koven Bowen, *Growing Up with a City* (repr., New York: Macmillan, 1926; Urbana: University of Illinois Press, 2002), 20. See also Mrs. Joseph Frederick Ward, "As I Remember It," in *Chicago Yesterdays: A Sheaf of Reminiscences,* ed. Caroline Kirkland (Chicago: Daughaday, 1919), 89.

73. Glessner Journal, Dec. 16, 1883.

74. Civic Federation of Chicago, *The Street Railways of Chicago* (New York, 1901), 7; Greg Borzo, *Chicago Cable Cars* (Charleston, S.C.: History Press, 2012), 62.

75. Carter H. Harrison, "A Kentucky Colony," in Kirkland, *Chicago Yesterdays,* 163.

76. Borzo, *Chicago Cable Cars,* 83–84; Civic Federation, *Street Railways of Chicago,* 7–8; Hoyt, *One Hundred Years of Land Values,* 146.

77. Miller, *City of the Century,* 270; Borzo, *Chicago Cable Cars,* 85; Hoyt, *One Hundred Years of Land Values in Chicago,* 144–149, 183; Marco D'Eramo, *The Pig and the Skyscraper: Chicago; A History of Our Future* (London: Verso, 2002), 103.

78. Stead, *If Christ Came to Chicago,* 197.

79. Theodore Dreiser, *The Titan* (New York: John Lane, 1914), 485.

80. Glessner Journal, Jan. 30, 1898.

81. For cable route maps, see Borzo, *Chicago Cable Cars,* 84–85; *Chicago Tribune's Columbian Souvenir Map of Chicago and the World's Fair* (Chicago: Rand, McNally, 1893), available at http://pi.lib.uchicago.edu/1001/cat/bib/1595319.

82. "America's Thanksgiving Dinner Market," *Chicago Tribune*, Nov. 24, 1895, 51. See also Max Grinnell, "Retail Geography," in Grossman, Keating, and Reiff, *Encyclopedia of Chicago*, 703; Genevieve Forbes Herrick, "South Water St. Passes; Ancient Glory Recalled," *Chicago Tribune*, Aug. 30, 1925, 4.

83. "The Marketing Problem," *Chicago Tribune*, Dec. 28, 1884, 9, quoted in Deutsch, *Building a Housewife's Paradise*, 24.

84. Louis Schick, *Chicago and Its Environs: A Handbook for the Traveler* (Chicago: L. Schick, 1891), 90.

85. See, for example, Glessner Journal, Feb. 7, 1901; Mar. 1, 1891; Mar. 7, 1891; Dec. 1, 1894; Apr. 28, 1901.

86. "The New Music Hall," *Chicago Tribune*, Dec. 7, 1879, 4; Carl W. Condit, *The Chicago School of Architecture: A History of Commercial and Public Building in the Chicago Area, 1875–1925* (Chicago: University of Chicago Press, 1973), 32–33; David Garrard Lowe, *Lost Chicago* (Chicago: University of Chicago Press, 2000), 123; Dominic A. Pacyga, *Chicago: A Biography* (Chicago: University of Chicago Press, 2009), 133–134.

87. "Sweet Crumbs of Comfort," *Chicago Tribune*, May 18, 1884, 15.

88. Benson, *Counter Cultures*, 18.

89. Schick, *Chicago and Its Environs*, 100; Twyman, *History of Marshall Field*, 175.

90. Glessner Journal, Jan. 26, 1881.

91. See, for example, Glessner Journal, Mar. 29, 1882; Nov. 28, 1886; Apr. 25, 1891; Dec. 24, 1893.

92. On Marshall Field's catering to elite tastes and selling imported products, see Twyman, *History of Marshall Field*, 107; Pierce, *History of Chicago*, 177. On private showings, see, for example, Glessner Journal, Dec. 24, 1893; Dec. 31, 1894; Dec. 18, 1898; Dec. 17, 1899.

93. Harold Richard Vynne, *Chicago by Day and Night: The Pleasure Seeker's Guide to the Paris of America* (Chicago: Thomas and Zimmerman, 1892), 120.

94. Siry, *Carson Pirie Scott*, 34–35.

95. Glessner Journal, May 2, 1886; Dec. 12, 1897; Feb. 11, 1898.

96. Pierce, *History of Chicago*, 176, 180.

97. Siry, *Carson Pirie Scott*, 32; Twyman, *History of Marshall Field*, 108.

98. Whitaker, *Service and Style*, 9; Duncan, *Culture and Democracy*, 127–128.

99. Vynne, *Chicago by Day and Night*, 120.

100. Based on 1892 Chicago city directory. See *The Lakeside Directory of Chicago* (Chicago: Chicago Directory Company, 1892).

101. *The Artistic Guide to Chicago and the World's Columbian Exposition* (Chicago: Columbian Art, 1892), 151–152; Vynne, *Chicago by Day and Night*, 33.

102. See, for example, Glessner Journal, Mar. 26, 1881; Mar. 28, 1881; Mar. 17, 1903; Feb. 3, 1895; Apr. 17, 1891; Feb 3, 1892.

103. Glessner Journal, Nov. 12, 1893.

104. Glessner Journal, Mar. 22, 1891. On the Visiting Nurse Association, see "Chicago: A Sociological Survey," *Chicago Commerce* 10 (Dec. 11, 1914): 33.

105. *U.S. Census Office, Report on Population of the United States at the Eleventh Census: 1890* (Washington, D.C.: Government Printing Office, 1897), 1:708, 714, 720, 726, 728.

106. Meeker, *Chicago, with Love,* 25.

107. Benson, *Counter Cultures,* 23.

108. Margaret Garb, "The Great Chicago Waiters' Strike: Producing Urban Space, Organizing Labor, Challenging Racial Divides in 1890s Chicago," *Journal of Urban History* 40 (June 2014): 1092.

109. Spear, *Black Chicago,* 31, 34; Garb, "Great Waiters' Strike," 1081; Reed, *Black Chicago's First Century,* 247–255; Louise de Koven Bowen, *The Colored People of Chicago: An Investigation Made for the Juvenile Protective Association* (Chicago: Rogers & Hall, 1913), 5–6.

110. Spear, *Black Chicago,* 30.

111. Meeker, *Chicago, with Love,* 286.

112. Spear, *Black Chicago,* 12, 29–30; Garb, "Great Waiters' Strike," 1081.

113. Bowen, *Colored People of Chicago,* 6.

114. "Colored Men," *Broad Ax,* May 6, 1905, 1. See also Knupfer, *Toward a Tenderer Humanity,* 58–59.

115. Glessner Journal, Dec. 20, 1896; Jan. 3, 1897; Jan. 17, 1897.

116. Glessner Journal, Feb. 11, 1898.

117. Glessner Journal, May 13, 1888. Sherwood later married a Chicagoan and relocated to the prairie city.

118. Joseph J. Korom, *The American Skyscraper, 1850–1940: A Celebration of Height* (Boston: Branden Books, 2008), 93–96; Carol Willis, *Form Follows Finance: Skyscrapers and Skylines in New York and Chicago* (New York: Princeton Architectural Press, 1995), 50–51.

119. Fuller, *Cliff-Dwellers,* 4–5.

120. Ralph, "Chicago—the Main Exhibit," 425, 428.

121. Herrick, *Gospel of Freedom,* 103.

2. The Hoopskirt War of 1893

1. Harriet Monroe, ed., biographical introduction to *Harlow Niles Higinbotham: A Memoir with Brief Autobiography and Extracts from Speeches and Letters* (Chicago: R. F. Seymour, 1920), 19.

2. Robert W. Rydell, "World's Columbian Exposition," in Grossman, Keating, and Reiff, *Encyclopedia of Chicago,* 898–899.

3. On the crinoline revival as a "pestilence" or "plague," see, for example, *Journal of the House of Representatives of the 37th General Assembly of the State of Missouri, 1893* (Jefferson City, Mo.: Tribune Printing, 1893), 822; Helen Gilbert Ecob, "Crinoline Folly," *Cosmopolitan* 15 (May 1893): 117; Dick Law, "In Time of Peace," *Puck,* Apr. 19, 1893, 138.

4. "The Anti-Hoopskirt War," *Chicago Tribune,* Jan. 22, 1893, 28.

5. *Picturesque Chicago and Guide to the World's Fair,* xiii.

6. "Anti-Hoopskirt War," 28.

7. Joan L. Severa, *Dressed for the Photographer: Ordinary Americans and Fashion, 1840–1900* (Kent, Ohio: Kent State University Press, 1995), 97–98; Alison Gernsheim, *Victorian and Edwardian Fashion: A Photographic Survey* (London: Courier Dover, 1963), 54.

8. Patricia Marks, *Bicycles, Bangs, and Bloomers: The New Woman in the Popular Press* (Louisville: University of Kentucky Press, 1990), 151; Gernsheim, *Victorian and Edwardian Fashion*, 46–47.

9. "Life in Boston," *Inter Ocean*, Feb. 26, 1893, 35.

10. Leach, *Land of Desire*, xiii, 5–6.

11. On the Columbian Exposition as an expression of corporate capitalism, see especially Gilbert, *Perfect Cities*, 100–101, 105; Alan Trachtenberg, *The Incorporation of America: Culture and Society in the Gilded Age* (New York: Hill and Wang, 1982), 214–215, 220; Judith A. Adams, "The American Dream Actualized," in *The World's Columbian Exposition: A Centennial Bibliographic Guide*, ed. David J. Bertuca, Donald K. Hartman, and Susan M. Neumeister (New York: Greenwood Press, 1996), xx–xxii; Neil Harris, "Great American Fairs and American Cities: The Role of Chicago's Columbian Exposition," in *Cultural Excursions: Marketing Appetites and Cultural Tastes in Modern America* (Chicago: University of Chicago Press, 1990), 118–120.

12. Mrs. William J. Calhoun, "The World's Fair," in Kirkland, *Chicago Yesterdays*, 296.

13. Rydell, "World's Columbian Exposition," 899–900; Robert W. Rydell, *All the World's a Fair: Visions of Empire at American International Expositions, 1876–1916* (Chicago: University of Chicago Press, 1987), 42; Gilbert, *Perfect Cities*, 39.

14. "To Hoop or Not to Hoop?," *Chicago Herald*, Feb. 5, 1893, 28.

15. See, for example, "Crinolines Reach Chicago at Last," *Chicago Tribune*, Mar. 15, 1893, 1; "Heading Off Hoopskirts," *New York Times*, Feb. 4, 1893, 1; "The Crinoline Terror," *New York Times*, Feb. 14, 1893, 1; "Day of Disorder," *Inter Ocean*, Apr. 9, 1893, 1; "Hoopskirts Find No Favor," *Chicago Herald*, Feb. 16, 1893, 1.

16. "Life in Boston," 35.

17. Severa, *Dressed for the Photographer*, 17; Gernsheim, *Victorian and Edwardian Fashion*, 45.

18. Gernsheim, *Victorian and Edwardian Fashion*, 47–48; Phillipe Perrot, *Fashioning the Bourgeoisie: A History of Clothing in the Nineteenth Century* (Princeton, N.J.: Princeton University Press, 1994), 107–108; Marks, *Bicycles, Bangs, and Bloomers*, 148–149.

19. Gernsheim, *Victorian and Edwardian Fashion*, 46–47; Marks, *Bicycles, Bangs, and Bloomers*, 151.

20. "New Contrivance for Lady's Maids, Adapted to the Present Style of Fashions," *Harper's Weekly*, July 25, 1857, 480.

21. Perrot, *Fashioning the Bourgeoisie*, 107–108; Severa, *Dressed for the Photographer*, 310.

22. Hoganson, *Consumers' Imperium*, 61.

23. Severa, *Dressed for the Photographer*, 3–4.

24. Severa, 3–4, 296; Hoganson, *Consumers' Imperium*, 63–64; Wendy Gamber, *The Female Economy: The Millinery and Dressmaking Trades, 1860–1930* (Urbana: University of Illinois Press, 1997), 111; Patricia Cunningham, *Reforming Women's Fashion, 1850–1920* (Kent, Ohio: Kent State University Press, 2003), 12.

25. Gamber, *Female Economy*, 4, 97–98. On the size of the men's market in 1900, see Siry, *Carson Pirie Scott*, 124. On the development of men's ready-to-wear, see Michael Zakim, *Ready-Made Democracy: A History of Men's Dress in the American Republic, 1760–1860* (Chicago: University of Chicago Press, 2003).

26. Even imported dresses would still need to be customized for size and fit by local dressmakers. Katherine Joslin, *Edith Wharton and the Making of Fashion* (Durham: University of New Hampshire Press, 2009), 8; Cunningham, *Reforming Women's Fashion*, 11; "About Paris Gowns," *Chicago Tribune*, June 3, 1893, 16.

27. Hoganson, *Consumers' Imperium*, 59–60; Gamber, *Female Economy*, 4, 96, 99–100; Glessner Journal, Mar. 24, 1895; Mar. 14, 1897.

28. Gamber, *Female Economy*, 194.

29. *Chicago Tribune*, Feb. 5, 1894, 12.

30. Glessner Journal, Dec. 12, 1897.

31. Nancy L. Green, *Ready-to-Wear and Ready-to-Work: A Century of Industry and Immigrants in Paris and New York* (Durham, N.C.: Duke University Press, 1997), 45; John Leander Bishop, *A History of American Manufactures from 1608 to 1860*, vol. 3 (Philadelphia: Edward Young, 1868), 209–210; "Douglas & Sherwood's Hoop Skirt Factory," *Harper's Weekly*, Jan. 29, 1859, 68; "Ready for Business," *Inter Ocean*, Jan. 22, 1893, 4.

32. "Changing Styles," *Inter Ocean*, Nov. 13, 1892, 22.

33. "Now It's Victorian," *Chicago Tribune*, Nov. 19, 1892, 16.

34. *Chicago Daily News*, Feb. 7, 1893, 4.

35. "Ward McAllister Approves 'Em," *Chicago Herald*, Feb. 6, 1893, 3.

36. "Will Don Crinoline," *Saint Paul Globe*, Mar. 25, 1893, 8.

37. "The Crinoline Question," *Boston Post*, Feb. 18, 1893, 5.

38. "The Outrage of This Age," *Indiana State Sentinel*, Mar. 8, 1893, 10.

39. "Dr. Mary Walker and Crinoline," *Elmira Star-Gazette*, Feb. 23, 1893, 3.

40. Severa, *Dressed for the Photographer*, 88; Cunningham, *Reforming Women's Fashion*, 39–41, 61–62; Elizabeth Wilson, *Adorned in Dreams: Fashion and Modernity* (London: Virago Press, 1985), 209.

41. National Council of Women, *Transactions of the National Council of Women of the United States, Assembled in Washington, D.C., February 22 to 25, 1891*, ed. Rachel Foster Avery (Philadelphia: J. B. Lippincott, 1891), 45; Patricia A. Cunningham, "Redeeming the Voices of Reform," in *Fashion in Popular*

Culture: Literature, Media and Contemporary Studies, ed. Joseph Hancock, Toni Johnson-Woods, and Vicki Karaminas (Chicago: University of Chicago Press, 2013), 198.

42. National Council of Women, *History and Minutes of the National Council of Women of the United States, Organized in Washington, D.C., March 31, 1888*, ed. Louise Barnum Robbins (Boston: E. B. Stillings, 1898), 65.
43. Cunningham, *Reforming Women's Fashion*, 62–64.
44. Ecob, "Crinoline Folly," 122.
45. "To Hoop or Not to Hoop?," 28.
46. "Anti-Hoopskirt War," 28.
47. "Anti-Hoopskirt War," 28.
48. "A Horror Averted," *Inter Ocean*, Jan. 21, 1893, 11.
49. "The Anti-Crinoline Crusade," *Inter Ocean*, Feb. 5, 1893, 15; "War against the Crinoline Waxes Hot," *Chicago Tribune*, Jan. 15, 1893, 9.
50. Ellen Osborne, "Hoops Have Come for Sure," *Pittsburgh Post*, Feb. 12, 1893, 13.
51. "The Coming Plague," *Wilmington Morning News*, Jan. 21, 1893, 4.
52. Egbert Jamieson and Francis Adams, *Municipal Code of Chicago: Comprising the Laws of Illinois Relating to the City of Chicago and the Ordinances of the City Council* (Chicago: Beach, Barnard, 1881), 433; "Common Council," *Inter Ocean*, Aug. 11, 1874, 5.
53. Rodney Hitt, *Electric Railway Dictionary; Definitions and Illustrations of the Parts and Equipment of Electric Railway Cars and Trucks; Compiled under the Direction of a Committee Appointed by the American Electric Railway Association* (New York: McGraw, 1911), figs. 44–47; Borzo, *Chicago Cable Cars*, 41.
54. "They Abhor Them," *San Francisco Call*, Feb. 19, 1893, 6.
55. Iris Marion Young, "Throwing Like a Girl: A Phenomenology of Feminine Body Comportment Motility and Spatiality," *Human Studies* 3 (Apr. 1980): 149–150.
56. "The Coming Plague," 4.
57. "The Revival of Crinoline," *Current Literature* 12 (Mar. 1893): 340.
58. Helen Gale, "Late Fashion Tips," *Inter Ocean*, Jan. 22, 1893, 11.
59. Law, "In Time of Peace," 138.
60. "The Hoop Skirt," *Chicago Tribune*, Jan. 28, 1893, 12.
61. "Not Enough Room," *Chicago Tribune*, Apr. 2, 1893, 42.
62. "To Hoop or Not to Hoop?," 28.
63. Jeanette L. Gilder, "Hoops as a Plague," *Chicago Tribune*, Mar. 19, 1893, 26.
64. "Anti-Crinoline Crusade," 15; "War against the Crinoline Waxes Hot," 9.
65. "The Crinoline Craze," *Chicago Herald*, Feb. 13, 1893, 4.
66. "Two Anti-Crinoline Bills," *Buffalo Enquirer*, Feb. 14, 1893, 4.
67. "Anti-Hoopskirt War," 28.
68. "Broke Them All Up," *Chicago Tribune*, Mar. 19, 1893, 34.
69. *Inter Ocean*, Feb. 23, 1893, 6.
70. Eleanor Flexner, *Century of Struggle: The Woman's Rights Movement in the United States*, 3rd ed. (Cambridge, Mass.: Belknap Press, 1996), 214.

71. Christine Stansell, *The Feminist Promise: 1792 to the Present* (New York: Modern Library, 2010), 121.

72. Sarah Wadsworth and Wayne A. Wiegand, *Right Here I See My Own Books: The Woman's Building Library at the World's Columbian Exposition* (Amherst: University of Massachusetts Press, 2012), 109.

73. "Anti-Crinoline Crusade," 15; "War against the Crinoline Waxes Hot," 9.

74. "Extremes," *Youth's Companion*, Feb. 1, 1894, 48.

75. "Verbal Missiles Hurled at Hoops," *Chicago Tribune*, Apr. 16, 1893, 43.

76. [Caroline Kirkland,] "Illinois in Spring-time," *Atlantic Monthly* 2 (Sept. 1858): 488.

77. On nineteenth-century workingwomen's more frequent use of public space, see especially Wilson, "The Invisible Flâneur," 93; Elsa Barkley Brown and Gregg D. Kimball, "Mapping the Terrain of Black Richmond," *Journal of Urban History* 3 (Mar. 1995): 296–346; Stansell, *City of Women*; Ryan, *Women in Public*.

78. Herma Clark, *The Elegant Eighties: When Chicago Was Young* (Chicago: A. C. McClurg, 1941), x.

79. On women's public endeavors, see especially Ryan, *Women in Public*; Ginzberg, *Women and the Work of Benevolence*; Kathryn Kish Sklar, *Florence Kelley and the Nation's Work*; Deutsch, *Women and the City*; Flanagan, *Seeing with Their Hearts*.

80. Florence Hartley, *The Ladies' Book of Etiquette and Manual of Politeness* (1860; repr., Boston: Lee and Shepard, 1873), 114.

81. Emily Thornwell, *The Lady's Guide to Perfect Gentility* (New York: Derby & Jackson, 1856), 78; Arthur Martine, *Martine's Book of Etiquette and Guide to True Politeness* (New York: Dick & Fitzgerald, 1866), 131; S. L. Louis, *Decorum: A Practical Treatise on Etiquette and Dress of the Best American Society* (New York: Union, 1882), 119; Richard A. Wells, *Manners, Culture and Dress of the Best American Society* (Springfield, Mass.: King, Richardson, 1891), 129.

82. For more on the risks women faced at night, see Baldwin, *In the Watches of the Night*, 138–154.

83. Hartley, *Ladies' Book of Etiquette*, 113–114.

84. Hartley, 110–111, 113; Lydia E. White, *Success in Society: A Manual of Good Manners* (Boston: James H. Earle, 1889), 188; Walter R. Houghton et al., *Rules of Etiquette and Home Culture; or, What to Do and How to Do It* (Chicago: Rand, McNally, 1889), 96.

85. Eliza Bisbee Duffey, *Ladies' and Gentlemen's Etiquette: A Complete Manual of the Manners and Dress of American Society* (Philadelphia: Porter and Coates, 1877), 87. Also in John H. Young, *Our Deportment; or, The Manners, Conduct and Dress of the Most Refined Society* (Detroit: F. B. Dickerson, 1881), 143–144; Wells, *Manners, Culture, and Dress of the Best American Society*, 132.

86. Kasson, *Rudeness and Civility*, 123–124, 129–130.

87. De B. Randolph Keim, *Hand-Book of Official and Social Etiquette and Public Ceremonials at Washington,* 3rd ed. (Washington, D.C.: De B. Randolph Keim, 1889), 240.

88. "People and Things," *Inter Ocean,* Dec. 24, 1887, 12.

89. See especially Benjamin, "The Flâneur," 35–66.

90. Fuller, *With the Procession,* 140, 149.

91. *Handy Guide to Chicago and World's Columbian Exposition* (Chicago: Rand, McNally, 1892), 104–110.

92. Fuller, *With the Procession,* 136.

93. Glessner Journal, Nov. 6, 1892.

94. *Handy Guide to Chicago,* 54, 72.

95. *Woman's Directory, Purchasing and Chaperoning Society* (brochure), 1892, Trade Catalog Collection, Winterthur Museum, Garden, and Library, Wilmington, Del.

96. "To Chicago with Comfort: Chaperones and Guides Provided for Parties of Ladies," *New York Times,* Apr. 27, 1893, 1.

97. *Chicago Herald,* Feb. 4, 1893, 16.

98. "Fair Guides for Ladies," *Chicago Tribune,* May 22, 1890, 5.

99. Teresa Dean, *White City Chips* (Chicago: Warren, 1895), 111. Dean's World's Fair articles for the *Inter Ocean,* published between April and October 1893, are collected in this volume.

100. *Chicago Tribune,* Mar. 9, 1890, 13.

101. *Chicago Tribune,* Nov. 3, 1889, 31.

102. Mary Ryan identifies shopping as the "commonest everyday public diversion" in the late nineteenth century. See Ryan, *Women in Public,* 87.

103. Glessner Journal, Dec. 19, 1897; Mar. 25, 1894.

104. See, for example, Glessner Journal, Oct. 25, 1896; Jan. 17, 1897.

105. "Female Shopping Clubs," *Chicago Tribune,* Apr. 11, 1886, 4.

106. Anne Friedberg, *Window Shopping: Cinema and the Postmodern* (Berkeley: University of California Press, 1993), 36–37.

107. Glessner Journal, Apr. 19, 1899.

108. Fuller, *With the Procession,* 132.

109. Grinnell, "Retail Geography," 703. Lizabeth Cohen has shown that many working-class Chicagoans, particularly from ethnic communities, preferred to patronize small neighborhood stores until well into the 1920s. See Lizabeth Cohen, *Making a New Deal: Industrial Workers in Chicago, 1919–1939* (New York: Cambridge University Press, 1990), esp. 109–120.

110. Ray Stannard Baker, "The Color Line in the North," *American Magazine* 65 (Feb. 1908): 350.

111. *Handy Guide to Chicago,* 68.

112. "Day on State Street," *Chicago Tribune,* May 6, 1888, 25.

113. Schick, *Chicago and Its Environs,* 126, 103.

114. Flinn, *Chicago,* 587.

115. Veblen, *Theory of the Leisure Class,* 87.

116. Veblen, "Economic Theory of Woman's Dress," 200.

117. Veblen, 202.

118. Augusta Prescott, "Crinoline Coming," *Los Angeles Times,* Feb. 26, 1893, 21.

119. Leach, *Land of Desire,* 93.

120. *Dry Goods Economist,* Aug. 15, 1903. Quoted in Leach, *Land of Desire,* 94.

121. Leach, *Land of Desire,* 93, 17; Veblen, "Economic Theory of Woman's Dress," 202.

122. National Council of Women, *Transactions of the National Council of Women,* 153–156; Ralph, "Chicago's Gentle Side," 289–290; Dorcas J. Spencer, "Woman's Christian Temperance Union," *California Illustrated Magazine* 3 (Jan. 1893): 167; Paula Young Lee, "The Temperance Temple and Architectural Representation in Late Nineteenth-Century Chicago," *Gender and History* 17 (Nov. 2005): 796–798; Schultz and Hast, *Women Building Chicago,* 144; Lowe, *Lost Chicago,* 143; Korom, *American Skyscraper,* 166–167; "Woman's Temple to Be Torn Down," *Chicago Tribune,* May 1, 1926, 3.

123. Rand, McNally & Co., *Bird's-Eye Views and Guide to Chicago,* 40, 129.

124. "Shrine of Temperance," *Chicago Tribune,* Nov. 2, 1890, 1; "A Temperance Temple," *Inter Ocean,* Nov. 2, 1890, 1–2.

125. Lee, "Temperance Temple and Architectural Representation," 793, 797, 808–809; National Council of Women, *Transactions of the National Council of Women,* 154; "Lofty Temple to Temperance Falls in Debris," *Chicago Tribune,* Aug. 12, 1926, 25; Schultz and Hast, *Women Building Chicago,* 144.

126. Vynne, *Chicago by Day and Night,* 142.

127. "Fountain Girl," 1907, DN-0005310, Chicago Daily News Negatives Collection, Chicago History Museum, Chicago, Ill.

128. Marietta Holley, *Samantha at the World's Fair* (New York: Funk & Wagnalls, 1893), 164.

129. On women's prominence at the World's Fair, see especially Jeanne Madeline Weimann, *The Fair Women* (Chicago: Academy Chicago, 1981); Ralph, *Harper's Chicago and the World's Fair,* 161–170; Trachtenberg, *Incorporation of America,* 221–222; Wanda M. Corn, *Women Building History: Public Art at the 1893 Columbian Exposition* (Berkeley: University of California Press, 2011).

130. Maud Howe Elliott, "The Building and Its Decorations," *Art and Handicraft in the Woman's Building of the World's Columbian Exposition, Chicago, 1893* (Chicago: Rand, McNally, 1894), 25; Mary Pepchinski, "Woman's Buildings at European and American World's Fairs, 1893–1939," in *Gendering the Fair: Histories of Women and Gender at World's Fairs,* ed. T. J. Boisseau and Abigail M. Markwyn (Champaign: University of Illinois, 2010), 192–193; Sarah Wadsworth and Wayne A. Viegan, *Right Here I See My Own Books: The Woman's Building Library at the World's Columbian Exposition* (Amherst: University of Massachusetts, 2012), 47–48.

131. Trumball White and William Igleheart, *World's Columbian Exposition, Chicago, 1893* (Boston: J. K. Hastings, 1893), 445–455.

132. John J. Flinn, *Hand-Book of the World's Columbian Exposition* (Chicago: Standard Guide, 1892), 260–261.

133. On the Woman's Building's popularity, see, for example, "Through the Looking Glass," *Chicago Tribune,* Nov. 1, 1893, 10.

134. Miller, *City of the Century,* 549–550; Gilbert, *Perfect Cities,* 165; Korom, *American Skyscraper,* 167; "Woman's Temple to Be Torn Down," *Chicago Tribune,* May 1, 1926, 3.

135. Walter Lamb, reprinted from *Figaro,* in "Mrs. Potter Palmer," *Inter Ocean,* Mar. 7, 1891, 11.

136. Glessner Journal, Dec. 11, 1892; "For the Children: Auspicious Opening of the Columbian Bazaar," *Chicago Tribune,* Dec. 8, 1892, 1.

137. See especially Montgomery, *Displaying Women,* 163–170.

138. Fuller, *With the Procession,* 154.

139. On actresses pioneering new trends, see Marlis Schweitzer, *When Broadway Was the Runway: Theater, Fashion, and American Culture* (Philadelphia: University of Pennsylvania Press, 2009), 66–68; Severa, *Dressed for the Photographer,* 375; Hoganson, *Consumers' Imperium,* 74.

140. "Hoops Strike Town," *Chicago Tribune,* Feb. 5, 1893, 33.

141. Amy Leslie, "It Is Not a Great Play," *Chicago Daily News,* Feb. 14, 1893, 4.

142. "Prohibition of the Hoop-Skirt," *Chicago Tribune,* Feb. 4, 1893, 1.

143. "George M. Bleecker," Member Record, Minnesota Reference Library, accessed on Aug. 8, 2013, www.leg.state.mn.us/legdb/fulldetail.aspx?ID =11284. On sincerity, see "The Anti-Hoopskirt Crusade in Minnesota," *Chicago Tribune,* Feb. 5, 1893, 28.

144. "Heading Off Hoopskirts," *New York Times,* Feb. 4, 1893, 1.

145. "Heading Off Hoopskirts," 1.

146. "Anti-Hoopskirt Crusade in Minnesota," 28.

147. "Heading Off Hoopskirts," 1; "Prohibition of the Hoop-Skirt," 1.

148. "The Crinoline Terror," 1; "Hoopskirts Find No Favor," *Chicago Herald,* Feb. 16, 1893, 1; "Against Crinoline in Indiana," *Chicago Tribune,* Feb. 18, 1893, 2; "Laughter Kills a Crinoline Resolution," *Chicago Tribune,* Mar. 10, 1893, 1; "Work at the Capital," *San Francisco Chronicle,* Feb. 16, 1893, 4.

149. *Journal of the House of Representatives of the 37th General Assembly of the State of Missouri 1893,* 822.

150. "Laughter Kills a Crinoline Resolution," 1.

151. "Against Crinoline in Indiana," 2.

152. *Journal of the Indiana State Senate during the Fifty-Eighth Session of the General Assembly Commencing Thursday, January 5, 1893* (Indianapolis: Wm. B., Contractor for State Printing and Binding, 1893), 570–571.

153. "The Crinoline Terror," 1; *Journal of the Assembly of the State of New York at their One Hundred and Sixteenth Session* (Albany: James B. Lyon, State Printer, 1893), 409.

154. "Bill to Squelch the Crinoline," *Chicago Herald,* Feb. 14, 1893, 9.

155. "New York State Gets in Line," *Chicago Times,* Feb. 14, 1893, 1; "The Crinoline

Terror," 1; "Hoop Skirts: The New York Assembly Will Follow in the Path Blazed by Bleecker," *St. Paul Daily News,* Feb. 13, 1893, 8.

156. "Bill to Squelch the Crinoline," 9. The bill came up for a second reading in August, by which time the crinoline threat had effectively ended. "Autumn's New Modes: The Crinoline Microbe Has Not Yet Been Exterminated," *Chicago Tribune,* Aug. 19, 1893, 16. *Journal of the Assembly of the State of New York,* 409, 1192, 1586.

157. "Anti-Hoopskirt Crusade in Minnesota," 28.

158. *Inter Ocean,* Mar. 16, 1893, 6; *Chicago Tribune,* Feb. 22, 1893, 4.

159. "Anti-Hoopskirt War," 28.

160. "The White City," *Los Angeles Times,* Mar. 28, 1893, 10.

161. "Chicago Antihoop Skirt Society," *Chicago Herald,* Feb. 12, 1893, 28; "Anti-Hoopskirt War," 28.

162. "Dress Reform Notes," *Woman's Journal,* Apr. 15, 1893, 114; John Strange Winter, "The No-Crinoline League," *Detroit Free Press,* Apr. 30, 1893, 28.

163. "Kohl & Middleton's," *Chicago Tribune,* Mar. 19, 1893, 37; "Kohl & Middleton's," *Inter Ocean,* Mar. 19, 1893, 15; "Theatrical Gossip," *Inter Ocean,* Mar. 19, 1893, 17.

164. "Theatrical Gossip," *Inter Ocean,* Mar. 26, 1893, 17; "Howling Success at Kohl & Middleton's," *Chicago Tribune,* Mar. 26, 1893, 37.

165. "Hoops Strike Town," 33.

166. "Hoops Strike Town," 33.

167. "'Hoops' as Bugaboos," *Chicago Tribune,* Apr. 29, 1893, 16.

168. "Revival of Crinoline," 340.

169. Marie Evelyn, "Keep Out Hoops," *San Francisco Call,* Feb. 17, 1893, 6.

170. Mary McGuire, "About Hoop Skirts," repr. in *Logansport Pharos-Tribune,* Jan. 12, 1893, 19.

171. "Chicago Antihoop Skirt Society," 28.

172. "On a Hunt for a Hoop," *Chicago Tribune,* Feb. 12, 1893, 27.

173. "Dressing the Hair," *Chicago Tribune,* Apr. 1, 1893, 16.

174. Isabel A. Mallon, "Costumes of Early Spring," *Ladies' Home Journal* 10 (Apr. 1893): 29.

175. See, for example, "Notes from the French Capital," *Godey's Magazine* 126 (Apr. 1893): 514; "New York Fashions," *Harper's Bazaar* 26 (Apr. 1, 1893): 251.

176. "Seasonable Shopping Hints," *Inter Ocean Illustrated Supplement,* Apr. 30, 1893, 2.

177. "Revival of Crinoline," 340.

3. Consumer Rights and the Theater Hat Problem

1. "Hiss Off the High Hats," *Chicago Tribune,* Jan. 18, 1897, 1, 5.

2. On the Illinois bill, see, for example, "War on the Big Hat," *Chicago Herald,* Jan. 31, 1895, 5; "Death to High Hats," *Chicago Tribune,* Jan. 31, 1895, 1.

3. "Theater Hat Problem Up Again," *Chicago Tribune,* Sept. 27, 1896, 28.

4. "Women Defy the Hat Ordinance," *Chicago Tribune*, Jan. 7, 1897, 6.

5. On the emergence of a modern consumer movement in this period, see especially Lawrence B. Glickman, *Buying Power: A History of Consumer Activism in America* (Chicago: University of Chicago Press, 2009), 158–160; Cohen, *A Consumers' Republic*, 21; Michael J. Sandel, *Democracy's Discontent: America in Search of a Public Philosophy* (Cambridge, Mass.: Belknap Press, 1996), 225–232; Landon Storrs, *Civilizing Capitalism: The National Consumers' League, Women's Activism, and Labor Standards in the New Deal Era* (Chapel Hill: University of North Carolina Press, 2000), 2, 19–20.

6. See especially Stanley, "Revolutionizing Human Rights"; Dailey, "Deference and Violence in the Postbellum Urban South"; Dale, "'Social Equality Does Not Exist among Themselves, nor among Us'"; Sandoval-Strausz, "Travelers, Strangers, and Jim Crow"; Scott, "Public Rights, Social Equality, and the Conceptual Roots of the Plessy Challenge."

7. Dale, "'Social Equality Does Not Exist among Themselves, nor among Us,'" 311n1.

8. Henry T. Finck, "Musical Notes," *The Looker-On* 3 (Sept. 1896): 247, 246, 245.

9. Robin W. Doughty, *Feather Fashions and Bird Preservation: A Study in Nature Protection* (Berkeley: University of California Press, 1975), 17; Severa, *Dressed for the Photographer*, 470, 474.

10. Gernsheim, *Victorian and Edwardian Fashion*, 67. The Gainsborough hat received its name from the broad-brimmed millinery featured in the work of British portraitist Thomas Gainsborough. The term "picture hat" offered a shorthand referent for this style.

11. The popularity of feathers depleted the bird population and, ultimately, led to the founding of the Audubon Society in the late nineteenth century. However, there is no evidence that conservation concerns were ever invoked in the theater hat debate. On millinery and bird preservation, see especially Doughty, *Feather Fashions and Bird Preservation*; Dorceta E. Taylor, *The Rise of the American Conservation Movement: Power, Privilege, and Environmental Protection* (Durham, N.C.: Duke University Press, 2016), 189–223.

12. On contemporary hat styles, see especially Severa, *Dressed for the Photographer*, 386, 470–471; Anita A. Stamper and Jill Condra, *Clothing through American History: The Civil War through the Gilded Age, 1861–1899* (Santa Barbara: ABC-CLIO, 2011), 294–295; Georgine de Courtais, *Women's Hats, Headdresses, and Hairstyles* (Mineola, N.Y.: Dover, 1973), 132–144; R. Turner Wilcox, *The Mode in Hats and Headdresses* (1945; repr., Mineola, N.Y.: Dover, 2008), 264–283.

13. Glessner Journal, Feb. 2, 1897; Multigraph of Frances MacBeth Glessner, 1897, Glessner House Museum, Chicago, Ill.

14. See, for example, "Portrait of Bertha Honore Palmer," 1900, ICHi-012053, Chicago History Museum, Chicago, Ill.; "Mrs. Potter Palmer Walking

Down Steps," 1908, DN-0006592, Chicago Daily News Negatives Collection, Chicago History Museum, Chicago, Ill.; "Mrs. Potter Palmer, of Chicago and Newport," 1900, Miriam and Ira D. Wallach Division of Art, Prints, and Photographs, New York Public Library Digital Collections, http://digitalcollections.nypl.org/items/510d47e0-ed6f-a3d9-e040-e00a 18064a99.

15. Anzia Yezierska, *Bread Givers: A Novel,* 3rd ed. (1925; repr., New York: Persea Press, 2003), 2.

16. Enstad, *Ladies of Labor,* 78, 80–81.

17. Calculated comparing 1895 to 2017 using the Consumer Price Index available on the Federal Reserve's website. See "Consumer Price Index (Estimate)," Federal Reserve Bank of Minneapolis, accessed Feb. 19, 2018, www .minneapolisfed.org/community_education/teacher/calc/hist1800.cfm.

18. On women's hat production, see especially Gamber, *Female Economy,* 96–100, 182–188.

19. "Marshall Field & Co.," *Chicago Tribune,* May 4, 1895, 8. Calculated comparing 1895 to 2017. See "Consumer Price Index (Estimate)."

20. "Siegle-Cooper & Co.," *Chicago Tribune,* Apr. 11, 1897, 40. Calculated comparing 1895 to 2017. See "Consumer Price Index (Estimate)."

21. Gamber, *Female Economy,* 114; Jenna Weissman Joselit, *A Perfect Fit: Clothes, Character, and the Promise of America* (New York: Metropolitan Books, 2001), 107; Diana Crane, *Fashion and Its Social Agendas: Class, Gender, and Identity in Clothing* (Chicago: University of Chicago Press, 2000), 83.

22. Hartley, *Ladies' Book of Etiquette,* 173–174. See also Duffey, *Ladies' and Gentlemen's Etiquette,* 281.

23. Abby Buchanan Longstreet, *Social Etiquette of New York,* rev. and enl. ed. (New York: D. Appleton, 1888), 203.

24. Agnes H. Morton, *Etiquette: An Answer to the Riddle When? Where? How?* (Philadelphia: Penn, 1893), 164–165.

25. Young, *Our Deportment,* 151; Walter Raleigh Houghton et al., *American Etiquette and Rules of Politeness* (Chicago: Rand, McNally, 1889), 99.

26. Duffey, *Ladies' and Gentlemen's Etiquette,* 157.

27. H. F. Farny, "The Interior of the Chicago Auditorium," *Harper's Weekly* 33 (Dec. 28, 1889): 1032.

28. *McVicker's Observanda* (Chicago: W. J. Jefferson Press, 1891), 20–21.

29. See William Dean Howells, "Life and Letters," *Harper's Weekly* 40 (Feb. 1, 1896): 103; "Shuts Out All Hope," *Chicago Tribune,* Feb. 1, 1896, 12; "Vice of the Theater Hat," *Washington Post,* Feb. 1, 1896, 10; "W. D. Howells on the Theater Hat," *Los Angeles Times,* Feb. 5, 1896, 3.

30. *Argonaut,* quoted in "He Had a Sweet Revenge at Last," *Chicago Tribune,* May 10, 1896, 50; "Sweet Revenge," *Boston Globe,* May 17, 1896, 44.

31. Finck, "Musical Notes," 246.

32. "The Theater Hat: Some Apologies for Its Existence," *Chicago .Tribune,* Jan. 27, 1895, 39.

33. "Revenge Is Sweet," *Life* 29 (Mar. 25, 1897): 228.

34. "Matinee Hat Again," *Chicago Tribune,* May 29, 1898, 38.

35. *Munsey's Magazine,* quoted in "It Really Must Go," *Chicago Tribune,* Mar. 9, 1895, 16.

36. "Theater Hat Problem Up Again," 28.

37. "Her Ideal Supreme," *Chicago Tribune,* Apr. 2, 1893, 44. Calculated comparing 1893 to 2017. See "Consumer Price Index (Estimate)."

38. Glessner Journal, Apr. 9, 1893.

39. "Her Reasons for It," *Chicago Tribune,* Apr. 8, 1893, 16.

40. "The Hat Must Go," *Munsey's Magazine* 8 (Dec. 1892): 431.

41. "Plan Reefs in Headgear," *Chicago Tribune,* Oct. 2, 1896, 9.

42. Howells, "Life and Letters," 103.

43. Howells, 103.

44. "The Theater Hat," *Desert Weekly,* Dec. 24, 1892, 15.

45. "Big Theater Hat," *Inter Ocean,* Dec. 20, 1891, 12.

46. "That Theater Hat," *Chicago Tribune,* Feb. 5, 1893, 38.

47. "All Men Are Back of Jones," *Chicago Tribune,* Jan. 31, 1895, 1.

48. "Crusade against Theater Hats," *Chicago Tribune,* Feb. 12, 1893, 38.

49. "Theater Hats Were There Galore," *Chicago Tribune,* Feb. 7, 1893, 1.

50. "All the Men Are Back of Jones," 1.

51. "Theatrical Gossip," *Inter Ocean,* Mar. 5, 1893, 16.

52. "That Theater Hat," 38.

53. "Vindicated at Last," *Chicago Tribune,* Jan. 16, 1892, 16.

54. Harry Germaine, "Sworn at by Many," *Inter Ocean,* Nov. 16, 1896, 12.

55. "The Theater Hat," *Munsey's Magazine* 12 (Mar. 1895): 662.

56. Richard Butsch, *The Making of American Audiences: From Stage to Television, 1750–1990* (New York: Cambridge University Press, 2000), 66–67; Richard Allen, *Horrible Prettiness: Burlesque and American Culture* (Chapel Hill: University of North Carolina Press, 1991), 50–52.

57. J. Seymour Currey, *Chicago: Its History and Its Builders; A Century of Marvelous Growth* (Chicago: S. J. Clarke, 1912), 3: 244.

58. Butsch, *Making of American Audiences,* 68–69.

59. Butsch, 70; Allen, *Horrible Prettiness,* 53–55; Sewell, *Women and the Everyday City,* 96.

60. Cecil B. Hartley, *The Gentlemen's Book of Etiquette and Manual of Politeness* (Boston: G. W. Cottrell, 1860), 294–295.

61. Hartley, *Ladies' Book of Etiquette,* 173–174.

62. Morton, *Etiquette,* 152.

63. On "legitimate" theater, see Lawrence Levine, *Highbrow/Lowbrow: The Emergence of Cultural Hierarchy in America* (Cambridge, Mass.: Harvard University Press, 1988), 75–76. The term was freighted with class bias regarding what qualified as "art."

64. Levine, 190–197; Butsch, *Making of American Audiences,* 72–74, 78; Sewell, *Women and the Everyday City,* 96–97. See also Baldwin, *In the Watches of the*

Night, 164–165; Kasson, *Rudeness and Civility,* 227–228, 247–248. Allen shows that museum theaters, such as Barnum's American Museum, first applied these changes to court female audiences. Their success soon inspired traditional theaters to make similar adjustments. Allen, *Horrible Prettiness,* 65–70.

65. Butsch, *Making of American Audiences,* 73.
66. "Editor's Easy Chair," *Harper's New Monthly Magazine* 40 (Mar. 1870): 605.
67. "Hooley Redivivus," *Inter Ocean,* July 14, 1877, 10.
68. Chicago Association of Commerce, *A Guide to the City of Chicago* (Chicago: Chicago Association of Commerce, 1909), 94.
69. Pacyga, *Chicago,* 137–138; Miller, *City of the Century,* 354–366. See also Joseph M. Siry, *The Chicago Auditorium: Adler and Sullivan's Architecture and the City* (Chicago: University of Chicago Press, 2002); Jay Pridmore, *The Auditorium Building: A Building Book from the Chicago Architecture Foundation* (Chicago: Chicago Architecture Foundation, 2003).
70. Madame Léon Grandin, *A Parisienne in Chicago: Impressions of the World's Columbian Exposition,* trans. Mary Beth Raycraft (Urbana: University of Illinois Press, 2010), 57.
71. Vynne, *Chicago by Day and Night,* 39–40.
72. *Marquis' Hand-Book of Chicago: A Complete History, Reference Book, and Guide to the City,* 3rd ed. (Chicago: A. N. Marquis, 1887), 237–238.
73. Schick, *Chicago and Its Environs,* 374.
74. *McVicker's Observanda,* 13.
75. Dreiser, *Sister Carrie,* 34.
76. On variety houses and neighborhood theaters as working-class spaces, see especially Butsch, *Making of American Audiences,* 103–107, 114–115, 130–136.
77. For a helpful account of the details and significance of Curry's case, see Dale, "'Social Equality Does Not Exist among Themselves, nor among Us,'" 311–339.
78. "Chicago," *Western Appeal,* Mar. 24, 1888, 1.
79. Bowen, *Colored People of Chicago,* 6; Spear, *Black Chicago,* 12.
80. See especially Butsch, *Making of American Audiences,* 74–75; Schweitzer, *When Broadway Was the Runway,* 4–5.
81. Kate Chopin, "A Pair of Silk Stockings," *Vogue* 10 (Sept. 16, 1897): 191–192.
82. Butsch, *Making of American Audiences,* 68, 74–75.
83. Glessner Journal, Mar. 4, 1893.
84. "Best Known Matinee Girl in Chicago," *Chicago Tribune,* May 12, 1907, 43.
85. "An Incident of the Matinee," *Chicago Tribune,* Apr. 5, 1891, 14.
86. On the matinee girl, see Schweitzer, *When Broadway Was the Runway,* 34–37.
87. "The Matinée Girl," *Munsey's Magazine* 18 (Oct. 1897): 35, 39.
88. "The Matinée Girl," 35.
89. "Best Known Matinee Girl in Chicago," 43.

90. Butsch, *Making of American Audiences*, 79; Schweitzer, *When Broadway Was the Runway*, 37–42; Clayton Hamilton, "The Psychology of Theater Audiences," *Forum* 39 (Oct. 1907): 245–246.

91. "Music and Drama," *Chicago Tribune*, June 13, 1893, 4. On "The Black Crook," see Mark Caldwell, *New York Night: The Mystique and Its History* (New York: Simon and Schuster, 2005), 162.

92. Me Qui Vive, "Hooray for the 'Box Office Lady' Shouts the Matinee Girl," *Chicago Tribune*, May 8, 1910, 15; "Plan Reefs in Headgear," 9.

93. Schweitzer, *When Broadway Was the Runway*, 37.

94. Butsch, *Making of American Audiences*, 79; Schweitzer, *When Broadway Was the Runway*, 37.

95. "The Matinée Girl," 37.

96. Schweitzer, *When Broadway Was the Runway*, 4.

97. "Rebel against High Hat Legislation," *Chicago Tribune*, Nov. 10, 1895, 47.

98. Walter Prichard Eaton, "Women as Theater-Goers," *Woman's Home Companion* 27 (Oct. 1910): 13.

99. Hamilton, "Psychology of Theater Audiences," 245.

100. "The Matinée Girl," 37.

101. Schweitzer, *When Broadway Was the Runway*, 66–68.

102. "Her Face and Gowns," *Chicago Tribune*, Nov. 24, 1896, 3.

103. See, for example, "Lillian Russell's Dresses," *Inter Ocean*, Dec. 4, 1892, 5; "Lillian Russell's Gowns," *Inter Ocean*, Apr. 10, 1892, 22.

104. Veblen, *Theory of the Leisure Class*, 87.

105. Duffey, *Ladies' and Gentlemen's Etiquette*, 280–281.

106. Hartley, *Ladies' Book of Etiquette*, 175.

107. On the politics of promenading, see David Scobey, "Anatomy of the Promenade: The Politics of Bourgeois Sociability in Nineteenth-Century New York," *Social History* 17 (May 1992): 203–227.

108. Frank Norris, *The Pit: A Story of Chicago* (New York: Doubleday, 1903), 6, 23.

109. Garland, *Rose of Dutcher's Coolly*, 266, 268.

110. "The Theater Hat Again," *Munsey's Magazine* 14 (Jan. 1896): 493.

111. The *Tribune* reported that the number of hats actually increased after Davis began his campaign. "All the Men Are Back of Jones," 1.

112. "Plan Reefs in Headgear," 9.

113. On the modern consumer movement, see especially Glickman, *Buying Power*, 155–160; Cohen, *Consumers' Republic*, 21.

114. On state and local precedents to the Pure Food and Drug Act, see Lorine Swainston Goodwin, *The Pure Food, Drink, and Drug Crusaders, 1879–1914* (Jefferson, N.C.: McFarland, 1999), esp. 62–84.

115. See, for example, "Kennicott on 'Food Adulteration,'" *Chicago Tribune*, Jan. 23, 1897, 7; "Will Work for Pure Food Supplies," *Chicago Tribune*, Jan. 31, 1897, 12.

116. See, for example, "Chicago Bread Law Not Obeyed," *Chicago Tribune*, Jan. 10, 1897, 12.

117. Sinclair spent seven weeks in Chicago's packing houses in 1904. Lauren Coodley, *Upton Sinclair: California Socialist, Celebrity Intellectual* (Lincoln: University of Nebraska, 2013), 42.

118. "The Anti-Butterine Law," *Chicago Tribune,* July 18, 1897, 30.

119. "To Give Consumers Honest Butter," *Chicago Tribune,* Apr. 30, 1895, 6.

120. Miller, *City of the Century,* 271.

121. For more on the "traction problem," see Edward R. Kantowicz, "Carter H. Harrison II: The Politics of Balance," in *The Mayors: The Chicago Political Tradition,* ed. Paul M. Green and Melvin G. Holli (Carbondale: Southern Illinois University Press, 1987), 25–28; Harold L. Platt, "Traction Ordinances," in Grossman, Keating, and Reiff, *Encyclopedia of Chicago,* 825.

122. "All Hats to Come Off," *Chicago Times-Herald,* Jan. 5, 1897, 1; "Ban on High Hat," *Chicago Record,* Jan. 6, 1897, 6; "High Hats Must Go," *Inter Ocean,* Jan. 5, 1897, 1.

123. "Legislation against Hats," *Inter Ocean,* Feb. 24, 1895, 31.

124. "The Theater Hat," 662.

125. On the regulation of consumer practices to protect women's morality, see especially Stansell, *City of Women;* Peiss, *Cheap Amusements;* Meyerowitz, *Women Adrift;* Enstad, *Ladies of Labor, Girls of Adventure;* Hunter, *To 'Joy My Freedom.*

126. Editorial, *Chicago Tribune,* Feb. 21, 1895, 6.

127. "Will Not Take off His Theater Hat," *Chicago Tribune,* Aug. 25, 1896, 1.

128. "Would Abolish High Theater Hat," *Chicago Times,* Jan. 31, 1895, 2.

129. "Death to High Hats," 1.

130. "Death to High Hats," 1; "Come Lower That Theater Hat," *Chicago Tribune,* Jan. 14, 1895, 7; "The Massachusetts Legislature," *Inter Ocean,* Mar. 29, 1895, 6; "Leg for Alex Jones to Stand On," *Inter Ocean,* Feb. 21, 1895, 2. Although these bills sometimes gained approval from one or more houses of the legislature, none made it into law.

131. "Only One Defender of the High Hat," *Chicago Tribune,* Jan. 31, 1895, 1.

132. On the Civic Federation, see Sklar, *Florence Kelley and the Nation's Work,* 227. For biographical information on Jones, see Currey, *Chicago,* 4:614–619.

133. "A. J. Jones to Work on Labor Troubles," *Chicago Tribune,* Jan. 7, 1895, 2.

134. "War on the Big Hat," 5.

135. "Death to High Hats," 1.

136. "War on the Big Hat," 5.

137. "Death to High Hats," 1.

138. "Against the Big Hat," *Chicago Tribune,* Feb. 17, 1895, 11.

139. "Take the Jones Bill as a Joke," *Chicago Herald,* Jan. 31, 1895, 5.

140. "Suppressing the Theater Hat," *Chicago Tribune,* Feb. 1, 1895, 6.

141. "As to the Theater Hat," *Chicago Times,* Feb. 6, 1895, 4.

142. "Against the Big Hat," 11.

143. "Against the Big Hat," 11.

144. "One Woman's Big Hat Experience," *Chicago Tribune,* Feb. 15, 1895, 9.

145. Mary H. Krout, "Woman's Kingdom," *Inter Ocean*, Mar. 30, 1895, 13.

146. Mary H. Krout, "A New Sumptuary Law," *Inter Ocean*, Dec. 12, 1896, 16.

147. Krout, "Women's Kingdom," 13.

148. Krout, "A New Sumptuary Law," 16.

149. "High Hat Bill Causes Levity," *Inter Ocean*, Feb. 8, 1895, 7.

150. "Tights and the Big Theater Hats," *Chicago Tribune*, Feb. 8, 1895, 5.

151. Editorial, *Chicago Tribune*, Feb. 21, 1895, 6.

152. "Work in Committee," *Inter Ocean*, Mar. 13, 1895, 5.

153. On Ohio as first law, see *Cincinnati: "The Queen City"; Newspaper Reference Book* (Cincinnati: Cuvier Press Club, 1914), 137; S. C. Schenck, "Theater Millinery," *Harrisburg Telegraph*, Jan. 19, 1897, 2. Schenck's article was printed in several other newspapers across the country. On amending the law to target only managers, see "Hats Must Come Off," *Chicago Times-Herald*, Mar. 25, 1896, 1; "Bosler's Claim to Fame," *Chicago Tribune*, Mar. 26, 1896, 6.

154. "Ohio's Anti–High Hat Law," *New York Times*, Apr. 6, 1896, 9.

155. Schenck, "Theater Millinery," 2.

156. "Fosdick Law in Action," *Chicago Tribune*, Apr. 7, 1896, 3.

157. "To Crush the Theater Hat," *Chicago Times-Herald*, Jan. 6, 1897, 6.

158. Schenck, "Theater Millinery," 2.

159. "Hats Off to Ohio," *Chicago Times-Herald*, Mar. 26, 1896, 6.

160. "Bosler's Claim to Fame," 6.

161. "The Theater Hat," 662.

162. Plotke invoked European practices when justifying his proposal. "Plotke on the Big Hat," *Chicago Record*, Jan. 6, 1897, 3.

163. Finck, "Musical Notes," 245; "Theater Hat Problem Up Again," 28.

164. "Plan Reefs in Headgear," 9.

165. "That Theater Hat," 38.

166. "Her Reasons for It," 16.

167. Joselit, *A Perfect Fit*, 111.

168. Veblen, *Theory of the Leisure Class*, 171.

169. "A Woman's Reasons," *Life* 24 (Dec. 27, 1894): 27.

170. "Knox Hats," *The Rotarian* 22 (Mar. 1923): 171.

171. "O, My Milliner's Bill!," *Chicago Tribune*, Sept. 28, 1890, 25.

172. Schenck, "Theater Millinery," 2.

173. Jane Addams, *The Spirit of Youth and the City Streets* (New York: Macmillan, 1909), 8.

174. "Vindicated at Last," 16.

175. "Vindicated at Last," 16.

176. "Fuss over High Hat Feathers," *Chicago Tribune*, Feb. 9, 1895, 14.

177. *Proceedings of the City Council of the City of Chicago for the Municipal Year 1896–1897* (Chicago: John F. Higgins, 1897), 1308.

178. "Plotke on the Big Hat," 3.

179. For the vote tally, see *Proceedings of the City Council of the City of Chicago for the Municipal Year 1896–1897*, 1308.

180. "All Hats to Come Off," 1.
181. "Hats Off in Chicago Theaters," *Chicago Tribune*, Jan. 6, 1897, 6.
182. "High Hats Must Go," 1.
183. "All Hats to Come Off," 1; "High Hats Must Go," 1; "Ban on the High Hat," 6.
184. "Hat Law Is No Joke," *Chicago Times-Herald*, Jan. 6, 1897, 9.
185. Many southern business owners claimed they had a right to serve only white people and that the government could not dictate private commercial relations. See especially Lawrence Glickman, *The Free Enterprise System: A Cultural History* (New Haven, Conn.: Yale University Press, forthcoming).
186. "Harmony at Home," *Inter Ocean*, Jan. 6, 1897, 5.
187. "War on Theater Hats," *Chicago Tribune*, Jan. 5, 1897, 1.
188. "Harmony at Home," 5.
189. "Plotke on the Big Hat," 3.
190. "Mayor and High Hats," *Chicago Times-Herald*, Jan. 10, 1897, 2.
191. *Chicago Chronicle*, repr. in "The Anti–Theater Hat Law in Chicago," *St. Louis Republic*, Jan. 7, 1897, 6.
192. "Harmony at Home," 5.
193. "Plotke on the Big Hat," 3.
194. "Women of Society Oppose High Hats," *Chicago Journal*, Jan. 9, 1897, 6.
195. "Hat Law Is No Joke," 9.
196. "Will the High Hats Go?," *Chicago Tribune*, Jan. 7, 1897, 3.
197. "Hat Law Is No Joke," 9.
198. "Hat Law Is No Joke," 9.
199. Mary H. Krout, "Woman's Kingdom: Unconstitutional Legislation Directed against Disfranchised," *Inter Ocean*, Feb. 1, 1897, 11.
200. "Plotke on the Big Hat," 3.
201. "Yes, Take Off Your Hats Indoors," *Chicago Tribune*, Apr. 1, 1895, 8.
202. "Plotke on the Big Hat," 3.
203. "Plotke's Ordinance Is Doomed," *Chicago Times-Herald*, Jan. 11, 1897, 4.
204. For the mayor's veto message and text of the revised ordinance, see *Proceedings of the City Council of the City of Chicago for the Municipal Year 1896–1897*, 1369–1371. "Mayor and High Hats," 2; "Veto for Theater Hat Ordinance," *Chicago Tribune*, Jan. 10, 1897, 1.
205. "Amended Doom of the Theater Hat," *Chicago Tribune*, Jan. 16, 1897, 12.
206. *Proceedings of the City Council of the City of Chicago for the Municipal Year 1896–1897*, 1370; "High Hat Ordinance," *Chicago Journal*, Jan. 15, 1897, 7.
207. "Women Defy the Hat Ordinance," 6.
208. "Theaters and High Hats," *Washington Post*, Jan. 8, 1897, 6.
209. "Hiss Off the High Hats," 1.
210. Levine, *Highbrow/Lowbrow*, 68. See also Allen, *Horrible Prettiness*, 57–61.
211. "Hiss Off the High Hats," 5.
212. "Footlight View of Theater Hats," *Chicago Tribune*, Jan. 24, 1897, 30.
213. "Few Hats Seen in the Theaters," *Chicago Tribune*, Jan. 19, 1897, 9.
214. "Hiss Off the High Hats," 1.

215. "Big Hats Are Doffed," *Chicago Times-Herald,* Feb. 5, 1897, 7.

216. "High Hat Act in Force," *Chicago Tribune,* Feb. 5, 1897, 5.

217. John A. Howland, "The Selfishness of Women in Public," *Chicago Tribune,* Aug. 28, 1904, 25.

218. "Hair Hides the Stage," *Chicago Tribune,* Feb. 14, 1897, 26. See also *Chicago Chronicle,* quoted in "'Hats Off' Is the Fad," *Anaconda Standard,* Oct. 7, 1900, 13; *Chicago Times-Herald,* quoted in "How to Dress for the Theater," *Springfield Republican,* Nov. 3, 1898, 12. After Boston passed its own theater hat law, milliners there complained of decreased sales. "Theater Hats No More," *The Bystander,* June 3, 1898, 4.

219. See, for example, *Powers' Theater Program,* Feb. 26, 1900, 19, Lawrence J. Gutter Collection of Chicagoana, University of Illinois at Chicago.

220. See, for example, *Iroquois Theater Souvenir Program* (Chicago: Rand, McNally, 1903), 3.

221. Annie Randall White, *Twentieth Century Etiquette: An Up-to-Date Book for Polite Society* (Chicago: Monarch Book, 1900), 224.

222. "Let Her Have Her Way," *Inter Ocean,* Sept. 25, 1900, 6.

223. "Chicago Reform Measure Is Adopted," *Chicago Tribune,* Jan. 7, 1897, 3; "Will Follow Chicago's Lead," *Inter Ocean,* Jan. 7, 1897, 1; "Baltimore After High Hats," *Chicago Tribune,* Feb. 10, 1897, 3; "Theater Hat Bill Is Passed," *Chicago Tribune,* Mar. 24, 1897, 1. On the phrase "imitate Chicago," see "A Victory for the Big Theater Hats," *San Francisco Chronicle,* Mar. 22, 1897, 10.

224. "Theater Hats Must Come Down," *St. Louis Post-Dispatch,* Jan. 17, 1897, 5.

225. "Odd Bills Galore," *Chicago Tribune,* Feb. 21, 1897, 25.

4. Tippling Ladies and Public Pleasure

1. "Drink and Gaming Curse to Women," *Chicago Tribune,* Sept. 9, 1907, 6; "Women Who 'Booze' Caught by Hopkins," *Chicago Record-Herald,* Sept. 27, 1907, 2; "Reeling Woman Seen by Hopkins," *Chicago Tribune,* Sept. 18, 1907, 4. For national press coverage, see, for example, "Chicago Women as Drinkers," *New York Times,* Sept. 28, 1907, 7; "Counts Women Tipplers," *Washington Post,* Sept. 28, 1907, 2; "Pastor Sees Women Drink," *Los Angeles Times,* Oct. 8, 1907, I19.

2. To *tipple* was "to drink spirituous or strong liquors habitually; esp., to drink frequently, without absolute drunkenness." By contrast, to *booze* was "to drink excessively" or "guzzle." The former was often used to describe women, while the latter more often applied to men, who were assumed to be heavier drinkers. See Noah Webster, *Webster's Condensed Dictionary: A Condensed Dictionary of the English Language Giving the Correct Spelling, Pronunciation and Definitions of Words Based on the Unabridged Dictionary of Noah Webster, LL.D.,* ed. Noah Porter (Chicago: Reilly & Britton, 1910), 613, 56.

3. See, for example, Ian R. Tyrrell, *Sobering Up: From Temperance to Prohibition in Antebellum America, 1800–1860* (Westport, Conn.: Greenwood Press,

1979); Ruth M. Alexander, "'We Are Engaged as a Band of Sisters': Class and Domesticity in the Washingtonian Temperance Movement, 1840–1850," *Journal of American History* 75 (Dec. 1988): 763–785; Paul Boyer, "Battling the Saloon and the Brothel: The Great Coercive Crusades," in *Urban Masses and Moral Order in America, 1820–1920* (Cambridge, Mass.: Harvard University Press, 1978).

4. Helen Hale, "Do Women Drink?," *Advance,* Sept. 26, 1907, 371.

5. On drinking in public as a male privilege, see especially Perry Duis, *The Saloon: Public Drinking in Chicago and Boston, 1880–1920* (Urbana: University of Illinois Press, 1983); Roy Rosenzweig, *Eight Hours for What We Will: Workers and Leisure in an Industrial City, 1870–1920* (New York: Cambridge University Press, 1983); Madelon Powers, *Faces along the Bar: Lore and Order in the Workingman's Saloon, 1870–1920* (Chicago: University of Chicago Press, 1998); Elaine Frantz Parsons, "Risky Business: The Uncertain Boundaries of Manhood in the Midwestern Saloon," *Journal of Social History* 34 (Winter 2000): 283–307.

6. On the democratization of drinking and dining in this era, see especially Catherine Gilbert Murdock, *Domesticating Drink: Women, Men, and Alcohol in America, 1870–1940* (Baltimore: Johns Hopkins University Press, 1998); Lewis Erenberg, *Steppin' Out: New York Nightlife and the Transformation of American Culture, 1890–1930* (Westport, Conn.: Greenwood Press, 1981); Andrew Haley, *Turning the Tables: Restaurants and the American Middle Class, 1880–1920* (Chapel Hill: University of North Carolina Press, 2011).

7. See especially Alexander, "'We Are Engaged as a Band of Sisters'"; Ruth Bordin, *Woman and Temperance: The Quest for Power and Liberty, 1873–1900* (Philadelphia: Temple University Press, 1991); Ian R. Tyrrell, *Woman's World / Woman's Empire: The Woman's Christian Temperance Union in International Perspective, 1880–1930* (Chapel Hill: University of North Carolina Press, 1991).

8. See especially Scobey, "Nymphs and Satyrs"; Richter, *Home on the Rails;* Berger, *Hotel Dreams;* Baldwin, *Domesticating the Street;* Baldwin, *In the Watches of the Night.*

9. Smoking emphasized similar pleasures but remained on the "fringes of American society" until after World War I. See Cassandra Tate, *Cigarette Wars: The Triumph of "The Little White Slaver"* (New York: Oxford University Press, 1999), 6, 110.

10. Peiss, *Cheap Amusements;* Meyerowitz, *Women Adrift;* Wood, *Freedom of the Streets;* Erenberg, *Steppin' Out.*

11. G. Stanley Hall, "Flapper Americana Novissima," *Atlantic Monthly* 129 (June 1922): 776. On the modern woman, or flapper, see especially Paula Fass, *The Damned and the Beautiful: American Youth in the 1920s* (New York: Oxford University Press, 1977); Lynn Dumenil, *The Modern Temper: American Culture and Society in the 1920s* (New York: Hill and Wang, 1995).

12. Murdock, *Domesticating Drink,* 21; Bordin, *Woman and Temperance,* 45, 143.

13. Jane Brookshire, "Do Our 'Best' Women Drink?," *Wayside Tales* 9 (Feb. 1906): 593.

14. "Increasing Habits of Intoxication," *Chicago Tribune,* Oct. 23, 1892, 3; "The Drink Habit among Women," *Chicago Journal,* quoted in *Washington Post,* Dec. 31, 1899, 6; "Women Drinkers Are on Increase," *Chicago Tribune,* Jan. 6, 1908, 3.

15. Brookshire, "Do Our 'Best' Women Drink?," 593.

16. Jaher, *Urban Establishment,* 495–496.

17. On women's drinking practices in immigrant communities, see Margareta Matovic, "Embracing a Middle-Class Life: Swedish-American Women in Lake View," in *Peasant Maids, City Women: From the European Countryside to Urban America,* ed. Christiane Harzig (Ithaca, N.Y.: Cornell University Press, 1997), 266; Duis, *Saloon,* 153–156; Kathleen Neils Conzen, *Immigrant Milwaukee, 1836–1860: Accommodation and Community in a Frontier City* (Cambridge, Mass.: Harvard University Press, 1976), 157–158.

18. Norris, *The Pit,* 66.

19. Haley, *Turning the Tables,* 148–150, 155–156; Duncan, *Culture and Democracy,* 123; Miller, *City of the Century,* 140; Perry R. Duis, *Challenging Chicago: Coping with Everyday Life, 1837–1920* (Urbana: University of Illinois Press, 1998), 158.

20. "Women Lunch at Cafes," *Chicago Tribune,* June 19, 1896, 12.

21. On medicinal remedies at soda fountains, see Anne Cooper Funderburg, *Sundae Best: A History of Soda Fountains* (Bowling Green, Ohio: Bowling Green State University Press, 2002), 48–49, 67–81.

22. On patent medicines, see Cheryl Krasnick Warsh, "'Oh, Lord, Pour a Cordial in Her Wounded Heart': The Drinking Woman in Victorian and Edwardian Canada," in *Drink in Canada,* ed. Cheryl K. Warsh (Montreal: McGill-Queens University Press, 1993), 72. On women shoppers at soda fountains, see "The Soda-Water Habit," *Inter Ocean,* Aug. 12, 1888, 17; "Increasing Habits of Intoxication," 3; "Found a New Kind of Drunkenness," *Chicago Tribune,* Mar. 8, 1891, 17.

23. "Drinks in Drug Stores," *Inter Ocean,* Oct. 13, 1895, 6.

24. "The Soda Water Habit in Chicago," *Chicago Tribune,* Aug. 2, 1896, 29.

25. On licensing, see Richard Schneirov, *Labor and Urban Politics: Class Conflict and the Origins of Modern Liberalism in Chicago, 1864–97* (Urbana: University of Illinois Press, 1998), 165–166.

26. "'Sticks' in Soda Water: When You Drink Patent Combinations You Get Alcohol," *Chicago Tribune,* Aug. 5, 1888, 9.

27. Drugstore numbers are based on the 1881 and 1907 Chicago city directories. *The Lakeside Annual Directory of the City of Chicago* (Chicago: Chicago Directory Company, 1881); *The Lakeside Annual Business Directory of the City of Chicago* (Chicago: Chicago Directory Company, 1907).

28. "Flies to Her Head," *Chicago Tribune,* Jan. 17, 1897, 25.

29. Miller, *City of the Century,* 260–261; Ann Satterthwaite, *Going Shopping: Consumer Choices and Community Consequences* (New Haven, Conn.: Yale University Press, 2001), 43.

30. On the menu, see "Notes from Mrs. Clara Cady," n.d., folder 17, box 23007, Federated Department Stores' Records of Marshall Field & Company, Chicago History Museum, Chicago, Ill.; Twyman, *History of Marshall Field & Co.,* 125.

31. Whitaker, *Service and Style,* 226.

32. "Women Lunch at Cafes," 12.

33. "Grand Opening: Fish, Joseph & Co.," *Chicago Tribune,* Sept. 18, 1892, 24; "Siegel-Cooper & Co.," *Chicago Tribune,* June 10, 1894, 32.

34. Duis, *Challenging Chicago,* 158.

35. "Notice," *Chicago Tribune,* Nov. 22, 1885, 1; Duis, *Challenging Chicago,* 148; Royal L. LaTouche, *Chicago and Its Resources Twenty Years After, 1871–1891: A Commercial History Showing the Progress and Growth of Two Decades from the Great Fire to the Present Time* (Chicago: Chicago Times, 1892), 16–17.

36. "News of the Stores," *Inter Ocean,* July 19, 1898, 5.

37. Powers' Theater Program, Nov. 11, 1901, 24, Lawrence J. Gutter Collection of Chicagoana, Special Collections, University of Illinois at Chicago.

38. "Crowd Women Out," *Chicago Tribune,* Mar. 27, 1904, 37. Berger notes that men had untrammeled access to female-only spaces in hotels. Berger, *Hotel Dreams,* 126–127.

39. "The Soda-Water Habit," 17.

40. "Carte du Jour," Congress Hotel, Chicago, Ill., June 20, 1907, Digital ID 472881, Buttolph Collection, Rare Books Division, New York Public Library Digital Gallery, New York; "Grand Opening of Berry's New Candy Store," *Chicago Tribune,* June 16, 1901, 10. For typical recipes, see, for example, Charles Ranhofer, *The Epicurean: A Complete Treatise of Analytical and Practical Studies on the Culinary Art* (New York: Hotel Monthly Press, 1894), 1000–1003.

41. "Flies to Her Head," 25.

42. "Bits of Local Color: Candy Stores that Retail Liquor," *Chicago Herald,* Mar. 5, 1893, 7; "Candy Stores Secure Liquor Licenses," *Chicago Tribune,* Mar. 5, 1893, 7.

43. See especially Benson, *Counter Cultures,* 82–87; Kasson, *Rudeness and Civility,* 228–256; Baldwin, *In the Watches of the Night,* 164–169. On similar strategies at hotels, see Berger, *Hotel Dreams,* 125–135.

44. Charles B. Maugham, "Chicago," *American Carpet and Upholstery Journal* 21 (Nov. 1903): 85; "Schlesinger & Mayer Building," *Architectural Record* 16 (July 1904): 63; "Phases of the World's Affairs: Chicago Snap Shots," *National Magazine* 15 (Mar. 1902): 663.

45. "'The Hofbrau' in Chicago," *Indoors and Out: The Homebuilders' Magazine* 1 (Jan. 1906): 195; Press Club of Chicago, *Official Reference Book: Press Club of Chicago* (Chicago: Press Club of Chicago, 1922), 198; "Hotel Bismarck Ladies

Café and Restaurant," 1904 postcard (from author's private collection), available at "Teaching the *Journal of American History*: 'Tippling Ladies and the Making of Consumer Culture,'" Organization of American Historians, last updated June 2015, https://jah.oah.org/teaching-the-jah/201506/exercise-1/.

46. Grandin, *Parisienne in Chicago*, 99.

47. "Grand Opening of Berry's New Candy Store," 10.

48. "Gunther's New Building," *Chicago Tribune*, May 15, 1887, 17.

49. Funderburg, *Sundae Best*, 39–40.

50. "The Soda Water Habit in Chicago," 29.

51. "Clerk Draws Color Line," *Chicago Tribune*, Nov. 5, 1905, 7; "Girl Who Refused to Serve Negro Woman Faces Court," *Chicago Tribune*, Nov. 10, 1905, 6; "Girl Held to Grand Jury for Drawing Color Line," *Chicago Tribune*, Nov. 11, 1905, 5; Merritt Starr and Russell Curtis, eds., *Annotated Statutes of the State of Illinois, Supplement Embracing Session Laws of 1885–1892* (Chicago: Callaghan, 1892), 344.

52. Harry Germaine, "Swell Women's Café," *Inter Ocean*, Dec. 1, 1895, 14.

53. Anita de Campi, "Why Shouldn't a Woman Have a Good Time Just Like the Men?," *Chicago Tribune*, Dec. 29, 1907, 49.

54. Bonnie Royal, "When the Frost Is on the Fountain and the Soda's in the Glass," *Chicago Tribune*, Aug. 8, 1909, 54.

55. "Drinking Women," *Chicago Tribune*, Mar. 11, 1871, 5; "Over Stimulation in Women," *New York Evening Post*, reprinted in *Chicago Tribune*, Jan. 26, 1879, 3; "Lush," *Chicago Tribune*, July 17, 1881, 7; "What a Woman Saw While in Europe," *Chicago Tribune*, Aug. 2, 1891, 9; "Tippling in High Life," *Chicago Tribune*, Oct. 8, 1892, 5; "Demon in Fair France," *Chicago Tribune*, Sept. 13, 1896, 47.

56. "Paris Boulevards," *Inter Ocean*, July 10, 1892, 21.

57. "Sampling Wine in Stores," *Chicago Tribune*, Jan. 23, 1897, 14.

58. "Do Society Women Swear?," *Chicago Tribune*, Jan. 6, 1907, 57. For more on moneyed women as consumers of cosmopolitanism, see Hoganson, *Consumers' Imperium*.

59. Dean, *White City Chips*, 113, 246. Dean also claimed to have observed two young women at the German Village persuade their mother to drink alcohol for the first time. Dean, *White City Chips*, 128–129.

60. Glessner Journal, June 30, 1893.

61. "Cocktail Habit among Women," *Inter Ocean*, Feb. 10, 1901, 36.

62. "Drinking Decreasing among Men, Increasing among Women," *Chicago Tribune*, Sept. 2, 1906, F3.

63. De Campi, "Why Shouldn't a Woman Have a Good Time Just Like the Men?," 49.

64. "Drinking Decreasing among Men, Increasing among Women," F3.

65. "Cocktail Habit among Women," 29.

66. On the Temperance Crusades, see Jack S. Blocker, *American Temperance Movements: Cycles of Reform* (Boston: Twayne, 1989). Richard H. Chused,

"Courts and Temperance 'Ladies,'" *Yale Journal of Law and Feminism* 21 (2010): 339–371.

67. "The First Gun," *Inter Ocean,* Mar. 1, 1874, 5.

68. For a work that addresses women's alcohol consumption at private events and at home in the late nineteenth century, see Murdock, *Domesticating Drink.*

69. W. J. Rorabaugh, *The Alcoholic Republic: An American Tradition* (New York: Oxford University Press, 1979), 42.

70. George Makepeace Towle, *American Society* (London: Chapman and Hall, 1870), 1:327.

71. Towle, *American Society,* 2:52–53.

72. For an account of drinking and socializing, see "New Years Day," *Chicago Tribune,* Jan. 3, 1870, 4. On New Year's Day visits and class making, see Beckert, *Monied Metropolis,* 44–45.

73. Elisabeth Marbury, *Manners: A Hand-Book of Social Customs* (Chicago: Westminster, 1888), 41–42.

74. M. E. W. Sherwood, *The Art of Entertaining* (New York: Dodd, Mead, 1893), 27–28.

75. Annie Randall White, *Polite Society at Home and Abroad* (Chicago: Monarch, 1891), 99.

76. Mrs. John Sherwood, *Manners and Social Usages* (New York: Harper and Brothers, 1887), 275.

77. Glessner Journal, Jan. 20, 1889.

78. Ralph, "Chicago's Gentle Side," 288–289; "Chicago's Gentle Side," *Chicago Tribune,* July 16, 1893, 12; "The Gentle Side of Chicago," *Chicago Tribune,* July 25, 1893, 4.

79. Warsh, "'Oh, Lord, Pour a Cordial in Her Wounded Heart,'" 73; Martha Meir Allen, *Alcohol: A Dangerous and Unnecessary Medicine* (Marcellus, N.Y.: National Woman's Christian Temperance Union, 1900), 153.

80. "A Wonderful Cure," *Inter Ocean,* July 9, 1886, 3.

81. "The Cure of Consumption," *Inter Ocean,* Mar. 18, 1888, 9.

82. According to the *Oxford English Dictionary,* a bracer was a drink taken to "brace one up." See *Oxford English Dictionary Online,* "bracer, n.1," accessed Dec. 7, 2018, http://www.oed.com.proxy.library.nd.edu/view/Entry/22387?rskey=4pQ4Tv&result=1. On women and invalidism, see Barbara Berg, *The Remembered Gate: Origins of American Feminism; The Woman and the City, 1800–1860* (New York: Oxford University Press, 1978), 120.

83. Warsh, "'Oh, Lord, Pour a Cordial in Her Wounded Heart,'" 71–73.

84. "Drinking," *Inter Ocean,* Dec. 26, 1874, 10.

85. J. Milner Fothergill, *The Practitioner's Handbook of Treatment,* 3rd ed. (Philadelphia: Lea, 1887), 249.

86. Amelia E. Barr, "Women and Alcohol," *Chicago Tribune,* Jan. 28, 1894, 38.

87. Helen Brown, "Drinking among Women and in Families," *Centennial Temperance Volume: A Memorial of the International Temperance Conference, held in*

Philadelphia, June, 1876 (New York: National Temperance Society and Publication House, 1877), 181.

88. Fothergill, *Practitioner's Handbook*, 249.

89. Warsh, "'Oh, Lord, Pour a Cordial in Her Wounded Heart,'" 72.

90. "Vegetable Compound," *Chicago Tribune*, Dec. 16, 1881, 11.

91. "Fashionable Society," *Chicago Tribune*, Mar. 2, 1890, 5.

92. "Can I Assist You, Madam?," *Inter Ocean*, Mar. 27, 1891, 2.

93. Brown, "Drinking among Women and in Families," 180.

94. Warsh, "'Oh, Lord, Pour a Cordial in Her Wounded Heart,'" 72–73.

95. Quoted in Allen, *Alcohol*, 324.

96. Edward Bok, "A Few Words to the W.C.T.U.," *Ladies' Home Journal*, Sept. 1904, 16.

97. Murdock, *Domesticating Drink*, 67.

98. Chaim M. Rosenberg, *Goods for Sale: Products and Advertising in the Massachusetts Industrial Age* (Amherst: University of Massachusetts Press, 2007), 112; Murdock, *Domesticating Drink*, 53.

99. Allen, *Alcohol*, 299–301.

100. Edward Bok, "The Patent-Medicine Curse," *Ladies' Home Journal*, May 1904, 18.

101. Carry Amelia Nation, *The Use and Need of the Life of Carry A. Nation*, rev. ed. (Topeka: F. M. Steves & Sons, 1909), ii, 133–134; Herbert Asbury, *Carrie Nation* (New York: Knopf, 1929), 87. For her statements in the Pompeian Room, see "Carrie Nation Scares Annex," *Chicago Tribune*, July 14, 1908, 1. The Congress Hotel was originally the Auditorium Annex. For more on Carrie Nation, see Fran Grace, *Carry A. Nation: Retelling the Life* (Bloomington: Indiana University Press, 2001).

102. "Sees a Serpent in Soda," *Chicago Tribune*, Apr. 16, 1897, 13; "One of King Alcohol's Latest Devices," *Union Signal*, Apr. 22, 1897, 1; "Live Topics of Today," *Chicago Tribune*, Apr. 17, 1897, 12.

103. "Drinking Women Should Be Ostracized," *Chicago Tribune*, Sept. 2, 1906, 53.

104. Deborah A. Skok, *More Than Neighbors: Catholic Settlements and Day Nurseries in Chicago, 1893–1930* (DeKalb: Northern Illinois University Press, 2007), 4–6. On Irish stereotypes, see Tyrrell, *Sobering Up*, 297–299.

105. Duis, *The Saloon*, 99, 104, 260.

106. John D. Buenker, "Edward Dunne: The Limits of Municipal Reform," in Green and Holli, *The Mayors*, 42–43.

107. "Be Not Rash with Thy Mouth," *Chicago Tribune*, Sept. 15, 1903, 6; "Clubs a Danger to Home," *Chicago Tribune*, Sept. 7, 1903, 9; "Wrathy Women Route a Critic," *Chicago Tribune*, Oct. 7, 1903, 1.

108. Flanagan, *Seeing with Their Hearts*, 57–59.

109. *The Elite Directory and Club List of Chicago* (Chicago: Elite, 1885); *The Chicago Blue Book of Selected Names of Chicago and Suburban Towns* (Chicago: Chicago Directory Company, 1905).

110. "Clubs a Danger to Home," 9.

111. "Wrathy Women Route a Critic," 1.

112. "News of Woman's Clubs," *Chicago Tribune,* Oct. 11, 1903, 39.

113. "Wrathy Women Route a Critic," 1; "Club Women Rout Methodist Pastor," *Inter Ocean,* Oct. 7, 1903, 3.

114. "One Woman Joins in Drink Crusade," *Chicago Tribune,* Sept. 17, 1907, 3.

115. "Dr. Leach and Woman's Clubs," *Chicago Daily News,* Sept. 9, 1903, 8.

116. See, for example, "Echoes of Chicago Pulpit," *Advance,* Oct. 5, 1905, 393; "Rabbi in Christian Pulpit," *Chicago Tribune,* May 4, 1908, 14; "Englewood Vice Blotch on City," *Chicago Tribune,* Sept. 20, 1909, 3.

117. "Drink and Gaming Curse to Women," 6.

118. "Hopkins Catches Women Drinking," *Inter Ocean,* Sept. 27, 1907, 1; "Women Who Drink Publicly," *Inter Ocean,* Sept. 28, 1907, 6; "Women Who 'Booze' Caught by Hopkins," 2.

119. Hale, "Do Women Drink?," 371.

120. "Drinking Women and the WCTU," *Inter Ocean,* Sept. 27, 1907, 6.

121. "Those Cocktail Women Again," *Inter Ocean,* Oct. 1, 1907, 6.

122. "More from Anna Freiheit," *Inter Ocean,* Oct. 4, 1907, 6; "The Noun, Verb, and the New Woman," *Inter Ocean,* Oct. 3, 1907, 6.

123. "More from Anna Freiheit," 6.

124. "Individualism Right for Women," *Chicago Tribune,* Sept. 18, 1907, 9.

125. "Rev. Frederick E. Hopkins," *Englewood Times,* Sept. 27, 1907, 5; "The Rev. Mr. Hopkins and Cocktails," *Inter Ocean,* Sept. 25, 1907, 6; "Dr. Hopkins and His Critics," *Inter Ocean,* Oct. 3, 1907, 6; "Reeling Woman Seen by Hopkins," 4; "Hits Women Critics in New 'Booze' Talk," *Chicago Record-Herald,* Sept. 16, 1907, 1; "Women Who 'Booze' Caught by Hopkins," 2.

126. Flanagan, *Seeing with Their Hearts,* 81–82.

127. "Hits Women Critics in New 'Booze' Talk," 1.

128. "Splashes W.C.T.U. with War Paint," *Chicago Tribune,* Sept. 24, 1907, 3.

129. "Do Chicago Women Drink Too Many Cocktails?," *Inter Ocean Magazine,* Sept. 15, 1907, 1; "Rev. Frederick E. Hopkins," 5; "New Blow at Women's Booze," *Chicago Tribune,* Sept. 16, 1907, 1; "One Woman Joins in Drink Crusade," 3; "New Blow at Women's Booze," 1.

130. Both Leach and Hopkins claimed that women drinkers were also smoking and gambling. See "Club Women Rout Methodist Pastor," 3; "Do Chicago Women Drink Too Many Cocktails?," 1.

131. De Campi, "Why Shouldn't a Woman Have a Good Time Just Like the Men?," 49.

132. Chopin, "A Pair of Silk Stockings," 192.

133. Agnes Surbridge, *The Confessions of a Club Woman* (New York: Doubleday, Page, 1904), 48.

134. "Wants 'No Liquor' for Wife," *Chicago Tribune,* Apr. 3, 1910, 3; "Drinking Habit Grows on Women Who Cannot Resist Lure of Café," *Chicago Tribune,* Apr. 10, 1910, 70. Third parties could only recover damages if they could show "injury to means of support." As such, these laws were used

chiefly by the wives of husbands killed, injured, or otherwise incapacitated owing to drink. See Parsons, "Risky Business," 283–307.

135. Madison Peters, "Drinking Custom Bane of Nation," *Chicago Tribune,* Jan. 23, 1910, E3; "Drinking Habit Grows," I3.

136. Michael A. Lerner, *Dry Manhattan: Prohibition in New York City* (Cambridge, Mass.: Harvard University Press, 2007), 197–198. See also Daniel Okrent, *Last Call: The Rise and Fall of Prohibition* (New York: Simon & Schuster, 2010).

137. "Women Who Drink Publicly," 6.

138. On consumer capitalism and the creation of new desires, see especially Leach, *Land of Desire,* xiii, 3–4, 36–37; Kevin Floyd, *The Reification of Desire: Toward a Queer Marxism* (Minneapolis: University of Minnesota Press, 2009), 41–42, 50–55, 62–63; John D'Emilio, "Capitalism and Gay Identity," in *Powers of Desire: The Politics of Sexuality,* ed. Ann Barr Snitow, Christine Stansell, and Sharon Thompson (New York: Monthly Review Press, 1983), 104–105.

5. Mashers, Prostitutes, and Shopping Ladies

1. "Leading Women Hope to Arouse Sentiment That Will Put an End to the Growing Evil," *Chicago Tribune,* Feb. 4, 1906, 33.

2. Mrs. W. C. H. Keough, "Hunting Women Is Favorite Sport of Chicago Men," *Chicago Tribune,* Feb. 11, 1906, 32.

3. For demands that the city take action, see, for example, "Police Are Flayed; Women Demand Aid," *Chicago Record-Herald,* Feb. 23, 1906, 1–2; "Women to Work for High License," *Chicago Tribune,* Feb. 24, 1906, 1; "Roused to Curb Crime Carnival," *Chicago Tribune,* Feb. 25, 1906, 1–2.

4. Laura Jean Libbey, "The Annoying Masher," *Chicago Tribune,* Mar. 3, 1911, 6.

5. "'Mashers' Out in Force," *Chicago Tribune,* Apr. 20, 1903, 3.

6. On Progressive reform and capitalist development, see, for example, Meg Jacobs, *Pocketbook Politics: Economic Citizenship in Twentieth-Century America* (Princeton, N.J.: Princeton University Press, 2005); Martin J. Sklar, *The Corporate Reconstruction of American Capitalism, 1890–1916: The Market, the Law, and Politics* (New York: Cambridge University Press, 1988).

7. Estelle Freedman, *Redefining Rape: Sexual Violence in the Era of Suffrage and Segregation* (Cambridge, Mass.: Harvard University Press, 2013), 191–211; Georgina Hickey, "From Civility to Self-Defense: Modern Advice to Women on the Privileges and Dangers of Public Space," *Women's Studies Quarterly* (Spring / Summer 2011): 77–94; Kerry Segrave, *Beware the Masher: Sexual Harassment in American Public Places, 1880–1930* (Jefferson, N.C.: McFarland, 2014). On street harassment in London, see Judith R. Walkowitz, "Going Public: Shopping, Street Harassment, and Streetwalking in Late Victorian London," *Representations* 62 (Spring 1998): 1–30.

8. Dreiser, *Sister Carrie,* 4.

9. *Oxford English Dictionary Online,* s.v. "mash (n. 4) and (adj)," accessed Feb. 15, 2018, http://www.oed.com.proxy.library.nd.edu/view/Entry/114583; Freedman, *Redefining Rape,* 191.

10. For usage data, see Google n-gram, available at https://books.google.com /ngrams/graph?content=masher&year_start=1800&year_end=2000&cor pus=15&smoothing=3&share=&direct_url=t1%3B%2Cmasher%3B% 2Cc0.

11. *Oxford English Dictionary Online,* s.v. "masher (n. 2)," accessed Feb. 15, 2018, http://www.oed.com.proxy.library.nd.edu/view/Entry/114595.

12. Freedman separates physical assault from mashing in her study, but her contemporaries did not always make this distinction. On the masher defined, see Freedman, *Redefining Rape,* 191–192. For use of the term "goo goo eyes," see, for example, "What Are 'Goo Goo Eyes,'" *Chicago Tribune,* June 28, 1902, 12.

13. On mashers and race, see Freedman, *Redefining Rape,* 196.

14. "Chief Collins on the Masher," *Chicago Tribune,* Feb. 4, 1906, 32.

15. Sigmund Krausz, *Street Types of Chicago—Character Studies* (Chicago: Max Stern, 1892), 10.

16. Dreiser, *Sister Carrie,* 4, 6.

17. "Chicago Women Tell How Mashers Make Walk on State Street a Fearful Ordeal," *Chicago Tribune,* Feb. 4, 1906, 33.

18. "Police Save Two Alleged Mashers from Heavy Punishment by State Street Crowd," *Inter Ocean,* Jan. 6, 1904, 1; "Appears against Alleged 'Mashers,'" *Chicago Tribune,* Jan. 7, 1904, 5.

19. "Street Masher a Hyena," *Chicago Tribune,* May 13, 1901, 1.

20. Freedman, *Redefining Rape,* 81, 206–207; Mary Odem, *Delinquent Daughters: Protecting and Policing Adolescent Female Sexuality in the United States, 1885–1920* (Chapel Hill: University of North Carolina Press, 1995), 32–33; Crystal N. Feimster, *Southern Horrors: Women and the Politics of Rape and Lynching* (Cambridge, Mass.: Harvard University Press, 2009), 164–165; Deborah Gray White, *Ar'n't I a Woman: Female Slaves in the Plantation South* (New York: Norton, 1985), 27–61.

21. On working-class courtship rituals and sexuality, see especially Peiss, *Cheap Amusements,* 88–114; Meyerowitz, *Women Adrift,* 101–104; Odem, *Delinquent Daughters,* 24–25, 43–44.

22. "The Matinee Masher," *Inter Ocean,* Sept. 23, 1880, 8.

23. Willa Sibert Cather, *Song of the Lark* (Boston: Houghton Mifflin, 1915), 200–201.

24. W. L. Bodine, "How the Board of Education Is Trying to Protect School Girls," *Chicago Tribune,* Jan. 27, 1907, 52.

25. "Police Aim to Check Mashers," *Chicago Tribune,* May 7, 1901, 5.

26. "To Drive the Mashers Out of Chicago," *Chicago Tribune,* Jan. 27, 1907, 52.

27. Jane Brown, "Mashers of All Ages Make State Street a Sea of Eyes," *Inter Ocean Magazine,* May 31, 1903, 1.

28. See, for example, "The Throngs of Visitors from Abroad," *Chicago Tribune*, May 26, 1882, 6; "Masher Falls into a Trap," *Inter Ocean*, Sept. 1, 1902, 12.
29. "Police Aim to Check Mashers," 1.
30. "Getting Rid of Mashers," *Chicago Tribune*, Mar. 6, 1906, 4.
31. "'Mashers' Out in Force," 3.
32. "The Kind of Man Who Mashes and How He Insults His Victims," *Chicago Tribune*, Feb. 4, 1906, 32.
33. Brown, "Mashers of All Ages," 2.
34. "Police Aim to Check Mashers," 1.
35. "The Kind of Man Who Mashes and How He Insults His Victims," 32.
36. "Police Aim to Check Mashers," 1.
37. Dreiser, *Sister Carrie*, 5.
38. See, for example, "'James the Pincher' Is Fined $26," *Chicago Tribune*, Aug. 27, 1896, 7; "Hairclipper Plies His Shears in a State Street Store," *Chicago Tribune*, July 10, 1898, 2.
39. "Chicago Women Tell How Mashers Make Walk on State Street a Fearful Ordeal," 33.
40. Brown, "Mashers of All Ages," 1–2.
41. Brown, 1.
42. "No More 'Dates' for This Husband," *Chicago Tribune*, Jan. 17, 1904, 31.
43. "Chicago Women Tell How Mashers Make Walk on State Street a Fearful Ordeal," 33.
44. "Shopkeepers in Strenuous Campaign against State Street 'Mashers,'" *Inter Ocean Magazine*, July 20, 1902, 5.
45. "The Kind of Man Who Mashes and How He Insults His Victims," 32. Several words in the quotation "There is not a merchant . . ." are not legible but can be inferred from context.
46. On "legitimate" theater, see Levine, *Highbrow/Lowbrow*, 76.
47. "Matinee Masher," 8.
48. William H. Busbey, "The Chicago Inter Ocean," in *Discovery and Conquests of the Northwest with the History of Chicago*, ed. Rufus Blanchard, vol. 2 (Chicago: R. Blanchard, 1900), 238–239; Green B. Raum, "William Penn Nixon," *History of Illinois Republicanism* (Chicago: Rollins, 1900), 291–294; "Mrs. E. D. Nixon Leader in Civic Activities, Dies," *Chicago Tribune*, Mar. 24, 1918, 15.
49. "Matinee Masher," 8.
50. "Mashers," *Inter Ocean*, Sept. 30, 1880, 3.
51. "Mashers," 3.
52. "The Matinee Masher: Some Observations as to Their Reappearance at Yesterday's Matinees," *Inter Ocean*, Oct. 14, 1880, 8.
53. "The Masher," *Inter Ocean*, Dec. 23, 1880, 7.
54. "Why You Should Vote To-Day," *Inter Ocean*, Apr. 5, 1881, 4.
55. "A Disgrace to the City," *Inter Ocean*, Apr. 10, 1878, 8.

56. "Corner Loafers—Ladies Insulted," *Chicago Tribune*, Sept. 12, 1880, 10.

57. "Down with the Mashers," *Chicago Tribune*, Apr. 24, 1881, 19; "'Mashers' Vagrants," *Inter Ocean*, Apr. 25, 1881, 6.

58. Editorial, *Inter Ocean*, Apr. 25, 1881, 4.

59. "The 'Mashers' Mashed," *Inter Ocean*, May 5, 1881, 8.

60. "The 'Mashers' Mashed," 8.

61. *Report of the General Superintendent of the City of Chicago to the City Council for the Fiscal Year Ending December 31, 1879* (Chicago: McCann & O'Brien Printers, 1880), 17; *Report of the General Superintendent of the City of Chicago to the City Council for the Fiscal Year Ending December 31, 1881* (Chicago: Geo. K. Hazlitt, 1882), 22.

62. Editorial, *Inter Ocean*, Oct. 25, 1882, 4.

63. "A Black Picture," *Inter Ocean*, Feb. 21, 1882, 4.

64. Editorial, *Inter Ocean*, May 16, 1887, 4.

65. "Managers Up in Arms," *Chicago Tribune*, Sept. 2, 1888, 14.

66. "Mysterious Murder," *Inter Ocean*, Jan. 17, 1884, 3; "Drugged and Outraged," *Inter Ocean*, Jan. 23, 1884, 6.

67. "Amelia Olsen," *Chicago Tribune*, Feb. 9, 1884, 8.

68. "Amelia Olsen," *Inter Ocean*, Feb. 9, 1884, 4.

69. "Managers Up in Arms," 14.

70. Wilson, "The Invisible Flâneur," 93.

71. Stead, *If Christ Came to Chicago*, 378.

72. Blair, *I've Got to Make My Livin'*, 27, 50–51, 125; Bachin, *Building the South Side*, 255–256; Chad Heap, *Slumming: Sexual and Racial Encounters in American Nightlife, 1885–1940* (Chicago: University of Chicago Press, 2008), 37–39, 108.

73. Clifton R. Wooldridge, *Hands Up! In the World of Crime* (Chicago: Police Publishing Company, 1901), 243, 245.

74. "Sounds the Levee's Doom," *Chicago Tribune*, May 13, 1901, 3.

75. "Where Levee and Business District Mingle," *Chicago Tribune*, May 26, 1901, 29.

76. "Driving Out the Levee," *Chicago Tribune*, May 26, 1901, 29.

77. Carter H. Harrison, *Growing Up with Chicago* (Chicago: Ralph Fletcher Seymour, 1944), 291.

78. "Cleaning Out the Levee Dives," *Chicago Record-Herald*, June 22, 1901, 14.

79. "Beats Bon Marche," *Inter Ocean*, Mar. 6, 1892, 3; "Siegel-Cooper & Co.," *Chicago Tribune*, Mar. 6, 1892, 40.

80. "A Great Store," *Inter Ocean*, Sept. 18, 1891, 2.

81. "Beats Bon Marche," 3.

82. "Great Store," 2.

83. "Beats Bon Marche," 3.

84. "Beats Bon Marche," 3.

85. On Tuckhorn's saloon, see "To Clean Out the Levee," *Inter Ocean*, June 21, 1901, 12.

86. "Driving Out the Levee," 29.

87. Harrison, *Growing Up with Chicago*, 259, 260. On Harrison's attitude toward vice, see Kantowicz, "Carter H. Harrison II," 22–23.

88. On Harrison as an economic and civic reformer, see Kantowicz, "Carter H. Harrison II," 21, 24–25.

89. "O'Neill Is New Chief," *Chicago Chronicle*, Apr. 30, 1901, 1; "Captain O'Neill Chief of Police," *Chicago Tribune*, Apr. 30, 1901, 1. On O'Neill's background, see "Seven in Police Race," *Chicago Chronicle*, Apr. 29, 1901, 3; "O'Neill Shocks His Men," *Chicago Record-Herald*, May 3, 1901, 2; "Kipley Vacates Chief's Office," *Chicago Tribune*, Apr. 24, 1901, 1–2; June Sawyers, "The Chicago Cop Who Sure Loved His Irish Tunes," *Chicago Tribune Magazine*, Dec. 7, 1986, 12.

90. "Chief-of-Police O'Neill Promises to Serve the Mayor and the People," *Chicago Tribune*, Apr. 30, 1901, 13.

91. "Opinions of Experts on the Real Estate Situation in Chicago," *Chicago Tribune*, Sept. 8, 1901, 29.

92. "Thieves Leaving for New York," *Chicago Tribune*, May 15, 1901, 3. Timothy Gilfoyle has shown that commercial growth—and rising real estate values—did indeed tend to drive prostitution into less developed neighborhoods. Timothy J. Gilfoyle, *City of Eros: New York City, Prostitution, and the Commercialization of Sex, 1790–1920* (New York: Norton, 1992), 199–202.

93. "To Clean Out the Levee," 12.

94. "Another Blow for Vice," *Chicago Record-Herald*, June 25, 1901; "To Clean Out the Levee," 12.

95. "Ousts Tuckhorn; Rosen Is Next," *Chicago Tribune*, June 21, 1901, 9.

96. "To Keep Women Out of Saloons," *Inter Ocean*, June 29, 1901, 3.

97. "Levee Crusade on in Earnest," *Chicago Tribune*, June 29, 1901, 1.

98. "'Levee' Bows to Law," *Chicago Chronicle*, July 6, 1901, 1.

99. "'Levee' Bows to Law," 1.

100. "Drive Women from Levee," *Chicago Chronicle*, Sept. 1, 1901, 1.

101. "Has a Woman a Right to Drink?," *Chicago Record-Herald*, May 15, 1901, 15.

102. "Woman a Right on Levee," *Chicago Tribune*, July 7, 1901, 3. For more of Palmer's Denver decision, see "Warning to Reformers," *Colorado Springs Weekly Gazette*, June 12, 1901, 6.

103. "'Levee' Bows to Law," 1.

104. "Women Leaving the Levee, Says the Chief of Police," *Chicago Tribune*, July 14, 1901, 8.

105. "Reduce Levee Time Limit," *Chicago Record-Herald*, July 6, 1901, 7.

106. *Report of the General Superintendent of the City of Chicago to the City Council for the Fiscal Year Ending December 31, 1901* (Chicago: Department of Police, 1902), 6.

107. Blair, *I've Got to Make My Livin'*, 129.

108. "Opinions of Experts on the Real Estate Situation in Chicago," 29. On Keebler, see Rev. E. D. Daniels, *A Twentieth Century History and Biographical Record of LaPorte County, Indiana* (Chicago: Lewis, 1904), 490–491.

109. "Says Lower State Street Has Future," *Chicago Tribune*, Aug. 21, 1904, 27.

110. "Realty Deals and News of the Day," *Inter Ocean*, Aug. 20, 1904, 10.

111. "Business and Factory Sities [*sic*]," *Inter Ocean*, Oct. 9, 1904, 26. On Friend, see Vladimir F. Wertsman, *Salute to the Romanian Jews in America and Canada, 1850–2010* (self-pub., Xlibris, 2010), 73–74.

112. "Realty Deals of Week Reviewed," *Inter Ocean*, July 9, 1905, 21–22.

113. "Whisky Row," *Chicago Tribune*, Aug. 20, 1907, 8.

114. See especially Mara L. Keire, *For Business and Pleasure: Red-Light Districts and the Regulation of Vice in the United States, 1890–1933* (Baltimore: Johns Hopkins University Press, 2010), 90–92; Blair, *I've Got to Make My Livin'*, 146–147.

115. "Suppress Lake View Mashers," *Chicago Tribune*, May 6, 1901, 1; "Police Aim to Check Mashers," 5.

116. "Police Aim to Check Mashers," 1.

117. "Police Aim to Check Mashers," 1, 5.

118. "Women Applaud War on Mashers," *Chicago Tribune*, May 8, 1901, 9.

119. *Chicago Journal* article, repr. as "Smash the Mashers: Chicago League to Be Formed to Suppress the Pests," *Topeka Daily Capital*, May 19, 1901, 19.

120. "Athletic Girls Banded Together and with the Assistance of Ten Thousand Young Men Go After Chicago Mashers," *Cincinnati Enquirer*, May 10, 1901, 8. See also "To Avenge Insults," *Indianapolis News*, May 10, 1901, 1.

121. "Intend to Thrash Mashers," *Inter Ocean*, May 10, 1901, 7.

122. "'Masher' Beats an Officer," *Chicago Tribune*, Aug. 16, 1897, 4; "Woe among Mashers," *Chicago Tribune*, Aug. 17, 1897, 10. See also "Loafers Ousted from Palmer House," *Chicago Tribune*, Aug. 11, 1897, 9.

123. "Getting Rid of Mashers," 4.

124. "Masher Falls into a Trap," 12.

125. "Police Aim to Check Mashers," 5.

126. "Chicago Women Tell How Mashers Make Walk on State Street a Fearful Ordeal," 33.

127. "Police Aim to Check Mashers," 5.

128. "Shopkeepers in Strenuous Campaign against State Street 'Mashers,'" 5.

129. "The Kind of Man Who Mashes and How He Insults His Victims," 32.

130. "Shopkeepers in Strenuous Campaign against State Street 'Mashers,'" 5.

131. "Shopkeepers in Strenuous Campaign against State Street 'Mashers,'" 5; "Declare War against the Mashers," *Inter Ocean*, Oct. 26, 1904, 1.

132. "Declare War against the Mashers," 1.

133. "Crusade against Mashers," *Concord Times*, Nov. 1, 1904, 1.

134. "Crusade against Mashers," *Charlotte News*, Oct. 27, 1904, 3; "Chicago's Crusade against Mashers," *Washington Times*, Oct. 27, 1904, 6; "War on Masher in Big Chicago Stores," *Minneapolis Journal*, Oct. 26, 1904, 1, quoting *New York Sun*.

135. "New Dry Goods Store to Open," *Chicago Tribune*, Oct. 22, 1898, 3; "David M. Hackman, Who Gave Edward Hillman Start, Dies," *Chicago Tribune*, Apr. 12, 1911, 13.

136. "Declare War against the Mashers," 1.
137. "Declare War against the Mashers," 1.
138. "Declare War against the Mashers," 1.
139. "Crusade against Mashers," *Concord Times,* 1.
140. *First Annual Report of the Protective Agency for Women and Children* (Chicago: Woman's Temperance Publication Association, 1887), 11–12; Elizabeth Pleck, *Domestic Tyranny: The Making of American Social Policy against Family Violence from Colonial Times to the Present* (1987; repr., Champaign: University of Illinois Press, 2004), 95–98; Freedman, *Redefining Rape,* 61–62.
141. "Urge War on 'Mashers,'" *Chicago Tribune,* Apr. 17, 1903, 13.
142. "'Mashers' Out in Force," 3.
143. "Shopkeepers in Strenuous Campaign against State Street 'Mashers,'" 5.
144. "Work of the Chicago Police," *Chicago Record-Herald,* May 22, 1901, 6.
145. "The Anti-Masher Crusade," *Chicago Chronicle,* May 16, 1901, 6.
146. Dr. J. Sanderson Christison, *The Tragedy of Chicago: A Study in Hypnotism* (Chicago: J. Sanderson Christison, [1906]), 10–11, 28–29; "Youth Confesses Hollister Murder; Relative Tries to Kill Prisoner," *Inter Ocean,* Jan. 14, 1906, 1; "Seized in the Street and Choked to Death," *New York Times,* Jan. 14, 1906, 3; "Strangled with Copper Wire," *San Francisco Chronicle,* Jan. 14, 1906, 31. For a brief discussion of Hollister and Chicago's mashing problem, see Freedman, *Redefining Rape,* 198–199.
147. "Join to Fight Crime in Streets of City," *Chicago Record-Herald,* Jan. 15, 1906, 4.
148. Christison, *The Tragedy of Chicago,* 3.
149. "Plan to Check Crime," *Chicago Record-Herald,* Jan. 17, 1906, 11. For other "crime wave" references, see, for example, "Join to Fight Crime in Streets of City," 1; "More Police Needed," *Chicago Chronicle,* Jan. 15, 1906, 3; "Stop to Crime Wave Is Plan of Citizens," *Chicago Record-Herald,* Jan. 18, 1906, 1; "Anti-Crime Wave Reaching Climax," *Chicago Tribune,* Feb. 26, 1906, 1.
150. "Police Are Flayed; Women Demand Aid," 2. On additional homicides, see "Terror Due to Murders," *Chicago Tribune,* Jan. 14, 1906, 3; "Murders Arouse City," *Washington Post,* Jan. 15, 1906, 1.
151. "Join to Fight Crime in Streets of City," 1, 4; "Citizens Demand 1,000 More Police to Protect Women," *Inter Ocean,* Jan. 15, 1906, 1; "Demand Police Protect Women," *Chicago Tribune,* Jan. 15, 1906, 1.
152. "Leading Women Hope to Arouse Sentiment," 33.
153. "What to Do with a Masher," *Inter Ocean,* June 7, 1906, 6.
154. Ralph Wilder, "Chicago's Foremost Duty," *Chicago Record-Herald,* Jan. 16, 1906, 1.
155. "Protection for Evanston Women," *Chicago Tribune,* Feb. 24, 1906, 2.
156. "Council Renews License Battle in War on Crime," *Chicago Tribune,* Feb. 27, 1906, 2.
157. "Crime Crusade Rouses Chicago," *Chicago Tribune,* Jan. 31, 1906, 1; "Healy in Crime Probe," *Chicago Record-Herald,* Jan. 31, 1906, 2.

158. "More Police Needed," 3.

159. *Report of the General Superintendent of Police of the City of Chicago to the City Council for the Fiscal Year Ending December 31, 1905* (Chicago: Department of Police, 1906), 9.

160. Based on *Report of the General Superintendent of Police of the City of Chicago to the City Council for the Fiscal Year Ending December 31, 1905,* 9; *Report of the General Superintendent of Police of the City of Chicago to the City Council for the Fiscal Year Ending December 31, 1899* (Chicago: Department of Police, 1900), 4; *Vital Statistics of the City of Chicago for the Years 1899 to 1903 Inclusive* (Chicago: Department of Health, 1904), 1.

161. "More Police Needed," 3.

162. "Join to Fight Crime in Streets of City," 1, 4.

163. "Join to Fight Crime in Streets of City," 4.

164. "Join to Fight Crime in Streets of City," 1, 4; "Citizens to End Murder Carnival," *Inter Ocean,* Jan. 14, 1906, 2.

165. "500 More Police as a Crime Cure," *Chicago Tribune,* Jan. 18, 1906, 1; "Council Favors High Saloon Tax," *Chicago Tribune,* Jan. 23, 1906, 3; "Higher License and Better Collection," *Chicago Record-Herald,* Jan. 22, 1906, 6; "Increase the Saloon License Fee," *Chicago Record-Herald,* Jan. 19, 1906, 8; "Council Gets Plan to Raise Drink Fee," *Chicago Record-Herald,* Jan. 23, 1906, 5.

166. On influence of saloon and liquor men in municipal politics, see especially Duis, *The Saloon;* Powers, *Faces along the Bar.*

167. "Women to Work for High License," 1; "Higher License Up Tonight," *Chicago Record-Herald,* Feb. 26, 1906, 2.

168. "Roused to Curb Crime Carnival," 1; "Pastors to Preach on Crime Today," *Inter Ocean,* Feb. 25, 1906, 3.

169. "Police Are Flayed; Women Demand Aid," 1–2; "Women's Clubs Are Active," *Chicago Record-Herald,* Feb. 24, 1906, 2. On Arché Club, see Jane Croly, *History of the Woman's Club Movement in America* (New York: Henry G. Allen, 1898), 376–378.

170. "Police Are Flayed; Women Demand Aid," 2.

171. "Leading Women Hope to Arouse Sentiment," 33.

172. "Hints to Defenseless Women," *Chicago Chronicle,* Jan. 23, 1906, 6; "Human Life Cheap in Unsafe Chicago: Women in Peril in Lawless City," *Minneapolis Journal,* Jan. 15, 1906, 1.

173. "'Reform' and Murder," *Chicago Chronicle,* Jan. 17, 1906, 6.

174. "Chicago's Dangerous Streets," *Chicago Chronicle,* Jan. 16, 1906, 6.

175. "Four Ways in Which Women May Protect Themselves from Holdups," *Chicago Chronicle,* Mar. 6, 1906, 4.

176. "Join to Fight Crime in Streets of City," 4.

177. Keough, "Hunting Women Is Favorite Sport of Chicago Men," 32.

178. "Leading Women Hope to Arouse Sentiment," 33.

179. Keough, "Hunting Women Is Favorite Sport of Chicago Men," 32.

180. "Chicago as Seen by Herself," *McClure's Magazine* 29, no. 1 (May 1907): 71.

181. "Citizens Demand 1,000 More Police to Protect Women," 1.

182. "For a Greater Chicago," *Chicago Tribune,* May 6, 1907, 8.

183. "Human Life Cheap in Unsafe Chicago: Women in Peril in Lawless City," 1.

184. "For a Greater Chicago," 8.

185. "Stop to Crime Wave Is Plan of Citizens," 7.

186. "For a Greater Chicago," 8

187. "Judges Urge High Fee," *Chicago Record-Herald,* Mar. 3, 1906, 9.

188. "Will Make Charges against Policemen," *Inter Ocean,* Jan. 19, 1906, 12.

189. "Move against Crime," *Chicago Chronicle,* Mar. 7, 1906, 5; "Chicago Stirred Up for Higher License," *Chicago Record-Herald,* Feb. 3, 1906, 3; "Sunday Closing and a $1,000 Fee Menace Saloons," *Chicago Tribune,* Feb. 4, 1906, 1–2.

190. "Saloon License Divides Council," *Chicago Tribune,* Feb. 3, 1906, 1–2; "Police Watchdogs Ordered to Watch," *Chicago Record-Herald,* Feb. 27, 1906, 1–2; "Council Renews License Battle in War on Crime," 1. The Commercial Association became the Chicago Association of Commerce in 1908.

191. "Urge Work for High License," *Chicago Tribune,* Feb. 25, 1906, 2. On Hibbard, Spencer, Bartlett & Co., see "Hibbard, Spencer, Bartlett & Co.," in Grossman, Keating, and Reiff, *Encyclopedia of Chicago,* 928.

192. "Council Adopts $1,000 License; Mayor to Sign," *Chicago Tribune,* Mar. 6, 1906, 1–2; "$1,000 Saloon Tax Passes Council by Vote of 40 to 28," *Inter Ocean,* Mar. 6, 1906, 1–2.

193. "$1,000 Bar License Triumphs," *Chicago Record-Herald,* Mar. 6, 1906, 1–2.

194. "Crowds Throng Council Room," *Chicago Tribune,* Mar. 6, 1906, 2.

195. "Mrs. Hollister as Sacrifice for City," *Chicago Record-Herald,* Jan. 29, 1906, 4.

196. *Report of the General Superintendent of the City of Chicago to the City Council for the Fiscal Year Ending December 31, 1906* (Chicago: Department of Police, 1907), 5.

197. "Crime Still Rules; Cry for Aid Grows," *Chicago Record-Herald,* Jan. 19, 1906, 4.

198. "Police Face Inquiry," *Chicago Chronicle,* Jan. 19, 1906, 4.

199. "Sees Better Chicago in Passage of Ordinance," *Inter Ocean,* Mar. 6, 1906, 2.

200. Buenker, "Edward Dunne," 43–44; Maureen Flanagan, "Fred A. Busse: A Silent Mayor in Turbulent Times," in Green and Holli, *The Mayors,* 52–53. For sample criticism, see "Anti-Crime Wave Reaching Climax," 1; No Title, *Chicago Tribune,* Feb. 24, 1906, 8.

201. Buenker, "Edward Dunne," 45.

202. "Busse Takes Oath as Chicago Mayor," *Inter Ocean,* Apr. 7, 1907, 3; "Three 'Mayors' Shy at Running Chicago," *Inter Ocean,* Apr. 8, 1907, 2; "Collins Praises New Police Chief," *Chicago Tribune,* Apr. 8, 1907, 4; "Tribute from a Friend," *Inter Ocean,* Apr. 10, 1907, 6.

203. "Will He Keep His Word?," *Belleville News-Democrat,* July 6, 1907, 4.

204. "Shippy Puts End to Slot Machines," *Chicago Tribune,* Apr. 20, 1907, 3; "If All Idlers Are Suspected," *Inter Ocean,* July 2, 1907, 6; "Don't Loaf; You May Be Picked Up as an Ordinary Vag Today," *Inter Ocean,* July 1, 1907, 4.

205. "Rock Pile to Stop Crime," *Chicago Tribune,* Apr. 23, 1907, 1; "Don't Loaf; You May Be Picked Up as an Ordinary Vag Today," 4.

206. "Will He Keep His Word?," 4.

207. *Report of the General Superintendent of the City of Chicago to the City Council for the Fiscal Year Ending December 31, 1908* (Chicago: Department of Police, 1909), 37.

208. "War on Curbstone Masher," *Chicago Tribune,* May 23, 1909, 59; "Shop Girls Unite in Crusade Waged against Mashers," *Los Angeles Herald,* May 21, 1909, 10; "Object to Street 'Johnnies,'" *Salina Daily Union,* May 22, 1909, 2.

209. "Beware the Steely Glint in Eye of Girl You Ogle," *Chicago Tribune,* Sept. 16, 1916, 15.

210. "What to Do with a Masher," 6.

6. The Traffic of Women

1. "Women Give 'Civics Lunch,'" *Chicago Tribune,* Mar. 3, 1908, 5; "Clubs and Societies," *Chicago Daily News,* Mar. 9, 1908, 14; "Powder Puff Is Losing," *Chicago Daily News,* Mar. 10, 1908, 4; "Urges Shopping Time Limit," *Chicago Tribune,* Mar. 11, 1908, 9; "A Shopping Time Limit," *Chicago Tribune,* Mar. 15, 1908, G4.

2. "Plan a Shoppers' Paradise," *Chicago Tribune,* May 19, 1904, 12.

3. See especially Ryan, *Women in Public;* Stansell, *City of Women;* Peiss, *Cheap Amusements;* Meyerowitz, *Women Adrift;* Hunter, *To 'Joy My Freedom;* Lauren Rabinovitz, *For the Love of Pleasure: Women, Movies, and Turn-of-the-Century Chicago* (Camden, N.J.: Rutgers University Press, 1998).

4. On Chicago's significance to modern urban planning and the City Beautiful movement, see especially Smith, *Plan of Chicago,* 15–19.

5. John F. McDonald, *Chicago: An Economic History* (New York: Routledge, 2016), 32; Miller, *City of the Century,* 266; Mayer and Wade, *Chicago,* 128–132; Spain, *How Women Saved the City,* 210–211.

6. "Housekeeping in Chicago," *Harper's Bazaar,* June 18, 1892, 494.

7. Marvin A. Farr, "Sees Peril to City in Loop's Congestion," *Chicago Tribune,* Jan. 17, 1904, 34. On Farr, see Currey, *Chicago,* 4:37–38.

8. George E. Hooker, "Congestion and Its Causes," in *Proceedings of the Second National Conference on City Planning and the Problems of Congestion, Rochester, New York, May 2–4, 1910* (Boston: University Press, 1910), 42, 47.

9. "Traction Buncombe," *Inter Ocean,* Feb. 3, 1902, 6.

10. Board of Supervising Engineers, *Ninth Annual Report of the Board of Supervising Engineers: Chicago Traction Covering the Fiscal Year Ended January 31, 1916* (Chicago: Board of Supervising Engineers, 1918), 158.

11. Hoyt, *One Hundred Years of Land Values in Chicago,* 181–183, 208–210; Borzo, *Chicago Cable Cars,* 84–88; Greg Borzo, *The Chicago 'L'* (Charleston: Arcadia, 2007), 55.

12. "State St., World's Greatest Mart, Shows Amazing Growth," *Chicago Sunday Examiner,* Nov. 6, 1910, 40.

13. Hoyt, *One Hundred Years of Land Values in Chicago,* 172; Brigid Sweeney, "Can You Guess How Many People Walk Down State Street in a Week?," *Crain's Chicago Business,* Mar. 3, 2016, www.chicagobusiness.com/article/20160303 /NEWS07/160309955/can-you-guess-how-many-people-walk-down-state -street-in-a-week.

14. Fuller, *The Cliff Dwellers,* 1–2.

15. "State Street on a Busy Day," 1911 Postcard, Suhling Company, Chicago, Author's Private Collection.

16. William Archer, *America To-Day: Observations and Reflections* (London: William Heinemann, 1900), 90.

17. Paul Barrett, *The Automobile and Urban Transit: The Formation of Public Policy in Chicago, 1900–1930* (Chicago: Temple University Press, 1983), 15, 25.

18. See Chapter 1 for more on Frances Glessner's use of public transit.

19. Annette Reid, "English Woman's Shopping Unlike Chicagoan's," *Chicago Tribune,* Jan. 30, 1910, H7.

20. Thomas Johnson, *Chicago: A Satire* (Ann Arbor: Inland Press, 1901), 7–8.

21. "Nuisances Chicago People Endure with More or Less Patience," *Chicago Tribune,* Apr. 13, 1902, 71.

22. "Accidents Due to 'Rubbernecking,'" *Chicago Tribune,* Oct. 12, 1902, 46.

23. "Woman's Shopping Mania," *Inter Ocean,* June 15, 1902, 46.

24. "High Buildings in Chicago," *Chicago Tribune,* Feb. 6, 1902, 12.

25. Mona Domosh, *Invented Cities: The Creation of Landscape in Nineteenth-Century New York* (New Haven, Conn.: Yale University Press, 1998), 57–58; Edwin G. Burrows and Mike Wallace, *Gotham: A History of New York City to 1898* (New York: Oxford University Press, 1999), 668.

26. Siry, *Carson Pirie Scott,* 146–147; Thomas J. Misa, *Leonardo to the Internet: Technology and Culture from the Renaissance to the Present* (Baltimore: John Hopkins University Press, 2013), 163–167; Leach, *Land of Desire,* 61–64; Leach, "Transformations in a Culture of Consumption," 325; Peter Bacon Hales, "Grid, Regulation, Desire Line: Contests over Civic Space in Chicago," in *Public Space and the Ideology of Place in American Culture,* ed. Miles Orvell and Jeffrey L. Meikle (Amsterdam: Rodopi, 2009), 174–175.

27. Dreiser, *Sister Carrie,* 17, 75.

28. Leach, *Land of Desire,* 55–56, 64–67; Leach, "Transformations in a Culture of Consumption," 323. See also Abelson, *When Ladies Go A-Thieving,* 71– 73; Whitaker, *Service and Style,* 110–111.

29. Leach, *Land of Desire,* 59–60.

30. Leach, 67–70; Abelson, *When Ladies Go A-Thieving,* 71.

31. "Studied Carelessness," *Dry Goods Reporter,* May 16, 1903, 21.

32. See, for example, "Commercial, Psychological and Social Elements of Advertising as a Service Acquiring the Status of a Science," *Chicago Commerce* 8 (May 10, 1912): 27; "Chicago's Loop Is the Busiest Spot on Earth," *Chicago Tribune,* Apr. 28, 1907, 50; "Congested Loop Immensely Rich," *Chicago Tribune,* Nov. 30, 1910, 33; Gordon Seagrove, "Window Shopping at Its Height," *Chicago Tribune,* Dec. 4, 1910, H8.

33. John Thorpe, "Shop Windows Educators; State Street a Vast Museum," *Chicago Tribune,* Sept. 9, 1906, 45.

34. Schick, *Chicago and Its Environs,* 101.

35. L. Frank Baum, "The Window Gazer," *Show Window* 1 (Nov. 1897): 1.

36. "Keep to the Right," *Chicago Tribune,* Dec. 10, 1905, 16.

37. Thorpe, "Shop Windows Educators; State Street a Vast Museum," 45.

38. George Ade, *Artie: A Story of the Streets and Town* (Chicago: Herbert S. Stone, 1896), 61.

39. C. S. R., "State Street Pedestrianism: Her Line of March," *Chicago Tribune,* June 18, 1903, 12.

40. "Judge Scores Women Who Collide with Men in Rush for Bargains," *Inter Ocean,* Dec. 22, 1907, 8

41. Schick, *Chicago and Its Environs,* 103.

42. Reid, "English Woman's Shopping Unlike Chicagoan's," H7.

43. Fuller, *With the Procession,* 147.

44. "Marshall Field's Great Store and the Masonic Temple," 1909, LC-USZ62-51792, Prints and Photographs Division, Library of Congress, Washington, D.C.

45. "Christmas Shoppers, Women with Young Children in Their Arms Walking on the Sidewalk in Front of Marshall Field's Department Store on State Street," 1905, DN-0002541, Chicago Daily News Negatives Collection, Chicago History Museum, Chicago, Ill.

46. "Christmas Shoppers Including Three Women, Two Carrying Packages, Walking on a Sidewalk in Downtown Chicago," 1905, DN-0002549, Chicago Daily News Negatives Collection, Chicago History Museum, Chicago, Ill.

47. John A. Howland, "The Selfishness of Women in Public," *Chicago Tribune,* Aug. 28, 1904, 25.

48. C. S. R., "State Street Pedestrianism: Her Line of March," 12.

49. C. S. R., "State Street Pedestrianism: His Line of March," *Chicago Tribune,* June 24, 1903, 6.

50. Eliza Leslie, *Miss Leslie's Behaviour Book: A Guide and Manual for Ladies* (Philadelphia: T. B. Peterson and Brothers, 1859), 17, 83.

51. "Women Shopping," *Woman's Journal,* Apr. 26, 1873, 135.

52. "Through the Mails," *Inter Ocean,* Feb. 5, 1893, 36.

53. Leach, "Transformations in a Culture of Consumption," 325–326, 329–331; Leach, *Land of Desire,* 142–152; Benson, *Counter Cultures,* 82–85; Abelson, *When Ladies Go A-Thieving,* 54–59; Whitaker, *Service and Style,* 219–227.

54. "Retailing on State Street," *Dry Goods Reporter,* Apr. 23, 1904, 17.

55. "City Stores Sell Mud," *Dry Goods Reporter*, May 28, 1904, 24.

56. Leach, "Transformations in a Culture of Consumption," 323–325; Leach, *Land of Desire*, 74–90, 101–111; Whitaker, *Service and Style*, 131–158.

57. Grandin, *Parisienne in Chicago*, 97.

58. Thomas Wakefield Goodspeed, *The University of Chicago Biographical Sketches*, vol. 1 (Chicago: University of Chicago Press, 1922), 28.

59. George L. Lewis, "Making One Store Purchase Sell Another," *Sales Management* (1914; repr., Chicago: A. W. Shaw, 1917), 200. Quoted in Benson, *Counter Cultures*, 83.

60. Delia Austrian, "American Retail Store Leads; New Ideas Slow in Europe," *Chicago Tribune*, Feb. 2, 1908, C5.

61. "The Glory of Modern Shops," *Chicago Tribune*, Aug. 24, 1902, 18; "Fads and Fancies in Fashion's Realm," *Theater* 16 (Dec. 1912): xxvii; "Shopping and Showing," *Every Where* 26 (July 1910): 286; Blanche McManus, "The Economies of the French Housekeeper," *American Cookery* 11 (Apr. 1917): 670.

62. Reid, "English Woman's Shopping Unlike Chicagoan's," H7.

63. Veblen, *Theory of the Leisure Class*, esp. 35–67.

64. "Enormous Loss of Time by Congested Street Crossing," *Chicago Tribune*, Oct. 5, 1902, 45.

65. Mira L. Cobbe, "Against Shoppers," *Inter Ocean*, Jan. 6, 1894, 9.

66. Ellen Martin Henrotin, "The Ethics of Shopping," Nov. 6, 1908, folder 13, Ellen Martin Henrotin Papers, Schlesinger Library, Radcliffe Institute, Harvard University, Cambridge, Mass.

67. Lewis, "Making One Store Purchase Sell Another," 200.

68. "People Who Shop," *Woman's Home Companion* 25 (July 1908): 21.

69. Werrett Wallace Charters, *How to Sell at Retail* (Boston: Houghton Mifflin, 1922), 65.

70. "What a 'Looker' Means," *Inter Ocean*, Dec. 15, 1889, 3.

71. "Saunters through the Shops," *Chicago Tribune*, Dec. 11, 1899, 6; Charters, *How to Sell at Retail*, 30.

72. "State Street on a Busy Day," *Chicago Tribune*, May 2, 1897, 53.

73. Helen Gale, "Decrees of Fashion," *Inter Ocean*, Apr. 16, 1893, 27.

74. "Nuisances Chicago People Endure with More or Less Patience," 71.

75. "Enormous Loss of Time by Congested Street Crossing," 45.

76. Charles H. Wacker, prefatory note in *Creating a World Famous Street: Argument of Charles H. Wacker, Chairman of the Chicago Plan Commission, in behalf of widening and extending Michigan Avenue to Properly Connect the North and South Sides of Chicago; with Ordinance for Same, Detailed Drawings and Estimate of Cost as Prepared by the Board of Local Improvements of the City of Chicago* (Chicago: J. F. Higgins, 1913), iii.

77. "Relieving the Congestion," *Chicago Tribune*, Apr. 4, 1907, 8.

78. "State Street Improvement Association," *Dry Goods Reporter*, May 28, 1904, 13; "Model Street Is Aim," *Chicago Record-Herald*, May 18, 1904, 9; "Plan a

Model Street," *Chicago Tribune*, May 18, 1904, 1; "Plan a Shoppers' Paradise," 12.

79. "Asphalt for State Street," *Chicago Daily News*, May 23, 1904, 2; "Fine Road Is Assured," *Chicago Tribune*, May 25, 1904, 6. There was some dispute over cost. The *Daily News* estimated $50,000, while the *Chicago Tribune* put the number at $40,000.

80. For more on the advantages of asphalt, see Barrett, *Automobile and Urban Transit*, 51, 53–56; Clay McShane, *Down the Asphalt Path: The Automobile and the American City* (New York: Columbia University Press, 1994), 61, 109.

81. E. J. Hallock, "American and Foreign Asphalts," *Popular Science Monthly* 22 (Dec. 1882): 193; Thomas D. Weber, "Up to Date Horse Shoeing," *Chicago Tribune*, July 31, 1904, 11. For more on asphalt and horses, see Clay McShane, "Transforming the Use of Urban Space: A Look at the Revolution in Street Pavements, 1880–1924," *Journal of Urban History* 5 (May 1979): 279–307; Chris Otter, *The Victorian Eye: A Political History of Light and Vision in Britain, 1800–1910* (Chicago: University of Chicago Press, 2008), 92–96.

82. "Oppose Asphalt Pavements," *Chicago Tribune*, Jan. 6, 1903, 1.

83. John W. Alvord, *A Report to the Street Paving Committee of the Commercial Club on the Street Paving Problem of Chicago* (Chicago: R. R. Donnelley & Sons, 1904), 20, 18.

84. Barrett, *Automobile and Urban Transit*, 53–54.

85. "Would End Wild Driving," *Chicago Tribune*, Nov. 6, 1903, 10.

86. "Public Welcomes State St. Change," *Inter Ocean*, May 19, 1904, 7.

87. "See Larger Shopping Area," *Chicago Tribune*, Dec. 16, 1906, 10.

88. "Urge Boulevard in State Street," *Chicago Tribune*, Dec. 15, 1906, 5.

89. On Stumer's background, see Herbert E. Fleming, "The Literary Interests of Chicago: VI and VII," *American Journal of Sociology* 12 (July 1906): 89.

90. "Urge Boulevard in State Street," 5.

91. "Propose to Change State Street into a Boulevard," *Chicago Tribune*, Dec. 14, 1906, 4. See also "Street Change Is Aim," *Chicago Record-Herald*, Dec. 14, 1906, 5.

92. Bluestone, *Constructing Chicago*, 30–32, 35; Barrett, *Automobile and Urban Transit*, 51.

93. James Langland, *The Chicago Daily News Almanac and Year-Book for 1910* (Chicago: Chicago Daily News, 1909), 503–505; Andreas Simon, *Chicago, the Garden City: Its Magnificent Parks, Boulevards and Cemeteries* (Chicago: F. Gindele Printing, 1893), 56; *Report of the South Park Commissioners to the Board of County Commissioners of Cook County from December 1st, 1895, to December 1st, 1896* (Chicago: Cameron, Amberg, 1897), 6.

94. "Street Change Is Aim," 5; "State Street a Boulevard, Is War Cry of Merchants," *Inter Ocean*, Dec. 14, 1906, 7.

95. "Propose to Change State Street into a Boulevard," 4; "Street Change Is Aim," 5; "Better State Street," *Chicago Daily News*, Dec. 15, 1906, 2.

96. "See Larger Shopping Area," 10.

97. "State Street a Boulevard, Is War Cry of Merchants," 7.

98. Chicago Plan Commission, *Chicago's Greatest Issue: An Official Plan* (Chicago: Chicago Plan Commission, 1911), 55–56.

99. "'Show Street' Is Aim," *Chicago Record-Herald,* Dec. 15, 1906, 7; "Better State Street," 2.

100. "'Show Street' Is Aim," 7.

101. "Boulevard Plan Strikes a Snag," *Chicago Tribune,* Dec. 19, 1906, 8.

102. "Business Men in Protest," *Chicago Tribune,* Jan. 5, 1907, 2. For biographical background, see especially Albert Nelson Marquis, *The Book of Chicagoans: A Biographical Dictionary of Leading Living Men of the City of Chicago* (Chicago: A. N. Marquis, 1911).

103. "Boulevard Plan Strikes a Snag," 8.

104. "State Street Boulevard Plan Will Go to Council," *Chicago Tribune,* Jan. 27, 1907, 8; "To Fight Boulevard Plan," *Chicago Tribune,* Dec. 20, 1906, 9.

105. "Oppose Boulevard in State," *Chicago Record-Herald,* Dec. 21, 1906, 12.

106. "Condemns Plan for Boulevard," *Chicago Tribune,* Jan. 6, 1907, A5.

107. "More Warm Cars Win Aldermen," *Chicago Tribune,* Nov. 2, 1905, 7.

108. "Neither State nor LaSalle," *Chicago Tribune,* Jan. 30, 1907, 8.

109. "South Park Board Refuses to Talk State Street Boulevard," *Chicago Tribune,* Jan. 17, 1907, 16; "State Street Boulevard Plan Will Go to Council," 8; "16 'Link' Plans in Hand," *Chicago Tribune,* Jan. 29, 1907, 9.

110. "Members of the Chicago Real Estate Board," *Call Board Bulletin* 17 (Feb. 1908): 69–71; Pierce, *History of Chicago,* 207–208.

111. Chicago Real Estate Board, Regularly Monthly Meeting, *Call Board Bulletin* 17 (Feb. 1908): 67–68.

112. "To Oppose Loop Plans," *Chicago Record-Herald,* Feb. 6, 1908, 11.

113. "Jolts the Women Shoppers," *Chicago Tribune,* Feb. 6, 1908, 1.

114. "Chicago Man Takes Up Old Problem of Shopper and Toiler," *Los Angeles Herald,* Feb. 7, 1908, 1; "Regulating Shoppers," *Pittsburgh Post-Gazette,* Feb. 7, 1908, 4; "Women Shoppers," *Detroit Free Press,* Feb. 8, 1908, 4; "A Fruitless Task," *Benton Harbor News-Palladium,* Feb. 6, 1908, 2; "Chicago Man's Huge Task," *Asbury Park Press,* Feb. 12, 1908, 8.

115. "Regulation of Street Traffic," *Chicago Commerce* 5 (Dec. 31, 1909): 10.

116. Barrett, *Automobile and Urban Transit,* 55.

117. "Jolts the Women Shoppers," 1. See also "Blames Shoppers for Loop Crowding," *Chicago Examiner,* Feb. 6, 1908, 5.

118. "Shopping Eden Aim of Woman," *Wichita Daily Eagle,* Mar. 31, 1908, 9.

119. "Jolts the Women Shoppers," 1. For biographical information on Mills, see "Lincoln Club Names Leader," *Inter Ocean,* Apr. 9, 1905, 3; "Death of Well-Known Real Estate Operator," *Inter Ocean,* Apr. 26, 1914, 10; "Obituary," *Chicago Tribune,* Apr. 23, 1914, 14.

120. "Blames Shoppers for Loop Crowding," 5.

121. "W. D. Moody to Boom Chicago," *Chicago Tribune,* Dec. 1, 1907, E4.

122. "How Commerce Founds and Frames the World's Greatest Cities," *Chicago Commerce* 5 (Oct. 15, 1909): 22.

123. "Hub of All Industry, Future for Chicago," *Chicago Daily News*, Feb. 5, 1908, 1; "Chicago Industry Hub, Declare Business Men," *Chicago Record-Herald*, Feb. 6, 1908, 3.

124. For more on the CAC, see Currey, *Chicago*, 3:360–365.

125. On the rewards of circulation, see Daniel M. Bluestone, "'The Pushcart Evil': Peddlers, Merchants, and New York City's Streets, 1890–1940," *Journal of Urban History* 18 (Nov. 1991): 76.

126. For an autobiographical sketch, see Walter D. Moody, *Men Who Sell Things: Observations and Experiences of over Twenty Years as Travelling Salesman, European Buyer, Sales Manager, Employer* (Chicago: A. C. McClurg, 1907). See also "Walter Moody of City Plan Fame Is Dead," *Chicago Tribune*, Nov. 22, 1920, 17.

127. Moody, *Men Who Sell Things*, 240.

128. Report reprinted in George E. Plumbe, "Visit to the Land of Promise," *Chicago: The Great Central Market* 4 (July 1907): 83.

129. "Moody Asks Women to Take Up Fight for Subways," *Chicago Examiner*, Mar. 11, 1908, 2.

130. "Powder Puff Is Losing," 4.

131. "Moody Asks Women to Take Up Fight for Subways," 2.

132. "A Shopping Time Limit," G4.

133. For more on the NCL and the various state leagues, see Sklar, *Florence Kelley*, 306–315; Storrs, *Civilizing Capitalism*, esp. 20; Cecelia Tichi, *Civic Passions: Seven Who Launched Progressive America (and What They Teach Us)* (Chapel Hill: University of North Carolina Press, 2009), 140–163.

134. See, for example, Henrotin, "The Ethics of Shopping"; "Shop Early to Spare Clerk," *Chicago Tribune*, Nov. 29, 1908, 1; "Early Christmas Shopping," *Chicago Tribune*, Dec. 1, 1908, 10.

135. "News of Women's Clubs," *Chicago Tribune*, Dec. 25, 1898, 32. For more biographical information on Henrotin, see James, James, and Boyer, *Notable American Women*, 2:181–182.

136. "Woman as the Consumer," *Chicago Tribune*, Feb. 21, 1899, 8; "Talk on Holiday Buying," *Chicago Tribune*, Dec. 11, 1899, 7; "News of Women's Clubs," 32.

137. "City Home of 'Ungallant,'" *Chicago Tribune*, Feb. 7, 1908, 9.

138. "City Home of 'Ungallant,'" 9.

139. "This Will Detain Chicago Men for a Moment!," *Oakland Tribune*, Feb. 19, 1908, 7.

140. "Regulating Shoppers," 4.

141. "Shopping Eden Aim of Woman," 9. For biographical information, see 1900 United States Federal Census, Chicago Ward 18, Cook, Illinois, Ferdinand Batcher household, digital image, accessed Aug. 1, 2017, Ancestry .com; *Hull-House Year Book, 1905–1906* (Chicago, 1906), 17.

142. "Asks a Shoppers' Paradise," *Chicago Tribune*, Mar. 19, 1908, 1.

143. "Shopping Eden Aim of Woman," 9.

144. "State Street Shoppers' Paradise When Vehicles Are Barred," *Chicago Tribune,* Mar. 20, 1908, 1.

145. "Making a City Draw," *Chicago Commerce* 4 (May 15, 1908): 4.

146. "Problems in Street Traffic," *Chicago Commerce* 8 (Nov. 29, 1912): 6.

147. John Jacob Glessner, *The Commercial Club of Chicago: Its Beginning and Something of Its Work* (Chicago: privately printed, 1910), 14, 203.

148. Pierce, *A History of Chicago,* 190. In 1907, the Commercial Club absorbed the Merchants Club, which had been organized along the same lines but had a membership that was intentionally younger, with only men under forty-five eligible for inclusion. For more on the Commercial Club, see Smith, *Plan of Chicago,* 64–65.

149. For information on membership, see *The Commercial Club of Chicago: Year-Book 1911–1912* (Chicago: Executive Committee, 1912), 23–25.

150. Daniel H. Burnham and Edward H. Bennett, *The Plan of Chicago* (Chicago: Commercial Club, 1909), 1.

151. Burnham and Bennett, 98–99.

152. Burnham and Bennett, 68.

153. Burnham and Bennett, 63–64.

154. Burnham and Bennett, 65.

155. Walter D. Moody, *Wacker's Manual of the Plan of Chicago* (Chicago: Henneberry, 1911), 102; Burnham and Bennett, *Plan of Chicago,* 74, 102–103, 105.

156. Burnham and Bennett, *Plan of Chicago,* 101.

157. Burnham and Bennett, 83.

158. Burnham and Bennett, 102–103.

159. Burnham and Bennett, 106.

160. Smith, *Plan of Chicago,* 119, 122, 132–133.

161. Smith, 133.

Conclusion

1. Sarah Bernhardt, *My Double Life: Memoirs of Sarah Bernhardt* (London: William Heinemann, 1907), 385, 372, 399, 402, 417, 400.

2. Frederick, *Selling Mrs. Consumer,* 12, 43.

3. See, for example, Walter Friedman, *Birth of a Salesman: The Transformation of Selling in America* (Cambridge, Mass.: Harvard University Press, 2004), 190–224; Katherine J. Parkin, *Food Is Love: Food Advertising and Gender Roles in Modern America* (Philadelphia: University of Pennsylvania Press, 2006), 12–29; Davis, *Living Up to the Ads,* 80–104; Jennifer Scanlon, *Inarticulate Longings,* 169–196.

4. On the value of women's traffic in commercial real estate, see Isenberg, *Downtown America,* 78–123.

5. Spear, *Black Chicago,* 12.

6. On reasons for migration to Chicago, see Chicago Commission on Race Relations, *The Negro in Chicago: A Study of Race Relations and a Race Riot* (Chicago:

University of Chicago Press, 1922), 79–88; Grossman, *Land of Hope,* 66–97; Spear, *Black Chicago,* 140–146; James Grossman, "Great Migration," in Grossman, Keating, and Reiff, *Encyclopedia of Chicago,* 363–364.

7. Spear, *Black Chicago,* 12; Grossman, "Great Migration," 363–364.

8. Grossman, *Land of Hope,* 178–180; Andrew J. Diamond, *Mean Streets: Chicago Youths and the Everyday Struggle for Empowerment in the Multiracial City, 1908–1969* (Berkeley: University of California Press, 2009), 19–26, 47–49; Dominic A. Pacyga, "Chicago's 1919 Race Riot: Ethnicity, Class, and Urban Violence," in *The Making of Urban America,* ed. Raymond A. Mohl, 2nd ed. (London: SR Books, 1997), 187–196.

9. "Marshall Field's Drawing Color Line," *Chicago Defender,* June 10, 1916, 5.

10. Nella Larsen, *Passing* (New York: Alfred A. Knopf, 1929), 19.

11. African American women and girls concentrated their consumer spending in black commercial districts on Chicago's South Side. See especially Marcia Chatelain, *South Side Girls: Growing Up in the Great Migration* (Durham, N.C.: Duke University Press, 2015), 68–70.

12. Jens Jensen, "Regulating City Building," *Survey* 27 (Nov. 18, 1911): 1204. For more on Jensen's critique of the Chicago Planning Commission, see Samuel Kling, "Regional Plans and Regional Plants: Jens Jensen's Vernacular Landscape and Metropolitan Planning in Chicago, 1904–1920," *Journal of Urban History* 44 (Nov. 2018): 1154–1175.

13. In *Downtown America,* Isenberg shows that exclusion was an important theme of downtown development in the twentieth century. See Isenberg, *Downtown America,* 4–6.

14. On the dramatic rise of car ownership in Chicago between 1915 and 1925, see Barrett, *Automobile and Urban Transit,* 130.

15. On the development of suburban retail in the 1920s, see especially Richard Longstreth, *City Center to Regional Mall: Architecture, the Automobile, and Retailing in Los Angeles, 1920–1950* (Cambridge: MIT Press, 1997), 57–59, 116; Howard, *From Main Street to Mall,* 133–138.

16. Frederick, *Selling Mrs. Consumer,* 311–312.

17. "Marshall Field Opens Store for Oak Park Area," *Chicago Tribune,* Oct. 20, 1929, 67.

18. On branch stores as forerunners to shopping centers, see especially Longstreth, *City Center to Regional Mall;* Howard, *From Main Street to Mall.*

19. On the segmentation of consumption in the postwar era, see especially Cohen, *A Consumer's Republic;* Eric Avila, *Popular Culture in the Age of White Flight* (Berkeley: University of California Press, 2004); Victoria Wolcott, *Race, Riots, and Roller Coasters: The Struggle over Segregated Recreation in America* (Philadelphia: University of Pennsylvania Press, 2012).

20. Cohen, *Consumers' Republic,* 257–268, 278–283. On the architectural design of shopping centers, see David Smiley, *Pedestrian Modern: Shopping and American Architecture, 1925–1956* (Minneapolis: University of Minnesota Press, 2013).

Acknowledgments

My secret pleasure in the years spent researching and writing this book was to craft detailed acknowledgments in my head. Although the reality will undoubtedly fall far short of those elegantly worded fantasies, I am delighted to have this opportunity to convey my gratitude to the people and institutions that have helped me along the way.

This project began in the History Department at the University of Chicago. I will always feel extraordinarily fortunate to have had Amy Dru Stanley as my graduate adviser. Her criticism and support profoundly shaped this project. I am grateful for the exacting standards to which she held me, for the model of rigorous scholarship she continues to provide, and for her friendship. I also thank Craig Becker, Tom Stanley-Becker, and Isaac Stanley-Becker for welcoming me into their lives and home. Kathleen Neils Conzen never wavered in her enthusiasm for my work or her belief in my abilities. Her reassurance buoyed my spirits at several critical junctures, while her incisive feedback pushed me to refine many claims. James Grossman first spurred me to think about how historians craft ideas into actual books in his seminar on urban history, and I continue to benefit from his frank advice. Amy Lippert generously shared her expertise in cultural history and professional matters. Christine Stansell greatly influenced the conceptualization and early trajectory of this project. I remain incredibly thankful for her counsel and hope that the final product lives up to her expectations.

Many other colleagues and friends made my experience at the University of Chicago immensely rewarding. Katherine Turk's friendship sustained me through numerous milestones, both personal and professional. Her advice and example have made me a better historian. Sarah Miller-Davenport read nearly every word of the manuscript, some more than once. I thank her for her superb editorial instincts, as well as the meals and Skype chats we have shared. Susannah Engstrom continues to be one of the South Loop's strongest attractions, and I hope we will always be neighbors. My entire writing group—Chris Dingwall, Susannah Engstrom, Sarah Miller-Davenport, and Kathryn

Schumaker—encouraged me to think more broadly, craft my prose with greater clarity, and always bring plenty of wine. I also thank Leora Auslander, Jacob Betz, Jane Dailey, Rachel Feinmark, Korey Garibaldi, Adam Green, Sarah Gronningsater, Ramón Gutiérrez, Thomas Holt, Alison Lefkovitz, Jonathan Levy, Toussaint Losier, John McCallum, Monica Mercado, Celeste Moore, Traci Parker, Julie Saville, James Sparrow, Susan Gaunt Stearns, Emily Swafford, Marcia Walker, Sarah Weicksel, and many others. My work benefited from significant financial support from the University of Chicago, including the Harry Barnard Dissertation Year Fellowship in American History, the Center for the Study of Gender and Sexuality's Dissertation Fellowship, the Matthew Levin Dissertation Fellowship in the History of American Capitalism, the Century Fellowship, and a Freehling Research Grant.

I spent two rewarding years working on this project in Cambridge, Massachusetts, thanks to a Visiting Scholars fellowship at the American Academy of Arts and Sciences and a postdoctoral research fellowship from the University of Notre Dame. At the Academy, I am grateful to Larry Buell, Jonathon Fanton, John Tessitore, and fellow scholars Alex Acs, Michael Brownstein, Brent Cebul, Maggie Gram, Robin Scheffler, Claire Seiler, and especially Sunny Yang, who continues to respond to my frantic grammar and life queries. While in Cambridge, I greatly benefited from the advice and encouragement of Lizabeth Cohen, Nancy Cott, Walter Friedman, Lily Geismer, Casey Lurtz, Rebecca Marchiel, Katherine Marino, Joanne Meyerowitz, Caitlin Parton, Laura Phillips Sawyer, John Stauffer, and Susan Ware.

My colleagues at the University of Notre Dame have been particularly welcoming and supportive of my work. I am particularly grateful to two outstanding department chairs, Patrick Griffin and Jon Coleman. The mentorship of Thomas Tweed and Elisabeth Köll made my transition to junior faculty inestimably smoother. I continue to be awed by the generosity of the brilliant Gail Bederman. For their advice and cheer, I also thank Ted Beatty, Liang Cai, Mariana Candido, Catherine Cangany, Katlyn Carter, Annie Coleman, Yacine Daddi Addoun, John Deak, Darren Dochuk, Felipe Fernández-Armesto, Korey Garibaldi, Dan Graff, Karen Graubart, Brad Gregory, Dan Hobbins, Katie Jarvis, Jake Lundberg, Semion Lyandres, Alex Martin, John McGreevy, Rebecca McKenna, Nikhil Menon, Margaret Meserve, Abi Ocobock, Paul Ocobock, Jaime Pensado, Richard Pierce, Linda Przybyszewski, Evan Ragland, Francisco Robles, Sarah Shortall, Joshua Specht, Robert Sullivan, Julia Adeney Thomas, and many other terrific colleagues in the Department of History. A publishing grant from the Institute for Scholarship in the Liberal Arts in the School of Arts and Letters at the University of Notre Dame supported the final stages of indexing and production.

A number of venues offered the opportunity to receive feedback on portions of the manuscript. I thank Louis Galambos and Angus Burgin of the Johns Hopkins Institute for Applied Economics, Global Health, and the Study of Business Enterprise; Joshua Salzmann and Jeff Sklansky of the Newberry Seminar on the History of Capitalism; Bradford Hunt and Ann Durkin Keating of the Urban History Seminar at the Chicago History Museum; Michelle Nickerson and Joan Johnson of the Newberry Seminar on the History of Women, Gender, and Sexualities; Conrad Wright and Kate Viens of the Boston Seminar on the History of Women and Gender; the Newberry Urban History Dissertation Group; and the Social History Workshop and the Gender and Sexuality Studies Workshop at the University of Chicago. At conferences and seminars, I benefited from the thoughtful commentary of Eric Avila, Sarah Deutsch, Mona Domosh, Lawrence Glickman, Susan Johnson, Kevin Murphy, and Kathy Peiss, as well as from the questions, suggestions, or encouragement of Cathleen Cahill, Robin Einhorn, Timothy Gilfoyle, Vicki Howard, Samuel Kling, Richard Longstreth, Mark Rose, Mary Ryan, Andrew Sandoval-Strausz, Rima Lunin Schultz, Ellen Skerett, Carl Smith, Chloe Taft, Kyle Volk, Sandy Zipp, and many others.

At Harvard University Press, I am thankful for the support and keen advice of Joyce Seltzer. The insightful readings of Alison Isenberg and an anonymous reviewer greatly enhanced the book's argument and helped me clarify its stakes. I also thank Kathleen Drummy, Angela Piliouras, and the entire editorial team, as well as Isabelle Lewis, who created the wonderful maps. Chapter 4 reprints, with permission from Oxford University Press and with minor edits, "Tippling Ladies and the Making of Consumer Culture: Gender and Public Space in *Fin-de-Siècle* Chicago," *Journal of American History* 101 (Dec. 2014): 751–777. I am grateful to Edward Linenthal and the essay's reviewers—Elaine Abelson, Amy Richter, and anonymous readers—for their criticisms and suggestions. For their expert assistance, I thank librarians and archivists at the Chicago History Museum, the Newberry Library, the Regenstein Library at the University of Chicago, the Hesburgh Library at the University of Notre Dame, and the Schlesinger Library at the Radcliffe Institute for Advanced Study.

Many friends and mentors shaped this project long before I began writing it. At Swarthmore College, I thank the wonderful teacher-scholars who guided my early intellectual development, especially Alison Dorsey, Bruce Dorsey, Pieter Judson, Marjorie Murphy, and Robert Weinberg. Without the patience, love, and expert baking skills of Sarah Webb, I might never have made it through graduate school. I continue to cherish our friendship. Christina Procacci, Valerie Marone Smith, and Kelly Guzman were always willing to offer advice, encouragement, and sympathetic ears.

My deepest gratitude is reserved for my family. My parents, Jane and Ralph Remus, never doubted that I made the right choice in pursuing a career as a historian. Their conviction helped me weather many crises of confidence. My mother instilled in me a love of history and reading; my father nurtured my intellectual curiosity and taught me, through his example and advice, the importance of hard work. My sisters, Rebecca Cibulka and Margaret Remus, sustained this project by dragging me away from my work whenever I needed a break. They are my truest friends and fiercest allies. I thank Adam, Tyler, Mallory, and Peter Cibulka for their humor, kindness, and patience with my fondness for dance parties. Richard, Mindy, and the entire Goldstein family have been enthusiastic supporters, even when it seemed as though the finish line would never come. Not least, I thank my husband, Randy Goldstein. His intellectual companionship has immeasurably enriched this book and my life. To quote a favorite song, "And my love, that love is you."

Index